The Original Cleartype

United States
ZIP CODE
ATLAS

D1545427

Contents

American Map® Corporation

U.S. Post Office
Abbreviations for States and Territories

Alabama	AL	Nebraska	NE
Alaska	AK	Nevada	NV
American Samoa*	AS	New Hampshire	NH
Arizona	AZ	New Jersey	NJ
Arkansas	AR	New Mexico	NM
California	CA	New York	NY
Colorado	CO	North Carolina	NC
Connecticut	CT	North Dakota	ND
Delaware	DE	Northern Mariana Islands*	MP
District of Columbia	DC	Ohio	OH
Florida	FL	Oklahoma	OK
Georgia	GA	Oregon	OR
Guam*	GU	Palau*	PW
Hawaii	HI	Pennsylvania	PA
Idaho	ID	Puerto Rico*	PR
Illinois	IL	Rhode Island	RI
Indiana	IN	South Carolina	SC
Iowa	IA	South Dakota	SD
Kansas	KS	Tennessee	TN
Kentucky	KY	Texas	TX
Louisiana	LA	Utah	UT
Maine	ME	Vermont	VT
Maryland	MD	Virginia	VA
Massachusetts	MA	Virgin Islands*	VI
Michigan	MI	Washington	WA
Minnesota	MN	Washington, DC	DC
Mississippi	MS	West Virginia	WV
Missouri	MO	Wisconsin	WI
Montana	MT	Wyoming	WY

*Not included in atlas

Copyright 1997 American Map Corporation. All rights reserved. No part of this work may be reproduced or transmitted in any form or by any means, electronic or mechanical, including photocopying, recording, or by any information storage and retrieval system, without permission in writing from the publisher.

The information shown in this atlas has been obtained from various authoritative sources. Nevertheless, a work of this scope may contain some inaccuracies. Any errors and omissions called to our attention will be greatly appreciated.

Printed in Canada

The Zip Code as a Marketing Unit

Although counties have historically been used to define geographic marketing areas in the United States, there can be little doubt that technological advances combined with sophisticated marketing techniques, have made such macro measurements unsatisfactory. The motto for business success is "market segmentation". Segmentation by age, income, education, occupation, sex, marital status, psychographics, or geography is necessary in a society characterized by rapid changes in taste, attitude, and behavior. In such a business environment, the Zip Code has been advanced as a more definable, easy-to-use, and measurable marketing unit.

Use of the Zip Code as a marketing tool has permitted marketers to apply scientific principles to a business that has, traditionally, been judged an art, rather than a science. Economic, cultural, and attitudinal similarities may be seen to cluster around a geographic locus. The ability to identify and classify prospective customers in this way leads to better, more efficient business development.

The Zip Code System

The Zip Code System was originally developed by the U.S. Postal Service as an efficient means to classify and distribute mail. The first digit of each 5-digit Zip Code identifies one of the 10 national Zip Code areas (see map on page 122). The next two digits break down the national areas into smaller geographic units. These 3-digit units are served by Sectional Centers which are responsible for the distribution of mail to smaller post offices in the area. Due to their population density, some large cities have their own 3-digit Zip Code. Most of these are Multicoded Cities that have more than one 5-digit Zip Code within their city limits. A Multicoded City serves the same function as a Sectional Center but does so for neighborhood branches. In addition, some Multicoded Cities also serve as Sectional Centers for the area surrounding city limits. Currently there are more than 900 3-digit Zip Codes used by the Postal Service. The fourth and fifth digits of the Zip Code identify local delivery areas. With more than 43,000 5-digit Zip Codes, this identification system reaches down to small, local, neighborhoods.

The Zip Code Atlas Base Maps and Indexes

The Zip Code Atlas (ZCA) offers a clear, accurate, easy-to-read maps of each of the 50 states accompanied by corresponding indexes. Each index provides alphabetical listings of counties with their populations, and all places with populations of 1,000 and above that have been assigned 5-digit Zip Codes*, those respective codes, and keys to their map location. Maps show county outlines and all places of 1,000 population or more. Where room permits, places with populations under 1,000 are also shown although they do not appear in the index. County seats are always shown and are identified as such, regardless of size. Population ranges are indicated by special symbols explained in the map key. For improved readability, areas containing a great number of places in close proximity are shown in enlarged insets. Where insets were not sufficient to enhance clarity, states have been accommodated on more than one page .

The Zip Code Atlas

The ZCA has been designed to provide accurate, comprehensive, easy-to-use material for a broad audience. For the first time in any publication of this type, 5-digit Zip Code numbers have been included in each state map index*. The ability to identify and locate these 5-digit designations in their proper geographic locations brings a new utility to this publication. All 3-digit Zip Code area boundaries, Sectional Centers, and Multicoded Cities are shown in green on the maps. We have also included a special two-page 5-digit Zip Code map of New York City's 5 boroughs.

To enhance the value of the ZCA's maps and indexes, we have included 22 charts that provide important demographic informa-

*For Multicoded Cities ranges are given; i.e. Philadelphia 19101-99

tion by Zip Code. These charts numerically list all 3-digit Zip Code areas, indicate their population, population by age, number of households, and retail sales; define Black, Hispanic, and Gray Markets and more, 1-20 categories in all. (See table of contents for complete listing.)

In special situations we have combined demographic data for several 3-digit Zip Codes into ranges to present the data in a more meaningful manner. We have done this when a Sectional Center is associated with two or more 3-digit codes that in themselves do not represent logical geographic divisions. U.S. totals or averages for all categories listed are provided to permit the user to evaluate each Zip Code area relative to the entire country.

Naturally, it is up to each marketer to make the most of all this information. In every case, these data provide a means to effectively measure actual performance versus potential on a Zip Coded market-by-market basis. Anyone who does business by mail will find the American Map Cleartype Zip Code Atlas an indispensable marketing tool.

Notes on Places Shown on the Maps

1. Incorporated Places:
Those places which are incorporated under the laws of their respective states as cities, boroughs, towns, and villages.

2. Unincorporated Places:
a. CDPs (Census Designated Places) are closely settled population centers without corporate limits.
b. Additional population centers not classified by the Census as CDPs because they do not meet specific requirements but recognized by American Map as separate entities due to their significant population. Those places whose population is estimated to be above 1,000 are included in the index without population figures.

3. Townships:
In Pennsylvania, New Jersey, New York, and the New England states, many government functions are delegated to divisions within the counties called "towns" or "townships". Townships are shown on the map and listed in the index when they are areas of dense population and do not contain other localities within them.

4. Independent Cities:
Cities such as St. Louis, Missouri; Baltimore, Maryland; Carson City, Nevada; and 41 cities in Virginia are administered independently of their surrounding counties and have the legal status of separate counties. These independent cities are listed in the index following the state's other counties. Though independent, some of these cities serve as county seats for neighboring counties. To identify these cases in the index the name of county, following the name of the independent city, is placed in parentheses.

Explanation of Symbols Used in the Indexes:

● Census Designated Place (CDP)
▲ *Italics* Township shown on the map
● *Italics* Township shown which is also a CDP

For symbols used on maps see explanation on individual map pages.

Note:
Population-specific information on the state maps and indexes is based on 1990 census statistical data provided by the U.S. Department of Commerce Bureau of the Census.

The statistical data for 3-digit Zip Code areas on pages 125 through 146 are based on 1997 demographic and zip code data. The data are copyrighted by National Decision Systems, a national demographic company located in San Diego, California (Toll Free 1-800-866-6511) and are reproduced here by permission. Direct all other questions to the American Map Corporation at 718-784-0055.

COUNTIES

(67 Counties)

Name of County	Population	Location on Map
AUTAUGA	34,222	J-6
BALDWIN	98,280	O-3
BARBOUR	25,417	L-11
BIBB	16,576	H-5
BLOUNT	39,248	D-7
BULLOCK	11,042	K-9
BUTLER	21,892	L-6
CALHOUN	116,034	E-9
CHAMBERS	36,876	H-10
CHEROKEE	19,543	D-10
CHILTON	32,458	H-6
CHOCTAW	16,018	K-1
CLARKE	27,240	L-2
CLAY	13,252	G-9
CLEBURNE	12,730	E-10
COFFEE	40,240	M-8
COLBERT	51,666	B-2
CONECUH	14,054	M-5
COOSA	11,063	H-7
COVINGTON	36,478	N-7
CRENSHAW	13,635	L-7
CULLMAN	67,613	D-5
DALE	49,633	M-10
DALLAS	48,130	K-4
DEKALB	54,651	B-10
ELMORE	49,210	I-8
ESCAMBIA	35,518	O-4
ETOWAH	99,840	D-8
FAYETTE	17,962	E-3
FRANKLIN	27,814	C-2
GENEVA	23,647	O-8
GREENE	10,153	H-2
HALE	15,498	H-3
HENRY	15,374	M-11
HOUSTON	81,331	O-11
JACKSON	47,796	A-8
JEFFERSON	651,525	F-6
LAMAR	15,715	E-2
LAUDERDALE	79,661	A-2
LAWRENCE	31,513	B-4
LEE	87,146	I-10
LIMESTONE	54,135	A-5
LOWNDES	12,658	K-6
MACON	24,928	J-9
MADISON	238,912	A-7
MARENGO	23,084	J-3
MARION	29,830	D-2
MARSHALL	70,832	C-7
MOBILE	378,643	O-1
MONROE	23,968	M-4
MONTGOMERY	209,085	K-7
MORGAN	100,043	C-5
PERRY	12,759	I-4
PICKENS	20,699	F-2
PIKE	27,595	L-8
RANDOLPH	19,881	G-10
RUSSELL	46,860	J-11
SAINT CLAIR	50,009	E-8
SHELBY	99,358	G-7
SUMTER	16,174	I-1
TALLADEGA	74,107	G-8
TALLAPOOSA	38,826	H-9
TUSCALOOSA	150,522	F-3
WALKER	67,670	E-5
WASHINGTON	16,694	M-1
WILCOX	13,568	K-4
WINSTON	22,053	D-4
Total	4,040,587	

CITIES AND TOWNS

Note: The first name is that of the city or town, second, that of the county in which it is located, then the zip code area and location on the map.

Abbeville, Henry, 36310 ..... M-11
Adamsville, Jefferson, 35005 ..... P-6
Alabaster, Shelby, 35007 ..... G-6
Albertville, Marshall, 35950 ..... D-8
Alexander City, Tallapoosa, 35010 ..... H-9
Aliceville, Pickens, 35442 ..... H-2
Andalusia, Covington, 36420 ..... N-7
Anniston, Calhoun, 36201, 03, 06 ..... F-9
Anniston Northwest, Calhoun, 36201 ..... F-9
Arab, Cullman/Marshall, 35016 ..... C-7
Ardmore, Limestone, 35739 ..... A-6
Ashford, Houston, 36312 ..... O-11
Ashland, Clay, 36251 ..... G-9
Ashville, St. Clair, 35953 ..... E-8
Athens, Limestone, 35611 ..... B-6
Atmore, Escambia, 36502 ..... O-4
Attalla, Etowah, 35954 ..... E-8
Auburn, Lee, 36830 ..... J-10
Bay Minette, Baldwin, 36507 ..... P-3
Bay View, Jefferson, 35005 ..... Q-5
Bayou La Batre, Mobile, 36509 ..... R-1
Berry, Fayette, 35546 ..... F-4
Bessemer, Jefferson, 35020, 23 ..... G-6
Birmingham, Jefferson/Shelby, 35201-99 ..... F-6
Blountsville, Blount, 35031 ..... D-7
• Blue Ridge, Elmore, 36092 ..... J-8
Bluff Park, Jefferson, 35226 ..... R-7
Boaz, Etowah/Marshall, 35957 ..... D-8
Boylston, Montgomery, 36110 ..... J-8
Brantley, Crenshaw, 36009 ..... M-8
Brent, Bibb, 35034 ..... H-5
Brewton, Escambia, 36426 ..... O-5
Bridgeport, Jackson, 35740 ..... A-10
Brighton, Jefferson, 35020 ..... G-6
Brookside, Jefferson, 35036 ..... P-6
Brownville, Jefferson, 35020 ..... R-6
Brundidge, Pike, 36010 ..... M-9
Butler, Choctaw, 36904 ..... K-2
• Bynum, Calhoun, 36253 ..... F-9
• Cahaba Heights, Jefferson, 35243 ..... R-8
Calera, Shelby, 35040 ..... H-6
Camden, Wilcox, 36726 ..... L-5
Camp Hill, Tallapoosa, 36850 ..... I-10
Carbon Hill, Walker, 35549 ..... E-4
Carrollton, Pickens, 35447 ..... G-2
Cedar Bluff, Cherokee, 35959 ..... D-10
• Center Point, Jefferson, 35220 ..... P-8
Centre, Cherokee, 35960 ..... D-10
Centreville, Bibb, 35042 ..... H-5
Chatom, Washington, 36518 ..... N-2
• Chelsea, Shelby, 35043 ..... G-7
Cherokee, Colbert, 35616 ..... B-3
Chickasaw, Mobile, 36611 ..... P-2
Childersburg, Talladega, 35044 ..... G-8
Citronelle, Mobile, 36522 ..... O-2
Clanton, Chilton, 35045 ..... I-7
Clayton, Barbour, 36016 ..... L-11
Clio, Barbour, 36017 ..... M-10
Collinsville, Cherokee/DeKalb, 35961 ..... D-9
Columbiana, Shelby, 35051 ..... H-7
Concord, Jefferson, 35020 ..... R-5
Cordova, Walker, 35550 ..... E-5
Cottonwood, Houston, 36320 ..... O-11
Cowarts, Houston, 36321 ..... O-11
Craig, Dallas, 36701 ..... K-6
Creola, Mobile, 36525 ..... P-2
Crossville, DeKalb, 35962 ..... C-9
Cullman, Cullman, 35055 ..... D-6
Dadeville, Tallapoosa, 36853 ..... I-10
Daleville, Dale, 36322 ..... N-10
Daphne, Baldwin, 36526 ..... Q-3
Decatur, Limestone/Morgan, 35601, 03 ..... B-6
Demopolis, Marengo, 36732 ..... J-3
Dolomite, Jefferson, 35061 ..... R-6
Dora, Walker, 35062 ..... F-5
Dothan, Dale/Houston, 36301, 03 ..... O-11
Double Springs, Winston, 35553 ..... D-4
East Brewton, Escambia, 36426 ..... O-5
Eastern Valley, Jefferson, 35020 ..... G-6
Eclectic, Elmore, 36024 ..... J-9
Edgewater, Jefferson, 35203 ..... Q-6
Elba, Coffee, 36323 ..... N-9
Enterprise, Coffee/Dale, 36330 ..... N-9
Eufaula, Barbour, 36027 ..... L-12
Eutaw, Greene, 35462 ..... I-3
Evergreen, Conecuh, 36401 ..... N-6
Fairfield, Jefferson, 35064 ..... F-6
Fairhope, Baldwin, 36532 ..... Q-3
Falkville, Morgan, 35622 ..... C-6
Fayette, Fayette, 35555 ..... F-3
Flat Creek-Wegra, Jefferson/Walker, 35129-30 ..... F-5
Flint City, Morgan, 35601 ..... C-6
Flomaton, Escambia, 36441 ..... O-5
Florala, Covington, 36442 ..... O-8
Florence, Lauderdale, 35630, 33 ..... B-3
Foley, Baldwin, 36535 ..... R-3
• Forestdale, Jefferson, 35214 ..... Q-6
Fort Deposit, Lowndes, 36032 ..... L-7
• Fort McClellan, Calhoun, 36205 ..... F-9
Fort Payne, DeKalb, 35967 ..... C-10
• Fort Rucker, Dale, 36362 ..... N-10
Frisco City, Monroe, 36445 ..... N-4
Fultondale, Jefferson, 35068 ..... P-7
Fyffe, DeKalb, 35971 ..... C-9
Gadsden, Etowah, 35901-99 ..... E-9
Gardendale, Jefferson, 35071 ..... P-7
Geneva, Geneva, 36340 ..... O-9
Georgiana, Butler, 36033 ..... M-6
Glencoe, Calhoun/Etowah, 35905 ..... E-9
Good Hope, Cullman, 35055 ..... D-6
Goodwater, Coosa, 35072 ..... H-9
Gordo, Pickens, 35466 ..... G-3
• Grand Bay, Mobile, 36541 ..... Q-1
Graysville, Jefferson, 35073 ..... P-6
Greensboro, Hale, 36744 ..... I-4
Greenville, Butler, 36037 ..... M-7
Grove Hill, Clarke, 36451 ..... M-3
Guin, Marion, 35563 ..... E-3
Gulf Shores, Baldwin, 36542 ..... R-3
Guntersville, Marshall, 35976 ..... C-8
Gurley, Madison, 35748 ..... B-8
Hackleburg, Marion, 35564 ..... C-3
Haleyville, Marion/Winston, 35565 ..... D-4
Hamilton, Marion, 35570 ..... D-3
Hanceville, Cullman, 35077 ..... D-6
Hartford, Geneva, 36344 ..... O-10
Hartselle, Morgan, 35640 ..... C-6
• Harvest, Madison, 35749 ..... A-6
Hayneville, Lowndes, 36040 ..... K-7
• Hazel Green, Madison, 35750 ..... A-7
Headland, Henry, 36345 ..... N-11
Heflin, Cleburne, 36264 ..... F-10
Helena, Shelby, 35080 ..... G-6
Henagar, DeKalb, 35978 ..... B-9
Hokes Bluff, Etowah, 35903 ..... E-9
• Holt, Tuscaloosa, 35404 ..... G-4
Homewood, Jefferson, 35209 ..... F-6
Hoover, Jefferson/Shelby, 35236 ..... R-7
Hueytown, Jefferson, 35023 ..... R-5
• Huguley, Chambers, 36854 ..... I-11
Hunter, Montgomery, 36108 ..... J-7
Huntsville, Limestone/Madison, 35801-99 ..... B-7
• Inverness, Shelby, 35242 ..... G-6
Irondale, Jefferson, 35210 ..... Q-8
Jackson, Clarke, 36545 ..... N-3
Jacksonville, Calhoun, 36265 ..... E-10
Jasper, Walker, 35501 ..... E-5
Jemison, Chilton, 35085 ..... H-6
Killen, Lauderdale, 35645 ..... A-4
Kimberly, Jefferson, 35091 ..... E-6
Kinsey, Houston, 36303 ..... N-11
• Ladonia, Russell, 36869 ..... J-12
Lafayette, Chambers, 36862 ..... I-11
• Lake Purdy, Shelby, 35242 ..... G-6
Lanett, Chambers, 36863 ..... I-11
Leeds, Jefferson/St. Clair/Shelby, 35094 ..... F-7
Level Plains, Dale, 36322 ..... N-10
Lincoln, Talladega, 35096 ..... F-8
Linden, Marengo, 36748 ..... K-3
Lineville, Clay, 36266 ..... G-10
Lipscomb, Jefferson, 35020 ..... G-6
Livingston, Sumter, 35470 ..... J-2
Loxley, Baldwin, 36551 ..... Q-3
Luverne, Crenshaw, 36049 ..... M-8
Madison, Limestone/Madison, 35758 ..... B-6
Marion, Perry, 36756 ..... J-5
• Meadowbrook, Shelby, 35242 ..... G-6
• Meridianville, Madison, 35759 ..... A-7
Midfield, Jefferson, 35228 ..... G-6
Midland City, Dale, 36350 ..... N-11
• Mignon, Talladega, 35150 ..... G-8
Millbrook, Elmore, 36054 ..... J-8
Millport, Lamar, 35576 ..... F-2
• Minor, Jefferson, 35203 ..... F-6
Mobile, Mobile, 36601-99 ..... Q-2
Monroeville, Monroe, 36460 ..... N-4
Montevallo, Shelby, 35115 ..... H-6
Montgomery, Montgomery, 36101-99 ..... K-8
• Moody, St. Clair, 35004 ..... F-7
• Moores Mill, Madison, 35811 ..... B-7
Morris, Jefferson, 35116 ..... F-6
Mosses, Lowndes, 36040 ..... K-6
Moulton, Lawrence, 35650 ..... C-5
Moundville, Hale/Tuscaloosa, 35474 ..... H-4
Mount Olive, Jefferson, 35117 ..... F-6
Mountain Brook, Jefferson, 35223 ..... F-7
Muscle Shoals, Colbert, 35661 ..... B-4
New Brockton, Coffee, 36351 ..... N-9
New Hope, Madison, 35760 ..... C-7
• New Market, Madison, 35761 ..... A-7
Newton, Dale, 36352 ..... N-10
Normal, Madison, 35762 ..... B-7
Northport, Tuscaloosa, 35476 ..... G-4
Ohatchee, Calhoun, 36271 ..... E-8
Oneonta, Blount, 35121 ..... E-7
Opelika, Lee, 36801 ..... I-11
Opp, Covington, 36467 ..... N-8
Orange Beach, Baldwin, 36561 ..... R-3
Overton, Jefferson, 35203 ..... Q-8
Oxford, Calhoun/Talladega, 36203 ..... F-9
Ozark, Dale, 36360 ..... N-10
Parrish, Walker, 35580 ..... F-5
Pelham, Shelby, 35124 ..... G-6
Pell City, St. Clair, 35125 ..... F-8
Phenix City, Lee/Russell, 36067, 69 ..... J-12
Phil Campbell, Franklin, 35581 ..... C-3
Piedmont, Calhoun/Cherokee, 36272 ..... E-10
• Pinson-Clay-Chalkville, Jefferson, 35126 ..... F-7
Pleasant Grove, Jefferson, 35127 ..... Q-5
• Point Clear, Baldwin, 36564 ..... Q-3
Prattville, Autauga/Elmore, 36066-67 ..... J-7
Priceville, Morgan, 35603 ..... B-6
Prichard, Mobile, 36610 ..... P-2
Ragland, St. Clair, 35131 ..... F-8
Rainbow City, Etowah, 35906 ..... E-9
Rainsville, DeKalb, 35986 ..... C-9
Red Bay, Franklin, 35582 ..... C-2
• Redstone Arsenal, Madison, 35809 ..... B-7
Reform, Pickens, 35481 ..... G-2
Riverside, St. Clair, 35135 ..... F-8
Roanoke, Randolph, 36274 ..... H-11
Robertsdale, Baldwin, 36567 ..... Q-3
Rockford, Coosa, 35136 ..... I-8
Rogersville, Lauderdale, 35653 ..... B-5
Roosevelt, Jefferson, 35020 ..... R-6
Russellville, Franklin, 35653 ..... C-3
• Saks, Calhoun, 36201 ..... F-9
Samson, Geneva, 36477 ..... O-9
Saraland, Mobile, 36571 ..... P-2
Sardis City, DeKalb/Etowah/Marshall, 35957 ..... D-8
Satsuma, Mobile, 36572 ..... P-2
Scottsboro, Jackson, 35768 ..... B-9
Selma, Dallas, 36701-03 ..... J-6
• Selmont-West Selmont, Dallas, 36701 ..... J-6
Semmes, Mobile, 36575 ..... P-1
Sheffield, Colbert, 35660-61 ..... B-3
Shelby, Shelby, 35143 ..... H-7
Slocomb, Geneva, 36375 ..... O-10
• Smiths, Lee, 36877 ..... J-12
• Smoke Rise, Blount, 35180 ..... E-6
Southside, Calhoun/Etowah, 35901 ..... E-9
• Spanish Fort, Baldwin, 36527 ..... P-3
Springville, St. Clair, 35146 ..... E-7
Steele, St. Clair, 35987 ..... E-8
Stevenson, Jackson, 35772 ..... A-9
Sulligent, Lamar, 35586 ..... E-2
Sumiton, Jefferson/Walker, 35148 ..... E-5
Sylacauga, Talladega, 35150 ..... H-8
Sylvan Springs, Jefferson, 35118 ..... F-5
Talladega, Talladega, 35160 ..... G-9
Tallassee, Elmore/Tallapoosa, 36078 ..... J-9
Tarrant, Jefferson, 35217 ..... F-6
Taylor, Houston, 36301 ..... O-11
• Theodore, Mobile, 36582 ..... Q-2
Thomasville, Clarke, 36784 ..... L-3
Thorsby, Chilton, 35171 ..... I-6
• Tillmans Corner, Mobile, 36619 ..... Q-2
Town Creek, Lawrence, 35672 ..... B-4
Trinity, Morgan, 35673 ..... B-5
Troy, Pike, 36081 ..... L-9
Trussville, Jefferson, 35173 ..... P-8
Tuscaloosa, Tuscaloosa, 35401, 04-06 ..... H-4
Tuscumbia, Colbert, 35674 ..... B-3
Tuskegee, Macon, 36083 ..... J-10
• Underwood-Petersville, Lauderdale, 35630 ..... A-3
Union Springs, Bullock, 36089 ..... K-10
Uniontown, Perry, 36786 ..... J-4
Valley, Chambers, 36854 ..... I-10
Vernon, Lamar, 35592 ..... E-2
Vestavia Hills, Jefferson, 35216 ..... R-7
Vincent, St. Clair/Shelby/Talladega, 35178 ..... G-7
Warrior, Jefferson, 35180 ..... E-6
Weaver, Calhoun, 36277 ..... E-9
Webb, Houston, 36376 ..... N-11
Wedowee, Randolph, 36278 ..... G-10
West Blocton, Bibb, 35184 ..... H-5
• West End-Cobb Town, Calhoun, 35211 ..... F-9
Wetumpka, Elmore, 36092 ..... J-8
Wilsonville, Shelby, 35186 ..... G-7
Winfield, Fayette/Marion, 35594 ..... E-3
York, Sumter, 36925 ..... J-1

Explanation of symbols: • – Census Designated Place (CDP)

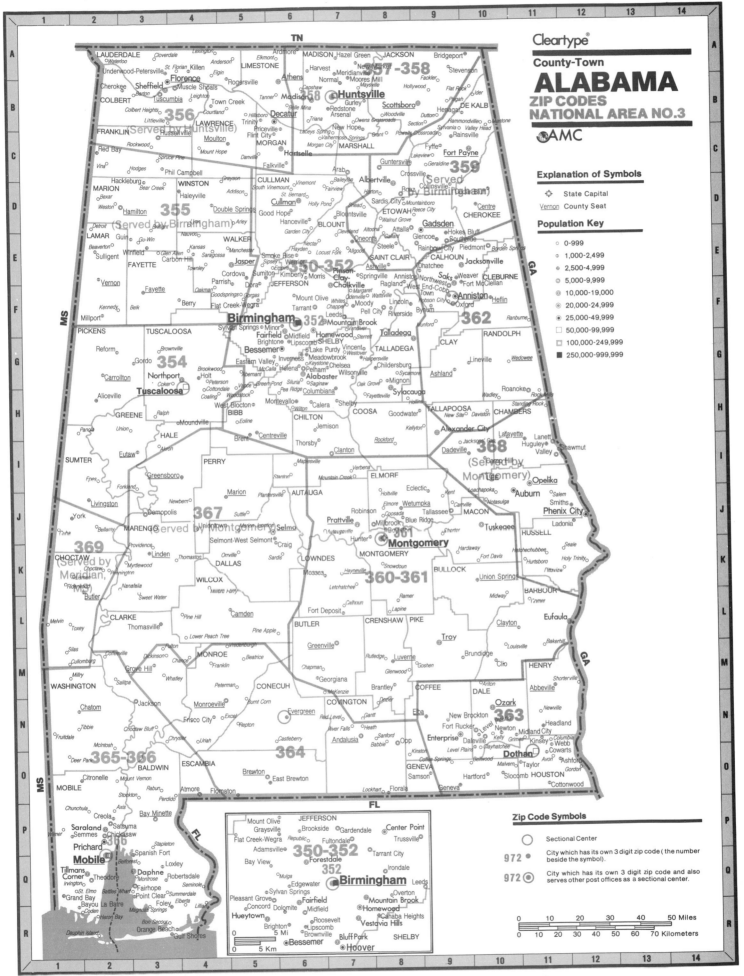

Cleartype®

County-Town

ALABAMA
ZIP CODES
NATIONAL AREA NO.3

AMC

Explanation of Symbols

◇ State Capital

Vernon County Seat

Population Key

- ⊙ 0-999
- ⊙ 1,000-2,499
- ⊙ 2,500-4,999
- ⊙ 5,000-9,999
- ⊙ 10,000-19,000
- ⊙ 20,000-24,999
- ⊙ 25,000-49,999
- □ 50,000-99,999
- □ 100,000-249,999
- ■ 250,000-999,999

Zip Code Symbols

○ Sectional Center

972 ● City which has its own 3 digit zip code (the number beside the symbol).

972 ◉ City which has its own 3 digit zip code and also serves other post offices as a sectional center.

0 10 20 30 40 50 Miles
0 10 20 30 40 50 60 70 Kilometers

Copyright American Map Corporation

BOROUGHS AND CENSUS AREAS

(25 Boroughs and Census Areas)

Name of Borough or Census Area	Population	Location on Map
ALEUTIANS EAST Borough	2,464	L-3
ALEUTIANS WEST Census Area	9,478	M-11
ANCHORAGE Borough	226,338	H-8
BETHEL Census Area	13,656	H-4
BRISTOL BAY Borough	1,410	J-6
DILLINGHAM Census Area	4,012	I-6
FAIRBANKS NORTH STAR Borough	77,720	E-10
HAINES Borough	2,117	I-15
JUNEAU Borough	26,751	I-15
KENAI PENINSULA Borough	40,802	I-8
KETCHIKAN GATEWAY Borough	13,828	K-17
KODIAK ISLAND Borough	13,309	K-7
LAKE AND PENINSULA Borough	1,668	J-7
MATANUSKA-SUSITNA Borough	39,683	G-8
NOME Census Area	8,288	E-4
NORTH SLOPE Borough	5,979	B-7
NORTHWEST ARCTIC Borough	6,113	C-6
PRINCE OF WALES-OUTER KETCHIKAN Census Area	6,278	L-15
SITKA Borough	8,588	K-15
SKAGWAY-YAKUTAT-ANGOON Census Area	4,385	H-13
SOUTHEAST FAIRBANKS Census Area	5,913	F-11
VALDEZ-CORDOVA Census Area	9,952	H-11
WADE HAMPTON Census Area	5,791	G-4
WRANGELL-PETERSBURG Census Area	7,042	J-16
YUKON-KOYUKUK Census Area	8,478	D-8
TOTAL	550,043	

CITIES AND TOWNS

Note: The first name is that of the city or town, second, that of the borough or census area in which it is located, then the zip code area and location on the map.

• Adak Station, Aleutians West Census Area, 96506 — N-12
Anchorage, Anchorage Borough, 99501-99 — H-9
Barrow, North Slope Borough, 99723 — A-7
Bethel, Bethel Census Area, 99559 — H-5
• Big Lake, Matanuska-Susitna Borough, 99652 — H-9
Butte, Matanuska-Susitna Borough, 99645 — H-9
• College, Fairbanks North Star Borough, 99708 — E-10
Cordova, Valdez-Cordova Census Area, 99574 — I-11
Craig, Prince of Wales-Outer Ketchikan Census Area, 99921 — K-16
Dillingham, Dillingham Census Area, 99576 — J-6
• Eielson AFB, Fairbanks North Star Borough, 99702 — F-10
Fairbanks, Fairbanks North Star Borough, 99701-12 — E-10
• Fritz Creek, Kenai Peninsula Borough, 99603 — I-9
Haines, Haines Borough, 99827 — I-14
Homer, Kenai Peninsula Borough, 99603 — I-9
Juneau, Juneau Borough, 99801 — I-15
Kenai, Kenai Peninsula Borough, 99611 — I-9
Ketchikan, Ketchikan Gateway Borough, 99901 — K-17
• Kodiak, Kodiak Island Borough, 99615 — K-8
• Kodiak Station, Kodiak Island Borough, 99619 — K-8
Kotzebue, Northwest Arctic Borough, 99752 — D-5
• Meadow Lakes, Matanuska-Susitna Borough, 99687 — G-9
• Metlakatla, Prince of Wales-Outer Ketchikan Census Area, 99926 — K-17
Mount Edgecumbe, Sitka, 99835 — J-15
• Nikiski, Kenai Peninsula Borough, 99635 — I-8
Nome, Nome Census Area, 99762 — E-4
North Pole, Fairbanks North Star Borough, 99705 — E-10
Palmer, Matanuska-Susitna Borough, 99645 — H-9
Petersburg, Wrangell-Petersburg Census Area, 99833 — J-16
• Ridgeway, Kenai Peninsula Borough, 99669 — I-9
Seward, Kenai Peninsula Borough, 99664 — I-9
Sitka, Sitka Borough, 99835 — J-16
Soldotna, Kenai Peninsula Borough, 99669 — I-9
• Sterling, Kenai Peninsula Borough, 99672 — I-9
Unalaska, Aleutians West Census Area, 99685 — M-3
Valdez, Valdez-Cordova Census Area, 99686 — H-10
Wasilla, Matanuska-Susitna Borough, 99654 — H-9
Wrangell, Wrangell-Petersburg Census Area, 99929 — K-16

Explanation of symbols: • – Census Designated Place (CDP)

Cleartype®
County-Town
ALASKA
ZIP CODES
NATIONAL AREA NO.9
AMC

Explanation of Symbols

✛ State Capital
Vernon County Seat

Population Key

○ 0-999
○ 1,000-2,499
⊕ 2,500-4,999
⊕ 5,000-9,999
◉ 10,000-19,000
◉ 20,000-24,999
◉ 25,000-49,999
□ 50,000-99,999
□ 100,000-249,999

Zip Code Symbols

○ Sectional Center

972 ● City which has its own 3 digit zip code (the number beside the symbol).

972 ◉ City which has its own 3 digit zip code and also serves other post offices as a sectional center.

300 Miles
500 Kilometers

250
400
200
300
150
200
100
100
50
0
0

CANADA

RUSSIA

Beaufort Sea

Chukchi Sea

Bering Strait

Bering Sea

Gulf of Alaska

Pacific Ocean

NORTH SLOPE

NORTHWEST ARCTIC

YUKON-KOYUKUK

997

995-996

NOME

WADE HAMPTON

BETHEL

DILLINGHAM

BRISTOL BAY

LAKE AND PENINSULA

KODIAK ISLAND

KENAI PENINSULA

ANCHORAGE

MATANUSKA-SUSITNA

SOUTHEAST FAIRBANKS

FAIRBANKS NORTH STAR

VALDEZ-CORDOVA

ALEUTIAN ISLANDS EAST

995-996 ALEUTIAN ISLANDS WEST

SITKA

JUNEAU

HAINES

WRANGELL PETERSBURG

KETCHIKAN GATEWAY

PRINCE OF WALES-OUTER KETCHIKAN

SKAGWAY YAKUTAT ANGOON

998

300

972

Barrow
Wainwright
Point Hope
Kivalina
Noatak
Kiana
Noorvik
Selawik
Kotzebue
Shishmaref
Gambell
Savoonga
Nome
Teller
Stebbins
Unalakleet
Nulato
Galena
Tanana
Nenana
Anderson
Healy
Fort Yukon
Two Rivers
North Pole
Eielson AFB
Salcha
College
Fairbanks
Big Delta
Delta Junction
Fort Greely
McGrath
Takotna
Sleetmute
St. Mary's
Mountain Village
Pilot Station
Chevak
Scammon Bay
Hooper Bay
Emmonak
Alakanuk
Toksook Bay
Tununak
Napakiak
Kwethluk
Akiachak
Akiak
Bethel
Kwigillingok
Kipnuk
Quinhagak
Togiak
New Stuyahok
Manokotak
Dillingham
Aleknagik
Naknek
King Salmon
Egegik
Perryville
Chignik
Old Harbor
Kodiak
Karluk
Larsen Bay
Port Lions
Kodiak Station
Seldovia
Homer
Ninilchik
Kasilof
Soldotna
Kenai
Nikiski
Seward
Hope
Sterling
Cooper Landing
Moose Pass
Whittier
Anchorage
Eagle River
Girdwood
Wasilla
Palmer
Butte
Big Lake
Houston
Willow
Talkeetna
Meadow Lakes
Glennallen
Copper Center
Chitina
Cordova
McCarthy
Valdez
Tatitlek
Tok
Northway
Gulkana
Yakutat
Hoonah
Gustavus
Elfin Cove
Pelican
Tenakee Springs
Angoon
Sitka
Port Alexander
Kake
Petersburg
Wrangell
Mount Edgecumbe
Skagway
Klukwan
Haines
Juneau
Craig
Klawock
Thorne Bay
Hollis
Metlakatla
Ketchikan
St. Paul
St. George
Cold Bay
King Cove
Sand Point
Nikolski
Unalaska
Atka
Adak Station
Shemya Station
Attu

Copyright American Map Corporation

COUNTIES

(15 Counties)

CITIES AND TOWNS

Note: The first name is that of the city or town, second, that of the county in which it is located, then the zip code area and location on the map.

Explanation of symbols: ● – Census Designated Place (CDP)

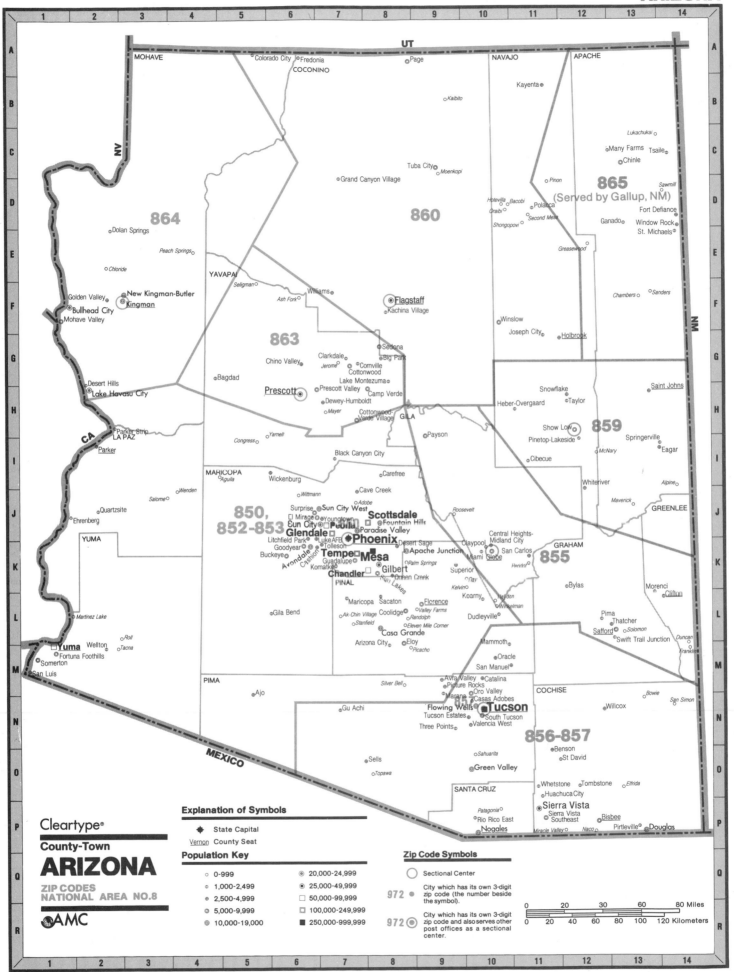

ARIZONA

UT

MOHAVE
COLORADO CITY Fredonia   Page   NAVAJO   APACHE
COCONINO
NV   Kayenta
Kaibito
Lukachukai
Many Farms Tsaile
865   Chinle
(Served by Gallup, NM)
Tuba City Moenkopi   Pinon
864   Grand Canyon Village   Hotevilla Bacobi   Sawmill
Dolan Springs   Oraibi Polacca   Fort Defiance
Shongopovi Second Mesa   Ganado   Window Rock
Peach Springs   **860**   St. Michaels
Chloride   Greasewood
YAVAPAI   Winslow
Golden Valley   Seligman   Williams   Joseph City Holbrook   Chambers Sanders
New Kingman-Butler
Kingman   Ash Fork   Flagstaff
Bullhead City   Kachina Village
Mohave Valley   Snowflake   Saint Johns
863   Sedona   Heber-Overgaard Taylor   **859**
Chino Valley   Clarkdale Big Park
Bagdad   Jerome Cornville   Show Low   Springerville
Desert Hills   Cottonwood   Pinetop-Lakeside McNary   Eagar
Lake Havasu City   Lake Montezuma   Cibecue
Prescott   Prescott Valley Camp Verde
CA   Dewey-Humboldt   Whiteriver   Alpine
Parker Strip   Mayer   Cottonwood-   GILA   Maverick   GREENLEE
LA PAZ   Verde Village   Payson
Parker   Congress Yarnell   Black Canyon City
MARICOPA   Carefree   Roosevelt
Aguila   Wickenburg
Quartzsite   Wenden   Cave Creek   Adobe   Central Heights-
Ehrenberg   Salome   Wittmann   Sun City West   Midland City   GRAHAM
YUMA   Surprise   Mirage Youngtown   Scottsdale   Claypool   San Carlos   **855**
850,   Sun City Peoria   Fountain Hills   Miami Globe
852-853   Glendale   Paradise Valley   Desert Sage   Superior   Perdin
Litchfield Park Luke AFB   Phoenix   Apache Junction   Bylas
Goodyear Tolleson   Palm Springs   Morenci
Buckeye   Tempe Mesa   Kelvin   Clifton
Avondale Cashion   Guadalupe   Gilbert   Kearny   Pima   Duncan
Komatke   Queen Creek   Hayden   Thatcher   Franklin
Chandler   Sun Lakes   Winkelman   Safford Solomon
PINAL   Kelvin   Swift Trail Junction
Maricopa Sacaton   Dudleyville
Gila Bend   Coolidge   Florence   Mammoth
Ak-Chin Village   Valley Farms   Oracle
Stanfield   Randolph   San Manuel
Eleven Mile Corner   COCHISE
Casa Grande   Avra Valley Catalina   Bowie San Simon
Arizona City Eloy   Picacho   Picture Rocks Oro Valley
Marana Casas Adobes   Willcox
PIMA   Silver Bell   Flowing Wells   Tucson
Ajo   Tucson Estates   South Tucson
Three Points   Valencia West   **856-857**
Gu Achi   Benson
Sells   Sahuarita   St David
Topawa   Green Valley   Whetstone Tombstone Elfrida
SANTA CRUZ   Huachuca City
MEXICO   Patagonia   Sierra Vista
Rio Rico East   Sierra Vista Southeast   Bisbee
Nogales   Miracle Valley Naco   Pirtleville Douglas

Cleartype®

County-Town

ARIZONA

ZIP CODES
NATIONAL AREA NO.8

AMC

Explanation of Symbols

State Capital
Vernon   County Seat

Population Key

○ 0-999	◉ 20,000-24,999
◦ 1,000-2,499	◉ 25,000-49,999
⊕ 2,500-4,999	□ 50,000-99,999
◌ 5,000-9,999	▫ 100,000-249,999
◉ 10,000-19,000	■ 250,000-999,999

Zip Code Symbols

○ Sectional Center

972 ● City which has its own 3-digit zip code (the number beside the symbol).

972 ◉ City which has its own 3-digit zip code and also serves other post offices as a sectional center.

0 20 30 60 80 Miles
0 20 40 60 80 100 120 Kilometers

Copyright American Map Corporation

COUNTIES

(75 Counties)

CITIES AND TOWNS

Note: The first name is that of the city or town, second, that of the county in which it is located, then the zip code area and location on the map.

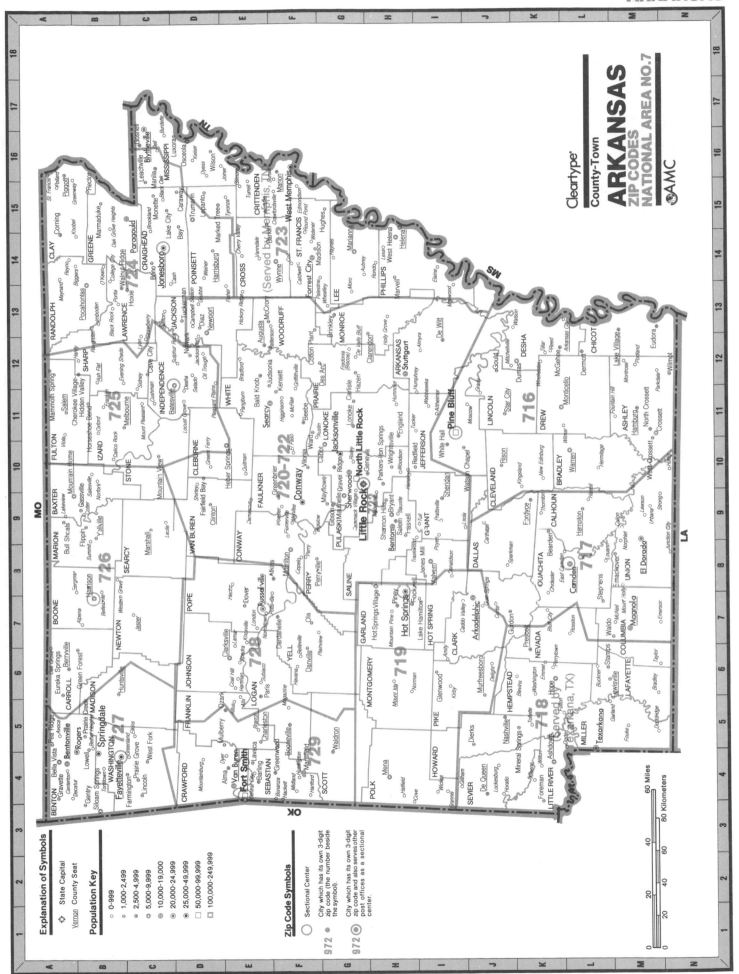

Cleartype®
County-Town
ARKANSAS
ZIP CODES
NATIONAL AREA NO.7

AMC

Explanation of Symbols

✧ State Capital
Vernon ⊛ County Seat

Population Key
○ 0-999
◦ 1,000-2,499
⊕ 2,500-4,999
◉ 5,000-9,999
⊛ 10,000-19,000
⊚ 20,000-24,999
● 25,000-49,999
□ 50,000-99,999
▣ 100,000-249,999

Zip Code Symbols

972 ○ Sectional Center

972 • City which has its own 3-digit zip code (the number beside the symbol).

972 ◉ City which has its own 3-digit zip code and also serves other post offices as a sectional center.

60 Miles
80 Kilometers

Copyright American Map Corporation

Citrus Heights

Folsom
Orangevale
Fair Oaks
Foothill Farms
Carmichael
Arden-Arcade
Rancho Cordova
Rancho Murieta
Mather AFB
North Highlands
La Riviera
Rosemont
Sacramento
Florin
Wilton
Laguna
Elk Grove
Parkway-South Sacramento

Santa Rosa

NAPA
Healdsburg
SONOMA **949,**
Guerneville
Guerneywood Park
Windsor
Larkfield-Wikiup
Monte Rio
Roseland
Graton
Sebastopol
Occidental
Rohnert Park
Cotati
954
South Park
Glen Ellen
Fetters Hot Springs-Agua Caliente
Boyes Hot Springs
Kenwood
North Bay
Sonoma
Petaluma
MARIN

Explanation of Symbols
* State Capital
Vernon County Seat

Population Key
○ 0-999
○ 1,000-2,499
□ 2,500-4,999
□ 5,000-9,999
● 10,000-19,000
● 20,000-24,999
◉ 25,000-49,999
□ 50,000-99,999
□ 100,000-249,999
■ 250,000-999,999
■ 1,000,000+

Zip Code Symbols
○ Sectional Center
972 City which has its own 3-digit zip code (the number beside the symbol).
972 City which has its own 3-digit zip code and also serves other post offices as a sectional center.

Cleartype®
County-Town
CALIFORNIA
(UPPER)
ZIP CODES
NATIONAL AREA NO.9
◎AMC

OR

955 HUMBOLT
DEL NORTE
SISKIYOU
MODOC
(Served by Reno, NV) **961**
SHASTA
TRINITY
960
Redding
TEHAMA
949, 954 MENDOCINO
LAKE
GLENN
Santa Rosa
Petaluma
SONOMA
NAPA
959
Chico
Paradise
BUTTE
PLUMAS
SIERRA
NEVADA
PLACER
EL DORADO
ALPINE 961
AMADOR
CALAVERAS
TUOLUMNE
MARIPOSA
Sacramento
Stockton
SAN JOAQUIN
Modesto
STANISLAUS
952-95
MERCED
Merced
MADERA
930-938
Fresno **936-938**
Clovis
FRESNO
TULARE
INYO
MONO
935
Bishop
MADERA
Madera

San Francisco
Oakland
Hayward
San Jose
Salinas
MONTEREY
SAN BENITO
SANTA CRUZ
Watsonville

940, 943-944
Military
APO South 962-966
FPO 966
951
939

Pacific Ocean

945-948
Concord
Antioch
CONTRA COSTA
Berkeley
Oakland
946-947
Alameda
San Leandro
Hayward
Union City
Fremont
Milpitas
SANTA CLARA
Mountain View
Sunnyvale
Santa Clara
950-951
San Jose
Morgan Hill
Campbell
Saratoga
Los Gatos
Palo Alto
Menlo Park
Redwood City
San Mateo
SAN MATEO
943-944
San Francisco
941
Military
APO 962-966
FPO 966
Daly City

948 Richmond
San Rafael
MARIN
949
San Pablo

Salinas
939
Marina
Seaside
Monterey
Pacific Grove
Carmel

Copyright American Map Corporation

For Explanation of Symbols see California (Upper), previous page.

Cleartype®
County-Town
CALIFORNIA
(LOWER)
ZIP CODES
NATIONAL AREA NO. 9
AMC

80 Miles
100 Kilometers

AZ
NV
MEXICO

923-925
922
935
924
912
913
915
916
917-918
926-928
930-951
939
923-925 (Moreno Valley)
934
936-938
914
913-916
919-921
921
904
907-908

San Bernardino
Riverside
Los Angeles
Orange
San Diego
Imperial
Inyo
Kern
Tulare
Kings
Monterey
San Benito
San Luis Obispo
Santa Barbara
Ventura
Fresno

Needles
East Blythe / Blythe
Fort Irwin
Barstow
Victorville
Apple Valley
Hesperia
Lancaster
Palmdale
Twentynine Palms
Palm Springs
Indio
Coachella
El Centro
Calexico
Brawley
Imperial
Bakersfield
Porterville
Visalia
Hanford
Ridgecrest
Mojave
Santa Maria
Lompoc
San Luis Obispo
Paso Robles
San Buenaventura (Ventura)
Oxnard
Camarillo
Simi Valley
Thousand Oaks
Santa Clarita
Burbank
Glendale
Pasadena
Los Angeles
East Los Angeles
Long Beach
Torrance
Inglewood
Santa Monica
Van Nuys
San Fernando
Hawthorne
Anaheim
Santa Ana
Irvine
Mission Viejo
San Clemente
Newport Beach
Costa Mesa
Huntington Beach
Fountain Valley
Garden Grove
Fullerton
Pomona
Rancho Cucamonga
Ontario
Chino
Redlands
Yucaipa
Rialto
Fontana
Colton
Escondido
Oceanside
Carlsbad
Encinitas
San Marcos
Vista
Poway
Temecula
Hemet
San Diego
Chula Vista
National City
Coronado
Imperial Beach
El Cajon
La Mesa
Santee
Lakeside

Pacific Ocean

Copyright American Map Corporation

13

COUNTIES

(58 Counties)

Name of County	Population	Location on Map
ALAMEDA	1,279,182	L-4
ALPINE	1,113	I-8
AMADOR	30,039	J-7
BUTTE	182,120	F-6
CALAVERAS	31,998	J-8
COLUSA	16,275	G-4
CONTRA COSTA	803,732	K-5
DEL NORTE	23,460	B-1
EL DORADO	125,995	I-8
FRESNO	667,490	N-7
GLENN	24,798	F-3
HUMBOLDT	119,118	B-2
IMPERIAL	109,303	V-15
INYO	18,281	L-11
KERN	543,477	Q-7
KINGS	101,469	P-7
LAKE	50,631	G-3
LASSEN	27,598	C-6
LOS ANGELES	8,863,164	S-10
MADERA	88,090	L-10
MARIN	230,096	J-3
MARIPOSA	14,302	L-8
MENDOCINO	80,345	F-1
MERCED	178,403	M-6
MODOC	9,678	A-6
MONO	9,956	J-9
MONTEREY	355,660	N-5
NAPA	110,765	I-4
NEVADA	78,510	G-7
ORANGE	2,410,556	V-11
PLACER	172,796	H-7
PLUMAS	19,739	E-6
RIVERSIDE	1,170,413	U-16
SACRAMENTO	1,041,219	I-6
SAN BENITO	36,697	N-6
SAN BERNARDINO	1,418,380	Q-14
SAN DIEGO	2,498,016	V-13
SAN FRANCISCO	723,959	K-3
SAN JOAQUIN	480,628	J-6
SAN LUIS OBISPO	217,162	P-5
SAN MATEO	649,623	L-4
SANTA BARBARA	369,608	S-7
SANTA CLARA	1,497,577	L-5
SANTA CRUZ	229,734	M-4
SHASTA	147,036	C-4
SIERRA	3,318	G-7
SISKIYOU	43,531	A-3
SOLANO	340,421	J-5
SONOMA	388,222	I-2
STANISLAUS	370,522	M-6
SUTTER	64,415	I-5
TEHAMA	49,625	E-3
TRINITY	13,063	C-3
TULARE	311,921	O-10
TUOLUMNE	48,456	J-8
VENTURA	669,016	S-8
YOLO	141,092	I-4
YUBA	58,228	G-6
TOTAL	29,760,021	

CITIES AND TOWNS

Note: The first name is that of the city or town, second, that of the county in which it is located, then the zip code area and location on the map.

- •Acton, Los Angeles, 93510 .... T-11
- Adelanto, San Bernardino, 92301 .... S-12
- Agoura Hills, Los Angeles, 91303 .... V-9
- Alameda, Alameda, 94501 .... C-11
- •Alamo, Contra Costa, 94507 .... C-13
- Albany, Alameda, 94706 .... B-11
- Alhambra, Los Angeles, 91801-03 .... W-5
- •Aliso Viejo, Orange, 92656 .... T-1
- •Alondra Park, Los Angeles, 90249 .... Z-3
- •Alpine, San Diego, 91901 .... X-13
- Alta Loma, San Bernardino, 91701, 37 .... P-12
- •Alta Sierra, Nevada, 95949 .... H-7
- •Altadena, Los Angeles, 91001 .... V-5
- Altaville, Calaveras, 95221 .... K-7
- Alturas, Modoc, 96101 .... B-8
- •American Canyon, Napa, 94589 .... J-4
- Anaheim, Orange, 92801-99 .... U-11
- Anderson, Shasta, 96007 .... E-4
- Angels, Calaveras, 95222 .... K-7
- •Angwin, Napa, 94508 .... I-4
- Antioch, Contra Costa, 94509 .... A-14
- Apple Valley, San Bernardino, 92307-08 .... T-12
- •Aptos, Santa Cruz, 95003 .... I-13
- •Aptos Hills-Larkin Valley, Santa Cruz, 95003 .... I-14
- •Arbuckle, Colusa, 95912 .... H-5
- Arcadia, Los Angeles, 91006-07 .... W-6
- Arcata, Humboldt, 95521 .... C-1
- •Arden-Arcade, Sacramento, 95821 .... B-17
- Argus, San Bernardino, 93562 .... Q-12
- •Armona, Kings, 93202 .... O-8
- •Arnold, Calaveras, 95223 .... J-8
- •Aromas, Monterey/San Benito, 95004 .... J-14
- Arroyo Grande, San Luis Obispo, 93420 .... R-6
- Artesia, Los Angeles, 90701 .... Z-5
- Arvin, Kern, 93203 .... R-9
- •Ashland, Alameda, 94541 .... D-12
- Atascadero, San Luis Obispo, 93422 .... Q-6
- Atherton, San Mateo, 94027 .... E-12
- Atwater, Merced, 95301 .... M-7
- •Auberry, Fresno, 93602 .... M-9
- Auburn, Placer, 95602-03 .... I-6
- •August, San Joaquin, 95201 .... K-6
- Avalon, Los Angeles, 90704 .... W-10
- Avenal, Kings, 93204 .... P-7
- •Avocado Heights, Los Angeles, 91746 .... X-6
- Azusa, Los Angeles, 91702 .... W-7
- Bakersfield, Kern, 93301-99 .... R-9
- Bakersfield East, Kern, 93305 .... Q-9
- Bakersfield South, Kern, 93304 .... R-9
- Baldwin Park, Los Angeles, 91706 .... W-6
- Banning, Riverside, 92220 .... U-12
- Barstow, San Bernardino, 92311 .... S-13
- •Bayview, Humboldt, 94124 .... C-1
- •Bayview-Montalvin, Contra Costa, 94806 .... A-11
- •Baywood-Los Osos, San Luis Obispo, 93402 .... R-5
- •Beale AFB, Yuba, 95903 .... H-6
- •Bear Valley Springs, Kern, 93561 .... R-10
- Beaumont, Riverside, 92223 .... U-12
- Bell, Los Angeles, 90201 .... X-5
- Bell Gardens, Los Angeles, 90201 .... X-5
- Bellflower, Los Angeles, 90706 .... Y-5
- Belmont, San Mateo, 94002 .... E-11
- Belvedere, Marin, 94920 .... B-10
- •Ben Lomond, Santa Cruz, 95005 .... H-13
- Benicia, Solano, 94510 .... K-5
- Berkeley, Alameda, 94701-99 .... B-11
- •Bermuda Dunes, Riverside, 92201 .... H-15
- •Bethel Island, Contra Costa, 94511 .... A-15
- Beverly Hills, Los Angeles, 90210-12 .... W-3
- •Big Bear City, San Bernardino, 92314 .... T-13
- Big Bear Lake, San Bernardino, 92315 .... T-13
- •Big Pine, Inyo, 93513 .... M-12
- Biggs, Butte, 95917 .... G-5
- Bishop, Inyo, 93514 .... M-11
- •Blackhawk, Contra Costa, 94506 .... C-13
- •Bloomington, San Bernardino, 92316 .... Q-3
- Blue Lake, Humboldt, 95525 .... C-1
- Blythe, Riverside, 92225 .... V-18
- •Bodega Bay, Sonoma, 94923 .... J-3
- •Bodfish, Kern, 93205 .... Q-10
- •Bolinas, Marin, 94924 .... B-9
- •Bonadelle Ranchos-Madera Ranchos, Madera, 93638 .... N-8
- •Bonita, San Diego, 91902 .... AA-12
- Bonnyview, Shasta, 96001 .... E-4
- •Bonsall, San Diego, 92003 .... W-12
- •Bootjack, Mariposa, 95338 .... L-9
- •Boron, Kern, 93516 .... R-12
- •Borrego Springs, San Diego, 92004 .... W-14
- •Bostonia, San Diego, 92021 .... Y-12
- •Boulder Creek, Santa Cruz, 95006 .... M-4
- •Boyes Hot Springs, Sonoma, 95416 .... E-18
- Brawley, Imperial, 92227 .... W-16
- Brea, Orange, 92621 .... Y-7
- Brentwood, Contra Costa, 94513 .... B-15
- Bridgeport, Mono, 93517 .... J-10
- Brisbane, San Mateo, 94005 .... D-11
- •Broadmoor, San Mateo, 94015 .... D-10
- •Buellton, Santa Barbara, 93427 .... T-7
- Buena Park, Orange, 90620-21 .... Z-6
- Bullard, Fresno, 93704 .... N-9
- Burbank, Los Angeles, 91501-99 .... T-10
- •Burbank, Santa Clara, 91500,03 .... G-13
- Burlingame, San Mateo, 94010 .... D-11
- •Burney, Shasta, 96013 .... D-6
- •Buttonwillow, Kern, 93206 .... Q-8
- Byron, Contra Costa, 94514 .... B-15
- •Cabazon, Riverside, 92230 .... H-13
- Calexico, Imperial, 92231 .... X-16
- California City, Kern, 93505 .... R-11
- Calimesa, Riverside, 92320 .... U-13
- Calipatria, Imperial, 92233 .... W-16
- Calistoga, Napa, 94515 .... I-4
- Camarillo, Ventura, 93310-12 .... U-9
- •Cambria, San Luis Obispo, 93428 .... Q-5
- •Cambrian Park, Santa Clara, 95154 .... G-13
- •Cameron Park, El Dorado, 95682 .... I-7
- •Camp Pendleton North, San Diego, 92055 .... W-12
- •Camp Pendleton South, San Diego, 92055 .... W-12
- Campbell, Santa Clara, 95008 .... G-13
- Campo, San Diego, 91906 .... X-14
- •Canyon Lake, Riverside, 92587 .... S-4
- Capitola, Santa Cruz, 95010 .... M-5
- Carlsbad, San Diego, 92007-08 .... W-12
- •Carmel Valley Village, Monterey, 93924 .... O-4
- Carmel Woods, Monterey, 93923 .... L-13
- Carmel-by-the-Sea, Monterey, 93923 .... L-13
- •Carmichael, Sacramento, 95608 .... A-17
- Carpinteria, Santa Barbara, 93013 .... T-8
- Carson, Los Angeles, 90745-46 .... Z-4
- •Caruthers, Fresno, 93609 .... O-7
- •Casa Conejo, Ventura, 91360 .... V-9
- •Casa de Oro-Mount Helix, San Diego, 92120 .... Z-12
- Castle, Merced, 95342 .... M-7
- •Castro Valley, Alameda, 94546-52 .... C-12
- •Castroville, Monterey, 95012 .... K-14
- Cathedral City, Riverside, 92234 .... V-14
- •Cayucos, San Luis Obispo, 93430 .... Q-5
- •Central Valley, Shasta, 96019 .... D-4
- Ceres, Stanislaus, 95307 .... L-7
- Cerritos, Los Angeles, 90703 .... Z-5
- •Challenge-Brownsville, Yuba, 95919 .... G-6
- •Channel Islands Beach, Ventura, 93030 .... U-9
- •Charter Oak, Los Angeles, 91724 .... W-8
- •Cherry Valley, Riverside, 92223 .... U-13
- •Cherryland, Alameda, 94541 .... D-12
- •Chester, Plumas, 96020 .... E-6
- Chico, Butte, 95926-28 .... G-5
- Chino, San Bernardino, 91709-10 .... Q-1
- •Chino Hills, San Bernardino, 91710 .... Q-1
- Chowchilla, Madera, 93610 .... M-8
- Chula Vista, San Diego, 91910-13 .... AA-11
- •Citrus, Los Angeles, 91702 .... W-7
- •Citrus Heights, Sacramento, 95616-21 .... A-17
- Claremont, Los Angeles, 91711 .... W-9
- Clayton, Contra Costa, 94517 .... B-13
- Clearlake, Lake, 95422 .... H-4
- •Clearlake Oaks, Lake, 95423 .... H-4
- Clifton, Los Angeles, 90277 .... Z-3
- Cloverdale, Sonoma, 95425 .... I-3
- Clovis, Fresno, 93611-12 .... N-9
- Coachella, Riverside, 92236 .... V-15
- Coalinga, Fresno, 93210 .... P-6
- •Cobb, Lake, 95426 .... I-4
- Colfax, Placer, 95713 .... H-6
- Colma, San Mateo, 94015 .... D-10
- Colton, San Bernardino, 92324 .... Q-3
- •Columbia, Tuolumne, 95310 .... K-8
- Colusa, Colusa, 95932 .... H-5
- Commerce, Los Angeles, 90040 .... X-5
- Compton, Los Angeles, 90220-22 .... Z-4
- Concord, Contra Costa, 94518-21 .... B-13
- •Concow, Butte, 95965 .... G-6
- Corcoran, Kings, 93212 .... P-8
- Corning, Tehama, 96021 .... F-5
- Corona, Riverside, 91719-20 .... R-2
- Coronado, San Diego, 92118 .... AA-10
- •Corralitos, Santa Cruz, 95076 .... I-14
- Corte Madera, Marin, 94925 .... B-10
- Costa Mesa, Orange, 92926-27 .... V-11
- Cotati, Sonoma, 94931 .... E-17
- •Coto De Caza, Orange, 92679 .... T-2
- •Cottonwood, Shasta, 96022 .... E-4
- •Country Club, San Joaquin, 94556 .... K-6
- •Covelo, Mendocino, 95428 .... F-3
- Covina, Los Angeles, 91722-24 .... W-7
- Crescent City, Del Norte, 95531 .... A-1
- •Crescent City North, Del Norte, 95531 .... A-1
- •Crestline, San Bernardino, 92325 .... T-12
- •Crockett, Contra Costa, 94525 .... A-12
- Cudahy, Los Angeles, 90201 .... Y-5
- Culver City, Los Angeles, 90230-32 .... X-3
- Cupertino, Santa Clara, 95014 .... G-13
- •Cutler, Tulare, 93615 .... O-9
- •Cutten, Humboldt, 95534 .... D-1
- Cypress, Orange, 90630 .... Z-4
- Dagget, San Bernardino,92327 .... S-13
- Daly City, San Mateo, 94014-15 .... C-10
- Dana Point, Orange, 92629 .... U-1
- Danville, Contra Costa, 94506,26 .... C-13
- Davis, Yolo, 95616 .... I-5
- •Day Valley, Santa Cruz, 96056 .... I-13
- •Deer Park, Napa, 94576 .... J-4
- •Del Aire, Los Angeles, 90250 .... Y-3
- Del Mar, San Diego, 92014 .... X-12
- •Del Monte Forest, Monterey, 93953 .... L-13
- •Del Rey, Fresno, 93616 .... N-9
- Del Rey Oaks, Monterey, 93940 .... L-13
- Delano, Kern, 93215 .... Q-8
- •Delhi, Merced, 95315 .... L-7
- •Denair, Stanislaus, 95316 .... L-7
- Desert Hot Springs, Riverside, 92240 .... U-14
- •Desert View Highlands, Los Angeles, 93550 .... S-11
- Diamond Bar, Los Angeles, 91765 .... X-8
- •Diamond Springs, El Dorado, 95619 .... I-7
- Dinuba, Tulare, 93618 .... O-8
- •Discovery Bay, Contra Costa, 94513 .... B-15
- Dixon, Solano, 95620 .... J-5
- •Dixon Lane-Meadow Creek, Inyo, 95620 .... L-11
- •Dollar Point, Placer, 96140 .... H-8
- Dominguez, Los Angeles,90810 .... Z-4
- Dos Palos, Merced, 93620 .... M-7
- Downey, Los Angeles, 90240-42 .... Y-5
- Downieville, Sierra,95936 .... G-7
- Duarte, Los Angeles, 91010 .... V-6
- Dublin, Alameda, 94568 .... D-13
- Dunsmuir, Siskiyou, 96025 .... C-5
- •Durham, Butte, 95938 .... G-5
- •Earlimart, Tulare, 93219 .... P-8
- •East Blythe, Riverside, 92225 .... V-18
- •East Compton, Los Angeles, 90221 .... Y-5
- •East Foothills, Santa Clara, 91501 .... F-14
- •East Hemet, Riverside, 92544 .... U-12
- •East La Mirada, Los Angeles, 90638 .... Y-6
- •East Los Angeles, Los Angeles, 90022 .... X-4
- East Palo Alto, San Mateo, 94303 .... E-12
- •East Pasadena, Los Angeles, 91117 .... W-5
- •East Porterville, Tulare, 93257 .... P-9
- •East Richmond Heights, Contra Costa, 94801 .... B-11
- •East San Gabriel, Los Angeles, 91775 .... W-6
- •East Sonora, Tuolumne, 95370 .... K-8
- •Easton, Fresno, 93706 .... N-9
- Edison, Kern,93220 .... R-9
- •Edwards AFB, Kern, 93523 .... S-11
- El Cajon, San Diego, 92019-20 .... Y-12
- El Centro, Imperial, 92243 .... X-16
- El Cerrito, Contra Costa, 94530 .... B-11
- •El Cerrito, Riverside, 91718-20 .... D-2
- •El Dorado Hills, El Dorado, 95762 .... I-6
- El Encanto Heights, Santa Barbara, 93117 .... T-7
- •El Granada, San Mateo, 94018 .... E-19
- El Monte, Los Angeles, 91731-33 .... W-6
- El Paso de Robles (Paso Robles), San Luis Obispo, 93446-47 .... Q-6
- El Porto, Los Angeles,90266 .... Y-3
- •El Rio, Ventura, 93030 .... T-9
- El Segundo, Los Angeles, 90245 .... Y-3
- •El Sobrante, Contra Costa, 94803 .... B-12
- •El Toro, Orange, 92610,30 .... T-1
- •El Toro Station, Orange, 92709 .... T-1
- •El Verano, Sonoma, 95433 .... J-4
- •Eldridge, Sonoma, 95431 .... J-4
- •Elk Grove, Sacramento, 95624 .... J-6
- •Elkhorn, Monterey, 93440 .... J-14
- •Emerald Lake Hills, San Mateo, 94061 .... E-11
- Emeryville, Alameda, 94608 .... C-11
- Empire, Stanislaus,95319 .... L-7
- Encinitas, San Diego, 92024 .... W-12
- Enterprise, Shasta, 96001 .... D-4
- Escalon, San Joaquin, 95320 .... K-7
- Escondido, San Diego, 92025-27 .... W-13
- •Esparto, Yolo, 95627 .... I-5
- Etiwanda, San Bernardino, 91739 .... P-2
- Eureka, Humboldt, 95501,03 .... D-1
- Exeter, Tulare, 93221 .... O-9
- •Fair Oaks, Sacramento, 95628 .... A-17
- Fairfax, Marin, 94930 .... A-10
- Fairfield, Solano, 94533 .... J-5
- •Fairview, Alameda, 94542 .... D-12
- •Fallbrook, San Diego, 92028 .... V-12
- Farmersville, Tulare, 93223 .... O-9
- •Felton, Santa Cruz, 95018 .... H-12
- Ferndale, Humboldt, 95536 .... D-1
- •Fetters Hot Springs-Agua Caliente, Sonoma, 95416 .... E-18
- Fig Garden, Fresno, 93704 .... N-9
- Fillmore, Ventura, 93015 .... T-9
- Firebaugh, Fresno, 93622 .... N-8
- •Florence-Graham, Los Angeles, 90001 .... Y-4
- •Florin, Sacramento, 95829 .... C-17
- Folsom, Sacramento, 95630 .... A-18
- Fontana, San Bernardino, 92334-36 .... P-3
- •Foothill Farms, Sacramento, 95841 .... A-17
- •Ford City, Kern, 93268 .... R-8
- •Foresthill, Placer, 95631 .... H-7
- •Forestville, Sonoma, 95436 .... J-3
- Fort Bragg, Mendocino, 95437 .... G-2
- Fort Irwin, San Bernardino, 92310 .... R-13
- Fortuna, Humboldt, 95540 .... B-1
- Foster City, San Mateo, 94404 .... E-11
- Fountain Valley, Orange, 92708 .... V-11
- Fowler, Fresno, 93625 .... N-9
- •Frazier Park, Kern, 93225 .... S-9
- •Freedom, Santa Cruz, 95019 .... I-14
- Fremont, Alameda, 94536-39,55 .... E-13
- •French Camp, San Joaquin, 95231 .... K-6
- Fresno, Fresno, 93701-94, 93844 .... N-9
- Fullerton, Orange, 92631-35 .... Z-7
- Galt, Sacramento, 95632 .... J-6
- Garberville, Humboldt, 95542 .... F-2
- •Garden Acres, San Joaquin, 95205 .... K-6
- Garden Grove, Orange, 92640-45 .... AA-7
- Gardena, Los Angeles, 90247-49 .... U-10
- •George AFB, San Bernardino, 92349 .... S-12
- •Gerber-Las Flores, Tehama, 96035 .... F-5
- Geyserville, Sonoma, 95441 .... I-3
- Gilroy, Santa Clara, 95020 .... M-6
- •Glen Avon, Riverside, 92509 .... Q-2
- •Glen Ellen, Sonoma, 95442 .... E-18
- Glendale, Los Angeles, 91201-99 .... V-4
- Glendora, Los Angeles, 91740 .... T-11
- •Glenshire-Devonshire, Nevada, 96162 .... G-8
- •Golden Hills, Kern, 93561 .... R-10
- Goleta, Santa Barbara, 93117 .... T-7
- Gonzales, Monterey, 93926 .... O-4
- Grand Terrace, San Bernardino, 92324 .... Q-3
- •Granite Hills, San Diego, 92120 .... Y-12
- Grass Valley, Nevada, 95945-49 .... H-7
- •Graton, Sonoma, 95444 .... E-16
- •Greenacres, Kern, 93307 .... Q-9
- Greenbrae, Marin, 94904 .... B-10
- Greenfield, Monterey, 93927 .... O-5
- •Greenville, Plumas, 95947 .... F-7
- Gridley, Butte, 95948 .... H-5
- •Groveland-Big Oak Flat, Tuolumne, 95321 .... K-8
- Grover City, San Luis Obispo, 93433 .... R-6
- Guadalupe, Santa Barbara, 93434 .... R-6
- •Guerneville, Sonoma, 95446 .... J-3
- Guernewood Park, Sonoma, 95446 .... D-16
- Gustine, Merced, 95322 .... M-7
- •Hacienda Heights, Los Angeles, 91745 .... X-7
- Half Moon Bay, San Mateo, 94019 .... E-10
- •Hamilton City, Glenn, 95951 .... G-5
- Hanford, Kings, 93230-32 .... O-8
- Hanford Northwest, Kings, 93230 .... O-8
- Hanford South, Kings, 93231 .... P-8
- •Harbison Canyon, San Diego, 92019-21 .... X-13
- Hatton Fields, Monterey, 93923 .... O-4
- Hawaiian Gardens, Los Angeles, 90716 .... Z-6
- Hawthorne, Los Angeles, 90250 .... U-10
- •Hayfork, Trinity, 96041 .... D-3
- Hayward, Alameda, 94541-45 .... L-5
- Healdsburg, Sonoma, 95448 .... I-3
- •Heber, Imperial, 92249 .... X-16
- Hemet, Riverside, 92543-45 .... V-13
- Hercules, Contra Costa, 94547 .... A-11
- Hermosa Beach, Los Angeles, 90254 .... Z-3
- Hesperia, San Bernardino, 92345 .... T-12
- Hidden Hills, Los Angeles, 91302 .... W-1
- •Hidden Meadows, San Diego, 92025 .... W-12
- •Hidden Valley Lake, Lake, 95650 .... I-4
- •Highgrove, Riverside, 92507 .... Q-3
- Highland, San Bernardino, 92346 .... U-12
- •Highlands, San Mateo, 93246 .... E-11
- Hillcrest Center, Kern, 93306 .... R-9
- Hillsborough, San Mateo, 94010 .... E-11
- •Hilmar-Irwin, Merced, 95324 .... L-7
- Hinkley, San Bernardino, 92347 .... S-12
- Hollister, San Benito, 95023 .... N-6
- Holtville, Imperial, 92250 .... X-16
- •Home Garden, Kings, 93239 .... O-8
- •Home Gardens, Riverside, 91720 .... R-2
- •Homeland, Riverside, 92548 .... S-5
- Hoopa, Humboldt, 95546 .... C-2
- Hughson, Stanislaus, 95326 .... L-7
- •Humboldt Hill, Humboldt, 95521 .... D-1
- Huntington Beach, Orange, 92646-49 .... AA-6
- Huntington Park, Los Angeles, 90255 .... X-4
- Huron, Fresno, 93234 .... O-7
- •Hydesville, Humboldt, 95547 .... D-1
- •Idyllwild-Pine Cove, Riverside, 92549 .... U-13
- Imperial, Imperial, 92251 .... X-16
- Imperial Beach, San Diego, 91932 .... BB-11
- Independence, Inyo, 93526 .... N-12
- Indian Wells, Riverside, 92210 .... V-14
- Indio, Riverside, 92201 .... V-15
- Inglewood, Los Angeles, 90301-99 .... Y-3
- •Interlaken, Santa Cruz, 95076 .... I-14
- •Inverness, Marin, 94937 .... K-3
- Ione, Amador, 95640 .... J-7
- Irvine, Orange, 92714-20 .... V-11
- Irwindale, Los Angeles, 91706 .... W-7
- •Isla Vista, Santa Barbara, 93117 .... T-7
- •Ivanhoe, Tulare, 93235 .... O-9
- Jackson, Amador, 95642 .... J-7
- Jamestown, Tuolumne, 95327 .... K-8
- •Jamul, San Diego, 91935 .... X-13
- •Joshua Tree, San Bernardino, 92252 .... T-14
- •Julian, San Diego, 92036 .... W-14
- •Kelseyville, Lake, 95451 .... H-3
- •Kensington, Contra Costa, 94707 .... B-11
- •Kentfield, Marin, 94904 .... B-10
- Kenwood, Sonoma, 95452 .... E-18
- Kerman, Fresno, 93630 .... N-8
- •Kernville, Kern, 93238 .... Q-10
- •Kettleman City, Kings, 93239 .... P-7
- •Keyes, Stanislaus, 95328 .... L-7
- King City, Monterey, 93930 .... O-5
- •Kings Beach, Placer, 96143 .... H-8
- Kingsburg, Fresno, 93631 .... O-8
- La Canada Flintridge, Los Angeles, 91011 .... V-5
- •La Crescenta-Montrose, Los Angeles, 91214 .... V-4
- La Habra, Orange, 90631 .... Y-7
- La Habra Heights, Los Angeles, 90631 .... Y-7
- La Mesa, San Diego, 91941-42 .... Z-11
- La Mirada, Los Angeles, 90638 .... Y-6
- La Palma, Orange, 90623 .... Z-6
- La Puente, Los Angeles, 91744-46,48 .... X-7
- La Quinta, Riverside, 92253 .... V-14
- •La Riviera, Sacramento, 95826 .... B-17
- La Verne, Los Angeles, 91750 .... W-8
- Ladera, San Mateo, 94028 .... F-12
- •Ladera Heights, Los Angeles, 90045 .... X-3
- Lafayette, Contra Costa, 94549 .... B-12
- •Laguna, Sacramento, 95824 .... C-17
- Laguna Beach, Orange, 92651,77 .... T-1
- •Laguna Hills, Orange, 92653 .... T-1
- Laguna Niguel, Orange, 92607 .... T-1
- •Lagunitas-Forest Knolls, Marin, 94938 .... A-9
- •Lake Arrowhead, San Bernardino, 92352 .... T-12
- Lake Elsinore, Riverside, 92530,32 .... S-3
- •Lake Isabella, Kern, 93240 .... Q-10
- •Lake Los Angeles, Los Angeles, 93535 .... S-11
- •Lake Nacimiento, San Luis Obispo, 93401 .... Q-5
- •Lake of the Pines, Nevada, 95603 .... H-6
- •Lake San Marcos, San Diego, 92069 .... W-12
- •Lakeland Village, Riverside, 92530 .... T-3
- Lakeport, Lake, 95453 .... H-3
- •Lakeside, San Diego, 92040 .... X-13
- •Lakeview, Riverside, 92567 .... R-4
- Lakewood, Los Angeles, 9712,13,15 .... Z-5
- •Lamont, Kern, 93241 .... R-9
- Lancaster, Los Angeles, 93534 .... S-11

Explanation of symbols: •– Census Designated Place (CDP)

Explanation of symbols: ● – Census Designated Place (CDP)

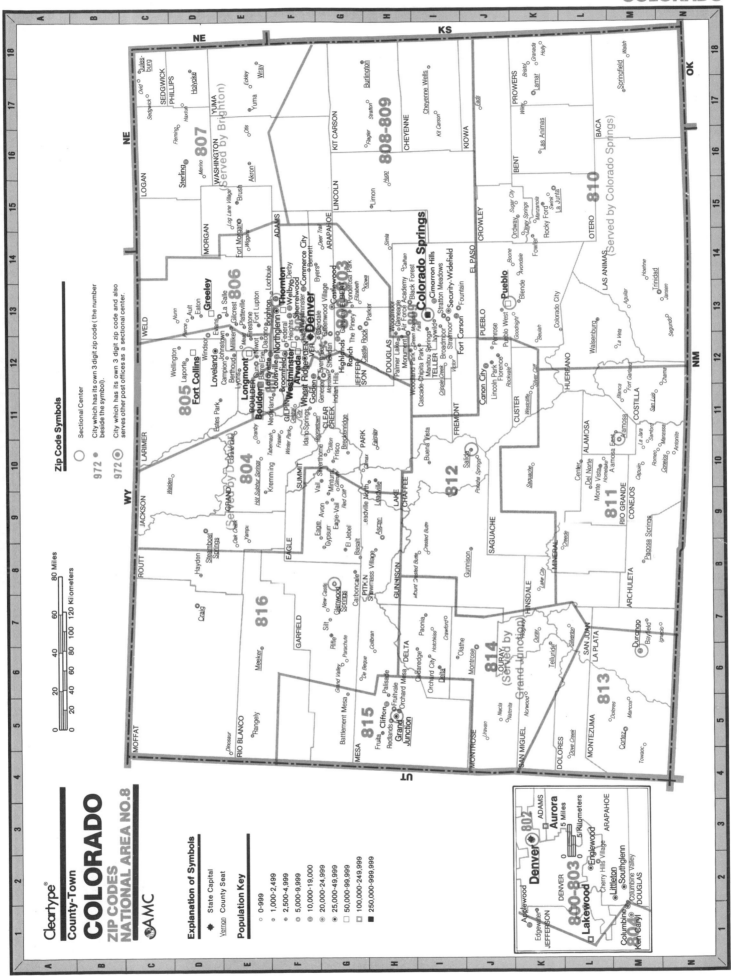

Cleartype®
County-Town
COLORADO
ZIP CODES
NATIONAL AREA NO. 8

AMC

Explanation of Symbols

✦ State Capital
Vernon County Seat

Population Key
○ 0-999
⊙ 1,000-2,499
⊕ 2,500-4,999
⊛ 5,000-9,999
⊚ 10,000-19,000
⊛ 20,000-24,999
⊙ 25,000-49,999
□ 50,000-99,999
▢ 100,000-249,999
■ 250,000-999,999

Zip Code Symbols

○ Sectional Center

972 ● City which has its own 3 digit zip code (the number beside the symbol).

972 ◉ City which has its own 3 digit zip code and also serves other post offices as a sectional center.

80 Miles
120 Kilometers

COUNTIES

(8 Counties)

Name of County	Population	Location on Map
FAIRFIELD	827,645	H-3
HARTFORD	851,783	A-7
LITCHFIELD	174,092	A-3
MIDDLESEX	143,196	F-10
NEW HAVEN	804,219	H-5
NEW LONDON	254,957	F-13
TOLLAND	128,699	A-12
WINDHAM	102,525	A-15
TOTAL	3,287,116	

CITIES AND TOWNS

Note: The first name is that of the city or town, second, that of the county in which it is located, then the zip code area and location on the map.

Explanation of symbols: ● – Census Designated Place (CDP) ● italics – Township shown which is also a CDP ▲ italics – Township (shown on the map)

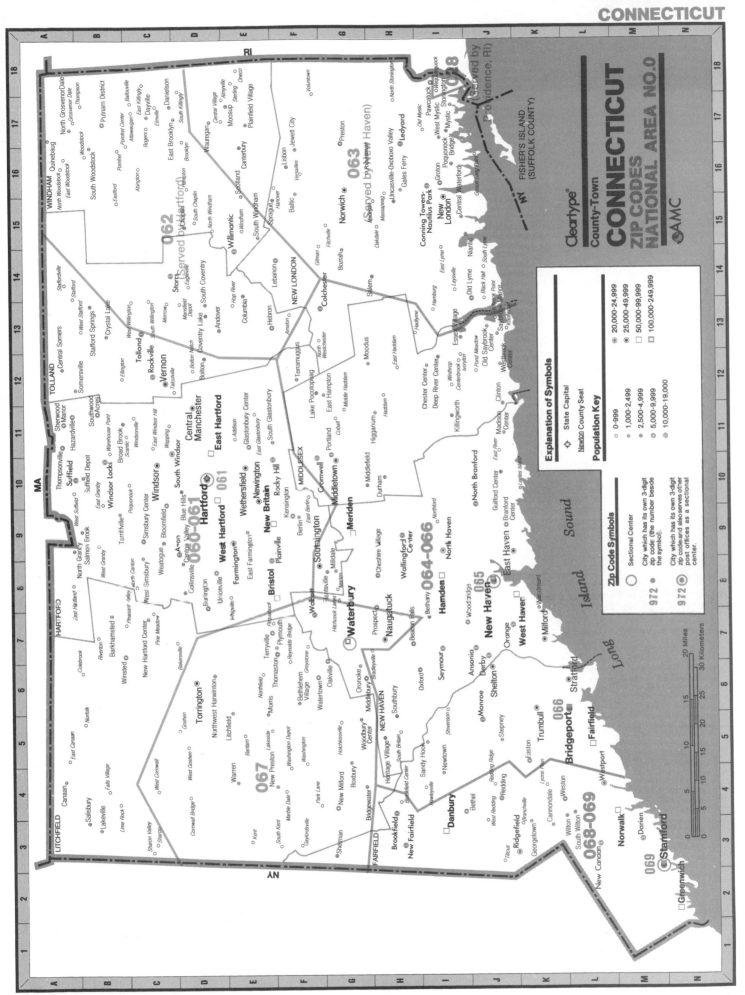

Copyright American Map Corporation

COUNTIES

(3 Counties)

Name	Population	Location on Map
KENT	110,993	H-5
NEW CASTLE	441,946	C-5
SUSSEX	113,229	M-5
TOTAL	666,168	

CITIES AND TOWNS

Note: The first name is that of the city or town, second, that of the county in which it is located, then the zip code area and location on the map.

Bellefonte, New Castle, 19809 .... B-8
Bridgeville, Sussex, 19933 .... N-7
Brookland Terrace, New Castle,
   19720 .... B-6
• Brookside, New Castle, 19713 .... C-5
Camden, Kent, 19934 .... J-7
• Claymont, New Castle, 19703 .... A-7
Clayton, Kent, 19938 .... H-6
Collins Park, New Castle, 19720 .... C-7
Delaware City, New Castle, 19706 ...... D-7
Dover, Kent, 19901-02 .... I-7
• Dover Base Housing, Kent, 19901 ...... J-8
• Edgemoor, New Castle, 19809 .... B-7
Elsmere, New Castle, 19805 .... B-7
Georgetown, Sussex, 19947 .... O-9
Harrington, Kent, 19952 .... L-7
• Highland Acres, Kent, 19720 .... J-7
Holloway Terrace, New Castle, 19720 . B-7
Holly Oak, New Castle, 19809 .... B-8
• Kent Acres, Kent, 19901 .... J-7
Laurel, Sussex, 19956 .... Q-7
Lewes, Sussex, 19958 .... N-11
Marshallton, New Castle, 19808 .... B-6
Middletown, New Castle, 19709 .... F-5
Milford, Kent/Sussex, 19963 .... L-8
Millsboro, Sussex, 19966 .... P-9
Milton, Sussex, 19968 .... N-9
Minquadale, New Castle, 19720 .... C-7
New Castle, New Castle, 19720 .... C-7
Newark, New Castle, 19702,11,13 ...... C-5
Newport, New Castle, 19804 .... B-6
• Pike Creek, New Castle, 19808 .... B-5
Rehoboth Beach, Sussex, 19971 ..... O-12
• Rising Sun-Lebanon, Kent,
   19901,34,62 .... J-8
• Riverview, Kent, 19962 .... K-7
• Rodney Village, Kent, 19901 .... I-7
Seaford, Sussex, 19973 .... O-6
Selbyville, Sussex, 19975 .... R-10
Smyrna, Kent/New Castle, 19977 .... H-7
• Stanton, New Castle, 19804 .... B-6
• Talleyville, New Castle, 19803 .... A-7
Wilmington, New Castle, 19801-99 ..... B-7
• Wilmington Manor, New Castle,
   19720 .... C-7
• Woodside East, Kent, 19980 .... J-7

Explanation of symbols: •– Census Designated Place (CDP)

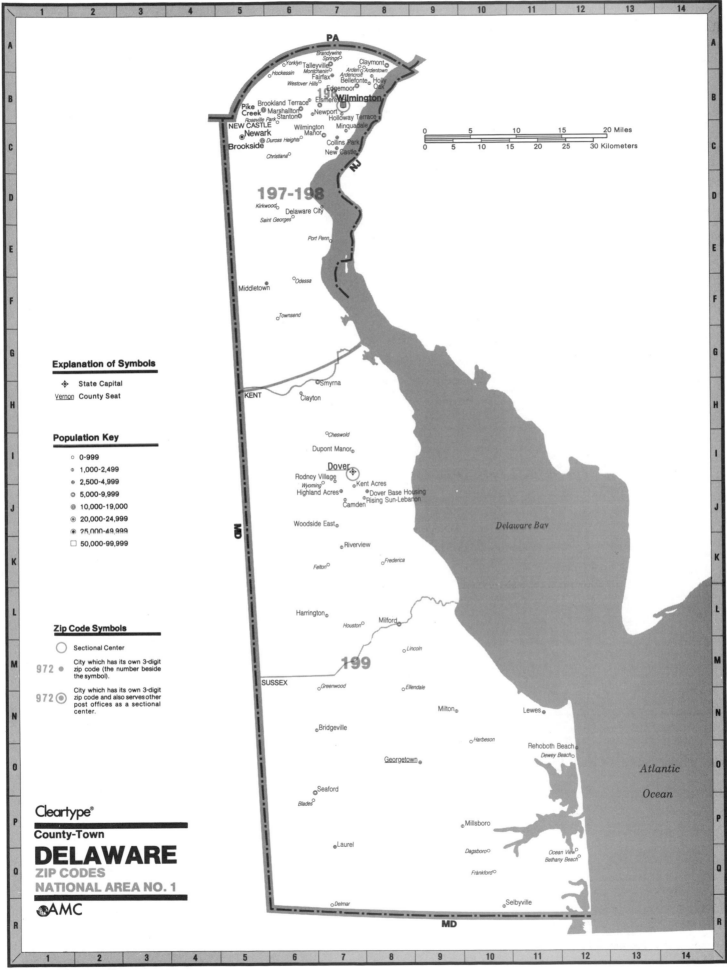

DELAWARE

Explanation of Symbols

✦ State Capital

Vernon County Seat

Population Key

○ 0-999
◉ 1,000-2,499
⊕ 2,500-4,999
◎ 5,000-9,999
⊕ 10,000-19,000
◉ 20,000-24,999
◉ 25,000-49,999
☐ 50,000-99,999

Zip Code Symbols

◯ Sectional Center

972 ● City which has its own 3-digit zip code (the number beside the symbol).

972 ◉ City which has its own 3-digit zip code and also serves other post offices as a sectional center.

Cleartype®

County-Town

DELAWARE
ZIP CODES
NATIONAL AREA NO. 1

◉AMC

197-198

199

PA

Brandywine Springs
Yorklyn Talleyville
Hockessin Montchanin Arden
Fairfax Ardentown
Westover Hills Edgemoor Ardencroft
Bellefonte Holly
198 Edgemoor Oak
Pike Brookland Terrace Elsmere Wilmington
Creek Marshallton Newport
Roseville Park Stanton Holloway Terrace
NEW CASTLE Wilmington
Newark Manor Minquadale
Brookside Duross Heights Collins Park
Christiana New Castle

Claymont

NJ

Kirkwood Delaware City
Saint Georges
Port Penn

Middletown Odessa

Townsend

Smyrna
KENT Clayton

Cheswold

Dupont Manor
Dover
Rodney Village Kent Acres
Wyoming Dover Base Housing
Highland Acres Rising Sun-Lebanon
Camden

Woodside East

Riverview

Felton Frederica

Harrington Milford
Houston
Lincoln

SUSSEX
Greenwood Ellendale

Milton Lewes

Bridgeville Harbeson
Rehoboth Beach
Georgetown Dewey Beach

Seaford
Blades

Millsboro

Laurel Dagsboro Ocean View
Bethany Beach
Frankford

Delmar Selbyville

MD

Delaware Bay

Atlantic Ocean

MD

0 5 10 15 20 Miles
0 5 10 15 20 25 30 Kilometers

Copyright American Map Corporation

Explanation of symbols: •– Census Designated Place (CDP)

Copyright American Map Corporation

Explanation of symbols: ● – Census Designated Place (CDP)

For Explanation of Symbols
See Florida, Main Map, Page 23

Top inset map:

15 16 17 18 19 20 21 22 23 24 25 26 27 28

CITRUS
Inverness
Lecanto
Homosassa Springs
Homosassa
Floral City
Lake Panasoffkee
Coleman
326
SUMTER
Wildwood
LAKE
Leesburg
Silver Lake
Sunnyside
Yalaha
Hawthorne
Eustis
Tavares
Apopka
Mount Plymouth
Mid Florida Lakes
Lake Monroe
Midway-Canaan
Sanford
VOLUSIA
327
SEMINOLE
Mid Florida
Longwood
Winter Springs
Altamonte Springs
Fern Park
Oviedo

HERNANDO
Brookridge
Mountain Park
High Point
North Brooksville
Brooksville
South Brooksville
South Weeki Wachee
Timber Pines
Ridge Manor
Spring Hill
Lacoochee
Weeki Wachee Gardens
Weeki Wachee Acres
Hernando Beach

Wekiva Springs
Forest City
South Apopka
Ocoee
Mascotte
Minneola
Clermont
Groveland
Winter Garden
Lockhart
Eatonville
Maitland
Fairvilla
ORANGE
Fern Park
Pine Hills
Fairview Shores
Union Park
Azalea Park
Orlando
328
Conway
Edgewood
Holden Heights
Oak Ridge
Sky Lake
Bay Hill
Tangelo Park
Doctor Phillips
Williamsburg
Lake Buena Vista
Meadow Wood
Bithlo

PASCO
Bayonet Point
Hudson
Jasmine Estates
316
St. Leo
Dade City North
Dade City
Dade City East

Port Richey
Gulf Harbors
New Port Richey
New Port Richey-East
(Served by Tampa)
Beacon Square
Elfers
Holiday Hills
Zephyrhills West
Zephyrhills North
Zephyrhills
Tahitian Gardens
Colonial Hills
Zephyrhills South
Country Estates
Buena Vista
Land O'Lakes
Forest Hills
Lutz

Kissimmee
Buena Ventura Lakes
OSCEOLA
Campbell
St. Cloud
Loughman
347
(Served by Orlando)
Polk City
Davenport
Poinciana Place

PINELLAS
Tarpon Springs
Palm Harbor
Ozona
Oldsmar
Dunedin
Clearwater
Belleair
Belleair Beach
Belleair Bluffs
Harbor Bluffs
Indian Rocks Beach
Indian Shores
Redington Shores
Seminole
North Redington Beach
Redington Beach
Madeira Beach
Treasure Island
St. Petersburg Beach

HILLSBOROUGH
Greater Northdale
Carrollwood Village
Egypt Lake
Town 'n' Country
West Park
Sweetwater Creek
Safety Harbor
Highpoint
Largo
Feather Sound
Candy
Bay Crest
Lake Magdalene
University West
Carrollwood
Del Rio
East Lake-Orient Park
Plant City
Mango
Dover
Seffner
Tampa
Brandon
Palm River-Clair Mel
Bloomingdale
Gibsonton
Riverview
335-336
St. Petersburg
Bardeen
Kenneth City
Pinellas Park
Baskin
Bay Pines
South Pasadena
Gulfport
337
Apollo Beach
Sun City Center
Ruskin

POLK
Kathleen
Gibsonia
Fussels Corner
West Auburndale
Auburndale
Winston
Inwood
West Winter Haven
Medulla
Crystal Lake
Lakeland
Lakeland Highlands
Willow Oak
Mulberry
Bartow
Haines City
North Winter Haven
Lake Alfred
Winter Haven
Cypress Gardens
Ian Phyl Village
Lake Wales
Babson Park
Crooked Lake Park
Bradley Junction
Fort Meade
Frostproof
338

MANATEE
Memphis
Palmetto
Ellenton
Palma Sola
West Bradenton
Bradenton
Samoset
West Samoset
Bradenton Beach
Bayshore Gardens
Whitfield
North Sarasota
Desoto Lakes
Tri Par Estates
The Meadows
342
Sarasota
Pinecraft
Kensington Park
Longboat Key
Southgate
Fruitville
Siesta Key
Sarasota Springs
South Sarasota
Ridge Wood Heights
Lake Sarasota
South Gate Ridge
Bee Ridge
SARASOTA
Vamo
Gulf Gate Estates
Osprey
Laurel
Nokomis
Venice Gardens
Venice
Plantation
North Port
Warm Mineral Springs
South Venice

HARDEE
Bowling Green
Wauchula
Zolfo Springs
HIGHLANDS
Avon Park
Sebring
Lake Placid
Placid Lakes
Sylvan Shores
Hiway Park
349

DE SOTO
Arcadia
Southeast Arcadia
Nocatee

GLADES
334

Gulf of Mexico

0 5 10 15 20 Miles
0 10 20 30 Kilometers

Lower-left inset map (330-332 / 333-334):

BROWARD
Parkland
Coral Springs
Deerfield Beach
Collier Manor-Cresthaven
Pompano Beach Highlands
Lighthouse Point
Margate
333
Kendall Green
Coconut Creek
Pompano Beach
North Lauderdale
Lauderdale-by-the-Sea
N. Andrews Gardens
Hillsboro Beach
334
Tamarac
Broadview-Pompano Park
Oakland Park
Lauderdale Lakes
Wilton Manors
Lauderhill
Fort Lauderdale
Sunrise
Browardale
Plantation
Washington Park
Fern Crest Village
Melrose Park
Dania
Pine Island Ridge
Davie
Pembroke Park
Hollywood
Cooper City
Broadview Park
Riverland
Hallendale
Miami Gardens-Utopia-Carver
Pembroke Pines
Lake Forest
South Florida
Miramar
Lake Lucerne
Aventura
DADE
Country Club
Carol City
Ives Estates
Sunny Isles
Palm Springs North
Scott Lake
Norland
North Miami Beach
Miami Lakes
Opa-locka North
Bunche Park
Golden Glades
Opa-locka
North Miami
330-332
Westview
Hialeah Gardens
Bay Harbor Islands
West Little River
Pinewood
Bal Harbour
Gladeview
Biscayne Park
Miami Springs
Miami Shores
Surfside
Doral
El Portal
North Bay Village
Virginia Gardens
Brownsville
Miami Beach
Sweetwater
West Miami
Miami
Military
Tamiami
Westchester
Coral Gables
APO-FPO 340
Kendale Lakes
Westwood Lakes
Coral Terrace
331-332
Kendall Lakes West
Sunset
Olympia Heights
Hammocks
Glenvar Heights
South Miami
Key Biscayne
Lindgren Acres
Richmond Heights
Kendall
Palmetto Estates
Cutler
South Miami Heights
Perrine
Lakes by the Bay
Naranja
Princeton
Homestead

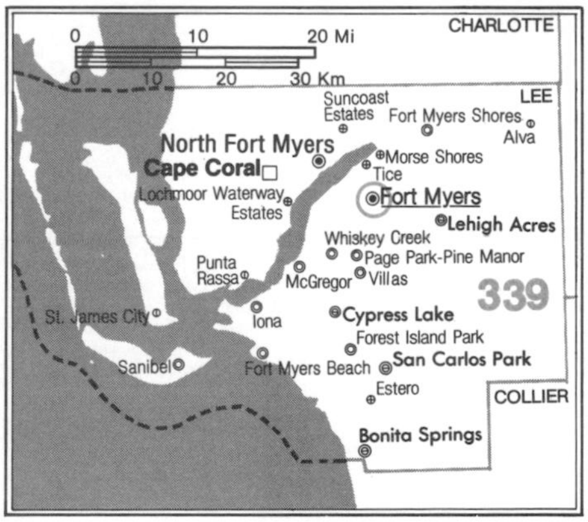

0 5 10 15 20 Miles
0 10 20 30 Kilometers

Lower-right inset map (339):

CHARLOTTE
0 10 20 Mi
0 10 20 30 Km
Suncoast Estates
Fort Myers Shores
LEE
Morse Shores
Alva
North Fort Myers
Tice
Cape Coral
Lochmoor Waterway Estates
Fort Myers
Whiskey Creek
Page Park-Pine Manor
Lehigh Acres
Punta Rassa
McGregor
Villas
339
St. James City
Iona
Cypress Lake
Forest Island Park
Sanibel
Fort Myers Beach
San Carlos Park
Estero
COLLIER
Bonita Springs

Cleartype®
County-Town
FLORIDA
INSET MAPS
ZIP CODES
NATIONAL AREA NO. 3
AMC

15 16 17 18 19 20 21 22 23 24 25 26 27 28

Copyright American Map Corporation

Explanation of symbols: ● – Census Designated Place (CDP)

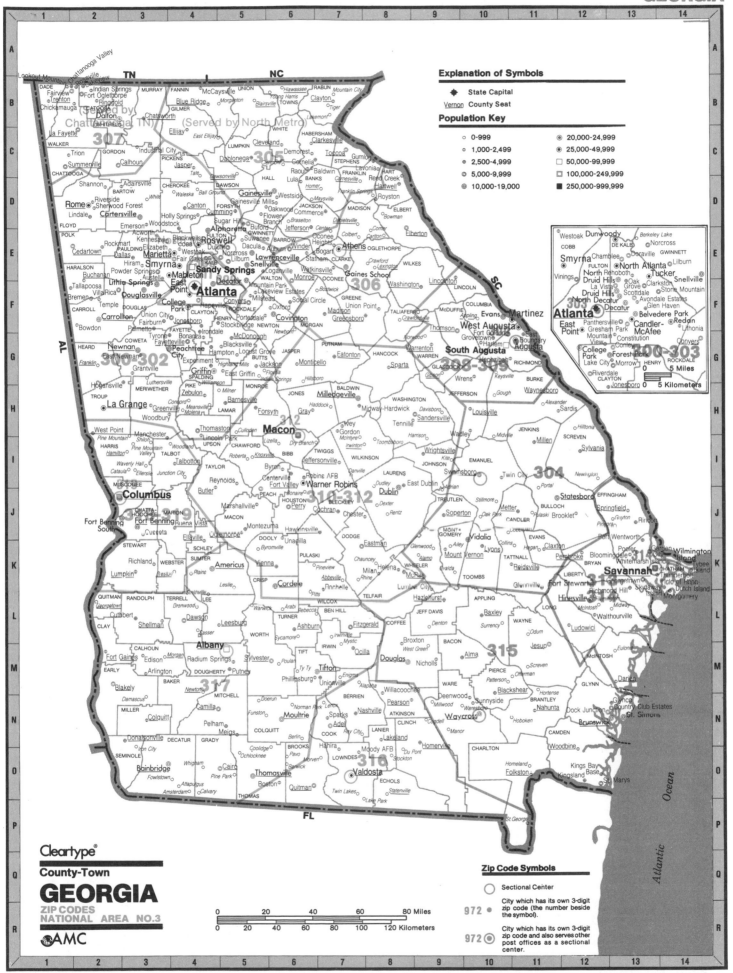

Copyright American Map.Corporation

COUNTIES

(5 Counties)

Name of County	Population	Location on Map
HAWAI'I	120,317	G-16
HONOLULU	836,231	B-7
KALAWAO	130	D-11
KAUAI	51,177	A-2
MAUI	100,374	G-13
TOTAL	1,108,229	

CITIES AND TOWNS

Note: The first name is that of the city or town, second, that of the county in which it is located, then the zip code area and location on the map.

Explanation of symbols: ● – Census Designated Place (CDP)

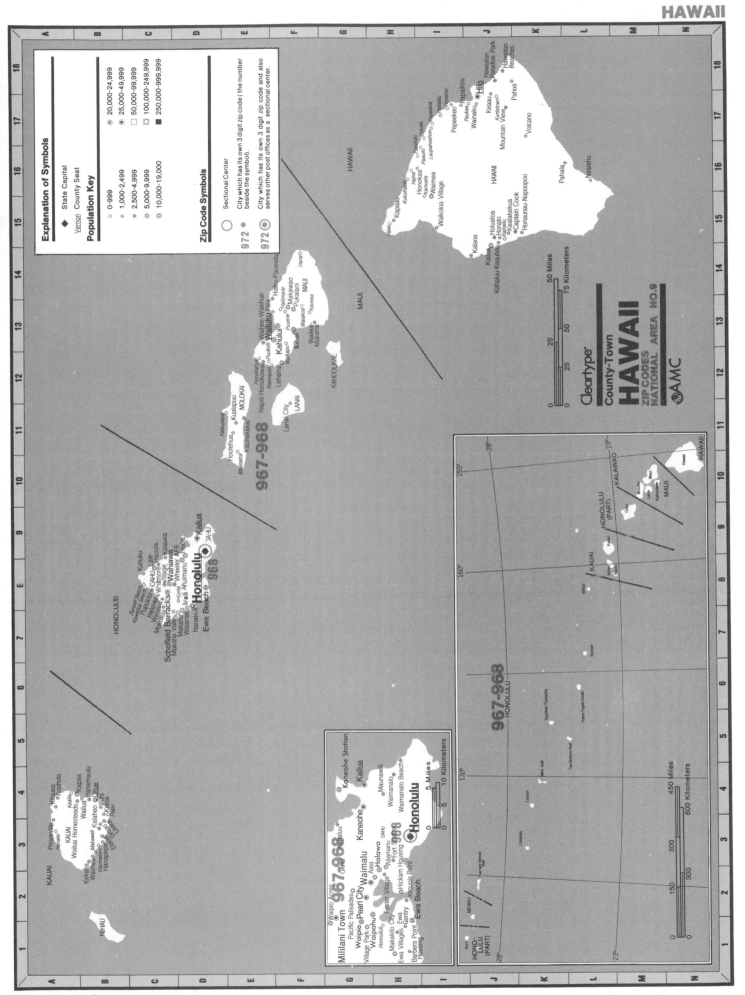

Explanation of Symbols

◆ State Capital
<u>Vernon</u> County Seat

Population Key

○ 0-999	◉ 20,000-24,999
⊙ 1,000-2,499	◉ 25,000-49,999
⊕ 2,500-4,999	☐ 50,000-99,999
⊚ 5,000-9,999	☐ 100,000-249,999
⊛ 10,000-19,000	■ 250,000-999,999

Zip Code Symbols

○ Sectional Center

972 ● City which has its own 3 digit zip code (the number beside the symbol).

972 ◉ City which has its own 3 digit zip code and also serves other post offices as a sectional center.

Cleartype®
County-Town
HAWAII
ZIP CODES
NATIONAL AREA NO. 9
◎AMC

Copyright American Map Corporation

COUNTIES

(44 Counties)

Name of County	Population	Location on Map
ADA	205,775	O-3
ADAMS	3,254	J-3
BANNOCK	66,026	P-11
BEAR LAKE	6,084	Q-13
BENEWAH	7,937	E-2
BINGHAM	37,583	O-10
BLAINE	13,552	N-6
BOISE	3,509	M-4
BONNER	26,622	B-3
BONNEVILLE	72,207	N-11
BOUNDARY	8,332	A-2
BUTTE	2,918	M-9
CAMAS	727	N-6
CANYON	90,076	O-2
CARIBOU	6,963	P-11
CASSIA	19,532	Q-7
CLARK	762	L-10
CLEARWATER	8,505	F-3
CUSTER	4,133	L-6
ELMORE	21,205	N-4
FRANKLIN	9,232	R-12
FREMONT	10,937	L-12
GEM	11,844	M-2
GOODING	11,633	O-6
IDAHO	13,783	H-3
JEFFERSON	16,543	M-10
JEROME	15,138	P-7
KOOTENAI	69,795	C-2
LATAH	30,617	F-2
LEMHI	6,899	J-6
LEWIS	3,516	G-3
LINCOLN	3,308	O-7
MADISON	23,674	N-12
MINIDOKA	19,361	P-8
NEZ PERCE	33,754	G-2
ONEIDA	3,492	R-10
OWYHEE	8,392	O-2
PAYETTE	16,434	M-2
POWER	7,086	P-10
SHOSHONE	13,931	D-3
TETON	3,439	N-13
TWIN FALLS	53,580	Q-6
VALLEY	6,109	J-4
WASHINGTON	8,550	L-2
TOTAL	**1,006,749**	

CITIES AND TOWNS

Note: The first name is that of the city or town, second, that of the county in which it is located, then the zip code area and location on the map.

Aberdeen, Bingham, 83210 .... P-10
American Falls, Power, 83211 .... P-10
Ammon, Bonneville, 83401 .... O-12
Arco, Butte, 83213 .... N-9
Ashton, Fremont, 83420 .... M-13
Bellevue, Blaine, 83313 .... O-7
Blackfoot, Bingham, 83221 .... O-11
Boise City, Ada, 83701-99 .... N-3
Bonners Ferry, Boundary, 83805 .... A-3
Buhl, Twin Falls, 83316 .... Q-6
Burley, Cassia/Minidoka, 83318 .... Q-8
Caldwell, Canyon, 83605 .... N-2
Cascade, Valley, 83611 .... L-4
Challis, Custer, 83226 .... L-7
Chubbuck, Bannock, 83202 .... P-11
Coeur d'Alene, Kootenai, 83814 .... D-3

Council, Adams, 83612 .... K-3
Dalton Gardens, Kootenai, 83814 .... D-3
Driggs, Teton, 83422 .... N-13
Dubois, Clark, 83423 .... M-11
Eagle, Ada, 83616 .... N-13
Emmett, Gem, 83617 .... N-3
Fairfield, Camas, 83327 .... O-6
Filer, Twin Falls, 83328 .... Q-6
● Fort Hall, Bannock/Bingham, 83203 ... P-11
Fruitland, Payette, 83619 .... M-2
Garden City, Ada, 83704 .... N-3
Glenns Ferry, Elmore, 83623 .... P-5
Gooding, Gooding, 83330 .... P-6
Grangeville, Idaho, 83530 .... H-4
Hailey, Blaine, 83333 .... N-7
Hayden, Kootenai, 83835 .... D-2
Heyburn, Minidoka, 83336 .... Q-8
Homedale, Owyhee, 83628 .... N-2
Idaho City, Boise, 83631 .... N-4
Idaho Falls, Bonneville, 83401-06 ...... N-11
Iona, Bonneville, 83427 .... N-12
Jerome, Jerome, 83338 .... P-7
Kamiah, Idaho/Lewis, 83538 .... H-4
Kellogg, Shoshone, 83837 .... D-4
Ketchum, Blaine, 83340 .... N-7
Kimberly, Twin Falls, 83341 .... Q-7
Kuna, Ada, 83634 .... O-3
Lewiston, Nez Perce, 83501 .... G-2
Malad City, Oneida, 83652 .... R-11
McCall, Valley, 83638 .... K-4
Meridian, Ada, 83642 .... N-3
Middleton, Canyon, 83644 .... N-2
Montpelier, Bear Lake, 83254 .... Q-13
Moscow, Latah, 83843 .... F-2
Mountain Home, Elmore, 83647 .... P-4
● Mountain Home AFB, Elmore, 83648 ... O-4
Murphy, Owyhee, 83650 .... O-3
Nampa, Canyon, 83685-87 .... N-3
New Plymouth, Payette, 83655 .... M-2
Nezperce, Lewis, 83543 .... H-3
Orofino, Clearwater, 83544 .... G-3
Osburn, Shoshone, 83849 .... D-4
Paris, Bear Lake, 83261 .... R-13
Parma, Canyon, 83660 .... N-2
Payette, Payette, 83661 .... M-2
Pinehurst, Shoshone, 83850 .... D-4
Pocatello, Bannock/Power,
    83201-02,04 .... P-11
Post Falls, Kootenai, 83850 .... D-2
Preston, Franklin, 83263 .... R-12
Priest River, Bonner, 83856 .... C-2
Rathdrum, Kootenai, 83858 .... D-2
Rexburg, Madison, 83440 .... N-12
Rigby, Jefferson, 83442 .... N-12
Rupert, Minidoka, 83350 .... Q-8
Saint Anthony, Fremont, 83445 .... M-12
Saint Maries, Benewah, 83861 .... E-3
Salmon, Lemhi, 83467 .... J-8
Sandpoint, Bonner, 83864 .... B-3
Shelley, Bingham, 83274 .... O-11
Shoshone, Lincoln, 83352 .... P-7
Soda Springs, Caribou, 83276 .... Q-12
Sugar City, Madison, 83448 .... N-12
Twin Falls, Twin Falls, 83301 .... Q-7
Wallace, Shoshone, 83873 .... D-4
Weiser, Washington, 83672 .... M-2
Wendell, Gooding, 83355 .... P-6
Wilder, Canyon, 83676 .... N-2

Explanation of symbols: ● – Census Designated Place (CDP)

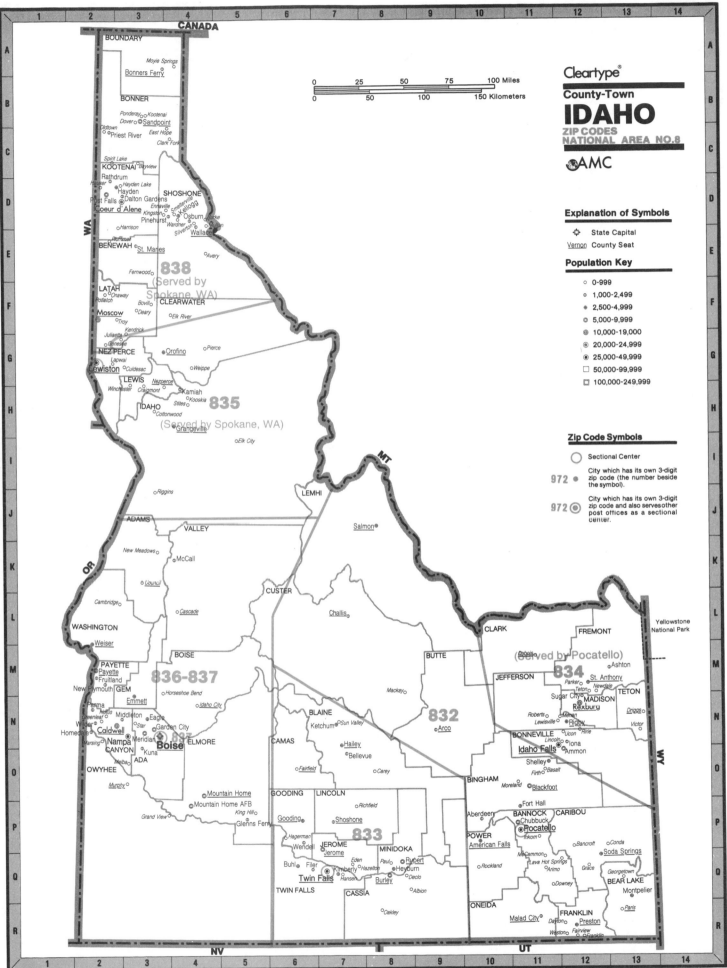

Cleartype®
County-Town
IDAHO
ZIP CODES
NATIONAL AREA NO.8

◈AMC

Explanation of Symbols

◇ State Capital

Vernon County Seat

Population Key

○ 0-999
◎ 1,000-2,499
⊕ 2,500-4,999
◉ 5,000-9,999
⊙ 10,000-19,000
◍ 20,000-24,999
◉ 25,000-49,999
□ 50,000-99,999
▣ 100,000-249,999

Zip Code Symbols

◯ Sectional Center

972 ● City which has its own 3-digit zip code (the number beside the symbol).

972 ◉ City which has its own 3-digit zip code and also serves other post offices as a sectional center.

Copyright American Map Corporation

31

ILLINOIS Index

COUNTIES

(102 Counties)

Name of County	Population	Location on Map
ADAMS	66,090	H-4
ALEXANDER	10,626	Q-9
BOND	14,991	L-9
BOONE	30,806	A-11
BROWN	5,836	H-6
BUREAU	35,688	D-8
CALHOUN	5,322	K-6
CARROLL	16,805	B-8
CASS	13,437	I-7
CHAMPAIGN	173,025	H-12
CHRISTIAN	34,418	J-9
CLARK	15,921	J-13
CLAY	14,460	L-11
CLINTON	33,944	M-9
COLES	51,644	J-12
COOK	5,105,067	B-12
CRAWFORD	19,464	L-13
CUMBERLAND	10,670	K-12
DE WITT	16,516	H-10
DEKALB	77,932	C-11
DOUGLAS	19,464	I-12
DUPAGE	781,666	C-12
EDGAR	19,595	I-13
EDWARDS	7,440	M-13
EFFINGHAM	31,704	K-11
FAYETTE	20,893	K-10
FORD	14,275	G-12
FRANKLIN	40,319	O-10
FULTON	38,080	G-7
GALLATIN	6,909	O-12
GREENE	15,317	K-6
GRUNDY	32,337	E-11
HAMILTON	8,499	N-11
HANCOCK	21,373	G-5
HARDIN	5,189	P-12
HENDERSON	8,096	F-5
HENRY	51,159	D-8
IROQUOIS	30,787	F-13
JACKSON	61,067	O-9
JASPER	10,609	K-12
JEFFERSON	37,020	N-10
JERSEY	20,539	L-6
JO DAVIESS	21,821	A-7
JOHNSON	11,347	Q-10
KANE	317,471	B-11
KANKAKEE	96,255	E-13
KENDALL	39,413	D-11
KNOX	56,393	E-7
LA SALLE	106,913	D-10
LAKE	516,418	A-12
LAWRENCE	15,972	L-13
LEE	34,392	C-9
LIVINGSTON	39,301	E-11
LOGAN	30,798	H-9
MACON	117,206	I-10
MACOUPIN	47,679	K-7
MADISON	249,238	L-8
MARION	41,561	M-10
MARSHALL	12,846	E-9
MASON	16,269	H-8
MASSAC	14,752	Q-11
MCDONOUGH	35,244	G-6
MCHENRY	183,241	B-11
MCLEAN	129,180	G-11
MENARD	11,164	H-8
MERCER	17,290	E-5
MONROE	22,422	N-7
MONTGOMERY	30,728	K-9
MORGAN	36,397	I-7
MOULTRIE	13,930	I-11
OGLE	45,957	B-9
PEORIA	182,827	F-8
PERRY	21,412	N-10
PIATT	15,548	I-11
PIKE	17,577	I-6
POPE	4,373	P-11
PULASKI	7,523	Q-10
PUTNAM	5,730	E-9
RANDOLPH	34,583	O-8
RICHLAND	16,545	L-12
ROCK ISLAND	148,723	D-5
SAINT CLAIR	262,852	M-8
SALINE	26,551	O-12
SANGAMON	178,386	I-9
SCHUYLER	7,498	H-6
SCOTT	5,644	J-6
SHELBY	22,261	J-10
STARK	6,534	E-8
STEPHENSON	48,052	A-8
TAZEWELL	123,692	G-9
UNION	17,619	P-9
VERMILION	88,257	G-13
WABASH	13,111	M-13
WARREN	19,181	G-6
WASHINGTON	14,965	N-9
WAYNE	17,241	M-11
WHITE	16,522	N-12
WHITESIDE	60,186	C-8
WILL	357,313	D-12
WILLIAMSON	57,733	P-10
WINNEBAGO	252,913	A-10
WOODFORD	32,653	F-9
TOTAL	11,430,602	

CITIES AND TOWNS

Note: The first name is that of the city or town, second, that of the county in which it is located, then the zip code area and location on the map.

Abingdon, Knox, 61410 F-7
Addison, DuPage, 60101 J-20
Albion, Edwards, 62806 N-13
Aledo, Mercer, 61231 E-6
Algonquin, Kane/McHenry, 60102 B-12
Alorton, St. Clair, 62207 D-2
Alsip, Cook, 60658 M-23
Altamont, Effingham, 62411 L-11
Alton, Madison, 62002 L-7
Amboy, Lee, 61310 C-10
Andalusia, Rock Island, 61232 D-6
Anna, Union, 62906 Q-10
Antioch, Lake, 60002 A-13
Arcola, Douglas, 61910 J-12
Arlington Heights, Cook, 60004-05 B-13
Aroma Park Northwest, Kankakee, 60910 E-13
Arthur, Douglas/Moultrie, 61911 J-12
Ashland, Cass, 62612 I-8
Ashton, Lee, 61006 C-10
Assumption, Christian, 62510 J-10
Astoria, Fulton, 61501 H-7
Athens, Menard, 62613 I-8
Atlanta, Logan, 61723 H-10
Atwood, Douglas/Piatt, 61913 I-12
Auburn, Sangamon, 62615 J-8
Aurora, DuPage/Kane, 60504-06 C-12
Bannockburn, Lake, 60015 F-22
Barrington, Cook/Lake, 60010 G-19
Barrington Hills, Cook/Kane/Lake/ McHenry, 60010 G-18
Barry, Pike, 62312 J-5
Bartlett, Cook/DuPage/Kane, 60103 I-18
Bartonville, Peoria, 61607 G-9
Batavia, DuPage/Kane, 60510 K-17
Beach, Lake, 60085 D-22
Beach Park, Lake, 60085 C-23
Beardstown, Cass, 62618 I-7
Beckemeyer, Clinton, 62219 M-9
Beecher, Will, 60401 E-14
Belleville, St. Clair, 62220-21, 23 M-8
Bellevue, Peoria, 62045 G-9
Bellwood, Cook, 60104 J-22
Belvidere, Boone, 61008 B-11
Bement, Piatt, 61813 I-11
Benld, Macoupin, 62009 L-8
Bensenville, Cook/DuPage, 60106 I-21
Benton, Franklin, 62812 O-11
Berkeley, Cook, 60163 J-21
Berwyn, Cook, 60402 C-13
Bethalto, Madison, 62010 B-2
Bethany, Moultrie, 61914 J-11
Bloomingdale, DuPage, 60108 I-20
Bloomington, McLean, 61701,04 G-10
Blue Island, Cook, 60406 C-14
Blue Mound, Macon, 62513 J-10
Bolingbrook, DuPage/Will, 60440 M-20
• Boulder Hill, Kendall, 60538 C-12
Bourbonnais, Kankakee, 60912 E-13
Bradley, Kankakee, 60915 E-13
Braidwood, Will, 60908 E-12
Breese, Clinton, 62230 M-9
Bridgeport, Lawrence, 62417 M-13
Bridgeview, Cook, 60455 L-22
Brighton, Jersey/Macoupin,62012 L-7
Broadview, Cook, 60153 K-22
Brookfield, Cook, 60513 K-22
Brooklyn, St. Clair, 62090 C-1
Brookport, Massac, 62910 R-11
Buffalo Grove, Cook/Lake, 60089 G-21
Bunker Hill, Macoupin, 62014 L-8
Burbank, Cook, 60459 L-23
Burnham, Cook, 60633 M-25
Burr Ridge, Cook/DuPage, 60521 L-21
Bushnell, McDonough, 61422 G-6
Butterfield, DuPage, 60148 K-20
Byron, Ogle, 61010 B-10
Cahokia, St. Clair, 62206 M-7
Cairo, Alexander, 62914 R-10
Calumet City, Cook, 60409 D-14
Calumet Park, Cook, 60643 M-24
Cambria, Williamson, 62915 P-10
Cambridge, Henry, 61238 E-7
Camp Point, Adams, 62320 H-5
Canton, Fulton, 61520 G-8
Carbon Cliff, Rock Island, 61239 D-7
Carbondale, Jackson, 62901 P-10
Carlinville, Macoupin, 62626 K-8
Carlyle, Clinton, 62231 M-9
Carmi, White, 62821 O-13
Carol Stream, DuPage, 60188, 99 J-19
Carpentersville, Kane, 60110 G-18
Carriers Mills, Saline, 62917 P-11
Carrollton, Greene, 62016 K-7
Carterville, Williamson, 62918 P-10
Carthage, Hancock, 62321 G-5
Cary, McHenry, 60013 B-12
Casey, Clark/Cumberland, 62420 K-13
Caseyville, St. Clair, 62232 C-2
Catlin, Vermilion,61817 I-14
Central City, Marion, 62801 M-10
Central Park, Vermilion, 61832 H-14
Centralia, Clinton/Marion, 62801 M-10
Centreville, St. Clair, 62207 D-2
Cerro Gordo, Piatt, 61818 I-11
Champaign, Champaign, 61820-21 H-12
Channahon, Grundy/Will, 60410 D-12
• Channel Lake, Lake, 60002 A-12
Charleston, Coles, 61920 J-12
Chatham, Sangamon,62629 J-8
Chatsworth, Livingston, 60921 F-12
Chebanse, Iroquois/Kankakee, 60922 F-13
Chenoa, McLean, 61726 F-11
Cherry Valley, Winnebago, 61016 B-10
Chester, Randolph, 62233 O-8
Chicago, Cook/DuPage, 60601-99 C-14
Chicago Heights, Cook,60411 O-24
Chicago Ridge, Cook, 60415 M-23
Chillicothe, Peoria, 61523 F-9
Chrisman, Edgar, 61924 I-14
Christopher, Franklin, 62822 O-10
Cicero, Cook, 60650 C-14
City Park, Christian, 62568 J-10
Clarendon Hills, DuPage, 60514 K-21
Clifton, Iroquois, 60927 F-13
Clinton, De Witt, 61727 H-10
Coal City, Grundy, 60416 E-12
Coal Valley, Henry/Rock Island, 61240 D-7
Cobden, Union, 62920 P-10
Colchester, McDonough, 62326 G-6
Collinsville, Madison/St. Clair, 62334 M-8
Colona, Henry, 61241 D-7
Columbia, Monroe, 62236 N-7
Cottage Hills, Madison, 62018 B-2
Country Club Hills, Cook, 60478 N-23
Countryside, Cook, 60525 L-22
Crainville, Williamson,62918 P-10
Crest Hill, Will, 60435 N-19
Crestwood, Cook, 60445 N-23
Crete, Will, 60417 D-14
Creve Coeur, Tazewell, 61611 G-9
Crystal Lake, McHenry, 60012,14 B-12
• Crystal Lawns, Will, 60435 O-19
Cuba, Fulton, 61427 G-7
Dallas City, Hancock/Henderson, 62330 G-5
Danville, Vermilion, 61832 H-14
Darien, DuPage, 60561 L-21
De Kalb, DeKalb, 60115 C-11
De Pue, Bureau, 61322 E-10
De Soto, Jackson, 62924 P-10
Decatur, Macon, 62521-23, 26 I-10
Deer Park, Lake, 60010 B-13
Deerfield, Cook/Lake, 60015 G-22
Delavan, Tazewell, 61734 H-9
Des Plaines, Cook, 60016,18 B-13
Diamond, Grundy/Will, 60416 E-12
Diamond Lake, Lake, 60060 F-20
Divernon, Sangamon, 62530 J-9
Dixmoor, Cook, 60426 N-24
Dixon, Lee, 61021 C-9
Dolton, Cook, 60419 M-25
Downers Grove, DuPage, 60515-17 C-13
Du Quoin, Perry, 62832 O-10
Dunlap Lake-Dewey Park, Madison, 61525 B-3
Dupo, St. Clair, 62239 D-1
Durand, Winnebago, 61024 A-9
Dwight, Grundy/Livingston, 60420 E-12
Earlville, La Salle, 60518 D-11
East Alton, Madison, 62024 L-7
East Chicago Heights, Cook, 60411 O-25
East Dubuque, Jo Daviess, 61025 A-7
East Dundee, Cook/Kane, 60118 H-18
East Hazel Crest, Cook, 60429 N-24
East Moline, Rock Island,61244 D-7
East Peoria, Tazewell, 61611 G-9
East St. Louis, St. Clair,62201-08 M-7
Edwardsville, Madison, 62025 L-8
Effingham, Effingham, 62401 L-11
El Paso, Woodford, 61738 F-10
Elburn, Kane, 60119 C-12
Eldorado, Saline, 62930 P-12
Elgin, Cook/Kane, 60120,23 B-12
Elizabethtown, Hardin, 62931 Q-12
Elk Grove Village, Cook/DuPage, 60007 I-21
Elmhurst, DuPage, 60126 J-21
Elmwood, Peoria, 61529 F-8
Elmwood Park, Cook, 60635 J-22
Energy, Williamson,62933 P-10
Erie, Whiteside, 61250 C-8
Eureka, Woodford, 61530 F-10
Evanston, Cook, 60201-99 H-24
Evergreen Park, Cook, 60642 C-14
Fairbury, Livingston, 61739 F-12
Fairfield, Wayne, 62837 N-12
• Fairmont, Will, 60441 N-20
Fairmont City, Madison/St. Clair,62201 C-2
Fairview Heights, St. Clair, 62208 D-3
Farmer City, De Witt, 61842 H-11
Farmington, Fulton, 61531 G-8
Fisher, Champaign, 61843 H-12
Flora, Clay, 62839 M-12
Flossmoor, Cook, 60422 O-24
Ford Heights, Cook, 60411 O-24
• Forest Lake, Lake, 60047 F-20
Forest Park, Cook, 60130 K-22
Forrest, Livingston, 61741 F-12
Forreston, Ogle, 61030 B-9
Forsyth, Macon, 62535 I-10
Fox Lake, Lake/McHenry, 60020 D-19
• Fox Lake Hills, Lake,60046 C-19
Fox River Grove, McHenry, 60021 F-18
Frankfort, Cook/Will, 60423 O-22
• Frankfort Square, Will, 60423 O-22
Franklin Park, Cook, 60131 J-22
Freeburg, St. Clair, 62243 N-8
Freeport, Stephenson, 61032 A-9
French Village, St. Clair, 62208 D-2
Fulton, Whiteside, 61252 C-8
• Gages Lake, Lake, 60030 D-21
Galena, Jo Daviess, 61036 A-7
Galesburg, Knox, 61401 F-7
Galva, Henry, 61434 E-8
Gardner, Grundy, 60424 E-12
Geneseo, Henry, 61254 D-8
Geneva, Kane, 60134 C-12
Genoa, DeKalb, 60135 B-11
Georgetown, Vermilion, 61846 I-14
Germantown, Clinton, 62245 M-9
Germantown Hills, Woodford, 61548 F-9
Gibson, Ford, 60936 G-12
Gillespie, Macoupin, 62033 K-8
Gilman, Iroquois, 60938 F-13
Girard, Macoupin, 62640 J-8
Glasford, Peoria, 61533 G-8
Glen Carbon, Madison, 62034 C-2
Glen Ellyn, DuPage, 60137 J-20
• Glenbard South, DuPage, 60187 K-6
Glencoe, Cook, 60022 G-23
Glendale Heights, DuPage, 60139 J-20
Glenview, Cook, 60025 H-22
Glenwood, Cook, 60425 O-24
Godfrey, Madison, 62035 L-7
Golconda, Pope, 62938 Q-11
• Goodings Grove, Will, 60434 N-21
Grandview, Sangamon,62702 I-9
• Grandwood Park, Lake,60031 D-20
Granite City, Madison, 62040 M-7
Grant Park, Kankakee, 60940 E-14
Granville, Putnam, 61326 E-10
Grayslake, Lake, 60030 D-20
Grayville, Edwards/White, 62844 N-13
Green Oaks, Lake, 60048 E-21
Green Rock, Henry, 61241 D-7
Greenfield, Greene, 62044 K-7
Greenup, Cumberland, 62428 K-13
Greenville, Bond, 62642 L-9
Gridley, McLean, 61744 F-11
Griggsville, Pike, 62340 J-6
Gurnee, Lake, 60031 D-21
Hamilton, Hancock, 62341 G-4
Hampshire, Kane, 60140 B-12
Hampton, Rock Island, 61256 D-7
Hanna City, Peoria, 61536 G-8
Hanover Park, Cook/DuPage, 60103 I-19
Hardin, Calhoun, 62047 K-6
Harrisburg, Saline, 62946 P-11
Harristown, Macon, 62537 I-10
Hartford, Madison, 62048 B-2
Harvard, McHenry, 60033. A-11
Harvey, Cook, 60426 D-14
Harwood Heights, Cook, 60656 I-22
Havana, Mason, 62644 H-8
Hawthorn Woods, Lake, 60047 F-20
Hazel Crest, Cook, 60429 N-24
Hennepin, Putnam, 61327 E-10
Henry, Marshall, 61537 E-9
Herrin, Williamson, 62948 P-10
Herscher, Kankakee,60941 E-13
Heyworth, McLean, 61745 H-10
Hickory Hills, Cook, 60457 L-22
Highland, Madison, 62249 M-9
Highland Hills, DuPage, 60148 K-20
Highland Park, Lake, 60035 B-13
Highwood, Lake, 60040 B-13
Hillsboro, Montgomery, 62049 K-9
Hillside, Cook, 60162 J-21
Hinckley, DeKalb, 60520 C-11
Hinsdale, Cook/DuPage, 60521-22 K-21
Hodgkins, Cook, 60525 L-22
Hoffman Estates, Cook/Kane, 60192, 95 H-20
Hollywood Heights, St. Clair, 62232 C-2
Homer, Champaign, 61849 I-13
Hometown, Cook, 60456 L-23
Homewood, Cook, 60430 O-24
Hoopeston, Vermilion, 60942 G-14
Hudson, McLean, 61748 G-10
Huntley, McHenry, 60142 B-12
Indian Head Park, Cook, 60525 L-21
• Ingalls Park, Will, 60431 O-20
Inverness, Cook,60067 G-20
Island Lake, Lake/McHenry, 60042 E-19
Itasca, DuPage, 60143 I-20
Jacksonville, Morgan, 62650 J-7

Explanation of symbols: •– Census Designated Place (CDP)

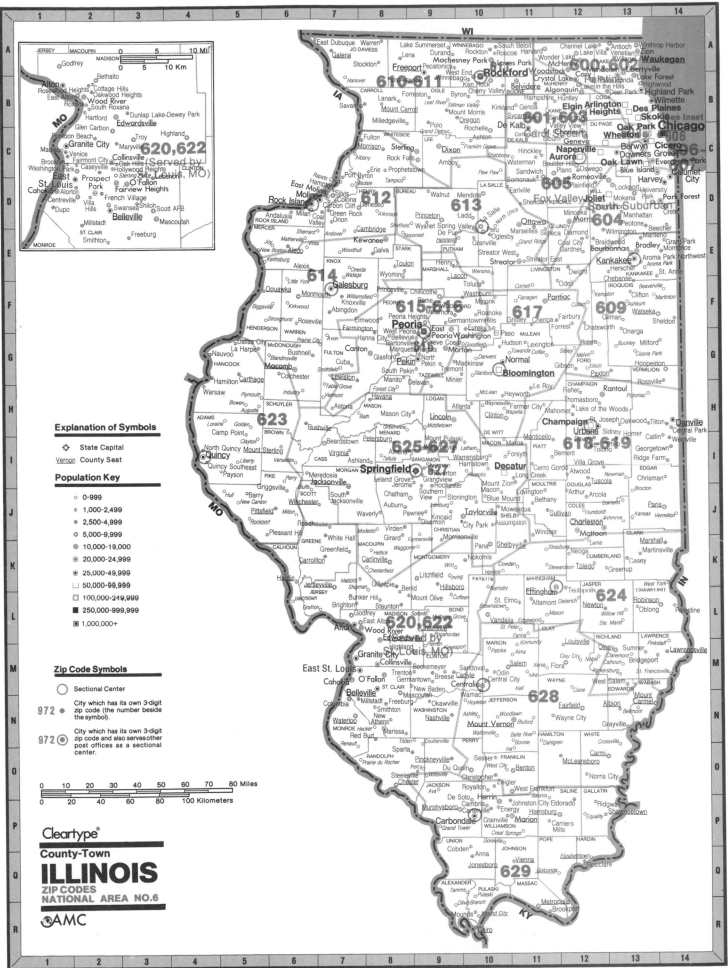

Explanation of Symbols

✥ State Capital
Vernon County Seat

Population Key

○ 0-999
⊙ 1,000-2,499
⊕ 2,500-4,999
⊖ 5,000-9,999
⊙ 10,000-19,000
⊛ 20,000-24,999
⊛ 25,000-49,999
☐ 50,000-99,999
☐ 100,000-249,999
■ 250,000-999,999
⊞ 1,000,000+

Zip Code Symbols

○ Sectional Center

972 ● City which has its own 3-digit zip code (the number beside the symbol).

972 ◉ City which has its own 3-digit zip code and also serves other post offices as a sectional center.

Cleartype®

County-Town

ILLINOIS

ZIP CODES
NATIONAL AREA NO.6

⊕AMC

Copyright American Map Corporation

Explanation of symbols: ● – Census Designated Place (CDP)

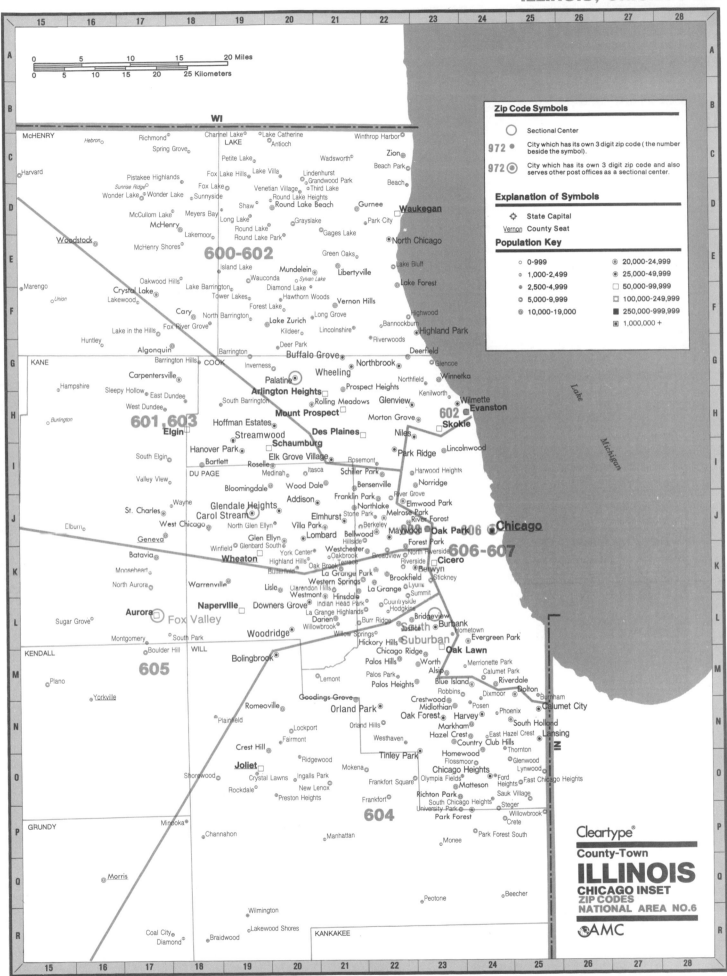

Copyright American Map Corporation

INDIANA Index

COUNTIES

(92 Counties)

Name of County	Population	Location on Map
ADAMS	31,095	E-11
ALLEN	300,836	C-10
BARTHOLOMEW	63,657	L-8
BENTON	9,441	F-3
BLACKFORD	14,067	F-10
BOONE	38,147	H-6
BROWN	14,080	L-7
CARROLL	18,809	F-6
CASS	38,413	E-6
CLARK	87,777	O-9
CLAY	24,705	K-4
CLINTON	30,974	G-6
CRAWFORD	9,914	P-6
DAVIESS	27,533	N-4
DE KALB	35,324	B-11
DEARBORN	38,835	L-11
DECATUR	23,645	L-9
DELAWARE	119,659	H-10
DUBOIS	36,616	O-4
ELKHART	156,198	B-8
FAYETTE	26,015	J-10
FLOYD	64,404	P-8
FOUNTAIN	17,808	H-4
FRANKLIN	19,580	K-11
FULTON	18,840	D-7
GIBSON	31,913	P-1
GRANT	74,169	F-9
GREENE	30,410	L-4
HAMILTON	108,936	H-7
HANCOCK	45,527	I-8
HARRISON	29,890	P-7
HENDRICKS	75,717	I-6
HENRY	48,139	I-10
HOWARD	80,827	F-7
HUNTINGTON	35,427	E-9
JACKSON	37,730	M-7
JASPER	24,960	C-4
JAY	21,512	F-11
JEFFERSON	29,797	N-10
JENNINGS	23,661	M-9
JOHNSON	88,109	K-7
KNOX	39,884	O-2
KOSCIUSKO	65,294	C-8
LA PORTE	107,066	B-6
LAGRANGE	29,477	A-10
LAKE	475,594	C-3
LAWRENCE	42,836	N-6
MADISON	130,669	G-9
MARION	797,159	I-7
MARSHALL	42,182	C-7
MARTIN	10,369	N-5
MIAMI	36,897	E-8
MONROE	108,978	L-6
MONTGOMERY	34,436	H-5
MORGAN	55,920	K-6
NEWTON	13,551	D-3
NOBLE	37,877	B-9
OHIO	5,315	M-11
ORANGE	18,409	N-6
OWEN	17,281	K-5
PARKE	15,410	I-4
PERRY	19,107	P-5
PIKE	12,509	O-3
PORTER	128,932	C-4
POSEY	25,968	Q-1
PULASKI	12,643	D-5
PUTNAM	30,315	J-5
RANDOLPH	27,148	H-11
RIPLEY	24,616	L-10
RUSH	18,129	J-10
SAINT JOSEPH	247,052	B-6
SCOTT	20,991	N-9
SHELBY	40,307	J-8
SPENCER	19,490	Q-4
STARKE	22,747	C-6
STEUBEN	27,446	B-11
SULLIVAN	18,993	M-3
SWITZERLAND	7,738	M-11
TIPPECANOE	130,598	F-4
TIPTON	16,119	H-7
UNION	6,976	J-11
VANDERBURGH	165,058	Q-2
VERMILLION	16,773	I-3
VIGO	106,107	K-3
WABASH	35,069	D-8
WARREN	8,176	G-3
WARRICK	44,920	P-4
WASHINGTON	23,717	N-7
WAYNE	71,951	I-11
WELLS	25,948	E-10
WHITE	23,265	E-5
WHITLEY	27,651	D-10
TOTAL	5,544,159	

CITIES AND TOWNS

Note. The first name is that of the city or town, second, that of the county in which it is located, then the zip code area and location on the map.

Akron, Fulton, 46910 ... D-8
Albany, Delaware/Randolph, 47320 ... G-11
Albion, Noble, 46701 ... C-10
Alexandria, Madison, 46001 ... H-9
Anderson, Madison, 46011-17 ... H-9
Andrews, Huntington, 46702 ... E-9
Angola, Steuben, 46703 ... A-11
Arcadia, Hamilton, 46030 ... H-8
Ardmore, St. Joseph, 46628 ... A-7
Argos, Marshall, 46501 ... C-7
Attica, Fountain, 47918 ... G-4
Auburn, De Kalb, 46706 ... C-11
Aurora, Dearborn, 47001 ... M-12
Austin, Scott, 47102 ... N-9
Avilla, Noble, 46710 ... C-11
Bargersville, Johnson, 46106 ... K-7
Batesville, Franklin/Ripley, 47006 ... L-11
Bedford, Lawrence, 47421 ... N-6
Beech Grove, Marion, 46107 ... J-8
Berne, Adams, 46711 ... F-12
Bicknell, Knox, 47512 ... N-3
Black Oak, Lake, 46406 ... B-3
Bloomfield, Greene, 47424 ... M-5
Bloomington, Monroe, 46011-13, 16, 17 ... L-6
Bluffton, Wells, 46714 ... E-11
Boonville, Warrick, 47601 ... Q-4
Bourbon, Marshall, 46504 ... C-8
Brazil, Clay, 47834 ... K-4
Bremen, Marshall, 46506 ... B-8
• Bright, Dearborn, 47025 ... L-12
Bristol, Elkhart, 46507 ... A-9
Brooklyn, Morgan, 46111 ... K-7
Brookston, White, 47923 ... F-5
Brookville, Franklin, 47012 ... K-11
Brownsburg, Hendricks, 46112 ... I-7
Brownstown, Jackson, 47220 ... M-8
Bunker Hill, Miami, 46914 ... F-8
Butler, De Kalb, 46721 ... B-12
Cambridge City, Wayne, 47327 ... I-11
Cannelton, Perry, 47520 ... R-5
Carmel, Hamilton, 46032-33 ... I-8
Cayuga, Vermillion, 47928 ... I-3
Cedar Lake, Lake, 46303 ... C-3
Centerville, Wayne, 47303 ... I-12
Chandler, Warrick, 47610 ... Q-3
Charlestown, Clark, 47111 ... O-9
Chesterfield, Delaware/Madison, 46017 ... H-9
Chesterton, Porter, 46304 ... B-4
Churubusco, Whitley, 46723 ... C-10
Cicero, Hamilton, 46634 ... H-8
Clarksville, Clark, 47129 ... P-9
Clermont, Marion, 46234 ... I-7
Clinton, Vermillion, 47842 ... J-3
Cloverdale, Putnam, 46120 ... K-5
Columbia City, Whitley, 46725 ... D-10
Columbus, Bartholomew, 47201, 03 ... L-8
Connersville, Fayette, 47331 ... J-11
Converse, Grant/Miami, 46919 ... F-9
Corydon, Harrison, 47112 ... P-8
Covington, Fountain, 47932 ... H-3
Crawfordsville, Montgomery, 47933 ... H-5
Crothersville, Jackson, 47229 ... N-9
Crown Point, Lake, 46307 ... B-3
Culver, Marshall, 46511 ... C-7
Cumberland, Hancock/Marion, 46229 ... I-8
Dale, Spencer, 47523 ... Q-5
Daleville, Delaware, 47334 ... H-10
Danville, Hendricks, 46122 ... J-6
Darmstadt, Vanderburgh, 47711 ... Q-2
De Motte, Jasper, 46310 ... C-4
Decatur, Adams, 46733 ... E-12
Delphi, Carroll, 46923 ... F-6
Dillsboro, Dearborn, 47018 ... M-11
Dunkirk, Blackford/Jay, 47336 ... G-11
• Dunlap, Elkhart, 46514 ... B-8
Dyer, Lake, 46311 ... B-3
East Chicago, Lake, 46312 ... A-3
Eaton, Delaware, 47338 ... G-10
Edgewood, Madison, 46011 ... H-9
Edinburgh, Bartholomew/ Johnson, 46124 ... L-8
Elkhart, Elkhart, 46514,16-17 ... A-8
Ellettsville, Monroe, 47429 ... L-6
Elwood, Madison/Tipton, 46036 ... G-9
Englewood, Lawrence, 47421 ... N-6
English, Crawford, 47118 ... P-6
Evansville, Vanderburgh, 47701-99 ... Q-2
• Fairland, Shelby, 46126 ... J-8
Fairmount, Grant, 46928 ... G-9
Fairview Park, Vermillion, 47842 ... J-3
Farmersburg, Sullivan, 47850 ... L-3
Farmland, Randolph, 47340 ... H-11
Ferdinand, Dubois, 47532 ... P-5
Fishers, Hamilton, 46038 ... I-8
Flora, Carroll, 46929 ... F-6
Fort Branch, Gibson, 47648 ... P-2
Fort Wayne, Allen, 46801-99 ... D-11
Fortville, Hancock, 46040 ... I-9
Fowler, Benton, 47944 ... F-4
Frankfort, Clinton, 46041 ... G-6
Franklin, Johnson, 46131 ... K-8
Frankton, Madison, 46044 ... H-9
Fremont, Steuben, 46737 ... A-12
French Lick, Orange, 47432 ... O-6
• Galena, Floyd, 46371 ... P-8
Galveston, Cass, 46932 ... F-7
Garrett, De Kalb, 46738 ... C-11
Gary, Lake, 46401-99 ... B-3
Gas City, Grant, 46933 ... G-9
Geneva, Adams, 46740 ... F-12
Georgetown, Floyd, 47122 ... P-8
• Georgetown, St. Joseph, 46614 ... A-7
Goodland, Newton, 47948 ... E-4
Goshen, Elkhart, 46526 ... B-9
• Granger, St. Joseph, 46530 ... A-7
Greencastle, Putnam, 46135 ... J-5
Greendale, Dearborn, 47025 ... L-12
Greenfield, Hancock, 46140 ... J-9
Greensburg, Decatur, 47240 ... K-10
Greentown, Howard, 46936 ... G-8
Greenwood, Johnson, 46142-43 ... J-8
Griffith, Lake, 46319 ... B-3
• Grissom AFB, Cass/Miami, 46971 ... F-7
• Gulivoire Park, St. Joseph, 46613 ... A-7
Hagerstown, Wayne, 47346 ... I-11
Hammond, Lake, 46320-24 ... B-3
Hanover, Jefferson, 47243 ... N-10
Hartford City, Blackford, 47348 ... G-10
Haubstadt, Gibson, 47639 ... P-2
Hebron, Porter, 46341 ... C-4
• Hidden Valley, Dearborn, 47014 ... L-12
Highland, Lake, 46322 ... B-3
• Highland, Vanderburgh, 47710 ... Q-2
Hobart, Lake, 46342 ... B-4
Home Place, Hamilton, 46240 ... I-8
Hope, Bartholomew, 47246 ... L-9
Huntertown, Allen, 46748 ... C-11
Huntingburg, Dubois, 47542 ... P-5
Huntington, Huntington, 46750 ... E-10
• Indian Heights, Howard, 46901-02 ... G-8
Indianapolis, Marion, 46201-99 ... I-8
Jasonville, Greene, 47438 ... L-4
Jasper, Dubois, 47546 ... P-5
Jeffersonville, Clark, 47130 ... P-9
Jonesboro, Grant, 46938 ... G-9
Kendallville, Noble, 46755 ... B-11
Kentland, Newton, 47951 ... E-3
Kingsford Heights, La Porte, 46346 ... B-6
Knightstown, Henry, 46148 ... J-10
Knox, Starke, 46534 ... C-6
Kokomo, Howard, 46901-02 ... G-8
• Koontz Lake, Marshall/Starke, 46574 ... B-6
Kouts, Porter, 46347 ... C-5
La Porte, La Porte, 46350 ... B-6
Ladoga, Montgomery, 47954 ... I-5
Lafayette, Tippecanoe, 47901, 05 ... G-5
Lagrange, Lagrange, 46761 ... A-10
• Lake Dalecarlia, Lake, 46356 ... C-3
Lake Station, Lake, 46405 ... B-4
• Lakes of the Four Seasons, Lake/Porter, 46307 ... C-4
Lapel, Madison, 46051 ... H-9
Lawrence, Marion, 46226 ... I-8
Lawrenceburg, Dearborn, 47025 ... M-12
Lebanon, Boone, 46052 ... H-6
Leo, Allen, 46765 ... C-11
Liberty, Union, 47353 ... J-12
Ligonier, Noble, 46767 ... B-9
Linton, Greene, 47441 ... M-4
Liverpool, Lake, 46408 ... B-4
Logansport, Cass, 46947 ... E-7
Long Beach, La Porte, 46360 ... A-5
Loogootee, Martin, 47533 ... N-5
Lowell, Lake, 46356 ... C-3
Lydick, St. Joseph, 46628 ... A-7
Lynn, Randolph, 47355 ... H-12
Madison, Jefferson, 47250 ... N-10
Marion, Grant, 46952-53 ... F-9
Markle, Huntington/Wells, 46770 ... E-10
Martinsville, Morgan, 46151 ... K-7
• Melody Hill, Vanderburgh, 47711 ... Q-3
Meridian Hills, Marion, 46260 ... I-7
Merrillville, Lake, 46410 ... B-3
• Mexico, Miami, 46958 ... E-8
Michigan City, La Porte, 46360 ... A-5
Middlebury, Elkhart, 46540 ... A-9
Middletown, Henry, 47356 ... H-10
Milan, Ripley, 47031 ... L-11
Milford, Kosciusko, 46542 ... B-9
Mishawaka, St. Joseph, 46544-45 ... A-8
Mitchell, Lawrence, 47446 ... N-6
Monon, White, 47959 ... E-5
Monroeville, Allen, 46773 ... D-12
Montezuma, Parke, 47862 ... I-3
Monticello, White, 47959 ... E-5
Montpelier, Blackford, 47359 ... F-11
Mooresville, Morgan, 46158 ... J-7
Morocco, Newton, 47963 ... D-3
Mount Vernon, Posey, 47620 ... Q-1
Mulberry, Clinton, 46058 ... G-6
Muncie, Delaware, 47302-05 ... H-10
Munster, Lake, 46321 ... B-3
Nappanee, Elkhart/Kosciusko, 46550 ... B-8
Nashville, Brown, 47448 ... L-7
New Albany, Floyd, 47150 ... P-9
New Carlisle, St. Joseph, 46552 ... A-6
New Castle, Henry, 47362 ... I-10
New Chicago, Lake, 46342 ... B-4
New Elliot, Lake, 46319 ... B-3
New Haven, Allen, 46774 ... D-11
• New Paris, Elkhart, 46553 ... B-9
New Pekin, Washington, 47192 ... O-8
New Whiteland, Johnson, 46184 ... K-8
Newburgh, Warrick, 47630 ... Q-3
Newport, Vermillion, 47966 ... I-3
Noblesville, Hamilton, 46060 ... H-8
North Judson, Starke, 46366 ... C-5
North Liberty, St. Joseph, 46554 ... B-7
North Manchester, Wabash, 46962 ... D-9
• North Terre Haute, Vigo, 47805 ... K-3
North Vernon, Jennings, 47265 ... M-9
• Oak Park, Clark, 47130 ... P-9
Oakland City, Gibson, 47660 ... P-3
Odon, Daviess, 47562 ... N-4
Ogden Dunes, Porter, 46368 ... B-4
Oolitic, Lawrence, 47451 ... M-6
Orleans, Orange, 47452 ... N-6
Osceola, St. Joseph, 46561 ... A-8
Osgood, Ripley, 47037 ... L-10
Ossian, Wells, 46777 ... E-11
Otterbein, Benton/Tippecanoe, 47970 ... G-4
Owensville, Gibson, 47453 ... P-2
Oxford, Benton, 47971 ... F-4
Paoli, Orange, 47454 ... O-6
Parker City, Randolph, 47368 ... H-11
Pendleton, Madison, 46064 ... I-9
Peru, Miami, 46970 ... E-8
Petersburg, Pike, 47567 ... O-4
Pierceton, Kosciusko, 46562 ... D-9
Plainfield, Hendricks, 46168 ... J-7
Plymouth, Marshall, 46563 ... C-7
Portage, Porter, 46368 ... B-4
Porter, Porter, 46304 ... B-4
Portland, Jay, 47371 ... G-12
Poseyville, Posey, 47633 ... P-2
Princes Lakes, Johnson, 46164 ... K-8
Princeton, Gibson, 47670 ... P-2
Redkey, Jay, 47373 ... G-11
Remington, Jasper, 47977 ... E-4
Rensselaer, Jasper, 47978 ... E-4
Richmond, Wayne, 47374 ... I-12
Rising Sun, Ohio, 47040 ... M-12
Roanoke, Huntington, 46783 ... D-10
Rochester, Fulton, 46975 ... D-7
Rockport, Spencer, 47635 ... R-4
Rockville, Parke, 47872 ... J-4
Rome City, Noble, 46784 ... B-10
Ross, Lake, 46410 ... B-3
Rossville, Clinton, 46065 ... G-6
Rushville, Rush, 46173 ... J-10
Saint John, Lake, 46373 ... B-3
Saint Paul, Decatur/Shelby, 47272 ... K-9
Salem, Washington, 47167 ... O-8
Schererville, Lake, 46375 ... B-3
Scottsburg, Scott, 47170 ... N-9
Seelyville, Vigo, 47878 ... K-4
Sellersburg, Clark, 47172 ... P-9
Seymour, Jackson, 47274 ... M-8
Shadeland, Tippecanoe, 47905 ... G-5
Shelburn, Sullivan, 47879 ... L-3
Shelbyville, Shelby, 46176 ... K-9
Sheridan, Hamilton, 46069 ... H-7
Shoals, Martin, 47581 ... N-5
• Simonton Lake, Elkhart, 46514 ... A-8
Smith Valley, Johnson, 46142 ... J-7
South Bend, St. Joseph, 46601-99 ... A-7
• South Haven, Porter, 46383 ... B-4
South Whitley, Whitley, 46787 ... D-9
Southport, Marion, 46227 ... J-8
Speedway, Marion, 46224 ... I-7
Spencer, Owen, 47460 ... L-5
Sullivan, Sullivan, 47882 ... L-3
Summitville, Madison, 46070 ... G-9
Swayzee, Grant, 46986 ... F-9
Syracuse, Kosciusko, 46567 ... B-9
• Taylorsville, Bartholomew, 47280 ... L-8
Tell City, Perry, 47586 ... Q-5
Terre Haute, Vigo, 47802-07 ... K-3
Thorntown, Boone, 46071 ... H-6
Tipton, Tipton, 46072 ... G-8
Trail Creek, La Porte, 46360 ... A-5
• Tri-Lakes, Whitley, 46725 ... C-10
Union City, Randolph, 47390 ... H-12
Upland, Grant, 46989 ... G-10
Valparaiso, Porter, 46383 ... B-4
Veedersburg, Fountain, 47978 ... H-4
Vernon, Jennings, 47282 ... M-9
Versailles, Ripley, 47042 ... M-11
Vevay, Switzerland, 47043 ... N-11
Vincennes, Knox, 47591 ... N-3
Wabash, Wabash, 46992 ... E-9
Wakarusa, Elkhart, 46573 ... B-8
Walkerton, St. Joseph, 46574 ... B-6
Walton, Cass, 46994 ... F-7
Warren, Huntington, 46792 ... F-10
Warren Park, Marion, 46219 ... I-8
Warsaw, Kosciusko, 46580 ... C-9
Washington, Daviess, 47501 ... N-4
Waterloo, De Kalb, 46793 ... B-11
West Glen Park, Lake, 46412 ... B-3
West Lafayette, Tippecanoe, 47906-07 ... G-5
West Terre Haute, Vigo, 47885 ... K-3
Westfield, Hamilton, 46074 ... H-8
Westport, Decatur, 47283 ... L-10
Westville, La Porte, 46391 ... B-5
Whiteland, Johnson, 46184 ... K-8
Whiting, Lake, 46394 ... A-3
Williamsport, Warren, 47993 ... G-4
Winamac, Pulaski, 46996 ... D-6
Winchester, Randolph, 47394 ... H-12
Winona Lake, Kosciusko, 46590 ... C-9
Woodburn, Allen, 46797 ... D-12
Worthington, Greene, 47471 ... L-5
Yorktown, Delaware, 47396 ... H-10
Zionsville, Boone, 46077 ... I-7

Explanation of symbols: •– Census Designated Place (CDP)

Explanation of Symbols

✦ State Capital
Vernon County Seat

Population Key

○ 0-999
⊙ 1,000-2,499
⊙ 2,500-4,999
⊙ 5,000-9,999
⊙ 10,000-19,000
⊙ 20,000-24,999
⊙ 25,000-49,999
□ 50,000-99,999
□ 100,000-249,999
■ 250,000-999,999

Zip Code Symbols

○ Sectional Center

972 • City which has its own 3-digit zip code (the number beside the symbol).

972 ⊙ City which has its own 3-digit zip code and also serves other post offices as a sectional center.

Cleartype®
County-Town

INDIANA
ZIP CODES
NATIONAL AREA NO.4

⊕AMC

0   10   20   30   40   50 Miles
0 10 20 30 40 50 60 70 80 Kilometers

Copyright American Map Corporation

Explanation of symbols: ●– Census Designated Place (CDP)

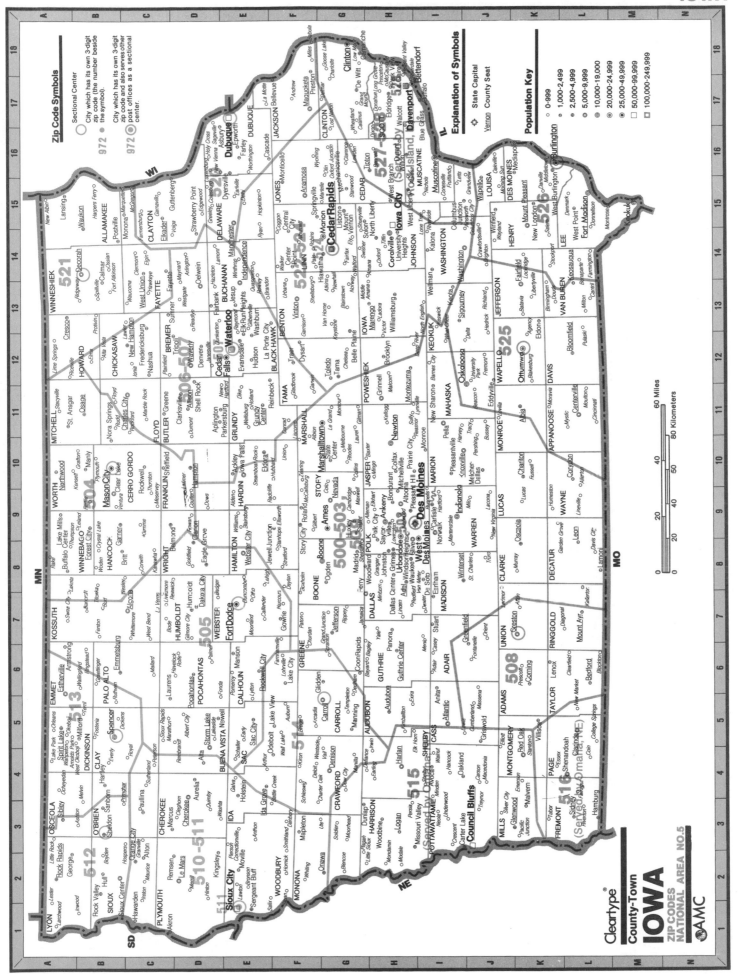

Clearype®
County-Town
IOWA
ZIP CODES
NATIONAL AREA NO.5
AMC

Copyright American Map Corporation

COUNTIES

(105 Counties)

Name of County	Population	Location on Map
ALLEN	14,638	G-16
ANDERSON	7,803	F-16
ATCHISON	16,932	B-16
BARBER	5,874	I-8
BARTON	29,382	E-8
BOURBON	14,966	G-17
BROWN	11,128	A-15
BUTLER	50,580	G-12
CHASE	3,021	F-13
CHAUTAUQUA	4,407	G-14
CHEROKEE	21,374	H-17
CHEYENNE	2,418	A-1
CLARK		I-6
CLAY	9,158	C-12
CLOUD	11,023	C-10
COFFEY	8,404	F-15
COMANCHE	2,313	I-7
COWLEY	36,915	I-12
CRAWFORD	35,568	H-17
DECATUR	4,021	A-4
DICKINSON	18,958	D-12
DONIPHAN	8,134	B-16
DOUGLAS	81,798	D-16
EDWARDS	3,787	H-7
ELK	3,327	I-14
ELLIS	26,004	D-7
ELLSWORTH	6,586	E-9
FINNEY	33,070	G-3
FORD	27,463	H-5
FRANKLIN	21,994	E-16
GEARY	30,453	E-13
GOVE	3,231	D-4
GRAHAM	3,543	C-5
GRANT	7,159	H-2
GRAY	5,396	H-4
GREELEY	1,774	E-1
GREENWOOD	7,847	G-14
HAMILTON	2,388	G-1
HARPER	7,124	J-9
HARVEY	31,028	G-11
HASKELL	3,886	H-3
HODGEMAN	2,177	G-5
JACKSON	11,525	C-15
JEFFERSON	15,905	C-16
JEWELL	4,251	B-10
JOHNSON	355,054	E-17
KEARNY	4,027	G-2
KINGMAN	8,292	H-9
KIOWA	3,660	H-7
LABETTE	23,693	I-16
LANE	2,375	E-4
LEAVENWORTH	64,371	C-17
LINCOLN	3,653	D-9
LINN	8,254	F-17
LOGAN	3,081	D-2
LYON	34,732	E-14
MARION	12,888	F-12
MARSHALL	11,705	A-13
McPHERSON	27,268	F-10
MEADE	4,247	I-4
MIAMI	23,466	E-17
MITCHELL	7,203	C-9
MONTGOMERY	38,816	I-15
MORRIS	6,198	E-13
MORTON	3,480	I-1
NEMAHA	10,446	A-14
NEOSHO	17,035	I-16
NESS	4,033	F-5
NORTON	5,947	A-5
OSAGE	15,248	E-15
OSBORNE	4,867	C-8
OTTAWA	5,634	D-11
PAWNEE	7,555	G-7
PHILLIPS	6,590	B-7
POTTAWATOMIE	16,128	C-13
PRATT	9,702	H-8
RAWLINS	3,404	A-2
RENO	62,389	G-10
REPUBLIC	6,482	A-11
RICE	10,610	F-9
RILEY	67,139	C-13
ROOKS	6,039	C-7
RUSH	3,842	E-7
RUSSELL	7,835	D-8
SALINE	49,301	E-10
SCOTT	5,289	E-3
SEDGWICK	403,662	H-11
SEWARD	18,743	I-3
SHAWNEE	160,976	D-15
SHERIDAN	3,043	C-4
SHERMAN	6,926	C-1
SMITH	5,078	A-8
STAFFORD	5,365	G-8
STANTON	2,333	I-1
STEVENS	5,048	I-1
SUMNER	25,841	I-11
THOMAS	8,258	C-3
TREGO	3,694	D-5
WABAUNSEE	6,603	D-14
WALLACE	1,821	D-1
WASHINGTON	7,073	A-12
WICHITA	2,758	E-2
WILSON	10,289	H-15
WOODSON	4,116	G-15
WYANDOTTE	161,993	D-17
TOTAL	**2,477,574**	

CITIES AND TOWNS

Note: The first name is that of the city or town, second, that of the county in which it is located, then the zip code area and location on the map.

Abilene, Dickinson, 67410 — D-12
Alma, Wabaunsee, 66401 — D-14
Altamont, Labette, 67330 — J-16
Andover, Butler, 67002 — H-12
Anthony, Harper, 67003 — J-10
Arkansas City, Cowley, 67005 — J-13
Arma, Crawford, 66712 — J-18
Ashland, Clark, 67831 — J-6
Atchison, Atchison, 66002 — B-17
Atwood, Rawlins, 67730 — B-3
Augusta, Butler, 67010 — H-13
Baldwin City, Douglas, 66006 — E-16
Basehor, Leavenworth, 66007 — D-17
Baxter Springs, Cherokee, 66713 — J-18
Bel Aire, Sedgwick, 67220 — H-12
Belle Plaine, Sumner, 67013 — I-12
Belleville, Republic, 66935 — B-11
Beloit, Mitchell, 67420 — C-10
Blue Rapids, Marshall, 66411 — B-13
Bonner Springs, Johnson/Wyandotte, 66012 — D-17
Buhler, Reno, 67522 — G-11
Burlingame, Osage, 66413 — F-12
Burlington, Coffey, 66839 — F-8
Caldwell, Sumner, 67022 — C-11
Camp Forsyth, Geary, 66442 — G-3
Caney, Montgomery, 67333 — G-15
Carbondale, Osage, 66414 — C-11
Chanute, Neosho, 66720 — G-7
Chapman, Dickinson, 67431 — E-15
Cheney, Sedgwick, 67025 — J-11
Cherryvale, Montgomery, 67335 — G-15
Chetopa, Labette, 67336 — H-8
Cimarron, Gray, 67835 — A-2
Clay Center, Clay, 67432 — A-10
Clearwater, Sedgwick, 67026 — F-9
Coffeyville, Montgomery, 67337 — C-13
Colby, Thomas, 67701 — C-7
Coldwater, Comanche, 67029 — E-7
Columbus, Cherokee, 66725 — D-8
Colwich, Sedgwick, 67030 — J-7
Concordia, Cloud, 66901 — E-10
Conway Springs, Sumner, 67460 — E-3
Cottonwood Falls, Chase, 66845 — H-11
Council Grove, Morris, 66846 — I-3
De Soto, Johnson, 66018 — D-15
Derby, Sedgwick, 67037 — C-4
Dighton, Lane, 67839 — C-1
Dodge City, Ford, 67801 — A-8
Douglass, Butler, 67039 — G-8
Downs, Osborne, 67437 — I-1
Edgerton, Johnson, 66021 — I-11
Edwardsville, Wyandotte, 66113 — C-3
El Dorado, Butler, 67042 — D-5
Elkhart, Morton, 67950 — D-14
Ellinwood, Barton, 67526 — D-1
Ellis, Ellis, 67637 — A-12
Ellsworth, Ellsworth, 67439 — E-2
Elwood, Doniphan, 66024 — H-15
Emporia, Lyon, 66801 — G-15
Erie, Neosho, 66733 — D-17
Eudora, Douglas, 66025 — D-13
Eureka, Greenwood, 67045 — B-10
Fairway, Johnson, 66205 — F-12
Fort Riley-Camp Whiteside, Geary, 66442 — B-13
Fort Riley North, Geary/Riley, 66442 — F-11

Fort Scott, Bourbon, 66701 — G-17
Fredonia, Wilson, 66736 — H-15
Frontenac, Crawford, 66762 — H-18
Galena, Cherokee, 66739 — J-18
Garden City, Finney, 67846 — H-3
Gardner, Johnson, 66030 — E-17
Garnett, Anderson, 66032 — F-16
Girard, Crawford, 66743 — H-17
Goddard, Sedgwick, 67052 — H-11
Goodland, Sherman, 67735 — C-2
Gove City, Gove, 67736 — D-4
Grandview Plaza, Geary, 66441 — D-13
Great Bend, Barton, 67530 — F-8
Greensburg, Kiowa, 67054 — I-7
Halstead, Harvey, 67056 — G-11
Harper, Harper, 67058 — J-10
Haven, Reno, 67543 — H-11

Hays, Ellis, 67601 — E-7
Haysville, Sedgwick, 67060 — I-11
Herington, Dickinson/Morris, 67449 — E-12
Hesston, Harvey, 67062 — G-11
Hiawatha, Brown, 66434 — B-16
Hill City, Graham, 67642 — C-6
Hillsboro, Marion, 67063 — F-12
Hoisington, Barton, 67544 — F-8
Holcomb, Finney, 67851 — G-3
Holton, Jackson, 66436 — C-15
Horton, Brown, 66439 — B-16
Howard, Elk, 67349 — I-14
Hoxie, Sheridan, 67740 — C-4
Hugoton, Stevens, 67951 — J-2
Humboldt, Allen, 66748 — H-16
Hutchinson, Reno, 67501-02 — G-10
Independence, Montgomery, 67301 — I-15
Inman, McPherson, 67546 — G-10
Iola, Allen, 66749 — H-16
Jetmore, Hodgeman, 67854 — G-6
Johnson City, Stanton, 67855 — I-1
Junction City, Geary, 66441 — D-13
Kansas City, Wyandotte, 66101-99 — D-18
Kingman, Kingman, 67068 — H-11
Kinsley, Edwards, 67547 — H-7
Kiowa, Barber, 67070 — K-9
La Crosse, Rush, 67548 — F-7
La Cygne, Linn, 66040 — F-17
Lakin, Kearny, 67860 — H-3
Lansing, Leavenworth, 66043 — C-17
Larned, Pawnee, 67550 — G-7
Lawrence, Douglas, 66044-49 — D-16
Leavenworth, Leavenworth, 66048 — C-17
Leawood, Johnson, 66209 — C-9
Lenexa, Johnson, 66215 — M-17
Leoti, Wichita, 67861 — F-2
Liberal, Seward, 67901 — J-3
Lincoln Center, Lincoln, 67455 — D-10
Lindsborg, McPherson, 67456 — F-11
Louisburg, Miami, 66450 — D-7
Lyndon, Osage, 66451 — E-9
Lyons, Rice, 67554 — F-10
Maize, Sedgwick, 67101 — H-11
Manhattan, Pottawatomie/Riley, 66502 — D-13
Mankato, Jewell, 66956 — B-10
Marion, Marion, 66861 — F-12
Marysville, Marshall, 66508 — B-13
McPherson, McPherson, 67460 — F-11
Meade, Meade, 67864 — J-5
Medicine Lodge, Barber, 67104 — J-9
Merriam, Johnson, 66202 — D-7
Midland Park, Sedgwick, 67216 — I-12
Minneapolis, Ottawa, 67467 — D-11
Mission, Johnson, 66202 — L-17
Mission Hills, Johnson, 66205, 08 — M-17
Mound City, Linn, 66056 — G-17
Moundridge, McPherson, 67107 — G-11
Mulvane, Sedgwick, 67110 — I-12
Neodesha, Wilson, 66757 — I-15
Ness City, Ness, 67560 — F-6
Newton, Harvey, 67114 — G-12
Nickerson, Reno, 67561 — G-10
North Newton, Harvey, 67114 — G-12
Norton, Norton, 67654 — B-6
● Oaklawn-Sunview, Sedgwick, 66616 — I-12
Oakley, Logan/Thomas, 67748 — D-4
Oberlin, Decatur, 67749 — B-4

Ogden, Riley, 66517 — D-13
Olathe, Johnson, 66061-62 — E-17
Osage City, Osage, 66523 — E-15
Osawatomie, Miami, 66064 — F-17
Osborne, Osborne, 67473 — C-8
Oskaloosa, Jefferson, 66066 — D-16
Oswego, Labette, 67356 — J-17
Ottawa, Franklin, 66067 — E-16
Overland Park, Johnson, 66020 — D-18
Oxford, Sumner, 67119 — J-11
Paola, Miami, 66071 — F-17
Park City, Sedgwick, 67219 — H-12
Parsons, Labette, 67357 — J-16
Peabody, Marion, 66866 — G-12
Phillipsburg, Phillips, 67661 — B-7
Pittsburg, Crawford, 66762 — J-18
Plainville, Rooks, 67663 — D-7
Pleasanton, Linn, 66075 — G-18
Prairie Village, Johnson, 66208 — M-17
Pratt, Pratt, 67124 — I-9
Riverview, Sedgwick, 67204 — H-12
Roeland Park, Johnson, 66202 — L-17
Rose Hill, Butler, 67133 — I-12
Rossville, Shawnee, 66533 — D-15
Russell, Russell, 67665 — E-8
Sabetha, Brown/Nemaha, 66534 — A-15
Saint Francis, Cheyenne, 67756 — A-1
Saint John, Stafford, 67576 — G-8
Saint Marys, Pottawatomie, 66536 — D-14
Salina, Saline, 67401 — E-11
Satanta, Haskell, 67870 — I-3
Scott City, Scott, 67871 — F-3
Sedan, Chautauqua, 67361 — J-14
Sedgwick, Harvey/Sedgwick, 67135 — H-11
Seneca, Nemaha, 66538 — B-14
Sharon Springs, Wallace, 67758 — E-2
Shawnee, Johnson, 66201-99 — L-16
Silver Lake, Shawnee, 66539 — D-15
Smith Center, Smith, 66967 — B-8
South Hutchinson, Reno, 67505 — G-10
Spring Hill, Johnson/Miami, 66083 — E-17
Stafford, Stafford, 67578 — H-9
Sterling, Rice, 67579 — G-10
Stockton, Rooks, 67669 — C-7
Sublette, Haskell, 67877 — I-3
Sunset Park, Sedgwick, 67060 — I-11
Syracuse, Hamilton, 67878 — G-1
Tonganoxie, Leavenworth, 66086 — D-17
Topeka, Shawnee, 66601-99 — D-15
Towanda, Butler, 67144 — H-12
Tribune, Greeley, 67879 — F-1
Troy, Doniphan, 66087 — B-17
Ulysses, Grant, 67880 — I-2
Valley Center, Sedgwick, 67147 — H-12
Valley Falls, Jefferson, 66088 — C-16
Victoria, Ellis, 67671 — E-7
Wakeeney, Trego, 67672 — D-6
Wamego, Pottawatomie, 66547 — D-14
Washington, Washington, 66968 — B-12
Wathena, Doniphan, 66090 — B-17
Wellington, Sumner, 67152 — J-12
Wellsville, Franklin, 66092 — E-7
West Plains, Meade, 67852 — J-4
Westmoreland, Pottawatomie, 66549 — C-13
Westwood, Johnson, 66205 — L-17
Wichita, Sedgwick, 67201-99 — J-12
Winfield, Cowley, 67156 — J-12
Yates Center, Woodson, 66783 — H-15

Explanation of symbols: ●– Census Designated Place (CDP)

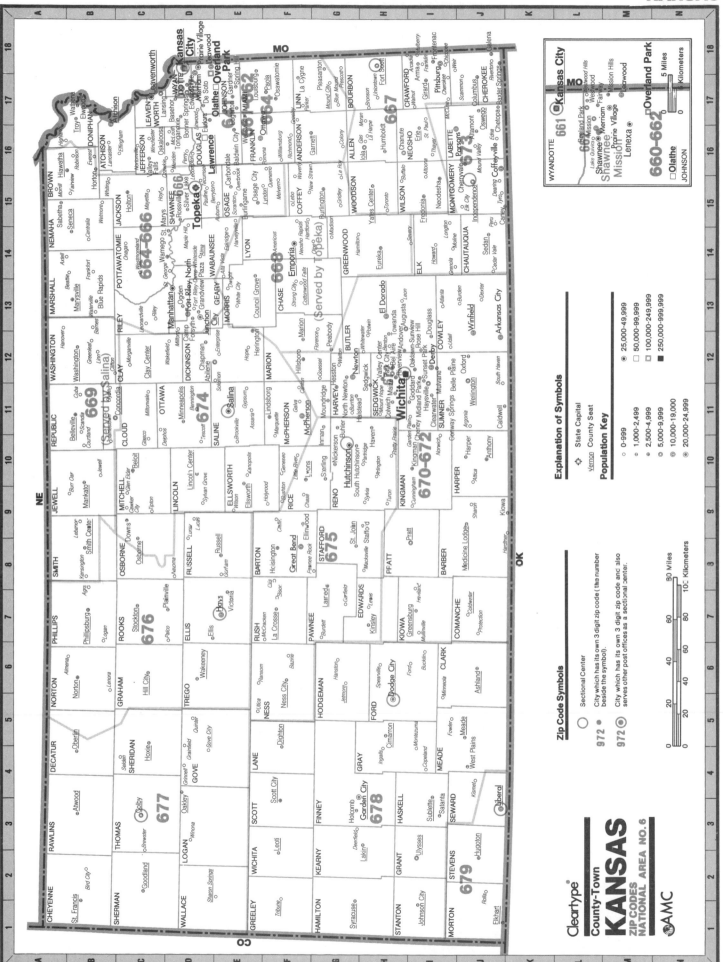

Copyright American Map Corporation

COUNTIES

(120 Counties)

Name of County	Population	Location on Map
ADAIR	15,360	I-8
ALLEN	14,628	J-5
ANDERSON	14,571	E-9
BALLARD	7,902	L-14
BARREN	34,001	J-6
BATH	9,692	D-13
BELL	31,506	J-13
BOONE	57,589	B-10
BOURBON	19,236	D-11
BOYD	51,150	D-16
BOYLE	25,641	G-9
BRACKEN	7,766	B-12
BREATHITT	15,703	G-14
BRECKINRIDGE	16,312	G-4
BULLITT	47,567	E-7
BUTLER	11,245	H-4
CALDWELL	13,232	K-17
CALLOWAY	30,735	M-16
CAMPBELL	83,866	B-11
CARLISLE	5,238	M-14
CARROLL	9,292	C-9
CARTER	24,340	D-15
CASEY	14,211	H-9
CHRISTIAN	68,941	I-1
CLARK	29,496	E-12
CLAY	21,746	H-13
CLINTON	9,135	J-9
CRITTENDEN	9,196	K-17
CUMBERLAND	6,784	J-8
DAVIESS	87,189	G-3
EDMONSON	10,357	H-5
ELLIOTT	6,455	E-15
ESTILL	14,614	F-12
FAYETTE	225,366	E-11
FLEMING	12,292	C-12
FLOYD	43,586	F-15
FRANKLIN	43,781	D-9
FULTON	8,271	N-13
GALLATIN	5,393	B-10
GARRARD	11,579	G-10
GRANT	15,737	B-10
GRAVES	33,550	M-15
GRAYSON	21,050	G-4
GREEN	10,371	H-7
GREENUP	36,742	C-15
HANCOCK	7,864	F-4
HARDIN	89,240	F-6
HARLAN	36,574	I-15
HARRISON	16,248	C-11
HART	14,890	H-6
HENDERSON	43,044	F-1
HENRY	12,823	C-9
HICKMAN	5,566	M-14
HOPKINS	46,126	H-1
JACKSON	11,955	G-12
JEFFERSON	664,937	D-7
JESSAMINE	30,508	F-10
JOHNSON	23,248	E-15
KENTON	142,031	B-10
KNOTT	17,906	H-15
KNOX	29,676	I-13
LARUE	11,679	G-7
LAUREL	43,438	I-12
LAWRENCE	13,998	D-16
LEE	7,422	G-13
LESLIE	13,642	H-14
LETCHER	27,000	I-15
LEWIS	13,029	C-14
LINCOLN	20,045	G-10
LIVINGSTON	9,062	K-16
LOGAN	24,416	I-3
LYON	6,624	L-17
MADISON	57,508	F-11
MAGOFFIN	13,077	F-15
MARION	16,499	G-8
MARSHALL	27,205	M-16
MARTIN	12,526	F-17
MASON	16,666	C-12
MCCRACKEN	62,879	L-15
MCCREARY	15,603	J-11
MCLEAN	9,628	G-2
MEADE	24,170	E-5
MENIFEE	5,092	F-13
MERCER	19,148	F-9
METCALFE	8,963	I-7
MONROE	11,401	J-7
MONTGOMERY	19,561	E-12
MORGAN	11,648	E-14
MUHLENBERG	31,318	I-2
NELSON	29,710	F-7
NICHOLAS	6,725	D-12
OHIO	21,105	G-3
OLDHAM	33,263	D-8
OWEN	9,035	C-9
OWSLEY	5,036	H-13
PENDLETON	12,036	B-11
PERRY	30,283	H-14
PIKE	72,583	F-17
POWELL	11,686	F-12
PULASKI	49,489	H-10
ROBERTSON	2,124	C-12
ROCKCASTLE	14,803	H-11
ROWAN	20,353	D-14
RUSSELL	14,716	I-9
SCOTT	23,867	D-10
SHELBY	24,824	D-8
SIMPSON	15,145	J-4
SPENCER	6,801	E-8
TAYLOR	21,146	H-8
TODD	10,940	I-2
TRIGG	10,361	M-17
TRIMBLE	6,090	C-8
UNION	16,557	J-17
WARREN	76,673	I-4
WASHINGTON	10,441	F-8
WAYNE	17,468	J-9
WEBSTER	13,955	G-1
WHITLEY	33,326	J-11
WOLFE	6,503	F-13
WOODFORD	19,955	E-10
TOTAL	3,685,296	

CITIES AND TOWNS

Note: The first name is that of the city or town, second, that of the county in which it is located, then the zip code area and location on the map.

Albany, Clinton, 42602 ... K-9
Alexandria, Campbell, 41001 ... A-11
Anchorage, Jefferson, 40223 ... B-4
Ashland, Boyd, 41101-02 ... C-16
Auburn, Logan, 42206 ... J-4
Audubon Park, Jefferson, 40213 ... C-2
Augusta, Bracken, 41002 ... B-12
Barbourmeade, Jefferson, 40222 A-3
Barbourville, Knox, 40906 ... J-13
Bardstown, Nelson, 40004 ... F-8
Bardwell, Carlisle, 42023 ... M-14
Beattyville, Lee, 41311 ... G-13
Beaver Dam, Ohio, 42320 ... H-3
Bedford, Trimble, 40006 ... C-8
Beechwood Village, Jefferson, 40207 ... B-3
Bellevue, Campbell, 41073 ... A-6
Benton, Marshall, 42025 ... M-16
Berea, Madison, 40403 ... G-11
Booneville, Owsley, 41314 ... G-13
Bowling Green, Warren, 42101-04 ... I-5
Brandenburg, Meade, 40108 ... A-6
• Breckinridge Center, Union, 42437 ... J-18
Brodhead, Rockcastle, 40409 ... H-11
Bromley, Kenton, 41016 ... A-10
• Brooks, Bullitt, 40109 ... E-7
Brooksville, Bracken, 41004 ... B-12
Brownsville, Edmonson, 42210 ... I-5
• Buechel, Jefferson, 40261 ... C-3
Burgin, Mercer, 40310 ... F-10
Burkesville, Cumberland, 42717 .. J-8
• Burlington, Boone, 41005 ... A-10
Cadiz, Trigg, 42211 ... M-18
Calhoun, McLean,42327 ... G-2
Calvert City, Marshall, 42029 ... L-17
Camargo, Montgomery, 40353 .. E-12
Campbellsville, Taylor, 42718 ... H-8
Campton, Wolfe, 41301 ... F-14
Carlisle, Nicholas, 40311 ... D-12
Carrollton, Carroll, 41008 ... C-9
Catlettsburg, Boyd, 41129 ... C-16
Cave City, Barren, 42127 ... I-6
Central City, Muhlenberg, 42330 . H-3
• Claryville, Campbell, 41001 ... B-11
Clay, Webster, 42404 ... G-1
Clay City, Powell, 40312 ... F-12
Clinton, Hickman, 42301 ... N-14
Cloverport, Breckinridge, 40111 .. F-4
Cold Spring, Campbell, 41076 ... A-6
Columbia, Adair, 42728 ... I-8
• Concord, McCracken, 42001 ... L-15
Corbin, Knox/Whitley, 40701 ... I-12
Covington, Kenton, 41011-18 ... A-11
Crescent Springs, Kenton, 41016 ... A-5
Crestview Hills, Kenton, 41017 ... B-5
Crestwood, Oldham, 40014 ... D-8
Cumberland, Harlan, 40823 ... I-15
Cynthiana, Harrison, 41031 ... D-11
Danville, Boyle, 40422 ... D-10
Dawson Springs, Hopkins, 42408 ... I-1
Dayton, Campbell, 41074 ... A-6
Dixon, Webster, 42409 ... G-1
Douglass Hills, Jefferson, 40243 ... B-3
Dry Ridge, Grant, 41035 ... B-10
Earlington, Hopkins, 42410 ... H-1
Eddyville, Lyon, 42038 ... L-17
Edgewood, Kenton, 41017 ... B-5
Edmonton, Metcalfe, 42129 ... I-7
Elizabethtown, Hardin, 42701 ... G-7
Elkton, Todd, 42220 ... J-3
Elsmere, Kenton, 41018 ... B-5
Eminence, Henry, 40019 ... D-9
Erlanger, Kenton, 41018 ... B-5
Evarts, Harlan, 40828 ... J-15
• Fairdale, Jefferson,40118 ... D-2
Falmouth, Pendleton, 41040 ... C-11
• Fern Creek, Jefferson, 40291 ... E-7
Flatwoods, Greenup, 41139 ... C-16
Flemingsburg, Fleming, 41041 .. D-13
Flemming-Neon, Letcher, 41840 ... H-16
Florence, Boone, 41042 ... A-10
• Fort Campbell North, Christian, 42223 ... K-2
• Fort Knox, Hardin/Meade, 40121 ... F-6
Fort Mitchell, Kenton, 41017 ... A-5
Fort Thomas, Campbell, 41075 ... A-11
Fort Wright, Kenton, 41011 ... A-6
Frankfort, Franklin, 40601-99 ... D-9
Franklin, Simpson, 42134 ... K-4
Frenchburg, Menifee, 40322 ... E-13
Fulton, Fulton, 42041 ... N-15
Georgetown, Scott, 40324 ... D-10
Glasgow, Barren, 42141 ... I-6
• Goshen, Oldham, 40026 ... D-7
Graymoor-Devondale, Jefferson, 40222 ... B-3
Grayson, Carter, 41143 ... D-15
Greensburg, Green, 42743 ... H-8
Greenup, Greenup, 41144 ... C-15
Greenville, Muhlenberg, 42345 ... I-3
Guthrie, Todd, 42234 ... K-3
Hardinsburg, Breckinridge, 40143 ... F-5
Harlan, Harlan, 40831 ... J-14
Harrodsburg, Mercer, 40330 ... F-10
Hartford, Ohio, 42327 ... H-3
Hawesville, Hancock, 42348 ... F-4
Hazard, Perry,41701 ... H-15
Henderson, Henderson, 42420 ... F-2
• Hendron, McCracken, 42001 ... L-15
Hickman, Fulton, 42050 ... N-14
Highland Heights, Campbell, 41076 ... B-6
• Highview, Jefferson, 40228 ... C-3
Hillview, Bullitt, 40229 ... E-7
Hindman, Knott, 41822 ... H-15
Hodgenville, Larue, 42748 ... G-7
Hopkinsville, Christian, 42240 ... J-2
Horse Cave, Hart, 42749 ... I-6
Hurstbourne, Jefferson, 40222 ... B-3
Hurstbourne Acres, Jefferson, 40220 ... B-3
Hyden, Leslie, 41749 ... I-14
Independence, Kenton, 41051 .. B-10
Indian Hills, Jefferson, 40207 ... B-2
Indian Hills Cherokee Section, Jefferson, 40207 ... B-3
Inez, Martin, 41224 ... F-17
Irvine, Estill, 40336 ... F-12
Irvington, Breckinridge, 40146 ... F-5
Jackson, Breathitt, 41339 ... G-14
Jamestown, Russell, 42629 ... I-9
Jeffersontown, Jefferson, 40269 ... C-3
Jeffersonville, Montgomery, 40337 ... E-13
Jenkins, Letcher, 41537 ... H-16
Junction City, Boyle/Lincoln, 40440 ... D-10
La Center, Ballard, 42056 ... L-14
La Grange, Oldham, 40031 ... D-8
Lakeside Park, Kenton, 41017 ... B-5
Lancaster, Garrard, 40444 ... G-10
Lawrenceburg, Anderson, 40342 ... E-9
Lebanon, Marion, 40033 ... G-8
Lebanon Junction, Bullitt, 40150 . F-7
• Ledbetter, Livingston, 42058 ... L-16
Leitchfield, Grayson, 42754 ... G-5
Lewisport, Hancock, 42351 ... I-3
Lexington-Fayette, Fayette, 40501-99 ... E-11
Liberty, Casey, 42539 ... H-9
Livermore, McLean, 42352 ... G-3
London, Laurel, 40741 ... I-12
Louisa, Lawrence, 41230 ... E-16
Louisville, Jefferson, 40201-99 ... D-7
Loyall, Harlan, 40854 ... J-14
Ludlow, Kenton,41016 ... A-5
Lynch, Harlan, 40855 ... I-16
Lyndon, Jefferson, 40252 ... B-3
Lynnview, Jefferson, 42063 ... C-2
Madisonville, Hopkins, 42431 ... H-2
Manchester, Clay, 40962 ... I-13
Marion, Crittenden, 42064 ... K-17
• Masonville, Daviess, 42376 ... G-3
• Massac, McCracken, 42001 ... M-15
Mayfield, Graves, 42066 ... M-16
Maysville, Mason, 41056 ... C-13
McKee, Jackson, 40447 ... H-12
• McRoberts, Letcher, 41835 ... H-16
Middlesborough, Bell, 40965 ... K-13
Middletown, Jefferson, 40253 ... B-4
Midway, Woodford, 40347 ... E-10
Minor Lane Heights, Jefferson, 40213 ... D-1
Monticello, Wayne, 42633 ... J-9
Morehead, Rowan, 40351 ... D-14
Morganfield, Union, 42437 ... J-18
Morgantown, Butler, 42261 ... H-4
Mount Olivet, Robertson, 41064 ... C-12
Mount Sterling, Montgomery, 40353 ... E-12
Mount Vernon, Rockcastle, 40456 ... H-11
Mount Washington, Bullitt, 40047 ... E-7
Muldraugh, Hardin/Meade, 40155 ... F-6
Munfordville, Hart, 42765 ... H-6
Murray, Calloway, 42071 ... N-17
New Castle, Henry,40050 ... D-9
• Newburg, Jefferson, 40218 ... C-2
Newport, Campbell, 41071-76 ... A-6
Nicholasville, Jessamine, 40356 ... F-10
• North Corbin, Knox/Laurel, 40701 ... I-12
Nortonville, Hopkins, 42442 ... I-2
Oak Grove, Christian, 42262 ... K-2
• Oakbrook, Boone, 41005,41042 ... A-10
• Okolona, Jefferson, 40259 ... E-7
Olive Hill, Carter, 41164 ... D-15
Orchard Grass Hills, Oldham, 40031 ... D-8
Owensboro, Daviess, 42301,03 .. F-3
Owensboro East, Daviess,42301 F-3
Owenton, Owen, 40359 ... C-10
Owingsville, Bath, 40360 ... E-13
Paducah, McCracken, 42001,03 L-16
Paintsville, Johnson, 41240 ... F-16
Paris, Bourbon, 40361 ... D-11
Park Hills, Kenton, 41015 ... A-10
Pewee Valley, Oldham, 40056 ... D-7
• Phelps, Pike, 41553 ... G-18
Pikeville, Pike,41501 ... G-17
• Pine Knot, McCreary, 42635 ... K-11
Pineville, Bell, 40977 ... J-13
Pioneer Village, Bullitt, 40165 ... E-7
• Pleasure Ridge Park, Jefferson .. G-5
40268 ... E-7
Prairie Village, Jefferson,40272 .. D-1
Prestonsburg, Floyd, 41653 ... G-16
Princeton, Caldwell, 42445 ... L-18
Prospect, Jefferson, 40059 ... A-3
Providence, Webster, 42450 ... J-1
Raceland, Greenup, 41169 ... C-16
Radcliff, Hardin, 40160 ... F-6
• Reidland, McCracken, 42003 ... L-16
Richmond, Madison, 40475 ... F-11
Rolling Hills, Jefferson, 40222 ... B-3
Russell, Greenup, 41169 ... C-16
Russell Springs, Russell, 42642 ... I-9
Russellville, Logan, 42276 ... J-3
• Saint Dennis, Jefferson, 40216 ... C-1
Saint Matthews, Jefferson, 40206 ... B-3
Saint Regis Park, Jefferson, 40220 ... B-3
Salyersville, Magoffin, 41465 ... F-15
Sandy Hook, Elliott, 41171 ... E-15
Scottsville, Allen, 42164 ... J-6
Sebree, Webster, 42455 ... G-1
Shelbyville, Shelby, 40065 ... E-8
Shepherdsville, Bullitt, 40165 ... E-7
Shively, Jefferson, 40256 ... E-7
Silver Grove, Campbell, 41085 ... B-7
Smithland, Livingston, 42081 ... L-16
Somerset, Pulaski, 42501 ... I-10
South Shore, Greenup, 41175 .. B-15
• South Wallins, Harlan, 40873 ... J-14
Southgate, Campbell, 41071 ... B-6
Springfield, Washington, 40069 .. G-8
Stanford, Lincoln, 40484 ... G-10
Stanton, Powell, 40380 ... F-13
• Stearns, McCreary, 42647 ... K-11
Sturgis, Union, 42459 ... J-18
Summer Shade, Metcalfe, 42166. J-7
Taylor Mill, Kenton, 41015 ... B-6
Taylorsville, Spencer, 40071 ... E-8
Tompkinsville, Monroe, 42167 ... K-7
Union, Boone, 41091 ... B-10
Uniontown, Union, 42461 ... I-18
• Valley Station, Jefferson, 40272 ... E-7
Valley Village, Jefferson, 40272 .. C-2
• Van Lear, Johnson, 41265 ... F-16
Vanceburg, Lewis, 41179 ... C-14
Versailles, Woodford, 40383 ... E-10
Villa Hills, Kenton, 41016 ... A-5
Vine Grove, Hardin, 40175 ... F-6
Walton, Boone, 41094 ... B-10
Warsaw, Gallatin, 41095 ... B-9
Watterson Park, Jefferson, 40213 ... C-2
West Buechel, Jefferson, 40218 . C-2
West Liberty, Morgan, 41472 ... F-14
West Point, Hardin, 40177 ... E-6
• Westwood, Boyd, 41101 ... C-16
Whitesburg, Letcher, 41858 ... I-16
• Whitley City, McCreary, 42653 ... J-11
Wickliffe, Ballard, 42087 ... L-14
Williamsburg, Whitley, 40769 ... J-12
Williamstown, Grant, 41097 ... C-10
Wilmore, Jessamine, 40390 ... F-10
Winchester, Clark, 40391 ... E-12
Windy Hills, Jefferson, 40207 ... B-3
Woodlawn Park, Jefferson, 40207 ... B-3
• Woodlawn-Oakdale, McCracken, 42001 ... L-16
Worthington, Greenup, 41183 ... C-15
Wurtland, Greenup, 41144 ... C-15

Explanation of symbols: • – Census Designated Place (CDP)

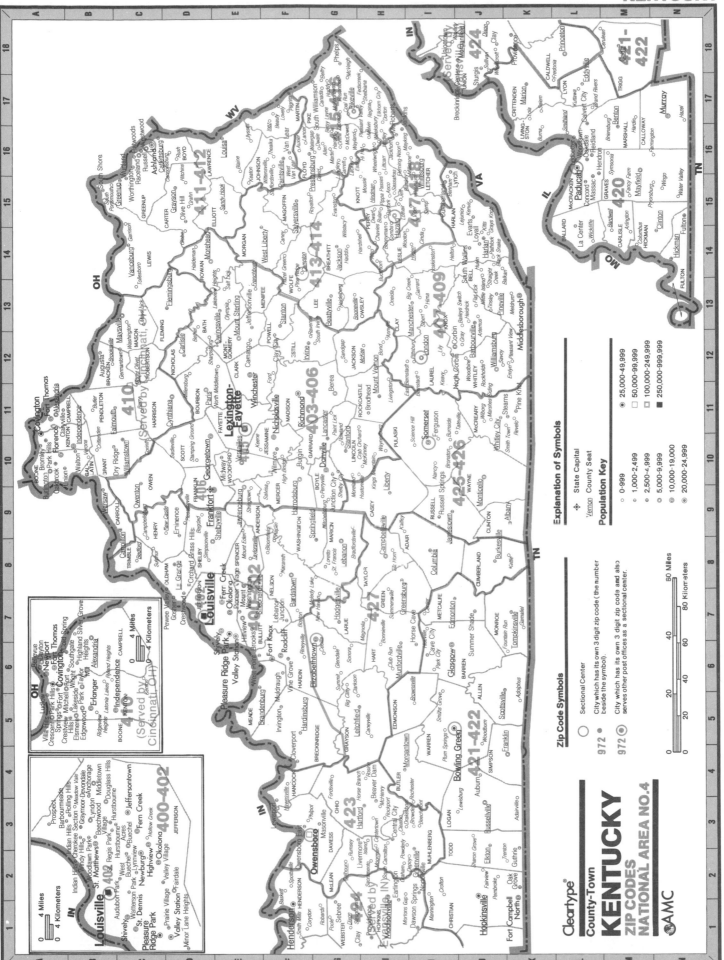

Cleartype®

County-Town

KENTUCKY

ZIP CODES
NATIONAL AREA NO.4

◆AMC

Zip Code Symbols

○ Sectional Center

972 • City which has its own 3 digit zip code (the number beside the symbol).

972 ◉ City which has its own 3 digit zip code and also serves other post offices as a sectional center.

Explanation of Symbols

★ State Capital

Vernon County Seat

Population Key

○ 0-999
◉ 1,000-2,499
● 2,500-4,999
◉ 5,000-9,999
◉ 10,000-19,000
◉ 20,000-24,999
◉ 25,000-49,999
□ 50,000-99,999
□ 100,000-249,999
■ 250,000-999,999

Explanation of symbols: ● – Census Designated Place (CDP)

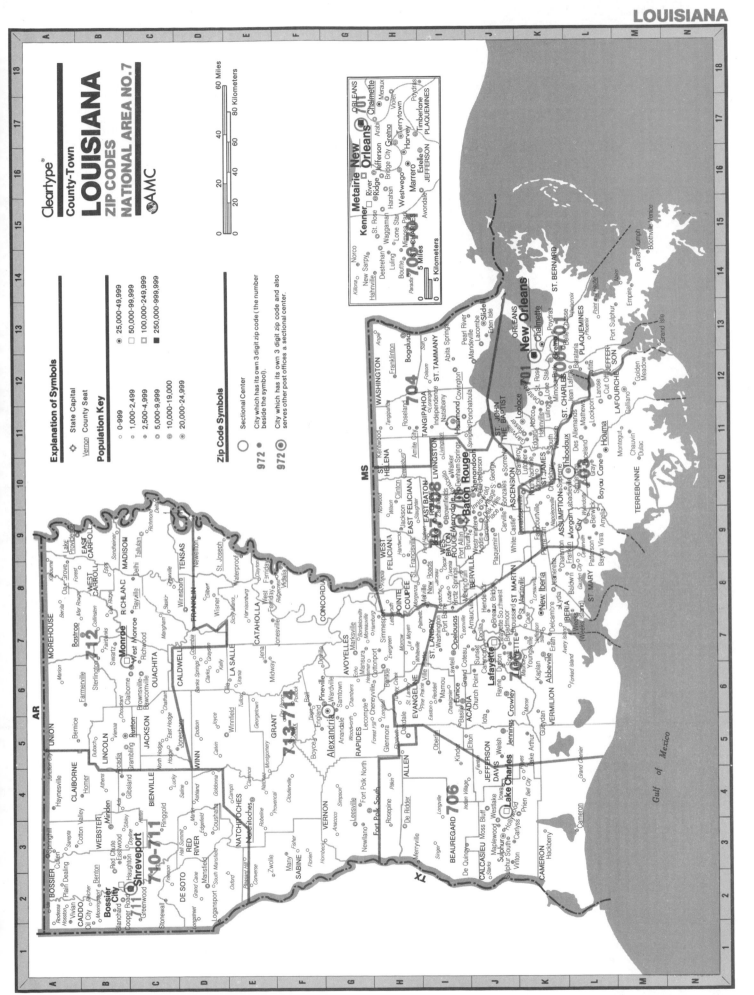

Copyright American Map Corporation

COUNTIES

(16 Counties)

CITIES AND TOWNS

Note: The first name is that of the city or town, second, that of the county in which it is located, then the zip code area and location on the map.

Explanation of symbols: ●– Census Designated Place (CDP)   ● *italics* – Township shown which is also a CDP   ▲ *italics* – Townships (shown on the map)

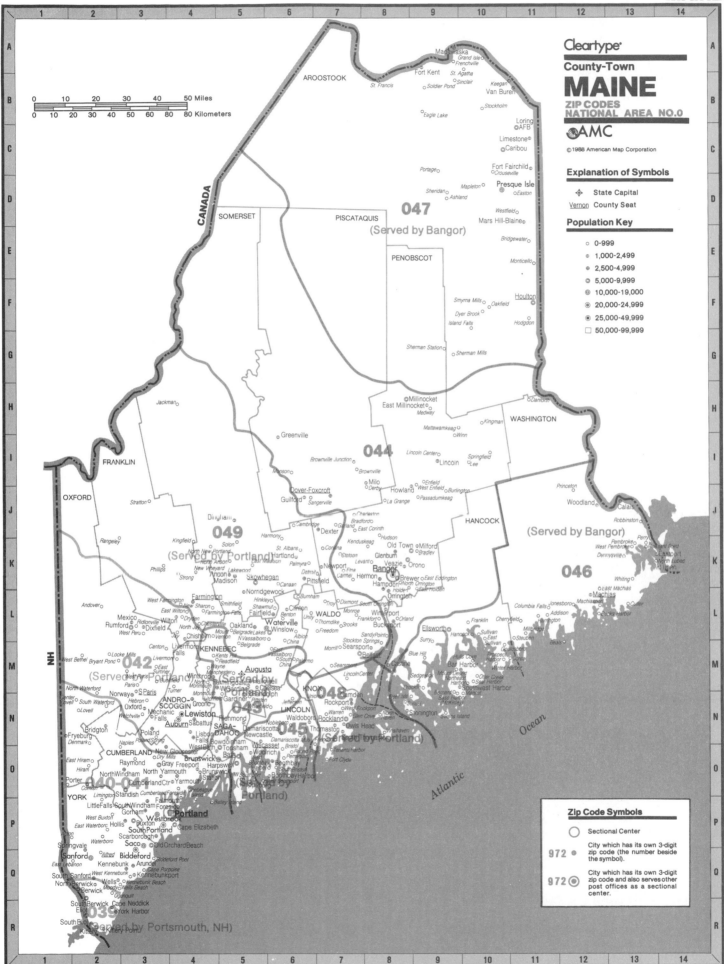

Cleartype®

County-Town

MAINE

ZIP CODES
NATIONAL AREA NO.0

AMC

©1988 American Map Corporation

Explanation of Symbols

✦ State Capital
Vernon County Seat

Population Key

○ 0-999
⊕ 1,000-2,499
⊕ 2,500-4,999
⊕ 5,000-9,999
⊕ 10,000-19,000
● 20,000-24,999
● 25,000-49,999
□ 50,000-99,999

Zip Code Symbols

○ Sectional Center

972 ● City which has its own 3-digit zip code (the number beside the symbol).

972 ◉ City which has its own 3-digit zip code and also serves other post offices as a sectional center.

Copyright American Map Corporation

Explanation of symbols: ● — Census Designated Place (CDP)

48

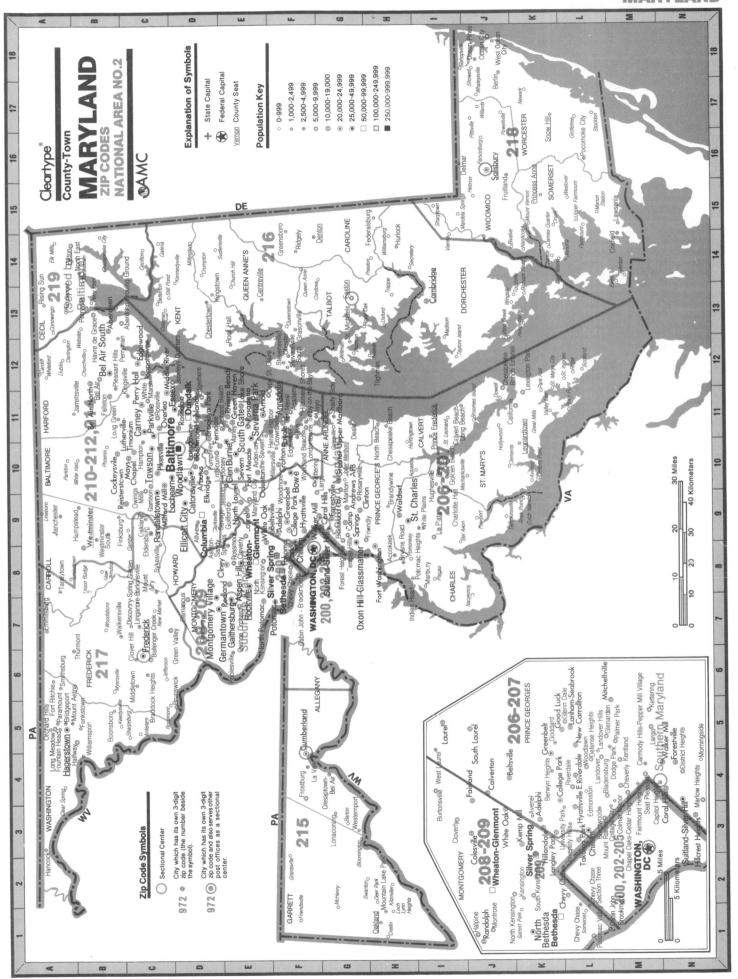

Cleartype®
County-Town
MARYLAND
ZIP CODES
NATIONAL AREA NO.2
AMC

Explanation of Symbols

✦ State Capital
★ Federal Capital
Vernon County Seat

Population Key
○ 0-999
● 1,000-2,499
◉ 2,500-4,999
◎ 5,000-9,999
◉ 10,000-19,000
◉ 20,000-24,999
◉ 25,000-49,999
□ 50,000-99,999
□ 100,000-249,999
■ 250,000-999,999

Zip Code Symbols

○ Sectional Center

972 ● City which has its own 3-digit
      zip code (the number beside
      the symbol).

972 ◉ City which has its own 3-digit
      zip code and also serves other
      post offices as a sectional
      center.

Copyright American Map Corporation

49

COUNTIES

Name of County (14 Counties)	Population	Location on Map
BARNSTABLE	186,605	J-15
BERKSHIRE	139,352	D-2
BRISTOL	506,325	I-12
DUKES	11,639	L-15
ESSEX	670,080	C-12
FRANKLIN	70,092	C-3
HAMPDEN	456,310	G-3
HAMPSHIRE	146,568	E-3
MIDDLESEX	1,398,468	C-9
NANTUCKET	6,012	M-17
NORFOLK	616,087	G-11
PLYMOUTH	435,276	I-13
SUFFOLK	663,906	F-13
WORCESTER	709,705	E-7
TOTAL	6,016,425	

CITIES AND TOWNS

Note: The first name is that of the city or town, second, that of the county in which it is located, then the zip code area and location on the map.

Explanation of symbols: ●– Census Designated Place (CDP) ● *italics* – Township shown which is also a CDP ▲ *italics* – Township (shown on the map)

Copyright American Map Corporation

Explanation of symbols: ● — Census Designated Place (CDP)

Explanation of Symbols

✧ State Capital
Vernon County Seat

Population Key

○ 0-999
◔ 1,000-2,499
◑ 2,500-4,999
◉ 5,000-9,999
◉ 10,000-19,000
◉ 20,000-24,999

◉ 25,000-49,999
□ 50,000-99,999
□ 100,000-249,999
■ 250,000-999,999
■ 1,000,000+

Cleartype®
County-Town
MICHIGAN
ZIP CODES
NATIONAL AREA NO.4
◉AMC

0   25   50   75   100 Miles
0   25   50   75   100   125 Kilometers

Zip Code Symbols

◯ Sectional Center

972 • City which has its own 3-digit zip code (the number beside the symbol).

972 ◉ City which has its own 3-digit zip code and also serves other post offices as a sectional center.

Copyright American Map Corporation

COUNTIES

(87 Counties)

CITIES AND TOWNS

Note: The first name is that of the city or town, second, that of the county in which it is located, then the zip code area and location on the map.

Explanation of symbols: ● – Census Designated Place (CDP)

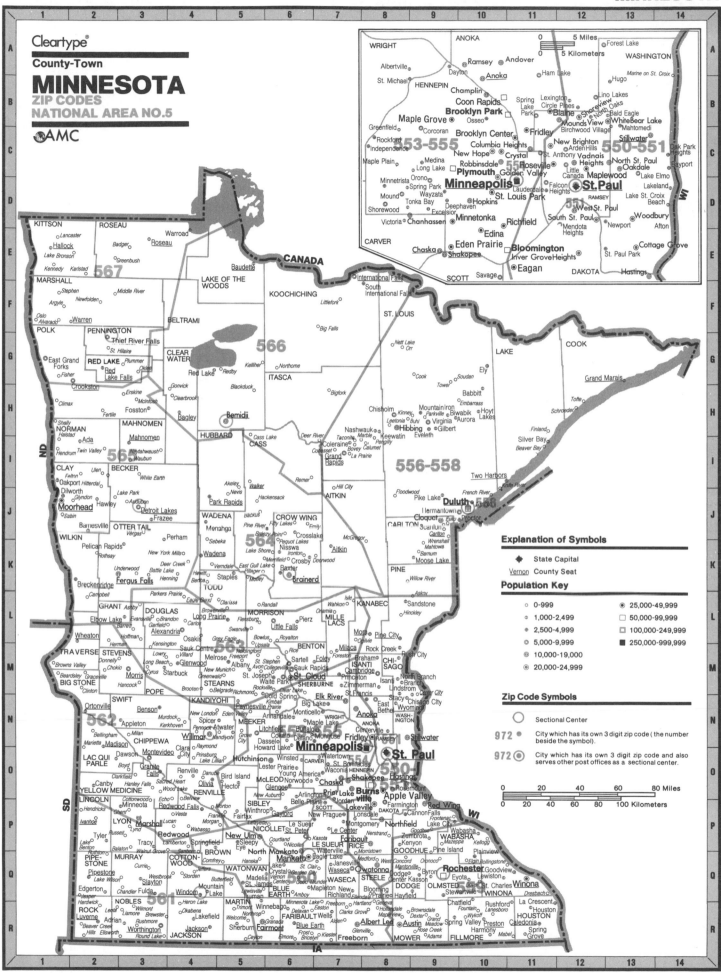

Cleartype®
County-Town
MINNESOTA
ZIP CODES
NATIONAL AREA NO.5
AMC

Explanation of Symbols

✚ State Capital

Vernon County Seat

Population Key

○ 0-999	◉ 25,000-49,999
⊕ 1,000-2,499	☐ 50,000-99,999
⊕ 2,500-4,999	▢ 100,000-249,999
◉ 5,000-9,999	■ 250,000-999,999
◉ 10,000-19,999	
◉ 20,000-24,999	

Zip Code Symbols

○ Sectional Center

972 ● City which has its own 3 digit zip code (the number beside the symbol).

972 ◉ City which has its own 3 digit zip code and also serves other post offices as a sectional center.

Copyright American Map Corporation

55

Explanation of symbols: ● – Census Designated Place (CDP)

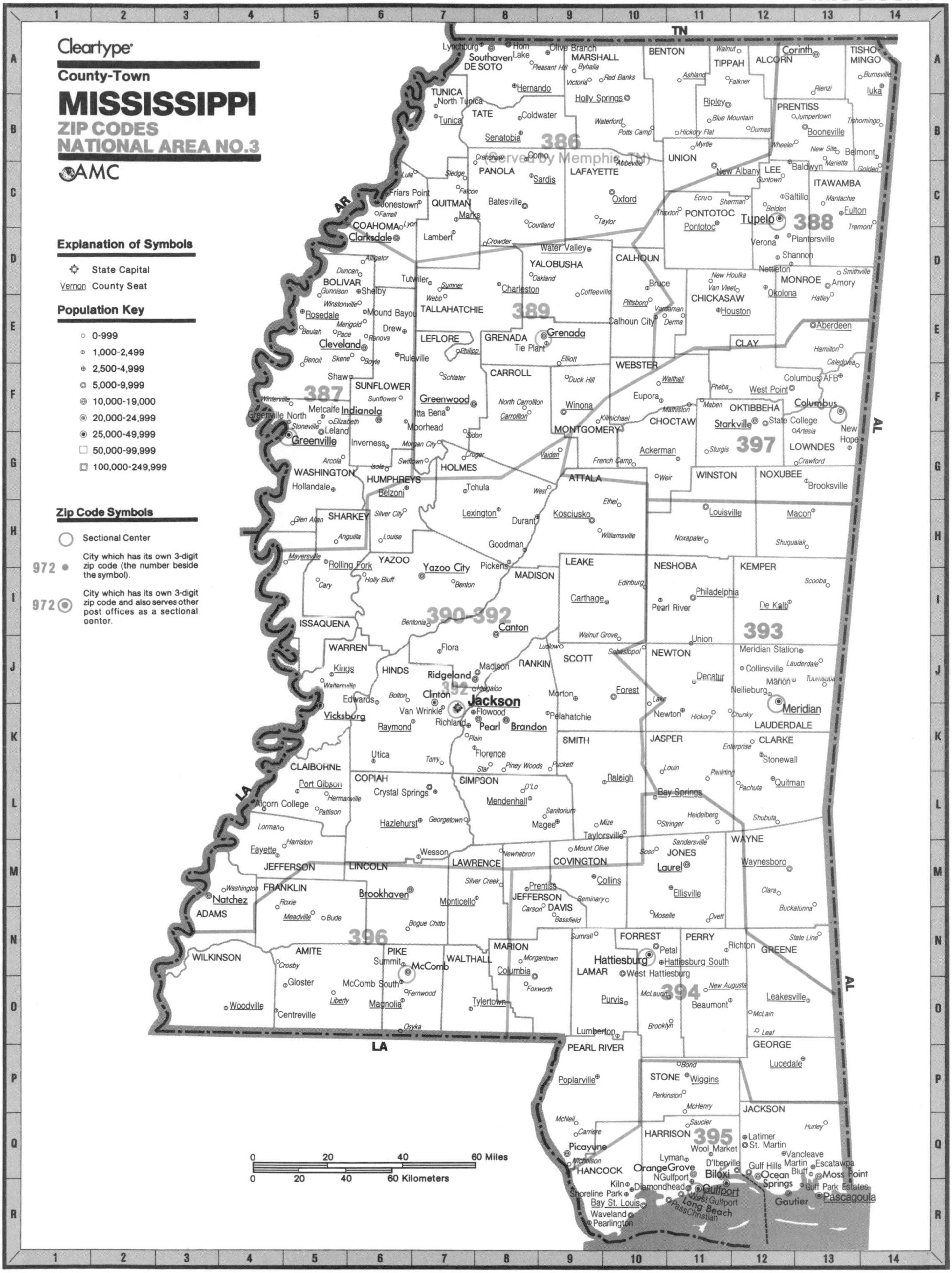

Cleartype
County-Town
MISSISSIPPI
ZIP CODES
NATIONAL AREA NO.3
AMC
Explanation of Symbols
State Capital
Vernon County Seat
Population Key
0-999
1,000-2,499
2,500-4,999
5,000-9,999
10,000-19,000
20,000-24,999
25,000-49,999
50,000-99,999
100,000-249,999
Zip Code Symbols
Sectional Center
972 City which has its own 3-digit zip code (the number beside the symbol).
972 City which has its own 3-digit zip code and also serves other post offices as a sectional center.
1 2 3 4 5 6 7 8 9 10 11 12 13 14
A B C D E F G H I J K L M N O P Q R
TN
AR
LA
AL
386
(Served by Memphis, TN)
387
388
389
390-392
393
394
395
396
397
DE SOTO
MARSHALL
BENTON
TIPPAH
ALCORN
TISHOMINGO
TUNICA
TATE
PRENTISS
PANOLA
LAFAYETTE
UNION
LEE
ITAWAMBA
COAHOMA
QUITMAN
PONTOTOC
YALOBUSHA
CALHOUN
BOLIVAR
TALLAHATCHIE
CHICKASAW
MONROE
LEFLORE
GRENADA
CLAY
CARROLL
WEBSTER
SUNFLOWER
OKTIBBEHA
MONTGOMERY
CHOCTAW
LOWNDES
WASHINGTON
HUMPHREYS
HOLMES
ATTALA
WINSTON
NOXUBEE
SHARKEY
YAZOO
MADISON
LEAKE
NESHOBA
KEMPER
ISSAQUENA
WARREN
HINDS
RANKIN
SCOTT
NEWTON
LAUDERDALE
SMITH
JASPER
CLARKE
CLAIBORNE
COPIAH
SIMPSON
JEFFERSON
LINCOLN
LAWRENCE
COVINGTON
JONES
WAYNE
ADAMS
FRANKLIN
JEFFERSON DAVIS
WILKINSON
AMITE
PIKE
WALTHALL
MARION
FORREST
LAMAR
PERRY
GREENE
PEARL RIVER
STONE
GEORGE
HARRISON
JACKSON
HANCOCK
Jackson
Greenville
Vicksburg
Hattiesburg
Meridian
Tupelo
Columbus
Natchez
McComb
Biloxi
Gulfport
Pascagoula
Clarksdale
Greenwood
Starkville
Oxford
Corinth
Yazoo City
Canton
Brookhaven
Laurel
Grenada
Cleveland
Indianola
Southaven
Hernando
Holly Springs
Ripley
Booneville
Iuka
Senatobia
Batesville
Sardis
New Albany
Pontotoc
Okolona
Houston
Aberdeen
West Point
Winona
Kosciusko
Louisville
Macon
Philadelphia
Carthage
De Kalb
Lexington
Belzoni
Rolling Fork
Port Gibson
Fayette
Hazlehurst
Mendenhall
Raleigh
Bay Springs
Quitman
Waynesboro
Collins
Monticello
Prentiss
Ellisville
Magnolia
Columbia
Tylertown
Woodville
Liberty
Purvis
Leakesville
Lucedale
Wiggins
Poplarville
Bay St. Louis
Brandon
Pearl
Clinton
Ridgeland
Madison
Forest
Decatur
Charleston
Water Valley
Calhoun City
Pittsboro
Lambert
Marks
Tunica
Rosedale
Mayersville
Copyright American Map Corporation
60 Miles
0 20 40
0 20 40 60 Kilometers

Explanation of symbols: ● – Census Designated Place (CDP)

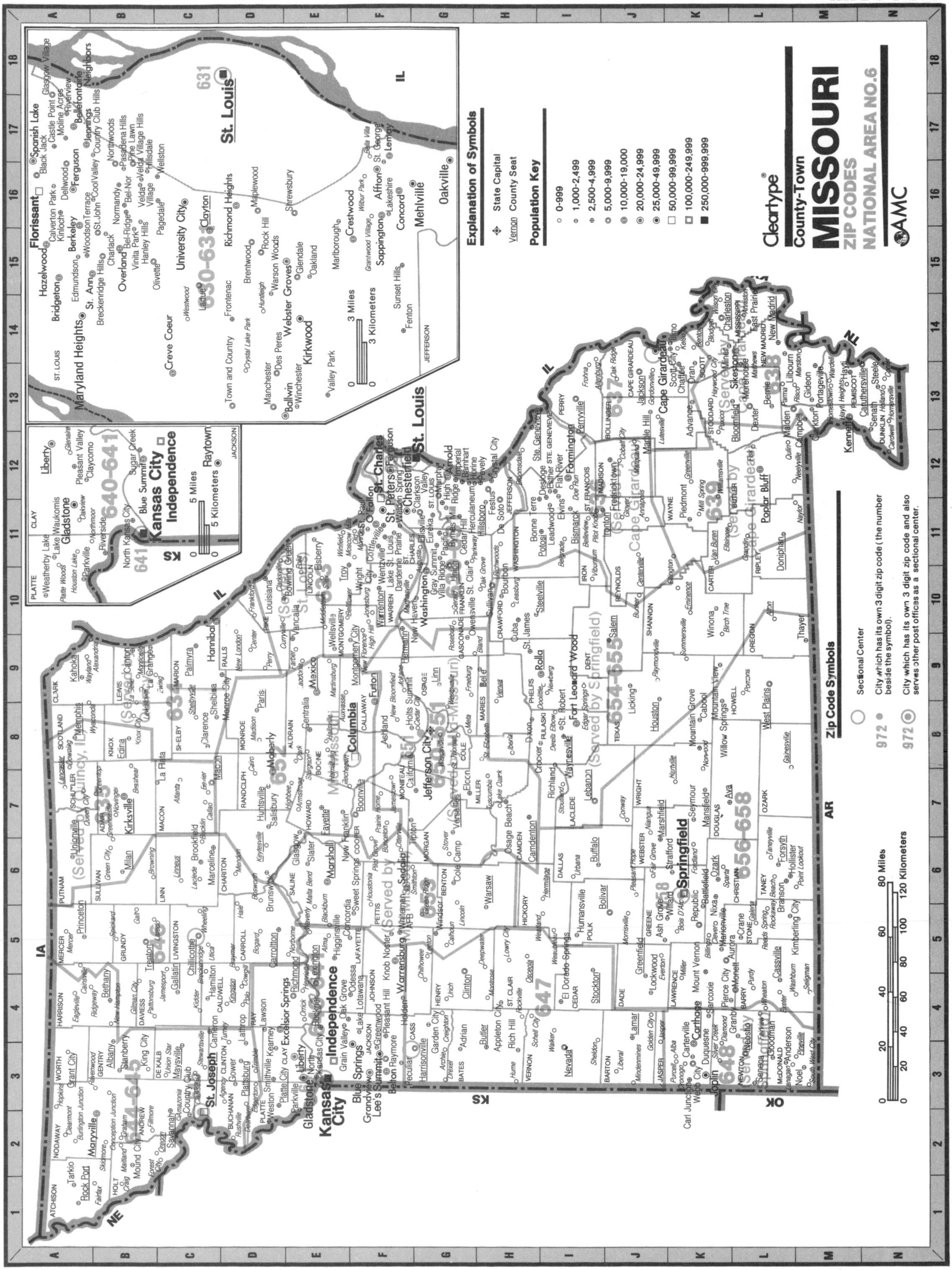

ClearType®

County-Town

MISSOURI
ZIP CODES
NATIONAL AREA NO.6

AMC

Explanation of Symbols

◆ State Capital

Vernon County Seat

Population Key

- ○ 0-999
- ◦ 1,000-2,499
- ⊙ 2,500-4,999
- ◉ 5,000-9,999
- ⊚ 10,000-19,000
- ⊛ 20,000-24,999
- ◎ 25,000-49,999
- □ 50,000-99,999
- ▣ 100,000-249,999
- ■ 250,000-999,999

Zip Code Symbols

○ Sectional Center

972 ● City which has its own 3 digit zip code (the number beside the symbol).

972 ◉ City which has its own 3 digit zip code and also serves other post offices as a sectional center.

IL
IA
NE
KS
OK
AR
TN
IL

St. Louis 631
630-631
640-641
641 KS
633
634
635
636
637
638
639
644-645
646
647
648
650-651
652
653
654-655
656-658

Kansas City
Independence
St. Joseph
Joplin
Springfield
Columbia
Jefferson City
Cape Girardeau

(Served by St. Louis-Missouri)
(Served by Kansas City-Missouri)
(Served by Springfield)
(Served by Cape Girardeau)

80 Miles
120 Kilometers

Copyright American Map Corporation

CITIES AND TOWNS

Note: The first name is that of the city or town, second, that of the county in which it is located, then the zip code area and location on the map.

Explanation of symbols: ● – Census Designated Place (CDP)

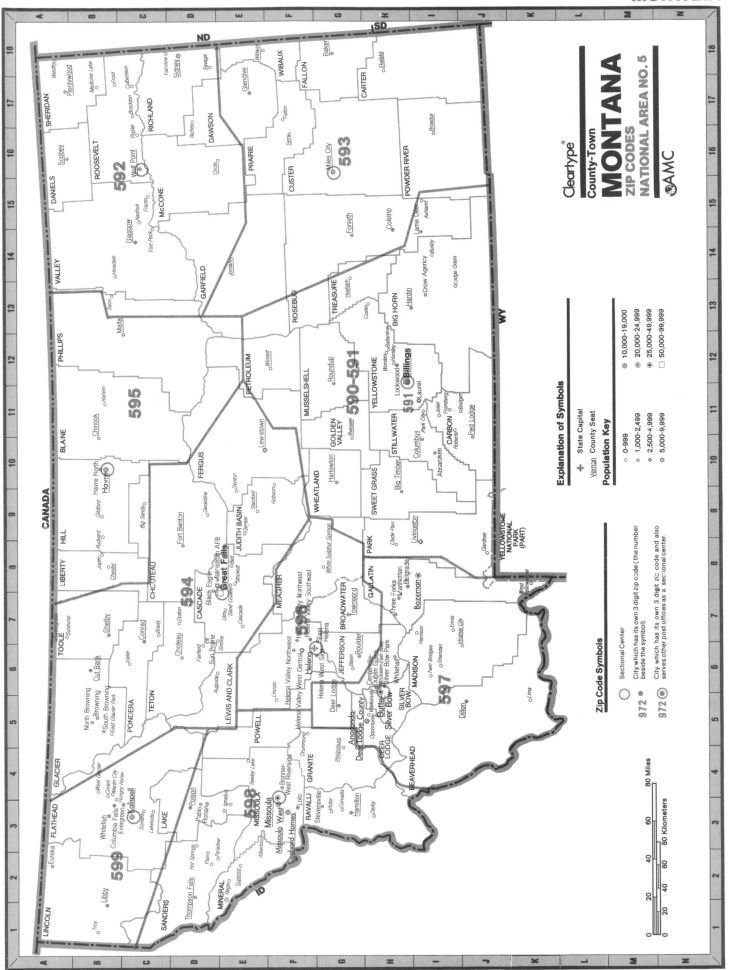

Cleartype®
County-Town
MONTANA
ZIP CODES
NATIONAL AREA NO. 5

⊕AMC

Explanation of Symbols

⟡ State Capital

Vernon County Seat

Population Key

○ 0-999	⊚ 10,000-19,000
○ 1,000-2,499	⊛ 20,000-24,999
⊕ 2,500-4,999	◉ 25,000-49,999
⊚ 5,000-9,999	□ 50,000-99,999

Zip Code Symbols

◯ Sectional Center

972 ● City which has its own 3 digit zip code (the number beside the symbol).

972 ◉ City which has its own 3 digit zip code and also serves other post offices as a sectional center.

80 Miles

Copyright American Map Corporation

COUNTIES

(93 Counties)

Name of County	Population	Location on Map
ADAMS	29,625	I-11
ANTELOPE	7,965	D-12
ARTHUR	462	F-5
BANNER	852	F-1
BLAINE	675	E-8
BOONE	6,667	E-12
BOX BUTTE	13,130	D-2
BOYD	2,835	B-10
BROWN	3,657	C-8
BUFFALO	37,447	H-10
BURT	7,868	E-16
BUTLER	8,601	G-14
CASS	21,318	H-16
CEDAR	10,131	B-14
CHASE	4,381	I-5
CHERRY	6,307	B-5
CHEYENNE	9,494	F-2
CLAY	7,123	I-12
COLFAX	9,139	F-14
CUMING	10,117	D-15
CUSTER	12,270	F-8
DAKOTA	16,742	C-15
DAWES	9,021	B-3
DAWSON	19,940	H-8
DEUEL	2,237	G-4
DIXON	6,143	C-15
DODGE	34,500	F-15
DOUGLAS	416,444	F-16
DUNDY	2,582	J-5
FILLMORE	7,103	H-13
FRANKLIN	3,938	J-11
FRONTIER	3,101	I-8
FURNAS	5,553	J-9
GAGE	22,794	I-15
GARDEN	2,460	E-3
GARFIELD	2,141	E-10
GOSPER	1,928	I-9
GRANT	769	E-5
GREELEY	3,006	E-11
HALL	48,925	H-12
HAMILTON	8,862	H-13
HARLAN	3,810	J-10
HAYES	1,222	I-6
HITCHCOCK	3,750	J-6
HOLT	12,599	D-11
HOOKER	793	E-6
HOWARD	6,055	G-11
JEFFERSON	8,759	J-14
JOHNSON	4,673	I-16
KEARNEY	6,629	I-11
KEITH	8,584	G-5
KEYA PAHA	1,029	B-8
KIMBALL	4,108	G-1
KNOX	9,534	C-12
LANCASTER	213,641	G-15
LINCOLN	32,508	G-6
LOGAN	878	F-7
LOUP	683	E-9
MADISON	32,655	D-13
McPHERSON	546	F-6
MERRICK	8,042	G-13
MORRILL	5,423	E-2
NANCE	4,275	F-12
NEMAHA	7,980	I-17
NUCKOLLS	5,786	J-12
OTOE	14,252	H-16
PAWNEE	3,317	J-16
PERKINS	3,367	H-5
PHELPS	9,715	I-10
PIERCE	7,827	D-14
PLATTE	29,820	E-13
POLK	5,675	G-14
RED WILLOW	11,705	J-7
RICHARDSON	9,937	J-17
ROCK	2,019	C-9
SALINE	12,715	I-14
SARPY	102,583	G-16
SAUNDERS	18,285	F-15
SCOTTS BLUFF	36,025	E-1
SEWARD	15,450	G-14
SHERIDAN	6,750	B-3
SHERMAN	3,718	G-10
SIOUX	1,549	B-1
STANTON	6,244	D-14
THAYER	6,635	J-13
THOMAS	851	E-7
THURSTON	6,936	D-15
VALLEY	5,169	F-10
WASHINGTON	16,607	F-16
WAYNE	9,364	D-14
WEBSTER	4,279	J-12
WHEELER	948	E-11
YORK	14,428	G-13
TOTAL	**1,578,385**	

CITIES AND TOWNS

Note: The first name is that of the city or town, second, that of the county in which it is located, then the zip code area and location on the map.

City/Town, County, ZIP	Location
Ainsworth, Brown, 69210	C-9
Albion, Boone, 68620	F-13
Alliance, Box Butte, 64301	D-3
Alma, Harlan, 68920	J-10
Arapahoe, Furnas, 68922	J-9
Arlington, Washington, 68002	F-16
Arthur, Arthur, 69121	F-5
Ashland, Saunders, 68003	G-16
Atkinson, Holt, 68713	C-11
Auburn, Nemaha, 68305	I-17
Aurora, Hamilton, 68818	H-13
Bartlett, Wheeler, 68622	E-12
Bassett, Rock, 68714	C-10
Bayard, Morrill, 69334	E-2
Beatrice, Gage, 68310	I-15
Beaver City, Furnas, 68926	J-9
Bellevue, Sarpy, 68005	G-17
Benkelman, Dundy, 69021	J-6
Blair, Washington, 68008	F-17
Bloomfield, Knox, 68718	C-13
Brewster, Blaine, 68821	E-9
Bridgeport, Morrill, 69336	F-3
Broken Bow, Custer, 68822	F-10
Burwell, Garfield, 68823	E-11
Butte, Boyd, 68722	B-11
Cambridge, Furnas, 69022	J-8
Center, Knox, 68724	C-13
Central City, Merrick, 68826	G-13
Chadron, Dawes, 69331	B-3
●Chalco, Sarpy, 68046	G-16
Chappell, Deuel, 69129	G-4
Clay Center, Clay, 68933	I-13
Columbus, Platte, 68601	F-14
Cozad, Dawson, 69130	H-9
Crawford, Dawes, 69339	C-2
Creighton, Knox, 68729	C-13
Crete, Saline, 68333	I-15
Dakota City, Dakota, 68731	C-16
David City, Butler, 68632	F-15
Eagle, Cass, 68347	G-16
Elkhorn, Douglas, 68022	G-16
Elmwood, Cass, 68349	H-16
Fairbury, Jefferson, 68352	J-14
Falls City, Richardson, 68355	J-18
Franklin, Franklin, 68939	J-11
Fremont, Dodge, 68025	F-16
Friend, Saline, 68359	I-14
Fullerton, Nance, 68638	F-13
Geneva, Fillmore, 68361	I-14
Genoa, Nance, 68640	F-13
Gering, Scotts Bluff, 69341	E-1
Gibbon, Buffalo, 68840	H-11
Gordon, Sheridan, 69343	B-4
Gothenburg, Dawson, 69138	H-9
Grand Island, Hall, 68801, 03	H-12
Grant, Perkins, 69140	H-5
Greeley Center, Greeley, 68842	F-12
Gretna, Sarpy, 68028	G-17
Harrisburg, Banner, 69345	F-1
Harrison, Sioux, 69346	C-1
Hartington, Cedar, 68739	B-14
Hastings, Adams, 68901	I-12
Hayes Center, Hayes, 69032	I-7
Hebron, Thayer, 68370	J-14
Hickman, Lancaster, 68372	I-15
Holdrege, Phelps, 68949	I-10
Humboldt, Richardson, 68376	J-17
Hyannis, Grant, 69350	E-5
Imperial, Chase, 69033	I-5
Kearney, Buffalo, 68847	H-11
Kimball, Kimball, 68145	G-1
La Vista, Sarpy, 68128	G-17
Lexington, Dawson, 68850	H-9
Lincoln, Lancaster, 66501-99	G-15
Loup City, Sherman, 68853	G-11
Lyons, Burt, 68038	E-16
Madison, Madison, 68748	E-14
McCook, Red Willow, 69001	J-8
Milford, Seward, 68405	H-15
Mitchell, Scotts Bluff, 69357	E-1
Mullen, Hooker, 69152	E-7
Nebraska City, Otoe, 68410	H-17
Neligh, Antelope, 68756	D-13
Nelson, Nuckolls, 68961	J-13
Norfolk, Madison, 68701	E-14
North Bend, Dodge, 68649	F-15
North Platte, Lincoln, 69101	G-7
Oakland, Burt, 68045	E-16
●Offutt AFB West, Sarpy, 68113	G-17
Ogallala, Keith, 69153	G-5
Omaha, Douglas, 68101-99	G-17
O'Neill, Holt, 68763	C-11
Ord, Valley, 68862	F-11
Osceola, Polk, 68651	G-14
Oshkosh, Garden, 69154	F-4
Papillion, Sarpy, 68046	G-17
Pawnee City, Pawnee, 68420	J-17
Pender, Thurston, 68047	D-15
Peru, Nemaha, 68421	I-18
Pierce, Pierce, 68767	D-14
Plainview, Pierce, 68769	D-13
Plattsmouth, Cass, 68048	G-17
Ponca, Dixon, 68770	C-15
Ralston, Douglas, 68127	G-17
Ravenna, Buffalo, 68869	H-11
Red Cloud, Webster, 68970	J-12
Rushville, Sheridan, 69360	C-4
Saint Paul, Howard, 68873	G-12
Schuyler, Colfax, 68661	F-15
Scottsbluff, Scotts Bluff, 69361	E-1
Seward, Seward, 68434	G-15
Sidney, Cheyenne, 69162	G-3
●Skyline, Douglas, 68022	G-16
South Sioux City, Dakota, 68716	C-16
Springfield, Sarpy, 68059	G-17
Springview, Keya Paha, 68778	B-9
Stanton, Stanton, 68779	E-14
Stapleton, Logan, 69163	F-8
Stockville, Frontier, 69042	I-8
Stromsburg, Polk, 68666	G-14
Superior, Nuckolls, 68978	J-13
Sutherland, Lincoln, 69165	G-6
Sutton, Clay, 68979	I-13
Syracuse, Otoe, 68446	H-16
Taylor, Loup, 68879	E-10
Tecumseh, Johnson, 68450	I-17
Tekamah, Burt, 68061	E-16
Thedford, Thomas, 69166	E-8
Trenton, Hitchcock, 69044	J-7
Tryon, McPherson, 69167	F-7
Valentine, Cherry, 69201	B-8
Valley, Douglas, 68064	G-16
Wahoo, Saunders, 68066	G-16
Wakefield, Dixon/Wayne, 68784	D-15
Waverly, Lancaster, 68462	G-15
Wayne, Wayne, 68787	D-15
Weeping Water, Cass, 68463	H-17
West Point, Cuming, 68788	E-15
Wilber, Saline, 68465	I-15
Wisner, Cuming, 68791	E-15
Wood River, Hall, 68883	H-12
Wymore, Gage, 68466	J-16
York, York, 68467	G-13

Explanation of symbols: ● – Census Designated Place (CDP)

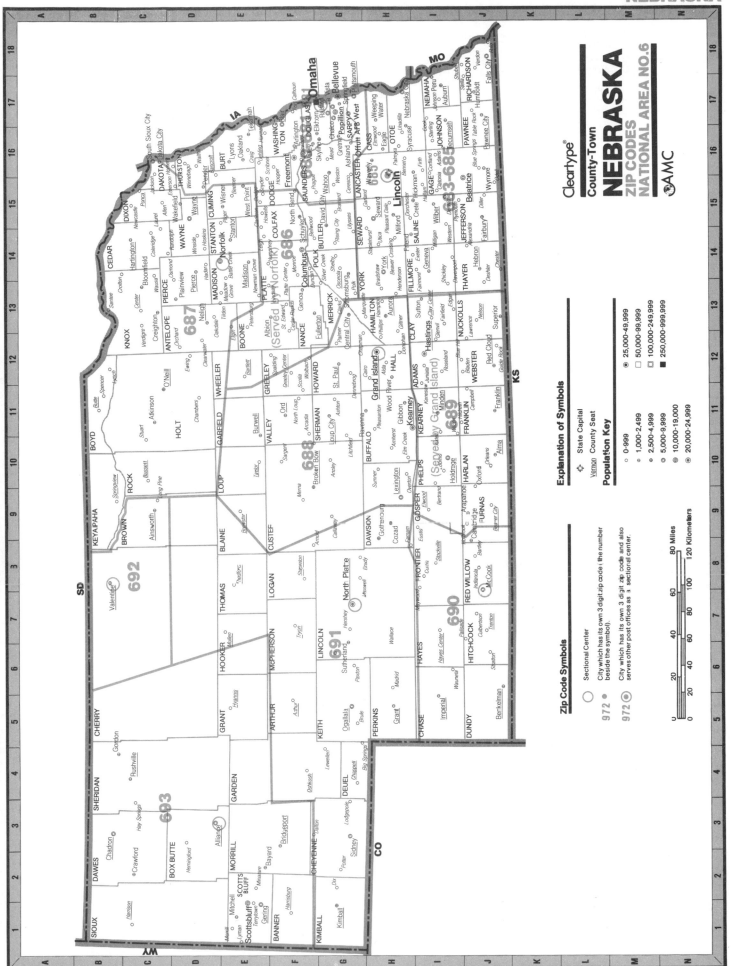

Cleartype®

County-Town

NEBRASKA

ZIP CODES
NATIONAL AREA NO.6

AMC

Explanation of Symbols

◈ State Capital

Vernon County Seat

Population Key

○ 0-999
◉ 1,000-2,499
◉ 2,500-4,999
◉ 5,000-9,999
◉ 10,000-19,000
◉ 20,000-24,999
◉ 25,000-49,999
□ 50,000-99,999
□ 100,000-249,999
■ 250,000-999,999

Zip Code Symbols

○ Sectional Center

972 • City which has its own 3 digit zip code i the number beside the symbol).

972 ◉ City which has its own 3 digit zip code and also serves other post offices as a sectional center.

80 Miles
120 Kilometers

Copyright American Map Corporation

COUNTIES

(17 Counties)

Name of County	Population	Location on Map
CARSON CITY	40,443	H-2
CHURCHILL	17,938	H-2
CLARK	741,459	N-9
DOUGLAS	27,637	H-2
ELKO	33,530	A-7
ESMERALDA	1,344	J-6
EUREKA	1,547	D-8
HUMBOLDT	12,844	A-3
LANDER	6,266	D-7
LINCOLN	3,775	I-12
LYON	20,001	G-3
MINERAL	6,475	H-4
NYE	17,781	H-7
PERSHING	4,336	D-3
STOREY	2,526	G-2
WASHOE	254,667	A-Z
WHITE PINE	9,264	F-10
TOTAL	**1,201,833**	

CITIES AND TOWNS

Note: The first name is that of the city or town, second, that of the county in which it is located, then the zip code area and location on the map.

Explanation of symbols: • – Census Designated Place (CDP)

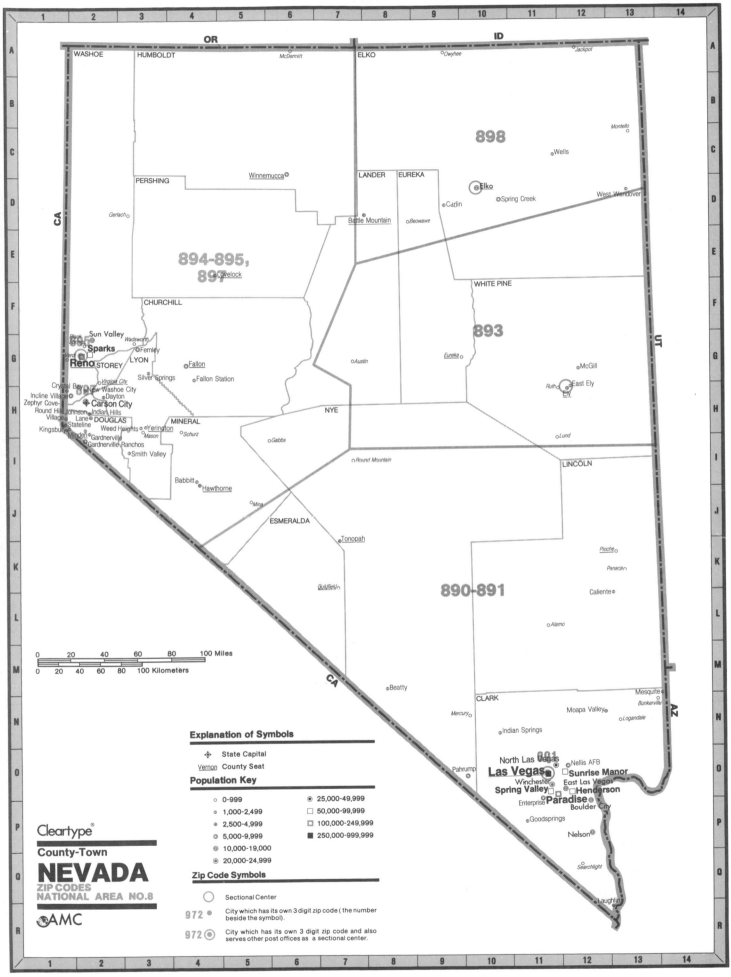

OR   **ID**

1 2 3 4 5 6 7 8 9 10 11 12 13 14

A

WASHOE HUMBOLDT ○McDermitt ELKO ○Owyhee Jackpot○

B

Montello○

898

C

○Wells

PERSHING LANDER EUREKA ○Elko West Wendover○

○Winnemucca ○Carlin Spring Creek○

D

○Gerlach Battle Mountain○ ○Beowawe

894-895,
897 ○Lovelock

E

WHITE PINE

CHURCHILL

F

893

Sun Valley ○Wadsworth ○Eureka McGill○

Black Sparks ○Fernley ○Austin Ruth○ ○East Ely

Sparks

G

Verdi **Reno** STOREY LYON ○Fallon Ely○

○Fallon Station

Crystal Bay ○Virginia City

Incline Village ○New Washoe City Silver Springs

Zephyr Cove ○Dayton NYE

Round Hill Johnson Indian Hills **Carson City**

H

Village Lane DOUGLAS MINERAL ○Schurz ○Lund

Kingsbury Minden ○Yerington

Stateline Weed Heights ○Mason

Gardnerville ○Gabbs ○Round Mountain LINCOLN

Gardnerville Ranchos Smith Valley

I

Babbitt○ ○Hawthorne

○Mina

J

ESMERALDA

Pioche○

K

○Tonopah Panaca○

L

○Goldfield **890-891** Caliente○

○Alamo

M

○Beatty Mesquite○

N

Bunkerville○

CLARK Moapa Valley○ ○Logandale

○Mercury ○Indian Springs

O

North Las Vegas○ Nellis AFB○

○Pahrump **891**

Las Vegas ☐**Sunrise Manor**

Winchester○ East Las Vegas

Spring Valley ☐☐**Henderson**

Enterprise **Paradise** Boulder City

P

○Goodsprings

Nelson○

Q

○Searchlight

R

Laughlin○

Explanation of Symbols

⬦ State Capital

Vernon County Seat

Population Key

○ 0-999 ◉ 25,000-49,999

◔ 1,000-2,499 ☐ 50,000-99,999

◑ 2,500-4,999 ☐ 100,000-249,999

◒ 5,000-9,999 ■ 250,000-999,999

◐ 10,000-19,000

◉ 20,000-24,999

Zip Code Symbols

○ Sectional Center

972 ● City which has its own 3 digit zip code (the number
      beside the symbol).

972 ◉ City which has its own 3 digit zip code and also
      serves other post offices as a sectional center.

Cleartype®

County-Town

NEVADA

ZIP CODES
NATIONAL AREA NO.8

◉AMC

0 20 40 60 80 100 Miles

0 20 40 60 80 100 Kilometers

Copyright American Map Corporation

COUNTIES

(10 Counties)

Name of County	Population	Location on Map
BELKNAP	49,216	L-6
CARROLL	35,410	H-8
CHESHIRE	70,121	P-2
COOS	34,828	A-7
GRAFTON	74,929	G-4
HILLSBOROUGH	336,073	P-4
MERRIMACK	120,005	M-4
ROCKINGHAM	245,845	O-8
STRAFFORD	104,233	M-8
SULLIVAN	38,592	L-2
TOTAL	**1,109,252**	

CITIES AND TOWNS

Note: The first name is that of the city or town, second, that of the county in which it is located, then the zip code area and location on the map.

Explanation of symbols: ● – Census Designated Place (CDP)   ▲ *italics* – Townships (shown on the map)

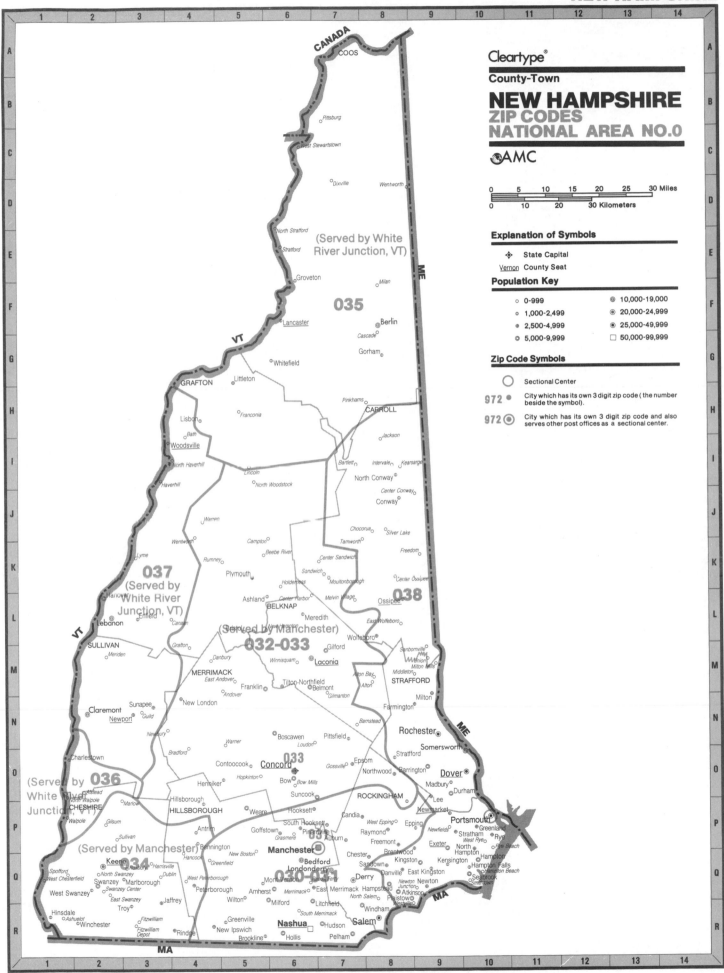

Cleartype®
County-Town
NEW HAMPSHIRE
ZIP CODES
NATIONAL AREA NO.0
AMC

0   5   10   15   20   25   30 Miles
0   10   20   30 Kilometers

Explanation of Symbols

State Capital
Vernon   County Seat

Population Key

○ 0-999
◔ 1,000-2,499
◑ 2,500-4,999
◕ 5,000-9,999
⊛ 10,000-19,000
⊛ 20,000-24,999
⊛ 25,000-49,999
☐ 50,000-99,999

Zip Code Symbols

○   Sectional Center

972 ●   City which has its own 3 digit zip code (the number beside the symbol).

972 ◉   City which has its own 3 digit zip code and also serves other post offices as a sectional center.

CANADA

COOS

Pittsburg

West Stewartstown

Dixville   Wentworth

North Stratford

Stratford   (Served by White River Junction, VT)

Groveton   Milan

035

VT

Lancaster   Berlin

Cascade

Whitefield   Gorham

GRAFTON   Littleton

Franconia   Pinkhams   CARROLL

Lisbon   Jackson

Bath

Woodsville

North Haverhill   Bartlett   Intervale   Kearsarge

Lincoln   North Conway

Haverhill   North Woodstock

Warren

037   Chocorua   Silver Lake

(Served by   Wentworth   Campton   Tamworth   Freedom

White River   Lyme   Rumney   Beebe River

Junction, VT)   Plymouth   Center Sandwich   Center Ossipee

Hanover   Sandwich   038

Ashland   Holderness   Moultonborough   Ossipee

Enfield   Center Harbor   Melvin Village

Lebanon   Canaan   BELKNAP   Meredith   East Wolfeboro

(Served by Manchester)   New Hampton

SULLIVAN   032-033   Gilford   Wolfeboro   Sanbornville

Grafton   Laconia   Alton Bay   Union   Milton Mills

Meriden   Danbury   Winnisquam   Middleton   Milton

MERRIMACK   Alton

East Andover   Tilton-Northfield   STRAFFORD

Franklin   Belmont

Andover   Gilmanton   Milton

Claremont   Sunapee   New London   Barnstead   Farmington

Newport   Guild   Rochester

Newbury   Boscawen   Pittsfield   Somersworth   ME

(Served by   036   Warner   Loudon   Stratford

White River   Bradford   Northwood   Dover

Junction, VT)   Charlestown   Contoocook   Concord   033   Gossville   Epsom   Barrington   Madbury   Durham

Alstead   Henniker   Hopkinton   Bow Mills   Northwood   Lee

North Walpole   Marlow   Hillsborough   Bow   Suncook   ROCKINGHAM   Newmarket

Walpole   Gilsum   HILLSBOROUGH   Weare   Hooksett   Candia   West Epping   Newfields   Portsmouth

(Served by Manchester)   Goffstown   South Hooksett   Raymond   Epping   Greenland

Sullivan   Antrim   Pinardville   03   Auburn   Freemont   Stratham   Rye

034   Bennington   Grasmere   Manchester   Chester   Brentwood   Exeter   North   West Rye   Rye Beach

Keene   Hancock   Greenfield   New Boston   Bedford   Sandown   Kingston   Kensington   Hampton

CHESHIRE   Harrisville   Dublin   Londonderry   Danville   East Kingston   Hampton Falls

Spofford   Roxbury   West Peterborough   030-03   Derry   Hampton Beach

West Chesterfield   North Swanzey   Mont Vernon   East Merrimack   Hampstead   Newton   Seabrook

Swanzey   Marlborough   Peterborough   Amherst   Merrimack   Newton Junction   Smithtown

West Swanzey   Swanzey Center   Jaffrey   Wilton   Litchfield   North Salem   Plaistow   Atkinson

East Swanzey   Milford   South Merrimack   Windham   Westville

Hinsdale   Troy   Fitzwilliam   Greenville

Ashuelot   Fitzwilliam Depot   New Ipswich   Nashua   Hudson   Salem

Winchester   Rindge   Brookline   Hollis   Pelham

MA

MA

NEW JERSEY Index

COUNTIES

(21 Counties)

Name of County	Population	Location on Map
ATLANTIC	224,327	M-9
BERGEN	825,380	C-12
BURLINGTON	395,066	J-9
CAMDEN	502,824	K-7
CAPE MAY	95,089	P-9
CUMBERLAND	138,053	N-6
ESSEX	778,206	D-12
GLOUCESTER	230,082	M-7
HUDSON	553,099	F-13
HUNTERDON	107,776	F-7
MERCER	325,824	H-9
MIDDLESEX	671,780	H-11
MONMOUTH	553,124	H-12
MORRIS	421,353	C-10
OCEAN	433,203	I-11
PASSAIC	453,060	B-11
SALEM	65,294	M-5
SOMERSET	240,279	F-10
SUSSEX	130,943	A-9
UNION	493,819	F-12
WARREN	91,607	C-8
TOTAL	7,730,188	

CITIES AND TOWNS

Note: The first name is that of the city or town, second, that of the county in which it is located, then the zip code area and location on the map.

Absecon, Atlantic, 08201 ... O-11
• Allamuchy-Panther Valley, Warren, 07820 ... D-9
Allendale, Bergen, 07401 ... C-13
Allentown, Monmouth, 08501 ... I-10
• Alloway, Salem, 08001 ... N-6
Almonesson, Gloucester, 08096 ... J-2
Alpha, Warren, 07814 ... F-7
Alpine, Bergen, 07627 ... C-14
• Annandale, Hunterdon, 08801 ... F-9
Asbury Park, Monmouth, 07712 ... I-14
Ashland, Camden, 08043 ... I-3
Atco, Camden, 08004 ... L-9
Atlantic City, Atlantic, 08401 ... O-11
Atlantic Highlands, Monmouth, 07716 ... H-6
Audubon, Camden, 08106 ... I-2
Audubon Park, Camden, 08106 ... K-7
Avalon, Cape May, 08202 ... Q-10
• Avenel, Middlesex, 07001 ... F-12
Avon-by-the-Sea, Monmouth, 07717 ... I-14
• Barnegat, Ocean, 08005 ... L-12
Barrington, Camden, 08007 ... I-2
Basking Ridge, Somerset, 07920 ... E-10
Bay Head, Ocean, 08004 ... J-13
Bayonne, Hudson, 07002 ... F-13
Beach Haven, Ocean, 08008 ... N-12
• Beach Haven West, Ocean, 08008 ... M-12
Beachwood, Ocean, 08722 ... K-13
• Beattyestown, Warren, 07840 ... E-9
• Beckett, Gloucester, 08085 ... M-6
Belford, Monmouth, 07718 ... H-6
• *Belleville, Essex, 07109* ... D-3
Bellmawr, Camden, 08031 ... I-2
Belmar, Monmouth, 07719 ... I-14
▲ *Belvidere, Warren, 07823* ... E-7
Bergenfield, Bergen, 07621 ... D-14
• *Berkeley Heights, Union, 07922* ... F-1
Berlin, Camden, 08009 ... L-8
Bernardsville, Somerset, 07924 ... E-10
Beverly, Burlington, 08010 ... J-8
• Blackwood, Camden, 08012 ... L-8
Blackwood Terrace, Gloucester, 08096 ... L-7
Blenheim, Camden, 08012 ... J-2
• *Bloomfield, Essex, 07003* ... E-12
Bloomingdale, Passaic, 07403 ... C-12
Bogota, Bergen, 07603 ... C-5
Boonton, Morris, 07005 ... D-11
Bordentown, Burlington, 08505 ... J-10
Bound Brook, Somerset, 08805 ... F-11
Bradley Beach, Monmouth, 07720 ... I-14
• Brass Castle, Warren, 07882 ... E-8
• *Brick, Ocean, 08723-24* ... J-13
Bridgeboro, Burlington, 08075 ... G-3
Bridgeton, Cumberland, 08302 ... O-7
Brielle, Monmouth, 08730 ... J-13
Brigantine, Atlantic, 08203 ... O-12
Brooklawn, Camden, 08030 ... I-2
• Brown Mills, Burlington, 08015 ... K-10
• Budd Lake, Morris, 07828 ... D-9
Buena, Atlantic, 08310 ... N-8
Burlington, Burlington, 08016 ... J-9
▲ *Burlington, Burlington, 08016* ... J-9
Butler, Morris, 07405 ... C-12
• *Caldwell, Essex, 07006* ... D-2
Califon, Hunterdon, 07830 ... E-9
Camden, Camden, 08101-99 ... K-7
Cape May, Cape May, 08204 ... R-8
• Cape May Court House, Cape May, 08210 ... Q-9
Carlstadt, Bergen, 07072 ... D-4
• Carneys Point, Salem, 08069 ... M-5
Carteret, Middlesex, 07008 ... F-12
• Cedar Glen Lakes, Ocean, 08759 ... J-11
• Cedar Glen West, Ocean, 08733 ... J-12
• *Cedar Grove, Essex, 07009* ... C-3
Cedar Knolls, Morris, 07927 ... E-11
Chatham, Morris, 07928 ... E-11
• Cherry Hill, Camden, 08002-03, 34 ... K-8
Chesilhurst, Camden, 08089 ... M-9
Chester, Morris, 07930 ... E-10
Churchtown, Salem, 08070 ... M-5
• *Cinnaminson, Burlington, 08108* ... K-8
• *Clark, Union, 07066* ... F-12
Clayton, Gloucester, 08312 ... M-7
• Clearbrook Park, Middlesex, 08831 ... H-11
Clementon, Camden, 08021 ... L-8
Cliffside Park, Bergen, 07010 ... D-5
• Cliffwood Beach, Monmouth, 07728 ... G-12
Clifton, Passaic, 07011-14 ... D-13
Clinton, Hunterdon, 08809 ... F-8
Closter, Bergen, 07624 ... C-14
• Collings Lakes, Atlantic, 08094 ... N-9
Collingswood, Camden, 08108 ... H-2
• Colonia, Middlesex, 07067 ... F-12
• Concordia, Middlesex, 08512 ... H-11
Convent Station, Morris, 07961 ... E-11
• Country Lake Estates, Burlington, 08015 ... K-10
▲ *Cranbury, Middlesex, 08512* ... H-11
• Crandon Lakes, Sussex, 07860 ... C-8
• Cranford, Union, 07016 ... F-2
Cresskill, Bergen, 07626 ... B-6
• Crestwood Village, Ocean, 08759 ... J-11
• Dayton, Middlesex, 08810 ... H-11
Deal, Monmouth, 07723 ... J-6
• *Delanco, Burlington, 08075* ... G-3
▲ *Delran, Burlington, 08075* ... G-4
Demarest, Bergen, 07627 ... D-14
▲ *Denville, Morris, 07834* ... D-11
Dover, Morris, 07801 ... D-10
Dumont, Bergen, 07628 ... B-5
Dunellen, Middlesex, 08812 ... F-11
• *East Brunswick, Middlesex, 08816* ... G-11
• East Freehold, Monmouth, 07728 ... I-12
▲ *East Greenwich, Gloucester, 08020* ... L-7
• *East Hanover, Morris, 07936* ... D-1
East Newark, Hudson, 07029 ... E-13
East Orange, Essex, 07017-18 ... E-3
East Rutherford, Bergen, 07073 ... D-4
▲ *Eastampton, Burlington, 08062* ... K-9
Eatontown, Monmouth, 07724 ... H-13
Edgewater, Bergen, 07020 ... D-5
• *Edgewater Park, Burlington, 07020* ... J-8
• *Edison, Middlesex, 08817,20,37* ... G-12
Egg Harbor City, Atlantic, 08215 ... N-10
Elizabeth, Union, 07201-99 ... F-12
Elmer, Salem, 08318 ... N-7
Elmwood Park, Bergen, 07407 ... C-4
• Elwood-Magnolia, Atlantic, 08424 ... N-10
Emerson, Bergen, 07630 ... B-5
Englewood, Bergen, 07631 ... D-14
Englewood Cliffs, Bergen, 07632 ... C-6
Englishtown, Monmouth, 07726 ... H-12
• Erma, Cape May, 08204 ... R-9
Espanong, Morris, 07849 ... D-10
▲ *Essex Fells, Essex, 07021* ... D-2
Estell Manor, Atlantic, 08319 ... O-9
• *Ewing, Mercer, 08618* ... I-9
Fair Haven, Monmouth, 07704 ... I-6
Fair Lawn, Bergen, 07410 ... B-4
• *Fairfield, Essex, 07004* ... C-2
• Fairton, Cumberland, 08320 ... O-7
Fairview, Bergen, 07022 ... D-5
• Fairview, Monmouth, 07701 ... I-6
Fanwood, Union, 07023 ... G-1
Farmingdale, Monmouth, 07727 ... I-13
Flemington, Hunterdon, 08822 ... G-9
• Florence-Roebling, Burlington, 08518,54 ... J-9
Florham Park, Morris, 07932 ... E-11
Folsom, Atlantic, 08037 ... N-9
• Fords, Middlesex, 08863 ... G-12
• Forked River, Ocean, 08731 ... L-13
• Fort Dix, Burlington, 08640 ... J-10
Fort Lee, Bergen, 07024 ... C-6
Franklin, Sussex, 07416 ... B-10
Franklin Lakes, Bergen, 07417 ... A-3
Franklinville, Gloucester, 08322 ... M-7
Freehold, Monmouth, 07728 ... I-12
Frenchtown, Hunterdon, 08825 ... G-8
Garfield, Bergen, 07026 ... D-13
Garwood, Union, 07027 ... F-2
Gibbsboro, Camden, 08026 ... I-4
• Gibbstown, Gloucester, 08027 ... L-6
• Gilford Park, Ocean, 08753 ... K-13
Gillette, Morris, 07933 ... F-11
Glassboro, Gloucester, 08028 ... M-7
Glen Gardner, Hunterdon, 08826 ... E-8
• *Glen Ridge, Essex, 07028* ... D-3
Glen Rock, Bergen, 07452 ... B-4
• Glendora, Camden, 08029 ... L-8
Gloucester City, Camden, 08030 ... K-7
• Great Meadows-Vienna, Warren, 07838 ... D-8
▲ *Greenwich, Warren, 08886* ... F-7
Guttenberg, Hudson, 07093 ... E-13
Hackensack, Bergen, 07601 ... C-5
Hackettstown, Warren, 07840 ... D-9
▲ *Haddon, Camden, 08108* ... I-2
Haddon Heights, Camden, 08035 ... I-2
Haddonfield, Camden, 08033 ... I-3
▲ *Hainesport, Burlington, 08036* ... K-9
Haledon, Passaic, 07508 ... B-3
Hamburg, Sussex, 07419 ... B-10
Hampton, Hunterdon, 08827 ... E-8
• *Hanover, Morris, 07981* ... D-1
Harrington Park, Bergen, 07640 ... B-6
Harrison, Hudson, 07029 ... E-4
Hasbrouck Heights, Bergen, 07604 ... C-5
Haworth, Bergen, 07649 ... B-5
Hawthorne, Passaic, 07506 ... D-13
• Heathcote, Middlesex, 08540 ... H-10
Helmetta, Middlesex, 08828 ... H-11
High Bridge, Hunterdon, 08827 ... F-8
• Highland Lake, Sussex, 07422 ... B-11
Highland Park, Middlesex, 08904 ... G-11
Highlands, Monmouth, 07732 ... H-6
Hightstown, Mercer, 08520 ... I-11
Hillsdale, Bergen, 07642 ... A-5
• *Hillside, Union, 07205* ... F-3
Hi-Nella, Camden, 08083 ... J-3
Ho-Ho-Kus, Bergen, 07423 ... C-13
Hoboken, Hudson, 07030 ... E-13
• Holiday City-Berkeley, Ocean, 08757 ... K-12
• Holiday City-Dover, Ocean, 08753 ... J-13
• Holiday City South, Ocean, 08757 ... K-12
Hopatcong, Sussex, 07843 ... D-10
Hopewell, Mercer, 08525 ... H-9
• Irvington, Essex, 07111 ... E-3
• Iselin, Middlesex, 08830 ... F-12
Island Heights, Ocean, 08732 ... K-13
Jamesburg, Middlesex, 08831 ... H-11
Jersey City, Hudson, 07301-99 ... E-13
Keansburg, Monmouth, 07734 ... G-13
Kearny, Hudson, 07302 ... E-4
• Kendall Park, Middlesex, 08824 ... G-10
Kenilworth, Union, 07033 ... F-2
Kenvil, Morris, 07847 ... D-10
Keyport, Monmouth, 07735 ... H-5
• Kingston, Middlesex, 08836 ... H-10
Kinnelon, Morris, 07405 ... C-11
Lake Hiawatha, Morris, 07034 ... C-1
• Lake Mohawk, Sussex, 07871 ... C-10
• Lake Telemark, Morris, 07866 ... D-11
Lakehurst, Ocean, 08733 ... J-12
• Lakewood, Ocean, 08701 ... J-13
Lambertville, Hunterdon, 08530 ... H-8
Landing (Shore Hills), Morris, 07850 ... D-10
Laurel Springs, Camden, 08021 ... L-8
• Laurence Harbor, Middlesex, 08879 ... G-12
Lavallette, Ocean, 08735 ... K-13
Lawnside, Camden, 08045 ... I-3
• Lawrenceville, Mercer, 08648 ... H-9
Lebanon, Hunterdon, 08833 ... F-9
Ledgewood, Morris, 07852 ... D-10
• Leisure Knoll, Ocean, 08733 ... J-12
• Leisure Village, Ocean, 08701 ... J-13
• Leisure Village East, Ocean, 08701 ... J-13
• Leisure Village West-Pine Lake Park, Ocean, 08733 ... K-12
• Leisuretowne, Burlington, 08088 ... K-9
• Leonardo, Monmouth, 07737 ... H-6
Leonia, Bergen, 07605 ... C-5
▲ *Liberty, Warren, 07863* ... D-8
Lincoln Park, Morris, 07035 ... B-2
• Lincroft, Monmouth, 07738 ... I-5
Linden, Union, 07036 ... F-12
Lindenwold, Camden, 08021 ... J-3
Linwood, Atlantic, 08221 ... O-10
• *Little Falls, Passaic, 07424* ... C-3
Little Ferry, Bergen, 07643 ... D-5
Little Silver, Monmouth, 07739 ... I-6
• *Livingston, Essex, 07039* ... E-12
Lodi, Bergen, 07644 ... C-4
Long Branch, Monmouth, 07740 ... H-14
▲ *Long Hill, Morris, 07946* ... F-11
• Long Valley, Morris, 07853 ... E-9
Longport, Atlantic, 08403 ... P-11
▲ *Lopatcong, Warren, 08865* ... F-7
▲ *Lumberton, Burlington, 08048* ... K-9
• *Lyndhurst, Bergen, 07071* ... D-4
Madison, Morris, 07940 ... E-11
• Madison Park, Middlesex, 08859 ... G-12
Magnolia, Camden, 08049 ... I-3
Mahwah, Bergen, 07430 ... C-13
• Manahawkin, Ocean, 08050 ... M-12
Manasquan, Monmouth, 08736 ... J-13
Manville, Somerset, 08835 ... G-10
• *Maple Shade, Burlington, 08052* ... H-3
• Maplewood, Essex, 07040 ... E-2
Margate City, Atlantic, 08402 ... P-11
• Marlton, Burlington, 08053 ... I-4
Matawan, Monmouth, 07747 ... H-12
• Mays Landing, Atlantic, 08330 ... O-10
Maywood, Bergen, 07607 ... C-5
• McGuire AFB, Burlington, 08641 ... J-10
Medford Lakes, Burlington, 08055 ... L-9
Mendham, Morris, 07945 ... E-10
• Mercerville-Hamilton Square, Mercer, 08619 ... I-9
Merchantville, Camden, 08109 ... H-2
Metuchen, Middlesex, 08840 ... G-12
Middlesex, Middlesex, 08846 ... F-11
Midland Park, Bergen, 07432 ... B-4
Milford, Hunterdon, 08848 ... F-7
• *Millburn, Essex, 07041* ... E-2
Millington, Morris, 07946 ... F-11
Milltown, Middlesex, 08850 ... G-11
Millville, Cumberland, 08332 ... O-8
▲ *Mine Hill, Morris, 07803* ... D-10
Monmouth Beach, Monmouth, 07750 ... I-7
• Monmouth Junction, Middlesex, 08852 ... H-10
• *Montclair, Essex, 07042-43* ... E-12
Montvale, Bergen, 07645 ... C-14
Moonachie, Bergen, 07074 ... D-5
• Moorestown-Lenola, Burlington, 08057 ... K-8
Morris Plains, Morris, 07950 ... E-11
▲ *Morristown, Morris, 07960* ... E-11
Mount Arlington, Morris, 07856 ... D-10
Mount Ephraim, Camden, 08059 ... I-2
Mount Freedom, Morris, 07970 ... E-10
• *Mount Holly, Burlington, 08060* ... K-9
Mountain Lakes, Morris, 07046 ... D-11
Mountainside, Union, 07092 ... F-1
• Mullica Hill, Gloucester, 08062 ... M-7
• Mystic Island, Ocean, 08067 ... N-12
National Park, Gloucester, 08014 ... L-7
Navesink, Monmouth, 07752 ... H-6
Neptune City, Monmouth, 07753 ... I-14
Netcong, Morris, 07857 ... D-9
New Brunswick, Middlesex, 08901 ... G-11
• New Egypt, Ocean, 08533 ... J-11
New Milford, Bergen, 07646 ... B-5
New Monmouth, Monmouth, 07748 ... H-5
New Providence, Union, 07974 ... E-11
Newark, Essex, 07101-99 ... E-13
Newfield, Gloucester, 08344 ... N-8
Newton, Sussex, 07860 ... C-9
Normandy Beach, Ocean, 08739 ... J-13
North Arlington, Bergen, 07031 ... D-4
• North Beach Haven, Ocean, 08008 ... N-12
• *North Bergen, Hudson, 07047* ... D-5
North Branch, Somerset, 08876 ... F-10
• *North Brunswick, Middlesex, 08902* ... G-11
• *North Caldwell, Essex, 07006* ... C-2
• North Cape May, Cape May, 08204 ... R-8
North Haledon, Passaic, 07508 ... B-3
• North Middletown, Monmouth, 07734 ... G-13
North Plainfield, Somerset, 07060 ... F-11
North Wildwood, Cape May, 08260 ... R-9
Northfield, Atlantic, 08225 ... O-11
Northvale, Bergen, 07647 ... C-14
Norwood, Bergen, 07648 ... C-14
• *Nutley, Essex, 07110* ... D-4
• Oak Valley, Gloucester, 08090 ... L-7
• Oakhurst, Monmouth, 07755 ... J-6
Oakland, Bergen, 07436 ... C-12
Oaklyn, Camden, 08107 ... I-2
• Ocean Acres, Ocean, 08005 ... L-12
Ocean City, Cape May, 08226 ... P-10
Ocean Gate, Ocean, 08740 ... K-13
• Ocean Grove, Monmouth, 07756 ... I-14
Oceanport, Monmouth, 07757 ... I-6
Ogdensburg, Sussex, 07439 ... C-10
• Old Bridge, Middlesex, 08857 ... H-12
Old Tappan, Bergen, 07675 ... A-5
• Olivet, Salem, 08318 ... N-7
Oradell, Bergen, 07649 ... B-5
• *Orange, Essex, 07050* ... E-12
• Oxford, Warren, 07863 ... E-8
Palisades Park, Bergen, 07650 ... D-5
Palmyra, Burlington, 08065 ... K-8
Paramus, Bergen, 07652 ... B-4
Park Ridge, Bergen, 07656 ... A-5
• *Parsippany-Troy Hills Township, Morris, 07054* ... D-11
Passaic, Passaic, 07055 ... D-13
Paterson, Passaic, 07501-99 ... D-13
Paulsboro, Gloucester, 08066 ... L-6
Peapack and Gladstone, Somerset, 07977 ... E-10
Pemberton, Burlington, 08068 ... K-10
• Pemberton Heights, Burlington, 08068 ... K-10
Pennington, Mercer, 08534 ... H-9
Penns Grove, Salem, 08069 ... M-5
• Pennsauken, Camden, 08110 ... K-8
• Pennsville, Salem, 08070 ... M-5
• *Pequannock Township, Morris, 07440* ... D-2
Perth Amboy, Middlesex, 08861 ... G-12
Phillipsburg, Warren, 08865 ... E-7
Pine Beach, Ocean, 08741 ... K-13
Pine Hill, Camden, 08021 ... L-8
• Pine Ridge at Crestwood, Ocean, 08733 ... K-12
Pitman, Gloucester, 08071 ... M-7
Plainfield, Union, 07060, 62-63 ... F-11
▲ *Plainsboro, Middlesex, 08536* ... H-10
• Pleasant Plains, Ocean, 08755 ... K-12
Pleasantville, Atlantic, 08232 ... O-11
▲ *Pohatcong, Warren, 08804* ... F-7
Point Pleasant, Ocean, 08742 ... J-13
Point Pleasant Beach, Ocean, 08742 ... J-13
• Pomona, Atlantic, 08240 ... N-10
Pompton Lakes, Passaic, 07442 ... A-2
Pompton Plains, Morris, 07444 ... B-2
• Port Monmouth, Monmouth, 07758 ... H-6
• Port Norris, Cumberland, 08349 ... P-8
• Port Reading, Middlesex, 07064 ... F-12
• Presidential Lakes Estates, Burlington, 08015 ... K-11
Princeton, Mercer, 08540,42 ... H-10
• Princeton Junction, Mercer, 08550 ... H-10
• Princeton North, Mercer, 08540 ... H-10
Prospect Park, Passaic, 07508 ... D-13
Rahway, Union, 07065 ... F-12
• Ramblewood, Burlington, 08054 ... K-9
Ramsey, Bergen, 07446 ... A-4
Raritan, Somerset, 08864 ... F-10
Red Bank, Monmouth, 07701 ... H-13
Ridgefield, Bergen, 07657 ... D-5
Ridgefield Park, Bergen, 07660 ... D-14
Ridgewood, Bergen, 07450 ... B-4
Ringwood, Passaic, 07456 ... B-12
• Rio Grande, Cape May, 08242 ... R-9
River Edge, Bergen, 07661 ... B-5
• *River Vale, Bergen, 07675* ... A-5
Riverdale, Morris, 07457 ... A-2
• *Riverside, Burlington, 08075* ... J-8
Riverton, Burlington, 08077 ... K-8
• Robertsville, Monmouth, 07726 ... H-12
• *Rochelle Park, Bergen, 07662* ... C-4
Rockaway, Morris, 07866 ... D-11
Roseland, Essex, 07068 ... D-2
Roselle, Union, 07203 ... F-2
Roselle Park, Union, 07204 ... F-2
• Rosenhayn, Cumberland, 08352 ... N-7
• Rossmoor, Middlesex, 08831 ... H-11
Rumson, Monmouth, 07760 ... I-6
Runnemede, Camden, 08078 ... I-2
Rutherford, Bergen, 07070 ... E-13
• *Saddle Brook, Bergen, 07662* ... C-4
Saddle River, Bergen, 07458 ... A-4
Salem, Salem, 08079 ... N-5
Sayreville, Middlesex, 08872 ... G-12
• *Scotch Plains, Union, 07076* ... F-11
Sea Bright, Monmouth, 07760 ... I-7
Sea Girt, Monmouth, 08750 ... J-14
Sea Isle City, Cape May, 08243 ... Q-10
• Seabrook Farms, Cumberland, 08361 ... N-7
Seaside Heights, Ocean, 08751 ... K-13
Seaside Park, Ocean, 08752 ... K-13
Secaucus, Hudson, 07004 ... D-5
• Sewaren, Middlesex, 07077 ... F-12
Sewell, Gloucester, 08080 ... L-7
• Shark River Hills, Monmouth, 07753 ... I-13
Ship Bottom, Ocean, 08008 ... M-13
Shrewsbury, Monmouth, 07702 ... I-6
• Silver Ridge, Ocean, 08753 ... K-12
• Silverton, Ocean, 08753 ... J-13
• Society Hill, Middlesex, 08854 ... G-11
Somerdale, Camden, 08083 ... J-3
Somers Point, Atlantic, 08244 ... P-10
• Somerset, Somerset, 08873 ... G-11
Somerville, Somerset, 08876 ... F-10
South Amboy, Middlesex, 08879 ... G-12
South Belmar, Monmouth, 07719 ... I-14
South Bound Brook, Somerset, 08880 ... G-11
▲ *South Hackensack, Bergen, 07606* ... C-5
• *South Orange, Essex, 07079* ... E-2
South Plainfield, Middlesex, 07080 ... F-11
South River, Middlesex, 08882 ... G-11
South Toms River, Ocean, 08757 ... K-13
Sparta, Sussex, 07871 ... C-10
Spotswood, Middlesex, 08884 ... H-11
Spring Lake, Monmouth, 07762 ... I-14
Spring Lake Heights, Monmouth, 07762 ... I-13
• *Springfield, Union, 07081* ... E-12
Stanhope, Sussex, 07874 ... D-9
Stanton, Hunterdon, 08885 ... F-9
Stockholm, Sussex, 07460 ... C-11
Stone Harbor, Cape May, 08247 ... R-9
Stratford, Camden, 08084 ... L-8
• Strathmore, Monmouth, 07735 ... H-12
• Succasunna-Kenvil, Morris, 07876, 47 ... D-10
Summit, Union, 07901 ... E-12
Surf City, Ocean, 08008 ... M-13
Sussex, Sussex, 07461 ... R-10
Swedesboro, Gloucester, 08085 ... L-6
Tabor (Mount Tabor), Morris, 07878 ... D-11
• *Teaneck, Bergen, 07666* ... C-5
Tenafly, Bergen, 07670 ... B-6
Tinton Falls, Monmouth, 07724 ... I-13
• Toms River, Ocean, 08753-57 ... K-13
Totowa, Passaic, 07152 ... C-13
Towaco, Morris, 07082 ... B-1
Trenton, Mercer, 08601-99 ... I-9
Tuckerton, Ocean, 08087 ... N-12
• Turnersville, Gloucester, 08012 ... L-8
• Twin Rivers, Mercer, 08520 ... I-11
• *Union, Union, 07083* ... F-2
Union Beach, Monmouth, 07735 ... H-5
Union City, Hudson, 07087 ... E-5
Upper Saddle River, Bergen, 07458 ... A-4
Ventnor City, Atlantic, 08406 ... O-11
• Vernon Valley, Sussex, 07462 ... B-11
• *Verona, Essex, 07044* ... D-3
Victory Gardens, Morris, 07801 ... D-11
• Victory Lakes, Gloucester, 08094 ... N-8
• Villas, Cape May, 08251 ... R-8
Vineland, Cumberland, 08360 ... N-8
▲ *Voorhees, Camden, 08043* ... I-3
Waldwick, Bergen, 07463 ... A-4
Wallington, Bergen, 07057 ... C-4
• Wanamassa, Monmouth, 07712 ... I-14
Wanaque, Passaic, 07465 ... C-12
• Waretown, Ocean, 08758 ... L-13
Washington, Warren, 07882 ... E-8
• *Washington Township, Bergen, 07675* ... A-4
Watchung, Somerset, 07060 ... F-11
• *Wayne, Passaic, 07470* ... B-2
• *Weehawken, Hudson, 07087* ... E-14
Wenonah, Gloucester, 08090 ... L-7
• West Belmar, Monmouth, 07719 ... I-13
West Berlin, Camden, 08091 ... L-8
• *West Caldwell, Essex, 07007* ... D-2
West Cape May, Cape May, 08204 ... R-8
• West Freehold, Monmouth, 07728 ... I-11
West Long Branch, Monmouth, 07764 ... I-6
• *West Milford, Passaic, 07480* ... B-12
West New York, Hudson, 07093 ... E-13
• *West Orange, Essex, 07052* ... D-3
West Paterson, Passaic, 07424 ... C-3
Westfield, Union, 07090 ... F-1
Westmont, Camden, 08108 ... I-2
Westville, Gloucester, 08093 ... L-7
Westwood, Bergen, 07675 ... B-5
▲ *Weymouth, Atlantic, 08317* ... O-9
Wharton, Morris, 07885 ... D-10
Whippany, Morris, 07981 ... D-11
• White Horse, Mercer, 08610 ... I-10
• White House Station, Hunterdon, 08889 ... F-9
• White Meadow Lake, Morris, 07866 ... D-11
• Whitesboro-Burleigh, Cape May, 08252 ... R-9
Wildwood, Cape May, 08260 ... R-9
Wildwood Crest, Cape May, 08260 ... R-9
• Williamstown, Gloucester, 08094 ... M-8
• *Willingboro, Burlington, 08046* ... J-9
▲ *Winfield, Union, 07036* ... F-2
Woodbine, Cape May, 08270 ... P-9
• Woodbridge, Middlesex, 07095 ... F-12
Woodbury, Gloucester, 08096 ... L-7
Woodbury Heights, Gloucester, 08097 ... J-1
Woodcliff Lake, Bergen, 07675 ... A-5
Woodlynne, Camden, 08107 ... H-2
Wood-Ridge, Bergen, 07075 ... C-4
Woodstown, Salem, 08098 ... M-6
Wrightstown, Burlington, 08562 ... J-10
• *Wyckoff, Bergen, 07481* ... A-3
• Yardville-Groveville, Mercer, 08620 ... I-10
• Yorketown, Monmouth, 07726 ... M-12

Explanation of symbols: • – Census Designated Place (CDP) • *italics* – Township shown which is also a CDP ▲ *italics* – Townships (shown on the map)

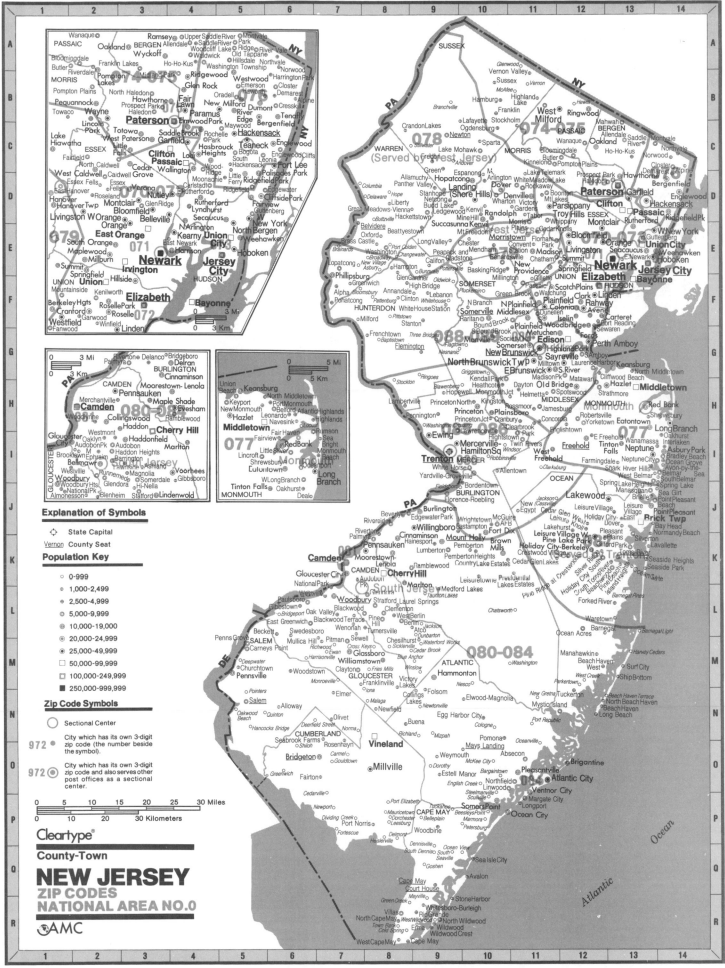

Explanation of Symbols

⟡ State Capital

Vernon County Seat

Population Key

- ○ 0-999
- ⊕ 1,000-2,499
- ⊕ 2,500-4,999
- ⊛ 5,000-9,999
- ⊛ 10,000-19,000
- ⊛ 20,000-24,999
- ⊡ 25,000-49,999
- ☐ 50,000-99,999
- ☐ 100,000-249,999
- ■ 250,000-999,999

Zip Code Symbols

○ Sectional Center

972 ● City which has its own 3-digit zip code (the number beside the symbol).

972 ◉ City which has its own 3-digit zip code and also serves other post offices as a sectional center.

0   5   10   15   20   25   30 Miles
0   10   20   30 Kilometers

Cleartype®

County-Town

NEW JERSEY
ZIP CODES
NATIONAL AREA NO.0

🜚 AMC

Copyright American Map Corporation

Explanation of symbols: ● – Census Designated Place (CDP)

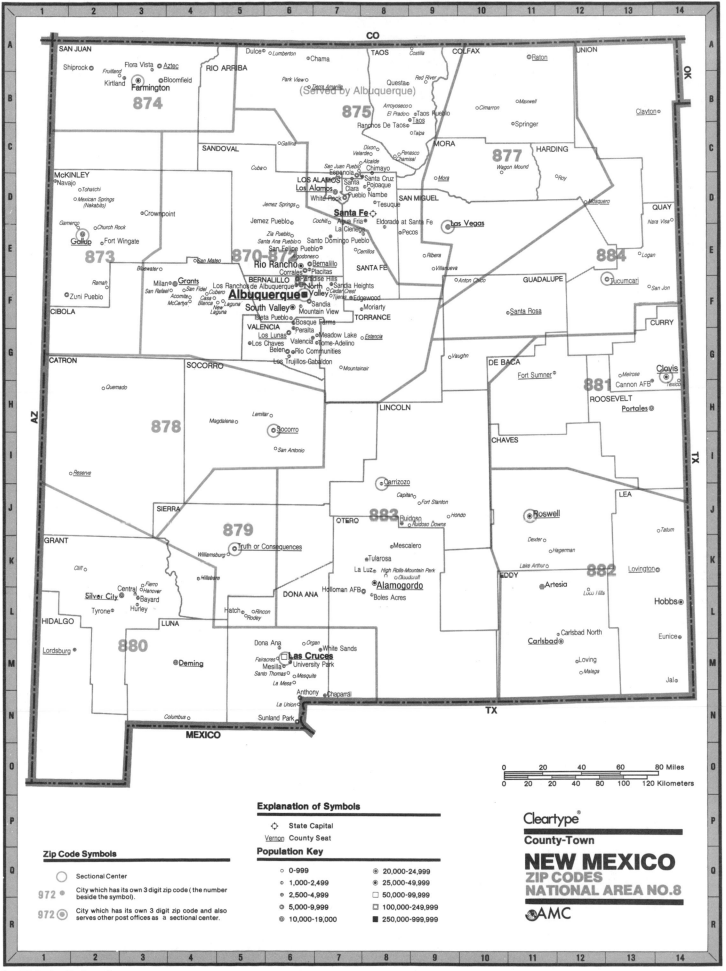

Explanation of Symbols

◇ State Capital
Vernon County Seat

Population Key

○ 0-999	◉ 20,000-24,999
⦶ 1,000-2,499	◉ 25,000-49,999
⦿ 2,500-4,999	☐ 50,000-99,999
◍ 5,000-9,999	☐ 100,000-249,999
◉ 10,000-19,000	■ 250,000-999,999

Zip Code Symbols

○ Sectional Center

972 ● City which has its own 3 digit zip code (the number beside the symbol).

972 ◉ City which has its own 3 digit zip code and also serves other post offices as a sectional center.

Cleartype®

County-Town

NEW MEXICO
ZIP CODES
NATIONAL AREA NO.8

AMC

Copyright American Map Corporation

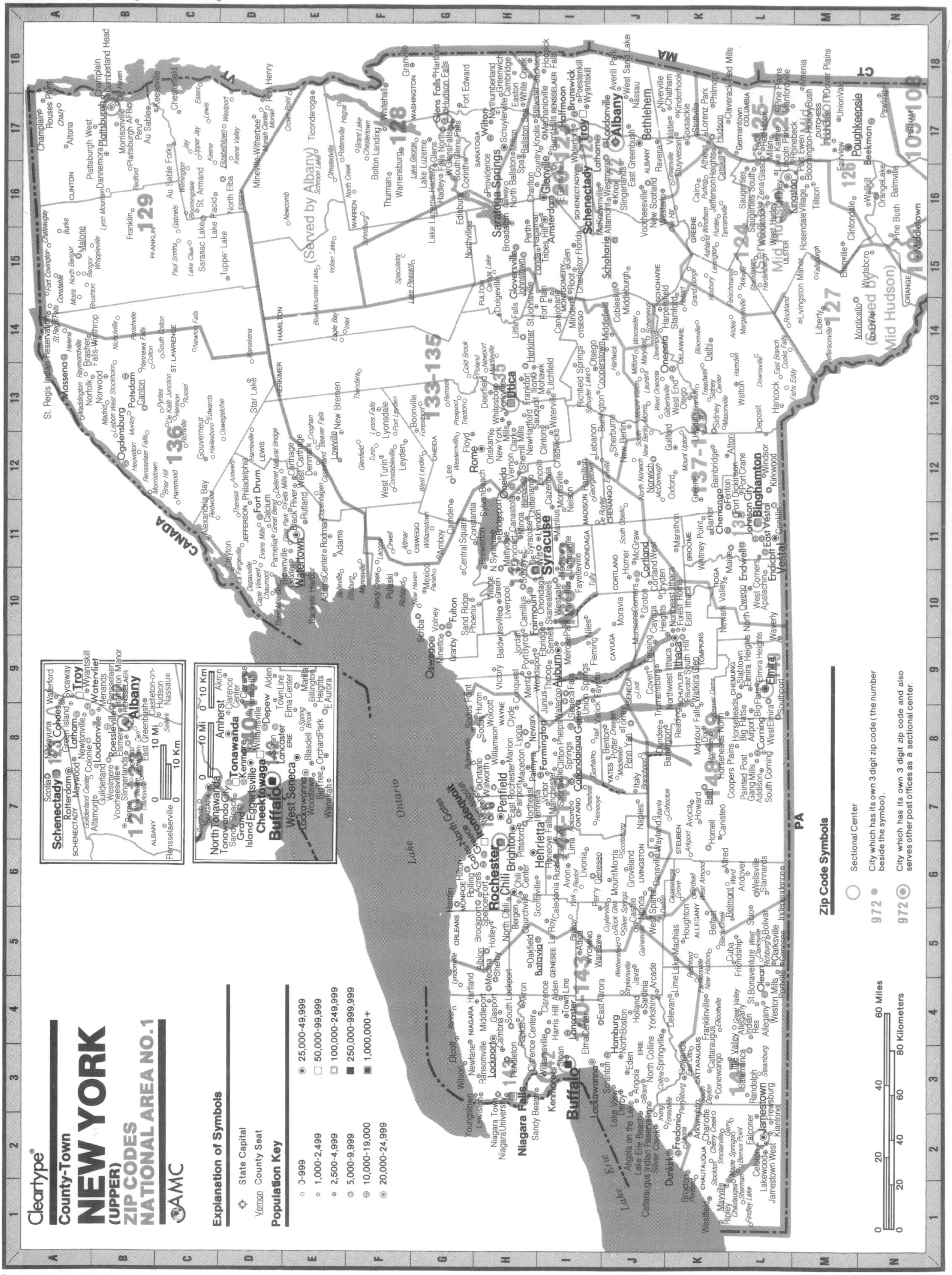

Cleartype®

County-Town

NEW YORK
(UPPER)

ZIP CODES
NATIONAL AREA NO. 1

◉ AMC

Explanation of Symbols

✧ State Capital
Vernon ◉ County Seat

Population Key

Symbol	Range
○	0-999
●	1,000-2,499
◉	2,500-4,999
◎	5,000-9,999
□	10,000-19,000
●	20,000-24,999
◉	25,000-49,999
□	50,000-99,999
▢	100,000-249,999
■	250,000-999,999
■	1,000,000 +

Zip Code Symbols

○ Sectional Center

972 ● City which has its own 3 digit zip code (the number beside the symbol).

972 ◉ City which has its own 3 digit zip code and also serves other post offices as a sectional center.

CANADA

MA   CT

VT

PA

Lake Ontario

Lake Erie

0   20   40   60   Miles
0   20   40   60   80 Kilometers

Copyright American Map Corporation

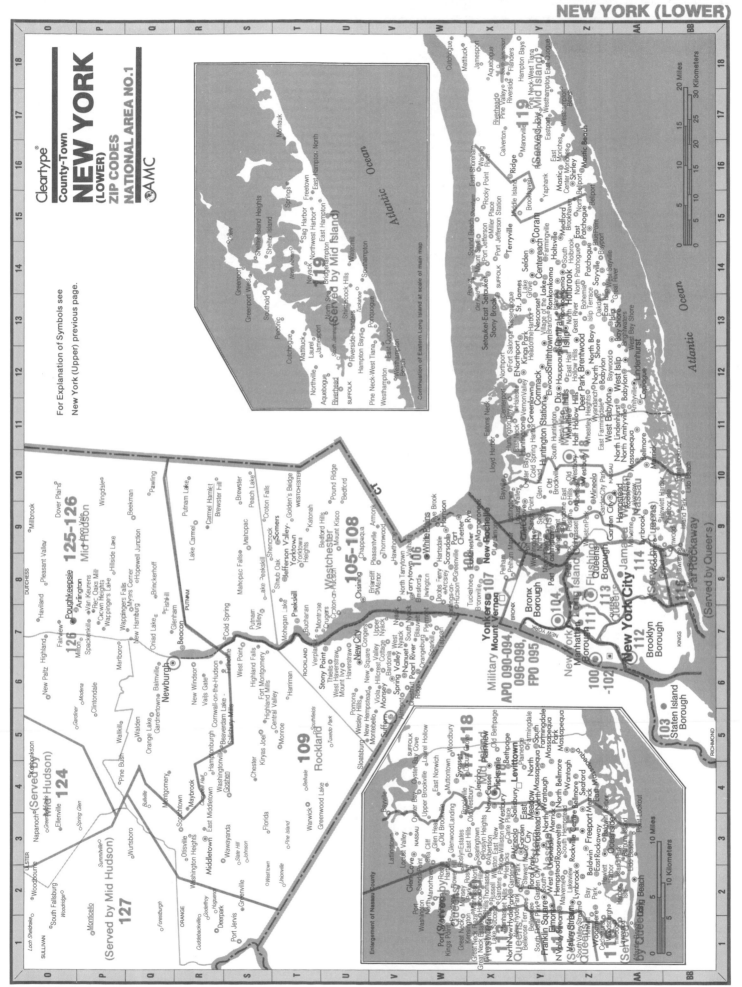

Cleartype®
County-Town
NEW YORK
(LOWER)
ZIP CODES
NATIONAL AREA NO.1
®AMC

For Explanation of Symbols see
New York (Upper) previous page.

Continuation of Eastern Long Island at scale of main map

COUNTIES

(62 Counties)

Name of County	Population	Location on Map
ALBANY	292,594	J-16
ALLEGANY	50,470	K-5
BRONX	1,203,789	Y-7
BROOME	212,160	K-11
CATTARAUGUS	84,234	K-3
CAYUGA	82,313	J-9
CHAUTAUQUA	141,895	K-2
CHEMUNG	95,195	L-9
CHENANGO	51,768	J-11
CLINTON	85,969	A-16
COLUMBIA	62,982	L-17
CORTLAND	48,963	J-10
DELAWARE	47,225	K-14
DUTCHESS	259,462	O-8
ERIE	968,532	J-3
ESSEX	37,152	D-16
FRANKLIN	46,540	B-15
FULTON	54,191	H-15
GENESEE	60,060	I-5
GREENE	44,739	K-16
HAMILTON	5,279	D-14
HERKIMER	65,797	D-13
JEFFERSON	110,943	D-11
KINGS	2,300,664	BB-7
LEWIS	26,796	D-12
LIVINGSTON	62,372	J-6
MADISON	69,120	I-11
MONROE	713,968	G-6
MONTGOMERY	51,981	I-15
NASSAU	1,287,348	Z-10
NEW YORK	1,487,536	Z-6
NIAGARA	220,756	G-4
ONEIDA	250,836	G-12
ONONDAGA	468,973	I-11
ONTARIO	95,101	I-7
ORANGE	307,647	R-1
ORLEANS	41,846	G-5
OSWEGO	121,771	G-11
OTSEGO	60,517	I-14
PUTNAM	83,941	R-7
QUEENS	1,951,598	AA-8
RENSSELAER	154,429	J-17
RICHMOND	378,977	BB-5
ROCKLAND	265,475	T-6
SAINT LAWRENCE	111,974	C-14
SARATOGA	181,276	H-17
SCHENECTADY	149,285	I-16
SCHOHARIE	31,859	J-15
SCHUYLER	18,662	K-9
SENECA	33,683	J-9
STEUBEN	99,088	K-6
SUFFOLK	1,321,864	X-14
SULLIVAN	69,277	N-14
TIOGA	52,337	K-10
TOMPKINS	94,097	K-9
ULSTER	165,304	L-15
WARREN	59,209	F-16
WASHINGTON	59,330	G-17
WAYNE	89,123	H-8
WESTCHESTER	874,866	T-9
WYOMING	42,507	I-5
YATES	22,810	J-7
TOTAL	17,990,455	

CITIES AND TOWNS

Note: The first name is that of the city or town, second, that of the county in which it is located, then the zip code area and location on the map.

Adams, Jefferson, 13605 ... E-11
• Adams Center, Jefferson, 13606 ... E-11
Addison, Steuben, 14801 ... L-7
• Airmont, Rockland, 10901,52,82 ... V-6
Akron, Erie, 14001 ... H-4
Albany, Albany, 12201-99 ... J-17
• Albertson, Nassau, 11501 ... Z-9
Albion, Orleans, 14411 ... H-5
Alden, Erie, 14004 ... I-4
Alexandria Bay, Jefferson, 13607 ... C-11
Alfred, Allegany, 14802 ... K-6
Allegany, Cattaraugus, 14706 ... L-4
Allegany Indian Reservation, Cattaraugus, 14707,81 ... L-4
Altamont, Albany, 12009 ... J-16
• Altona, Clinton, 12910 ... A-17
• Amenia, Dutchess, 12501 ... M-18
Amherst, Erie, 14226 ... D-8
Amityville, Suffolk, 11701 ... AA-11
Amsterdam, Montgomery, 12010 ... I-16
Andover, Allegany, 14806 ... L-6
Angola, Erie, 14006 ... J-3
• Angola on the Lake, Erie, 14006 ... J-3
• Apalachin, Tioga, 13732 ... L-10
• Aquebogue, Suffolk, 11931 ... X-18
Arcade, Wyoming,14009 ... J-4
Ardsley, Westchester, 10502 ... W-8
• Arlington, Dutchess, 12603 ... P-7
• Armonk, Westchester, 10504 ... V-10
Athens, Greene, 12015 ... K-17
Atlantic Beach, Nassau, 11509 ... BB-9
Attica, Genesee/Wyoming, 14011 ... I-5
Au Sable Forks, Clinton/Essex, 12912 ... C-17
Auburn, Cayuga, 13021 ... I-9
• Averill Park, Rensselaer, 12018 ... J-17
Avoca, Steuben, 14809 ... K-7
Avon, Livingston, 14414 ... I-6
Babylon, Suffolk, 11702 ... AA-12
Bainbridge, Chenango, 13733 ... K-12
• Baldwin, Nassau, 11510 ... Z-3
• Baldwin Harbor, Nassau, 11510 ... Z-3
Baldwinsville, Onondaga, 13027 ... H-10
Ballston Spa, Saratoga, 12020 ... H-17
• Balmville, Orange, 12550 ... N-16
• Bardonia, Rockland, 10954 ... V-7
• Barnum Island, Nassau, 11558 ... AA-3
Batavia, Genesee, 14020 ... I-5
Bath, Steuben, 14810 ... K-7
Bay Park, Nassau,11518 ... AA-9
• Bay Shore, Suffolk, 11706 ... Z-13
• Bayport, Suffolk, 11705 ... Z-14
Bayville, Nassau, 11709 ... X-10
• Baywood, Suffolk, 11931 ... Z-12
Beacon, Dutchess, 12508 ... R-7
• Beaverdam Lake-Salisbury Mills, Orange, 12553, 77 ... R-5
• Bedford, Westchester, 10506 ... U-9
Bedford Hills, Westchester, 10507 ... U-9
▲ Beekman, Dutchess, 12564 ... Q-9
Bellerose, Nassau, 11426 ... Y-2
Bellerose Terrace, Nassau, 11426 ... Y-2
• Bellmore, Nassau, 11710 ... AA-10
Bellport, Suffolk, 11713 ... Z-15
Belmont, Allegany, 14813 ... L-5
Bergen, Genesee, 14416 ... H-5
• Bethpage, Nassau, 11714 ... X-4
• Big Flats, Chemung, 14816 ... L-8
• Big Flats Airport, Chemung, 14814 ... L-8
Big Tree, Erie, 14219 ... E-8
• Billington Heights, Erie, 14052 ... E-8
Binghamton, Broome, 13901-99 ... L-11
Black River, Jefferson, 13612 ... E-11
Blasdell, Erie, 14219 ... E-8
• Blauvelt, Rockland, 10913 ... V-7
Bloomington-Hickory Bush, Ulster, 12411 ... M-16
• Blue Point, Suffolk, 11715 ... AA-13
• Bohemia, Suffolk, 11716 ... Z-14
Bolivar, Allegany, 14715 ... L-5
Bolton Landing, Warren, 12814 ... F-17
Boonville, Oneida, 13309 ... G-13
• Brasher Falls-Winthrop, St. Lawrence, 13613 ... A-14
• Brentwood, Suffolk, 11717 ... Z-13
• Brewerton, Onondaga/Oswego, 13029 ... H-11
Brewster, Putnam, 10509 ... S-9
• Brewster Hill, Putnam, 10509 ... R-10
Briarcliff Manor, Westchester, 10510 ... V-8
• Bridgehampton, Suffolk, 11932 ... U-14
• Bridgeport, Madison/Onondaga, 13030 ... H-11
• Brighton, Monroe, 14610 ... H-7
Brightwaters, Suffolk, 11718 ... Z-12
• Brinckerhoff, Dutchess, 12524 ... Q-8
Broadalbin, Fulton, 12025 ... H-16
Brockport, Monroe, 14420 ... H-6
Brocton, Chautauqua, 14716 ... K-2
Bronxville, Westchester, 10708 ... X-8
• Brookhaven, Suffolk, 11719 ... Y-16
Brookville, Nassau, 11545 ... W-3
Brownville, Jefferson, 13615 ... E-11
▲ Brunswick, Rensselaer, 12186 ... I-18
Buchanan, Westchester, 10511 ... T-7
Buffalo, Erie, 14201-99 ... I-3
Burnt Hills, Saratoga, 12027 ... I-16
• Cairo, Greene, 12413 ... K-16
• Calcium, Jefferson, 13616 ... D-11
Caledonia, Livingston, 14423 ... I-6
• Calverton, Suffolk, 11933 ... X-17
▲ Cambria, Niagara, 14094 ... H-3
Cambridge, Washington, 12816 ... H-18
Camden, Oneida, 13316 ... G-11
Camillus, Onondaga, 13031 ... H-10
Canajoharie, Montgomery, 11317 ... I-15
Canandaigua, Ontario, 11424-25 ... I-7
Canastota, Madison, 13032 ... H-12
Canisteo, Steuben, 14823 ... K-7
Canton, St. Lawrence, 13617 ... B-13
• Carle Place, Nassau, 11514 ... X-3
• Carmel Hamlet, Putnam, 10512 ... R-9
Carthage, Jefferson, 13619 ... E-12
Castile, Wyoming, 14427 ... J-5
Castleton-on-Hudson, Rensselaer, 12033 ... B-8
Catskill, Greene, 12414 ... K-17
Cattaraugus, Cattaraugus, 14719 ... K-3
Cattaraugus, Erie, 14719 ... J-3
Cayuga Heights, Tompkins, 14850 ... K-10
Cazenovia, Madison, 13035 ... I-11
Cedarhurst, Nassau, 11516 ... BB-9
Celoron, Chautauqua, 14720 ... L-2
• Center Moriches, Suffolk. 11934 ... Z-16
• Centereach, Suffolk, 11720 ... Y-14
• Centerport, Suffolk, 11721 ... X-11
• Central Islip, Suffolk, 11722 ... Z-13
Central Square, Oswego, 13036 ... G-10
• Central Valley, Orange, 10917 ... T-5
Chadwicks, Oneida, 13319 ... I-12
Champlain, Clinton, 12919 ... A-17
Chappaqua, Westchester, 10514 ... U-8
▲ Charlton, Saratoga, 12019 ... H-16
Chatham, Columbia, 12037 ... K-17
• Cheektowaga, Erie, 14225 ... D-8
▲ Chenango, Broome, 13745 ... K-11
Chester, Orange, 10918 ... S-4
Chestnut Ridge, Rockland, 10977 ... V-6
▲ Chili, Monroe, 14428 ... H-6
Chili Center, Monroe, 14674 ... H-6
Chittenango, Madison, 13037 ... I-11
Churchville, Monroe, 14428 ... H-6
Clarence, Erie, 14031 ... I-4
• Clarence Center, Erie, 14032 ... H-4
• Clark Mills, Oneida, 13321 ... H-13
• Claverack-Red Mills, Columbia, 12513 ... K-17
Clayton, Jefferson, 13624 ... D-10
Clifton Springs, Ontario, 14432 ... I-8
Clinton, Oneida, 13323 ... I-13
• Clintondale, Ulster, 12515 ... M-16
Clyde, Wayne, 14433 ... H-8
Cobleskill, Schoharie, 12043 ... J-15
Cohoes, Albany, 12047 ... A-8
Cold Spring, Putnam, 10516 ... S-7
• Cold Spring Harbor, Suffolk, 11724 ... Y-11
Colonie, Albany, 12212 ... A-8
• Commack, Suffolk, 11725 ... Y-12
• Congers, Rockland, 10920 ... V-7
▲ Conklin, Broome, 13748 ... L-11
• Constantia, Oswego, 13044 ... H-11
Coopers Plains, Steuben, 14827 ... L-8
Cooperstown, Otsego, 13326 ... J-14
• Copiague, Suffolk, 11726 ... AA-11
• Coram, Suffolk, 11727 ... Y-15
Corinth, Saratoga, 12822 ... G-16
Corning, Steuben, 14830 ... L-8
Cornwall on Hudson, Orange, 12520 ... R-6
Cortland, Cortland, 13045 ... J-10
• Cortland West, Cortland, 13045 ... J-10
• Country Knolls, Saratoga, 12019 ... I-17
Coxsackie, Greene, 12051 ... K-17
Croton Falls, Westchester, 10519 ... S-9
Croton-on-Hudson, Westchester, 10520 ... U-7
• Crown Heights, Dutchess, 12603 ... P-7
Crugers, Westchester, 10521 ... U-7
Cuba, Allegany, 14727 ... L-5
• Cumberland Head, Clinton, 12928 ... B-17
• Cutchogue, Suffolk, 11935 ... T-13
Dannemora, Clinton, 12929 ... B-17
Dansville, Livingston, 14437 ... J-6
• De Witt, Onondaga, 13214 ... I-11
• Deer Park, Suffolk, 11729 ... Z-12
▲ Deerfield, Oneida, 13503 ... H-13
▲ Deerpark, Orange, 12729 ... S-1
Delevan, Cattaraugus, 14042 ... K-4
Delhi, Delaware, 13753 ... K-14
• Delmar, Albany, 12054 ... B-8
Depew, Erie, 14043 ... D-8
Deposit, Broome/Delaware, 13754 ... L-12
Derby, Erie, 14047 ... E-11
• Dix Hills, Suffolk, 11746 ... Y-12
Dobbs Ferry, Westchester, 10522 ... W-8
Dolgeville, Fulton/Herkimer, 13329 ... H-14
• Dover Plains, Dutchess, 12522 ... M-14
Dryden, Tompkins, 13053 ... J-10
Dundee, Yates, 14837 ... J-8
Dunkirk, Chautauqua, 14048 ... K-2
East Aurora, Erie, 14052 ... J-4
• East Farmingdale, Suffolk, 11735 ... Z-11
• East Glenville, Schenectady, 12302 ... I-16
• East Greenbush, Rensselaer, 12061 ... J-17
East Half Hollow Hills, Suffolk, 11746 ... Z-12
East Hampton, Suffolk, 11937 ... T-15
• East Hampton North, Suffolk, 11937 ... T-15
East Hills, Nassau, 11576 ... Z-9
• East Islip, Suffolk, 11730 ... Z-13
• East Ithaca, Tompkins, 14650 ... K-10
• East Massapequa, Nassau, 11758 ... Z-5
• East Meadow, Nassau, 11554 ... Y-3
• East Middletown, Orange, 10940 ... R-3
• East Moriches, Suffolk, 11940 ... Y-17
East Neck, Suffolk, 11743 ... X-11
• East Northport, Suffolk, 11731 ... Y-12
• East Norwich, Nassau, 11732 ... W-4
• East Patchogue, Suffolk, 11772 ... Z-15
• East Quogue, Suffolk, 11942 ... Y-18
▲ East Rochester, Monroe, 14445 ... H-7
East Rochester, Monroe, 14445 ... H-7
East Rockaway, Nassau, 11518 ... Z-2
• East Shoreham, Suffolk, 11786 ... X-16
East Syracuse, Onondaga, 13057 ... H-11
East Vestal, Broome, 13902 ... L-11
East Williston, Nassau, 11596 ... X-3
• Eastchester, Westchester, 10709 ... X-8
Eastport, Suffolk, 11941 ... Y-17
• Eatons Neck, Suffolk, 11768 ... X-11
• Eden, Erie, 14057 ... J-3
Eggertsville, Erie, 14226 ... D-8
Elbridge, Onondaga, 13060 ... I-10
Ellenville, Ulster, 12428 ... M-15
• Elma Center, Erie, 14059 ... I-4
Elmira, Chemung, 14901-05 ... L-9
Elmira Heights, Chemun, 11003 ... Y-2
Elmsford, Westchester, 10523 ... W-8
Elmsmere, Albany, 12054 ... B-8
• Elwood, Suffolk, 11731 ... Y-12
Endicott, Broome, 13760 ... L-11
• Endwell, Broome, 13762 ... L-11
• Fairmount, Onondaga, 13031 ... H-10
Fairport, Monroe, 14450 ... H-7
• Fairview, Dutchess, 12601 ... M-17
Falconer, Chautauqua, 14733 ... L-2
Farmingdale, Nassau, 11735 ... Y-5
▲ Farmington, Ontario, 14425 ... I-7
• Farmingville, Suffolk, 11738 ... Y-14
Fayetteville, Onondaga, 13066 ... I-10
▲ Fenton, Broome, 13833 ... K-11
• Firthcliffe, Orange, 12584 ... R-6
Fishkill, Dutchess, 12524 ... Q-7
• Flanders, Suffolk, 11901 ... X-18
Floral Park, Nassau, 11001,03,04 ... Y-2
Florida, Orange, 10921 ... S-3
Flower Hill, Nassau, 11050 ... W-2
▲ Floyd, Oneida, 13440 ... G-12
Fonda, Montgomery, 12068 ... I-15
• Forest Home, Tompkins, 13440 ... K-10
• Fort Drum, Jefferson, 13603 ... D-11
Fort Edward, Washington, 12828 ... G-17
• Fort Montgomery, Orange, 10922 ... S-7
Fort Plain, Montgomery, 13339 ... I-14
• Fort Salonga, Suffolk, 11768 ... X-12
Frankfort, Herkimer, 13340 ... H-13
• Franklin Square, Nassau, 11010 ... Y-2
Franklinville, Cattaraugus, 14737 ... K-4
Fredonia, Chautauqua, 14063 ... K-2
Freeport, Nassau, 11520 ... Z-3
Freetown, Suffolk, 11937 ... T-15
• Frewsburg, Chautauqua, 14738 ... L-2
• Friendship, Allegany, 14739 ... L-5
Fulton, Oswego, 13069 ... G-10
• Gang Mills, Steuben, 14870 ... L-8
Garden City, Nassau, 11530 ... Z-10
• Garden City Park, Nassau, 11040 ... Z-9
• Garden City South, Nassau, 11040 ... Y-2
• Gardnertown, Orange, 12550 ... Q-6
• Gasport, Niagara, 14067 ... H-4
• Gates-North Gates, Monroe, 14626 ... H-6
Geneseo, Livingston, 14454 ... I-6
Geneva, Ontario, 14456 ... I-8
▲ Germantown, Columbia, 12526 ... L-17
• Glasco, Ulster, 12432 ... L-16
Glen Cove, Nassau, 11542 ... Y-9
• Glen Head, Nassau, 11545 ... Y-10
Glens Falls, Warren, 12801 ... G-17
• Glens Falls North, Warren, 12801 ... G-17
• Glenwood Landing, Nassau, 11547 ... W-3
Gloversville, Fulton, 12078 ... H-15
• Golden's Bridge, Westchester, 10526 ... T-9
Goshen, Orange, 10924 ... S-4
Gouverneur, St. Lawrence, 13642 ... C-12
Gowanda, Cattaraugus/Erie, 14070 ... K-3
▲ Granby, Oswego, 13069 ... G-9
▲ Grand Island, Erie, 14072 ... D-7
Granville, Washington, 12832 ... F-18
Great Neck, Nassau, 11020-24 ... Z-9
Great Neck Estates, Nassau, 11020 ... X-1
Great Neck Plaza, Nassau, 11022 ... X-1
Great River, Suffolk, 11739 ... AA-13
• Greece, Monroe, 14616 ... H-6
▲ Green Island, Albany, 12183 ... A-8
Green Island, Albany, 12183 ... A-8
Greene, Chenango, 13778 ... K-11
• Greenlawn, Suffolk, 11740 ... Y-12
Greenport, Suffolk, 11944 ... S-14
• Greenport West, Suffolk, 11944 ... S-14
▲ Greenville, Orange, 12771 ... S-2
• Greenville, Westchester, 10523 ... W-8
Greenwich, Washington, 12834 ... H-18
Greenwood Lake, Orange. 10925 ... U-4
Groton, Tompkins, 13073 ... J-10
Guilderland, Albany, 12084 ... B-8
Hagaman, Montgomery, 12086 ... I-16
• Halesite, Suffolk, 11743 ... X-11
Half Hollow Hills, Suffolk, 11746 ... Z-12
▲ Halfmoon, Saratoga, 12188 ... I-17
Hamburg, Erie, 14075 ... J-3
Hamilton, Madison, 13346 ... I-12
▲ Hamlin, Monroe, 14464 ... G-6
• Hampton Bays, Suffolk, 11946 ... Y-18
• Hampton Manor, Rensselaer, 12144 ... C-8
Hancock, Delaware, 13783 ... L-13
Harbor Hills, Nassau, 11023 ... X-2
Harbor Isle, Nassau, 11558 ... BB-9
Harriman, Orange, 10926 ... T-6
• Harris Hill, Erie, 14031 ... I-4
Harrison, Westchester, 10428 ... W-9
• Hartsdale, Westchester, 10530 ... W-8
Hastings-on-Hudson, Westchester, 10706 ... W-7
• Hauppauge, Suffolk, 11788 ... Y-12
Haverstraw, Rockland, 10927 ... U-7
• Haviland, Dutchess, 12538 ... O-7
• Hawthorne, Westchester, 10532 ... V-8
Head of the Harbor, Suffolk, 11743 ... Y-13
Hempstead, Nassau, 11550 ... AA-10
▲ Henrietta, Monroe, 14467 ... H-6
Herkimer, Herkimer, 13350 ... H-13
• Herricks, Nassau, 11040 ... X-2
• Hewlett, Nassau, 11557 ... Z-2
Hewlett Harbor, Nassau, 11557 ... AA-9
• Hicksville, Nassau, 11801-99 ... X-4
• Highland, Ulster, 12528 ... O-7
Highland Falls, Orange, 10928 ... S-7
• Highland Mills, Orange, 10930 ... S-5
• Hillcrest, Rockland, 10977 ... V-6
Hillside Lake, Dutchess, 12590 ... P-8
Hilton, Monroe, 14468 ... G-6
• Holbrook, Suffolk, 11741 ... Y-14
• Holland, Erie, 14080 ... J-4
Holley, Orleans, 14470 ... H-5
• Holtsville, Suffolk, 11742 ... Y-14
Homer, Cortland, 13077 ... J-10
Honeoye Falls, Monroe, 14472 ... I-7
Hoosick Falls, Rensselaer, 12090 ... I-18
• Hopewell Junction, Dutchess, 12533 ... Q-8
Hornell, Steuben, 14843 ... K-6
Horseheads, Chemung, 14845 ... L-9
• Horseheads North, Chemung, 14845 ... K-8
• Houghton, Allegany, 14744 ... K-5
Hudson, Columbia, 12534 ... K-17
Hudson Falls, Washington, 12839 ... G-17
• Huntington, Suffolk, 11743 ... Y-11
Huntington Bay, Suffolk, 11743 ... X-11
• Huntington Station, Suffolk, 11746 ... Y-11
• Hurley, Ulster, 12443 ... L-16
Ilion, Herkimer, 13357 ... H-13
• Inwood, Nassau, 11096,11696 ... BB-9
• Irondequoit, Monroe, 14617 ... H-6
Irvington, Westchester, 10533 ... W-8
Island Park, Nassau, 11558 ... BB-9
Islandia, Suffolk, 11722 ... Y-13
• Islip, Suffolk, 11751 ... Z-13
• Islip Terrace, Suffolk, 11752 ... Z-13
Ithaca, Tompkins, 14850 ... K-9
• Jamesport, Suffolk, 11947 ... X-18
Jamestown, Chautauqua, 14701,02 ... L-2
• Jamestown West, Chautauqua, 14701 ... L-2
Jamesville, Onondaga, 13078 ... I-11
• Jefferson Heights, Greene, 12414 ... K-17
• Jefferson Valley-Yorktown, Westchester, 10598 ... T-8
• Jericho, Nassau, 11753 ... X-4
Johnson City, Broome, 13790 ... L-11
Johnstown, Fulton, 12095 ... H-15
Jordan, Onondaga, 13080 ... H-10
Katonah, Westchester, 10536 ... T-9
Keeseville, Clinton/Essex, 12911 ... C-17
Kenmore, Erie, 14217 ... I-3
Kensington, Nassau, 11021 ... X-2
• Kerhonkson, Ulster, 12446 ... O-4
Kinderhook, Columbia, 12106 ... K-17
• Kings Park, Suffolk, 11754 ... Y-13
Kings Point, Nassau, 11024 ... Y-9
Kingston, Ulster, 12401 ... L-16
▲ Kirkwood, Broome, 13795 ... L-11
Kiryas Joel, Orange, 10950 ... S-5
Lackawanna, Erie, 14218 ... I-3
▲ LaFayette, Onondaga, 13084 ... I-11
• Lake Carmel, Putnam, 10512 ... R-9
• Lake Erie Beach, Erie, 14006 ... J-2
Lake George, Warren, 12845 ... G-17
Lake Grove, Suffolk, 11755 ... Y-14
• Lake Katrine, Ulster, 12449 ... L-16
• Lake Luzerne-Hadley, Saratoga/Warren, 12846 ... G-16
Lake Peekskill, Putnam, 10537 ... S-8
Lake Placid, Essex, 12946 ... C-16
Lake Pleasant, Hamilton, 12108 ... G-15
• Lake Ronkonkoma, Suffolk, 11779 ... Y-14
Lake Success, Nassau, 11020 ... X-2
Lake View, Erie, 14085 ... J-3
• Lakeview, Nassau, 11552 ... AA-9
Lakewood, Chautauqua, 14750 ... L-2
Lancaster, Erie, 14086 ... I-4
Lansing, Tompkins, 14882 ... J-9
Larchmont, Westchester, 10538 ... X-9
• Latham, Albany, 12110 ... I-17
Lattingtown, Nassau, 11771 ... X-10
• Laurel, Suffolk, 11948 ... T-13
Laurel Hollow, Nassau, 11791 ... W-4
Lawrence, Nassau, 11559 ... BB-9
Le Roy, Genesee, 14482 ... I-5
▲ Lee, Oneida, 13440 ... G-12
• Levittown, Nassau, 11756 ... Y-4
Lewiston, Niagara, 14092 ... H-3
Liberty, Sullivan, 12754 ... M-14
• Lido Beach, Nassau, 11561 ... BB-10
Lima, Livingston, 14485 ... I-6
• Lime Lake-Machias, Cattaraugus, 14042 ... K-4
• Lincoln Park, Ulster, 12401 ... L-16
Lindenhurst, Suffolk, 11757 ... AA-12
Little Falls, Herkimer, 13365 ... H-14

Explanation of symbols: • – Census Designated Place (CDP) • *italics* – Township shown which is also a CDP ▲ *italics* – Township (shown on the map)

Explanation of symbols: ● — Census Designated Place (CDP)   ● *italics* – Township shown which is also a CDP   ▲ *italics* – Township (shown on the map)

Explanation of symbols: ● – Census Designated Place (CDP)

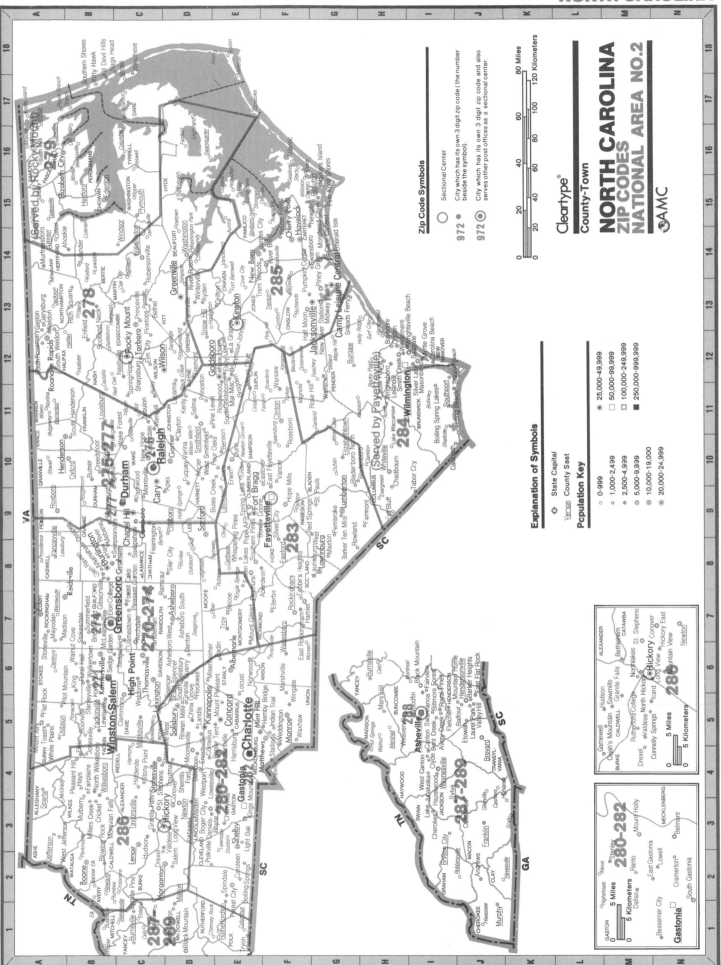

Copyright American Map Corporation

COUNTIES

(53 Counties)

CITIES AND TOWNS

Note: The first name is that of the city or town, second, that of the county in which it is located, then the zip code area and location on the map.

Explanation of symbols: ● – Census Designated Place (CDP)

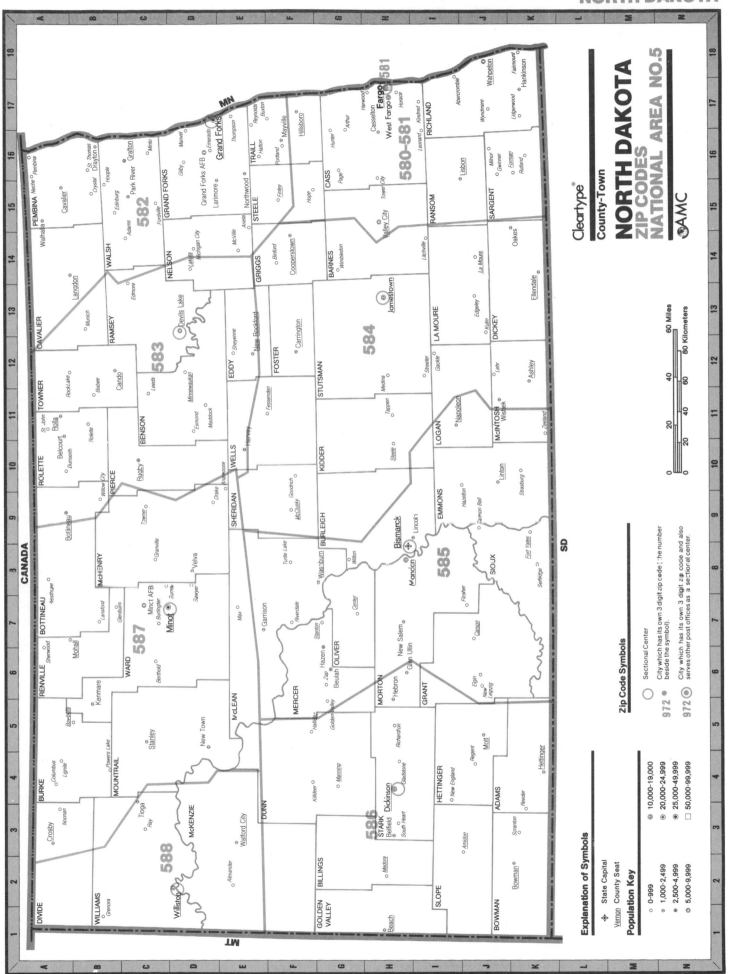

Cleartype®

County-Town

NORTH DAKOTA
ZIP CODES
NATIONAL AREA NO.5

AMC

Explanation of Symbols

★ State Capital

Vernon County Seat

Population Key

○ 0-999	⊚ 10,000-19,000
○ 1,000-2,499	⊛ 20,000-24,999
⊕ 2,500-4,999	⊛ 25,000-49,999
⊛ 5,000-9,999	☐ 50,000-99,999

Zip Code Symbols

○ Sectional Center

972 ● City which has its own 3 digit zip code (the number beside the symbol).

972 ⊚ City which has its own 3 digit zip code and also serves other post offices as a sectional center.

Copyright American Map Corporation

Explanation of symbols: ● – Census Designated Place (CDP)

Copyright American Map Corporation

Explanation of symbols: ● – Census Designated Place (CDP)

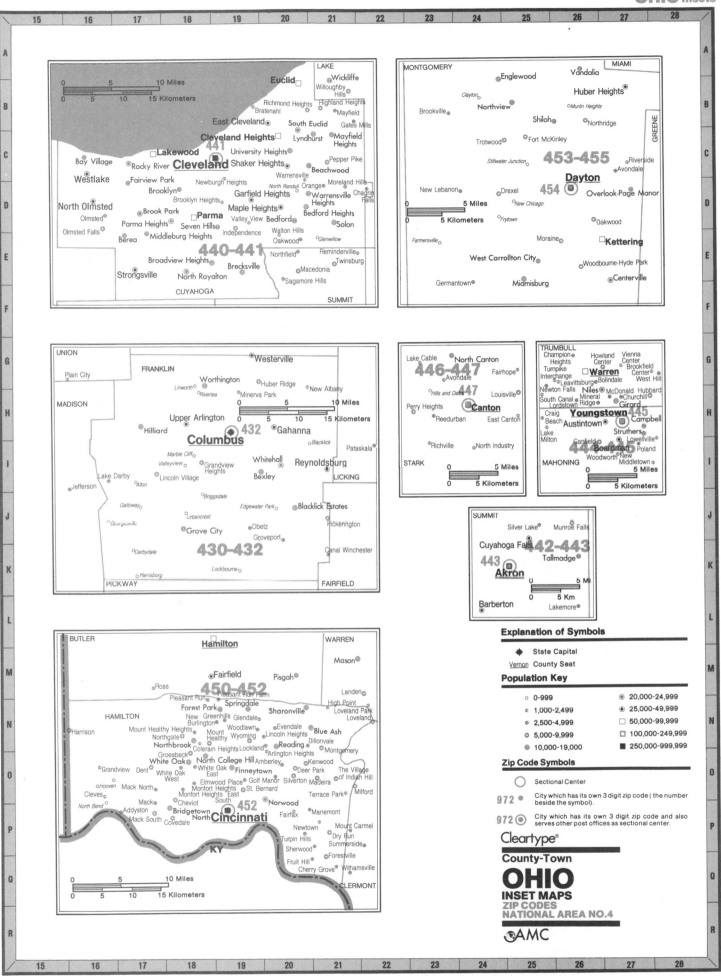

Copyright American Map Corporation

COUNTIES

(77 Counties)

CITIES AND TOWNS

Note: The first name is that of the city or town, second, that of the county in which it is located, then the zip code area and location on the map.

Explanation of symbols: ● – Census Designated Place (CDP)

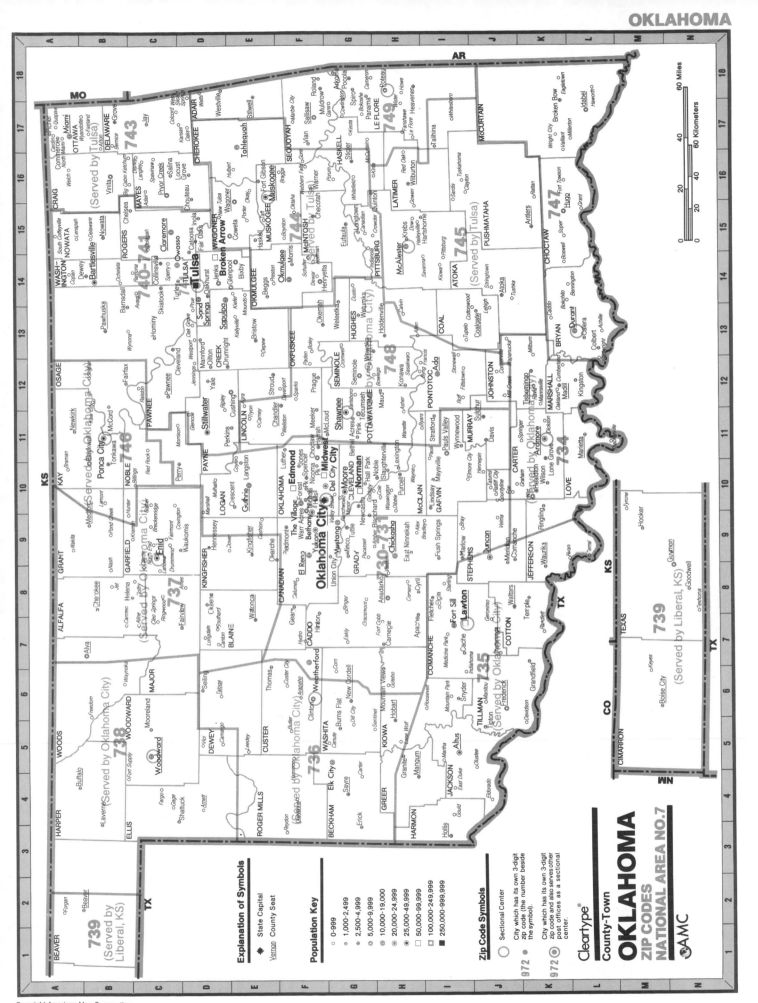

Copyright American Map Corporation

COUNTIES

(36 Counties)

Name of County	Population	Location on Map
BAKER	15,317	E-15
BENTON	70,811	G-6
CLACKAMAS	278,850	F-8
CLATSOP	33,301	C-5
COLUMBIA	37,557	C-6
COOS	60,273	I-4
CROOK	14,111	G-11
CURRY	19,327	K-4
DESCHUTES	74,958	I-9
DOUGLAS	94,649	H-5
GILLIAM	1,717	D-11
GRANT	7,853	F-13
HARNEY	7,060	H-13
HOOD RIVER	16,903	D-9
JACKSON	146,389	L-6
JEFFERSON	13,676	F-9
JOSEPHINE	62,649	L-5
KLAMATH	57,702	I-8
LAKE	7,186	I-10
LANE	282,912	G-5
LINCOLN	38,889	G-5
LINN	91,227	F-7
MALHEUR	26,038	G-16
MARION	228,483	F-8
MORROW	7,625	C-12
MULTNOMAH	583,887	D-8
POLK	49,541	F-6
SHERMAN	1,918	E-10
TILLAMOOK	21,570	D-5
UMATILLA	59,249	C-14
UNION	23,598	D-15
WALLOWA	6,911	C-16
WASCO	21,683	E-9
WASHINGTON	311,554	D-6
WHEELER	1,396	F-11
YAMHILL	65,551	D-6
TOTAL	2,842,321	

CITIES AND TOWNS

Note: The first name is that of the city or town, second, that of the county in which it is located, then the zip code area and location on the map.

Albany, Benton/Linn, 97321 .... F-6
● Aloha, Washington, 97006 .... B-8
● Altamont, Klamath, 97601 .... M-9
Amity, Yamhill, 97101 .... E-6
Ashland, Jackson, 97520 .... M-7
Astoria, Clatsop, 97103 .... B-5
Aumsville, Marion, 97325 .... F-7
Baker City, Baker, 97814 .... F-16
Bandor, Coos, 97411 .... J-4
● Barview, Coos, 97420 .... J-4
Bay City, Tillamook, 97107 .... D-5

Beaverton, Washington, 97005-07 .... D-7
Bend, Deschutes, 97701-02,07 .... H-10
Boardman, Morrow, 97818 .... C-13
Brookings, Curry, 97415 .... M-4
Brownsville, Linn, 97327 .... G-7
● Bunker Hill, Coos, 97420 .... J-4
Burns, Harney, 97720 .... I-14
Canby, Clackamas, 97013 .... E-7
Cannon Beach, Clatsop, 97110 .... C-5
Canyon City, Grant, 97820 .... G-14
Canyonville, Douglas, 97417 .... K-6
Carlton, Yamhill, 97111 .... E-6
Cave Junction, Josephine, 97523 .... M-5
● Cedar Hills, Washington, 97225 .... A-8
● Cedar Mill, Washington, 97291 .... L-7
Central Point, Jackson, 97501 .... L-7
Central Point West, Jackson, 97502 .... L-7
● Chenoweth, Wasco, 97502 .... D-10
City of the Dalles, Wasco, 97502 .... D-10
Clatskanie, Columbia, 97016 .... B-6
Columbia City, Columbia, 97018 .... C-7
Condon, Gilliam, 97823 .... E-12
Coos Bay, Coos, 97420 .... J-4
Coquille, Coos, 97423 .... J-4
Cornelius, Washington, 97113 .... D-6
Corvallis, Benton, 97330-31,33 .... G-6
Cottage Grove, Lane, 97424 .... I-6
Creswell, Lane, 97426 .... H-7
Dallas, Polk, 97338 .... F-6
Dayton, Yamhill, 97114 .... E-7
Deschutes River Woods, Deschutes, 97701 .... H-9
Drain, Douglas, 97435 .... I-6
Dundee, Yamhill, 97115 .... E-7
Dunes City, Lane, 97439 .... H-5
Eagle Point, Jackson, 97524 .... L-7
Eastside, Coos, 97420 .... J-4
Elgin, Union, 97827 .... D-16
Enterprise, Wallowa, 97828 .... D-17
Estacada, Clackamas, 97023 .... E-8
Eugene, Lane, 97401-05 .... H-6
Fairview, Multnomah, 97024 .... A-11
Florence, Lane, 97439 .... H-5
Forest Grove, Washington, 97116 .... D-7
Fossil, Wheeler, 97830 .... E-12
● Four Corners, Marion, 97301 .... F-7
● Garden Home-Whitford, Washington, 97223 .... B-8
Gearhart, Clatsop, 97138 .... B-5
Gilbert, Multnomah, 97266 .... B-10
Gladstone, Clackamas, 97027 .... D-7
Glendoveer, Multnomah, 97257 .... A-10
Gold Beach, Curry, 97444 .... L-4
Grants Pass, Josephine, 97526-27 .... L-6
● Green, Douglas, 97470 .... J-6
Gresham, Multnomah, 97030,80 .... B-11
Happy Valley, Clackamas, 97236 .... B-10
● Harbeck-Fruitdale, Josephine, 97526 .... L-6
● Harbor, Curry, 97415 .... M-4
Harrisburg, Linn, 97446 .... G-6
● Hayesville, Marion, 97303 .... E-7

Hazelwood, Multnomah, 97230 .... A-10
Heppner, Morrow, 97836 .... D-13
Hermiston, Umatilla, 97838 .... C-13
Hillsboro, Washington, 97123-24 .... D-7
Hines, Harney, 97738 .... I-14
Hood River, Hood River, 97031 .... D-9
Hubbard, Marion, 97032 .... E-7
Independence, Polk, 97351 .... F-6
Jacksonville, Jackson, 97530 .... M-7
Jefferson, Marion, 97352 .... F-7
Jennings Lodge, Clackamas, 97222 .... B-10
John Day, Grant, 97845 .... G-14
Joseph, Wallowa, 97846 .... D-17
Junction City, Lane, 97448 .... G-6
Keizer, Marion, 97303 .... E-7
Keno, Klamath, 97627 .... M-9
King City, Washington, 97224 .... B-8
Klamath Falls, Klamath, 97601,03 .... M-9
La Grande, Union, 97850 .... D-15
Lafayette, Yamhill, 97127 .... E-6
Lake Oswego, Clackamas/Multnomah/ Washington, 97034-35 .... B-9
Lakeside, Coos, 97449 .... I-4
Lakeview, Lake, 97630 .... M-12
Lebanon, Linn, 97355 .... G-7
Lincoln Beach, Lincoln, 97341 .... F-5
Lincoln City, Lincoln, 97367 .... F-5
Madras, Jefferson, 97741 .... F-10
May Park, Union,97850 .... D-15
McMinnville, Yamhill, 97128 .... E-6
Medford, Jackson, 97501,04 .... M-7
Metzger, Washington, 97223 .... M-7
Mill City, Linn/Marion, 97360 .... B-8
Milton-Freewater, Umatilla, 97862 .... F-8
Milwaukie, Clackamas/Multnomah, 97222 .... C-15
Molalla, Clackamas, 97038 .... D-7
Monmouth, Polk, 97361 .... E-7
Moro, Sherman, 97039 .... F-6
Mount Angel, Marion,97362 .... D-11
Mount Hood Village, Clackamas,97041 .... E-7
Myrtle Creek, Douglas, 97457 .... E-8
Myrtle Point, Coos, 97458 .... K-6
Newberg, Yamhill, 97132 .... K-4
Newport, Lincoln, 97365 .... E-7
● North Albany, Benton, 97321 .... F-5
North Bend, Coos, 97459 .... F-6
● North Springfield, Lane, 97477 .... J-4
Nyssa, Malheur, 97913 .... H-7
Oak Grove, Clackamas, 97267 .... H-17
● Oakridge, Lane, 97463 .... B-9
Oatfield, Clackamas, 97039 .... D-7
Ontario, Malheur, 97914 .... I-8
Oregon City, Clackamas, 97045 .... C-9
Pendleton, Umatilla, 97801 .... H-18
Philomath, Benton, 97370 .... D-7
Phoenix, Jackson, 97535 .... D-14
Pilot Rock, Umatilla, 97868 .... G-6
Port Orford, Curry, 97465 .... M-7
Portland, Clackamas/Multnomah/ 97201-99 .... D-14
 .... K-4
 .... D-7

● Powellhurst-Centennial, Multnomah, 97236 .... B-10
Prairie City, Grant, 97869 .... G-14
Pineville, Crook, 97754 .... G-10
Rainier, Columbia, 97048 .... C-7
● Raleigh Hills, Washington, 97225 .... B-8
Redmond, Deschutes, 97756 .... G-10
● Redwood, Josephine, 97526 .... L-6
Reedsport, Douglas, 97467 .... I-5
Riddle, Douglas, 97469 .... K-6
● River Road, Lane, 97404 .... H-6
● Rockcreek, Washington, 97812 .... D-7
Rogue River, Jackson, 97537 .... L-6
Rose Lodge, Lincoln, 97372 .... E-5
Roseburg, Douglas, 97470 .... J-6
Roseburg North, Douglas, 97470 .... J-6
Saint Helens, Columbia, 97051 .... C-7
Salem, Marion/Polk, 97301-06 .... E-7
Sandy, Clackamas, 97055 .... D-8
Santa Clara, Lane, 97404 .... H-6
Scappoose, Columbia, 97056 .... C-7
Seaside, Clatsop, 97138 .... C-5
Shady Cove, Jackson, 97539 .... L-7
Sheridan, Yamhill, 97378 .... E-6
Sherwood, Washington, 97140 .... D-7
Silverton, Marion, 97381 .... E-7
South Lebanon, Linn, 97355 .... G-7
Springfield, Lane, 97477-78 .... H-7
Stanfield, Umatilla, 97875 .... C-13
Stayton, Marion, 97383 .... F-7
Sublimity, Marion, 97385 .... F-7
Sunnyside, Clackamas,97015 .... B-10
Sutherlin, Douglas, 97424 .... J-6
Sweet Home, Linn, 97386 .... G-7
Talent, Jackson, 97540 .... M-7
Terrebonne, Deschutes, 97760 .... G-10
Three Rivers, Deschutes, 97023 .... H-10
Tigard, Washington, 97223 .... B-8
Tillamook, Tillamook, 97141 .... D-5
Toledo, Lincoln, 97391 .... F-5
● Tri-City, Douglas, 97457 .... K-6
Troutdale, Multnomah, 97060 .... A-11
Tualatin, Clackamas/Washington, 97062 .... C-8
Tumalo, Deschutes,97701 .... H-10
Turner, Marion, 97392 .... F-7
Umatilla, Umatilla, 97882 .... C-13
Union, Union, 97883 .... E-16
Vale, Malheur, 97918 .... H-17
Veneta, Lane, 97487 .... H-6
Vernonia, Columbia, 97064 .... C-6
Waldport, Lincoln, 97394 .... G-5
● Warm Springs, Jefferson, 97761 .... F-10
Warrenton, Clatsop, 97146 .... B-5
● West Haven-Sylvan, Washington,97225 .... A-8
West Linn, Clackamas, 97068 .... C-9
● West Slope, Washington, 97225 .... A-8
White City, Jackson, 97503 .... L-7
Willamina, Polk/Yamhill, 97396 .... E-6
Wilsonville, Clackamas/Washington, 97070 .... E-7
Winston, Douglas, 97496 .... J-6
Wood Village, Multnomah, 97060 .... A-11
Woodburn, Marion, 97071 .... E-7

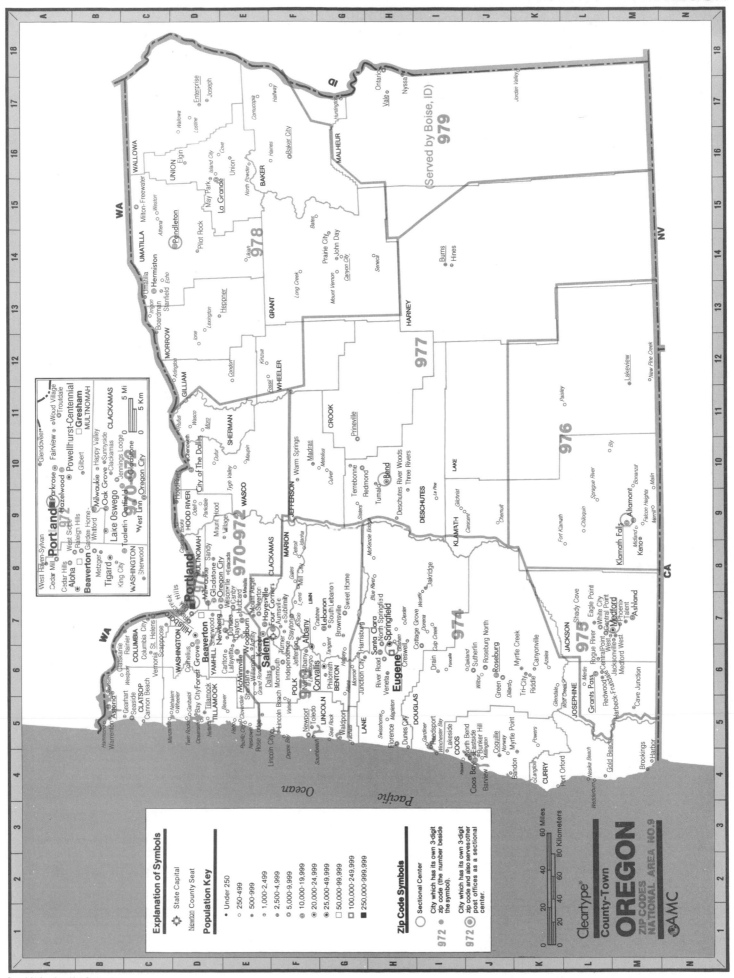

Explanation of Symbols

✦ State Capital

Newton County Seat

Population Key

- • Under 250
- ◦ 250-499
- ⊙ 500-999
- ⊕ 1,000-2,499
- ⊖ 2,500-4,999
- ⊕ 5,000-9,999
- ⊛ 10,000-19,999
- ⊗ 20,000-24,999
- ⊡ 25,000-49,999
- ☐ 50,000-99,999
- ☐ 100,000-249,999
- ■ 250,000-999,999

Zip Code Symbols

○ Sectional Center

972 • City which has its own 3-digit zip code (the number beside the symbol).

972 ⊙ City which has its own 3-digit zip code and also serves other post offices as a sectional center.

Served by Boise, ID) **979**

978

977

976

975

974

970-972

971

Cleartype®
County-Town
OREGON
ZIP CODES
NATIONAL AREA NO.9
◎AMC

Copyright American Map Corporation

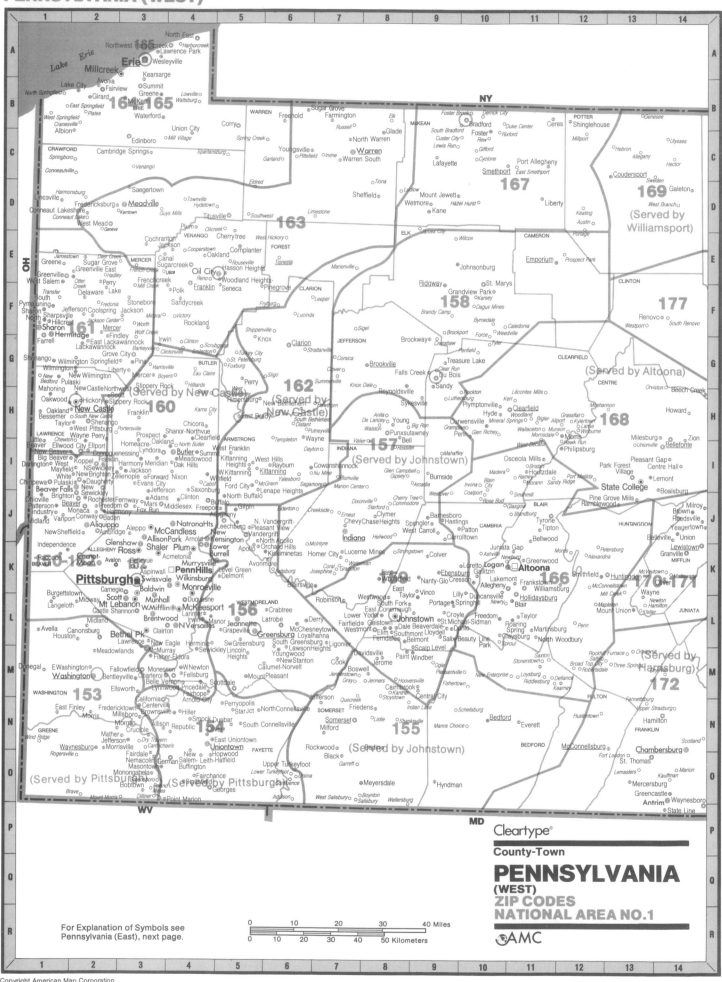

For Explanation of Symbols see
Pennsylvania (East), next page.

Cleartype®

County-Town

PENNSYLVANIA
(WEST)
ZIP CODES
NATIONAL AREA NO.1

AMC

Copyright American Map Corporation

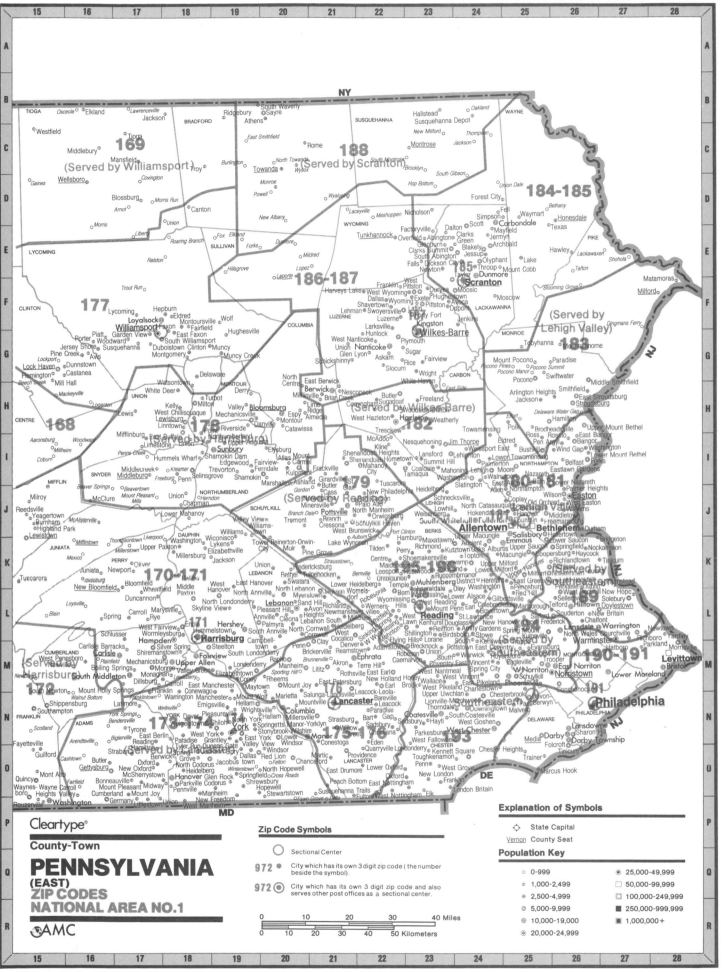

Zip Code Symbols

○ Sectional Center

972 ● City which has its own 3 digit zip code (the number beside the symbol)

972 ◉ City which has its own 3 digit zip code and also serves other post offices as a sectional center.

Explanation of Symbols

⬧ State Capital

Vernon County Seat

Population Key

○ 0-999	⊛ 25,000-49,999
⊙ 1,000-2,499	☐ 50,000-99,999
⊕ 2,500-4,999	▢ 100,000-249,999
⊙ 5,000-9,999	■ 250,000-999,999
⊙ 10,000-19,000	▪ 1,000,000+
◉ 20,000-24,999	

Cleartype®

County-Town

PENNSYLVANIA

(EAST)

ZIP CODES

NATIONAL AREA NO.1

🌐 AMC

0 10 20 30 40 Miles

0 10 20 30 40 50 Kilometers

Copyright American Map Corporation

COUNTIES

(67 Counties)

Name of County	Population	Location on Map
ADAMS	78,274	N-16
ALLEGHENY	1,336,449	K-2
ARMSTRONG	73,478	H-5
BEAVER	186,093	K-1
BEDFORD	47,919	N-11
BERKS	336,523	J-23
BLAIR	130,542	J-11
BRADFORD	60,967	B-18
BUCKS	541,174	K-26
BUTLER	152,013	G-4
CAMBRIA	163,029	J-10
CAMERON	5,913	E-11
CARBON	56,846	G-23
CENTRE	123,786	G-12
CHESTER	376,396	M-23
CLARION	41,699	F-6
CLEARFIELD	78,097	G-12
CLINTON	37,182	F-15
COLUMBIA	63,202	F-20
CRAWFORD	86,169	C-1
CUMBERLAND	195,257	M-15
DAUPHIN	237,813	K-18
DELAWARE	547,651	N-25
ELK	34,878	E-8
ERIE	275,572	B-3
FAYETTE	145,351	N-5
FOREST	4,802	E-6
FRANKLIN	121,082	N-13
FULTON	13,837	M-12
GREENE	39,550	N-1
HUNTINGDON	44,164	J-13
INDIANA	89,994	I-7
JEFFERSON	46,083	G-7
JUNIATA	20,625	J-17
LACKAWANNA	219,039	F-24
LANCASTER	422,822	M-20
LAWRENCE	96,246	H-1
LEBANON	113,744	K-19
LEHIGH	291,130	J-23
LUZERNE	328,149	F-21
LYCOMING	118,710	E-15
MC KEAN	47,131	B-8
MERCER	121,003	E-3
MIFFLIN	46,197	I-15
MONROE	95,709	G-24
MONTGOMERY	678,111	L-24
MONTOUR	17,735	H-19
NORTHAMPTON	247,105	I-25
NORTHUMBERLAND	96,771	I-18
PERRY	41,172	K-17
PHILADELPHIA	1,585,577	N-26
PIKE	27,966	E-26
POTTER	16,717	B-12
SCHUYLKILL	152,585	J-19
SNYDER	36,680	I-16
SOMERSET	78,218	N-7
SULLIVAN	6,104	E-19
SUSQUEHANNA	40,380	B-21
TIOGA	41,126	B-15
UNION	36,176	H-17
VENANGO	59,381	E-4
WARREN	45,050	B-5
WASHINGTON	204,584	M-1
WAYNE	39,944	B-25
WESTMORELAND	370,321	L-5
WYOMING	28,076	D-21
YORK	339,574	N-18
TOTAL	11,881,643	

CITIES AND TOWNS

Note: The first name is that of the city or town, second, that of the county in which it is located, then the zip code area and location on the map.

▲ *Abington, Lackawanna, 19001* E-23
Acmetonia, Allegheny, 15610 .... K-4
▲ *Adams, Butler, 16046* J-3
Adamstown, Berks/Lancaster, 19501 .... L-22
Akron, Lancaster, 17501 .... M-21
Albion, Erie, 16401 .... C-2
Alburtis, Lehigh, 18011 .... K-25
Aldan, Delaware, 18634 .... P-36
▲ *Aleppo, Allegheny, 15143* J-3
Aliquippa, Beaver, 15001 .... J-2
▲ *Allegheny, Blair, 16635* K-10
▲ *Allegheny, Westmoreland, 15656* .. J-5
▲ *Allen, Northampton, 18067* J-24
Allentown, Lehigh, 18101-99 .... J-25
Allison, Fayette, 15413 .... N-3
Allison Park, Allegheny, 15101 .... J-3
● Almedia, Columbia, 17815 .... H-20
Altoona, Blair, 16601-02 .... K-11
Ambler, Montgomery, 19002 .... I-38
Ambridge, Beaver, 15003 .... J-2
Ambridge Heights, Beaver, 15003 .... B-31
● Amity Gardens, Berks, 19518 .... I-9
● Ancient Oaks, Lehigh, 18062 .... K-24
Andalusia, Bucks, 19020 .... J-40
● *Annville, Lebanon, 17003* L-20
▲ *Antrim, Franklin, 17225* O-14
Apollo, Armstrong, 15613 .... K-5
Archbald, Lackawanna, 18403 .... E-24
● Ardmore, Delaware/Montgomery, 19003 .... K-37
● Arlington Heights, Monroe, 18360 .... H-26
Arnold, Westmoreland, 15068 .... K-4
Ashland, Columbia/Schuylkill, 17921 .... I-20
Ashley, Luzerne, 18706 .... M-31
Askam, Luzerne, 18706 .... G-22
Aspinwall, Allegheny, 15215 .... K-3
Athens, Bradford, 18810 .... B-20
● Audubon, Montgomery, 19407 .... J-36
Avalon, Allegheny, 15202 .... K-2
Avella, Washington, 15312 .... L-1
Avis, Clinton, 17721 .... G-16
Avoca, Luzerne, 18641 .... F-23
● Avon Heights, Lebanon, 17042 .... L-20
● Avonia, Erie, 16423 .... B-2
Avonmore, Westmoreland, 15618 .... K-6
Baden, Beaver, 15005 .... J-2
● Baldwin, Washington, 15327 .... F-34
Bala Cynwyd, Montgomery, 19004 .... K-38
Baldwin, Allegheny, 15234 .... D-34
Bangor, Northampton, 18013 .... I-26
Barnesboro, Cambria, 15714 .... J-9
▲ *Bart, Lancaster, 17503* N-22
Bath, Northampton, 18014 .... I-25
Bauerstown, Allegheny, 15209 .... C-34
Beaver, Beaver, 15009 .... J-2
Beaver Falls, Beaver, 15010 .... I-2
● Beaverdale-Lloydell, Cambria, 15921 .... L-9
Bedford, Bedford, 15522 .... N-10
▲ *Bedminster, Bucks, 18910* K-25
● Belfast, Northampton, 18064 .... I-26
▲ *Bell, Jefferson, 15767* H-8
▲ *Bell, Westmoreland, 15650* B-37
Bell Acres, Allegheny, 15143 .... B-32
Belle Vernon, Fayette, 15012 .... M-4
Bellefonte, Centre, 16823 .... I-14
● Belleville, Mifflin, 17004 .... J-14
Bellevue, Allegheny, 15202 .... K-3
Bellwood, Blair, 16617 .... J-11
● Belmont, Cambria, 15904 .... L-8
Ben Avon, Allegheny, 15202 .... B-32
Bentleyville, Washington, 15314 .... M-3
Berlin, Somerset, 15530 .... N-8
▲ *Bern, Berks, 19605* L-23
▲ *Berwick, Adams, 18603* O-18
Berwick, Columbia, 18603 .... H-21
Bessemer, Lawrence, 16112 .... H-1
▲ *Bethel, Delaware, 19507* R-34
Bethel Park, Allegheny, 11502 .... L-3
Bethlehem, Lehigh/Northampton, 18015,17-18 .... J-25
Big Beaver, Beaver, 15010 .... I-1
Birdsboro, Berks, 19508 .... L-23
▲ *Birmingham, Chester, 19380* Q-32
▲ *Birmingham, Delaware, 19317* L-25
● Black Lick, Indiana, 15716 .... K-7
▲ *Blair, Blair, 16635* K-11
Blairsville, Indiana, 15717 .... K-9
Blakely, Lackawanna, 18447 .... B-24
Blawnox, Allegheny, 15238 .... C-35
Bloomfield, Perry, 15761 .... L-16
Bloomsburg, Columbia, 17815 .... H-20
Blossburg, Tioga, 16912 .... D-17
● Blue Bell, Montgomery, 19422 .... I-37
● Boalsburg, Centre, 16827 .... I-14
● Boiling Springs, Cumberland, 17007 .... M-17
Bonneauville, Adams, 17325 .... O-17
● Boothwyn, Delaware, 19061 .... R-34
Boston, Allegheny, 15135 .... E-35
Boswell, Somerset, 15331 .... M-8
Boyertown, Berks, 19572 .... L-24
Brackenridge, Allegheny, 15014 .. B-35
Braddock, Allegheny, 15104 .... D-35
Braddock Hills, Allegheny, 15221 .... C-35
Bradford, Mc Kean, 16701 .... C-10
Bradfordwoods, Allegheny, 15015 .... A-33
▲ *Branch, Schuylkill, 17901* D-21
▲ *Brecknock, Berks, 19540* M-8
▲ *Brecknock, Lancaster, 17517* M-22
Brentwood, Allegheny, 15227 .... L-3
● Bressler-Enhaut-Oberlin, Dauphin, 17113 .... J-31
Briarcliff, Delaware, 19036 .... P-36
● Brickerville, Lancaster, 17543 .... M-21
Bridgeport, Montgomery, 19405 .... J-37
▲ *Bridgeton, Bucks, 18972* K-26
Bridgeville, Allegheny, 15017 .... D-33
▲ *Brighton, Beaver, 15009* J-2
Bristol, Bucks, 19007 .... M-28
● Brittany Farms-Highlands, Bucks, 18914 .... H-38
Brockway, Jefferson, 15824 .... G-9
● Brodheadsville, Monroe, 18322 .... H-25
Brookhaven, Delaware, 19015 .... Q-35
Brookville, Jefferson, 15825 .... G-8
● Broomall, Delaware, 19008 .... O-35
Broughton, Allegheny, 15236 .... E-34
Brownsville, Fayette, 15417 .... N-4
Bryn Athyn, Montgomery, 19009 .... M-26
● Bryn Mawr, Montgomery, 19010 .... O-35
▲ *Buckingham, Bucks, 18912* L-27
▲ *Buffalo, Butler, 15534* J-4
▲ *Buffalo, Washington, 15323* F-31
▲ *Bullskin, Fayette, 15666* G-37
Burgettstown, Washington, 15021 .... L-1
Burnham, Mifflin, 17009 .... J-15
▲ *Bushkill, Northampton, 18324* I-25
▲ *Butler, Adams, 17307* O-17
Butler, Butler, 16001 .... I-4
▲ *Butler, Luzerne, 18222* M-22
▲ *Butler, Schuylkill, 17921* I-20
▲ *Caernarvon, Berks, 19543* M-23
▲ *Caernarvon, Lancaster, 17555* M-23
California, Washington, 15418 .... N-3
● Calumet-Norvelt, Westmoreland, 15621 .... M-6
Cambridge Springs, Crawford, 16403 .... C-3
Camp Hill, Cumberland, 17001 .... M-18
● Campbelltown, Lebanon, 17010 .... L-20
Canonsburg, Washington, 15317 .... L-2
Canton, Bradford, 17724 .... D-18
Carbondale, Lackawanna, 18407 .. D-24
Carlisle, Cumberland, 17013 .... M-17
Carnegie, Allegheny, 15106 .... K-3
● Carnot-Moon, Allegheny, 15108 .... K-2
▲ *Carroll, Perry, 17090* L-17
▲ *Carroll, York, 17019* M-18
Carroll Valley, Adams, 17320 .... P-16
Carrolltown, Cambria, 15722 .... J-9
▲ *Cass, Schuylkill, 17901* J-21
● Castanea, Clinton, 17726 .... G-15
Castle Shannon, Allegheny, 15234 .... L-3
Catasauqua, Lehigh, 18032 .... J-25
Catawissa, Columbia, 17820 .... H-20
● Cecil-Bishop, Washington, 15321 D-32
Cedar Heights, Montgomery, 19428 .... J-37
Cedarbrook-Melrose Park, Montgomery, 19095 .... J-39
Cementon, Lehigh, 18052 .... J-24
▲ *Center, Beaver, 15001* A-31
Centerville, Washington, 16404 .... N-3
Central City, Somerset, 15926 .... M-9
Centre Hall, Centre, 16828 .... I-14
▲ *Centre, Berks, 19541* K-22
Chalfont, Bucks, 18914 .... L-26
Chambersburg, Franklin, 17201 .. N-14
▲ *Chanceford, York, 17309* O-20
▲ *Chapman, Snyder, 17864* J-18
Charleroi, Washington, 15022 .... M-3
▲ *Charlestown, Chester, 19460* M-24
● *Chester, Delaware, 19013-15,22* R-35
Chester, Delaware, 19013-15,22 .... Q-36
Chester Heights, Delaware, 19017 .... O-25
● Chesterbrook, Chester, 19333 .... M-25
Cheswick, Allegheny, 15024 .... B-34
● Chevy Chase Heights, Indiana, 15701 .... J-7
Chicora, Butler, 16025 .... H-4
▲ *Chippewa, Beaver, 15010* I-1
Christiana, Lancaster, 17509 .... N-22
Churchill, Allegheny, 15235 .... C-35
● Churchville, Bucks, 18966 .... L-27
Clairton, Allegheny, 15025 .... L-4
Clarion, Clarion, 16214 .... G-5
Clarks Green, Lackawanna, 18411 .... E-24
Clarks Summit, Lackawanna, 18411 .... E-23
▲ *Clay, Lancaster, 17522* M-21
● Claysburg, Blair, 16625 .... L-10
▲ *Clearfield, Butler, 16830* H-4
Clearfield, Clearfield, 16830 .... H-11
Cleona, Lebanon, 17042 .... L-20
Clifton Heights, Delaware, 19018 .... P-36
▲ *Clinton, Butler, 15026* J-4
▲ *Clinton, Lycoming, 17752* G-18
Clymer, Indiana, 15728 .... J-8
Coaldale, Schuylkill, 18218 .... I-23
Coatesville, Chester, 19320 .... N-23
Cochranton, Crawford, 16314 .... E-3
▲ *Codorus, York, 17311* O-19
▲ *Colebrookdale, Berks, 19512* L-24
Collegeville, Montgomery, 19426 .... M-25
▲ *Collier, Allegheny, 15106* L-3
Collingdale, Delaware, 19023 .... P-36
● Colonial Park, Dauphin, 17109 .... H-31
Columbia, Lancaster, 17512 .... N-20
● Colver, Cambria, 15927 .... K-9
Colwyn, Delaware, 19023 .... P-37
▲ *Concord, Delaware, 17217* O-26
▲ *Conemaugh, Cambria, 15902* L-9
▲ *Conewago, Dauphin, 17022* J-33
▲ *Conewago, York, 17404* N-19
● Conneaut Lakeshore, Crawford, 16316 .... D-2
Connellsville, Fayette, 15425 .... G-36
▲ *Conoy, Lancaster, 17502* N-19
Conshohocken, Montgomery, 19428 .... M-26
Conway, Beaver, 15027 .... J-2
Conyngham, Luzerne, 18219 .... I-21
▲ *Coolspring, Mercer, 15730* F-2
Coopersburg, Lehigh, 18036 .... K-25
Coplay, Lehigh, 18037 .... J-25
Coraopolis, Allegheny, 15108 .... B-32
Cornwall, Lebanon, 17016 .... L-20
● Cornwells Heights-Eddington, Bucks, 19020 .... J-40
Corry, Erie, 16407 .... B-5
Coudersport, Potter, 16915 .... C-13
Crabtree, Westmoreland, 15624 .... L-6
Crafton, Allegheny, 15205 .... C-32
▲ *Crescent, Allegheny, 15046* B-31
Cresson, Cambria, 16630 .... K-10
Cressona, Schuylkill, 17929 .... J-21
● Croydon, Bucks, 19021 .... J-40
▲ *Croyle, Cambria, 15944* L-9
Crucible, Greene, 15325 .... N-3
Crum Lynne, Delaware, 19022 .... Q-35
Cuddy, Allegheny, 15031 .... D-32
▲ *Cumberland, Adams, 17325* O-16
● Curtisville, Allegheny, 15032 .... A-35
Curwensville, Clearfield, 16833 .... H-10
Daisytown, Washington, 15427 .... G-34
Dale, Cambria, 15902 .... L-8
Dallas, Luzerne, 18612 .... F-22
Dallastown, York, 17313 .... O-19
Dalton, Lackawanna, 18414 .... E-23
Danville, Montour, 17821 .... H-19
Darby, Delaware, 19023 .... N-26
● *Darby Township, Delaware, 19036* N-26
▲ *Daugherty, Beaver, 15066* I-2
● Davidsville, Somerset, 15928 .... M-8
▲ *Delaware, Northumberland, 17777* H-18
Delmont, Westmoreland, 15626 .... K-5
Denver, Lancaster, 17517 .... L-22
Derry, Westmoreland, 15627 .... L-6
● Devon-Berwyn, Chester, 19333 .. N-25
Dickson City, Lackawanna, 18519 .... E-24
Dillsburg, York, 17019 .... M-17
▲ *District, Berks, 19512* K-24
Donora, Washington, 15033 .... F-34
Dormont, Allegheny, 15212 .... D-33
▲ *Douglass, Berks, 19464* L-22
Dover, York, 17315 .... N-18
Downingtown, Chester, 19335 .... N-24
Doylestown, Bucks, 18901 .... L-26
Dravosburg, Allegheny, 15034 .... D-35
● Drexel Hill, Delaware, 19026 .... P-36
Du Bois, Clearfield, 15801 .... G-9
Dublin, Bucks, 18917 .... L-26
Duboistown, Lycoming, 17701 .... F-17
Dunbar, Fayette, 15431 .... N-5
▲ *Dunbar, Fayette, 15431* N-5
Duncannon, Perry, 17020 .... L-17
Duncansville, Blair, 16635 .... K-10
Dunlo, Cambria, 15930 .... L-9
Dunmore, Lackawanna, 18512 .... E-24
● Dunnstown, Clinton, 17745 .... G-15
Dupont, Luzerne, 18641 .... F-23
Duquesne, Allegheny, 15110 .... L-32
▲ *Durham, Bucks, 18039* J-25
Duryea, Luzerne, 18642 .... F-23
● Eagleville, Montgomery, 19408 .... M-25
▲ *Earl, Berks, 19512* L-21
▲ *Earl, Lancaster, 17557* M-22
▲ *East Allen, Northampton, 18067* .. J-25
East Bangor, Northampton, 18013 .... I-26
East Berlin, Adams, 17316 .... N-18
● East Berwick, Luzerne, 18603 .... H-21
▲ *East Bradford, Chester, 19300* P-32
East Brady, Clarion, 16028 .... H-5
▲ *East Brandywine, Chester, 19335* O-31
▲ *East Caln, Chester, 19341* O-31
East Conemaugh, Cambria, 15909 .... K-9
▲ *East Coventry, Chester, 19457* M-23
▲ *East Deer, Allegheny, 15050* B-35
East Donegal, Lancaster, 17547 .... N-20
▲ *East Drumore, Lancaster, 17566* O-22
▲ *East Earl, Lancaster, 17519* M-22
▲ *East Fallowfield, Chester, 19036* P-30
East Greenville, Montgomery, 18041 .... K-25
▲ *East Hanover, Dauphin, 17028* K-20
▲ *East Huntingdon, Westmoreland, 15612* G-37
East Lansdowne, Delaware, 19050 .... P-37
▲ *East Manchester, York, 17347* N-24
▲ *East Marlborough, Chester, 19348* Q-31
East McKeesport, Allegheny, 15035 .... D-35
● *East Norriton, Montgomery, 19401* M-26
▲ *East Nottingham, Chester, 19363* O-23
East Petersburg, Lancaster, 17520 .... M-21
▲ *East Pikeland, Chester, 19460* N-23
East Pittsburgh, Allegheny, 15112 .... D-34
▲ *East Rockhill, Bucks, 18944* K-26
East Stroudsburg, Monroe, 18301 .... H-26
▲ *East Taylor, Cambria, 15909* L-8
● East Uniontown, Fayette, 15401 .... N-4
▲ *East Vincent, Chester, 19475* N-25
East Washington, Washington, 15301 .... M-2
▲ *East Wheatfield, Indiana, 15920* K-8
▲ *East Whiteland, Chester, 19355* .. O-33
● East York, York, 17402 .... N-19
● Eastlawn Gardens, Northampton, 18064 .... I-26
Easton, Northampton, 18042 .... J-26
Ebensburg, Cambria, 15937 .... K-9
Economy, Beaver, 15003,05 .... J-2
Eddystone, Delaware, 19022 .... Q-36
▲ *Eden, Lancaster, 17566* N-22
Edgely, Bucks, 19007 .... J-41
Edgewood, Allegheny, 15218 .... C-35
● Edgewood, Northumberland, 15218 .... I-19
Edgeworth, Allegheny, 15143 .... B-32
▲ *Edgmont, Delaware, 19028* P-33
Edinboro, Erie, 16412 .... C-3
Edwardsville, Luzerne, 18704 .... L-31
Egypt, Lehigh, 18052 .... J-24
▲ *Eldred, Lycoming, 16731* F-18
● Elim, Cambria, 17521 .... L-8
Elizabethtown, Lancaster, 17022 M-19
Elizabethville, Dauphin, 17023 .... K-19
▲ *Elizabeth, Allegheny, 15037* E-35
Elizabeth, Allegheny, 15037 .... E-35
▲ *Elk, Chester, 19351* O-23
Elkins Park, Montgomery, 19117 . J-39
Elkland, Tioga, 16920 .... B-16
Ellport, Lawrence, 16117 .... I-2
Ellsworth, Washington, 15331 .... M-3
Ellwood City, Beaver/Lawrence, 16117 .... I-2
Elwyn, Delaware, 19063 .... P-34
● Elysburg, Northumberland, 17824 .... I-20
● Emigsville, York, 17318 .... N-19
Emmaus, Lehigh, 18049 .... K-25
Emporium, Cameron, 15034 .... E-11
Emsworth, Allegheny, 15202 .... B-32
● Enola, Cumberland, 17025 .... L-18
Ephrata, Lancaster, 17522 .... M-22
Erie, Erie, 16501-99 .... A-3
● Espy, Columbia, 16424 .... H-20
Essington, Delaware, 19029 .... Q-36
Etna, Allegheny, 15223 .... C-34
Evans City, Butler, 16033 .... I-3
● Evansburg, Montgomery, 19426 . M-25
Everett, Bedford, 15537 .... N-11
▲ *Exeter, Luzerne, 18643* F-23
Exeter, Luzerne, 18643 .... F-23
● Exton, Chester, 19341 .... N-24
Factoryville, Wyoming, 18419 .... E-23
Fairchance, Fayette, 15436 .... O-4
● Fairdale, Greene, 15320 .... O-3
▲ *Fairfield, Lycoming, 17320* F-18
● Fairless Hills, Bucks, 19030 .... I-41
Fairview, Erie, 16415 .... B-2
▲ *Fairview, Luzerne, 19409* G-23
▲ *Fairview, York, 17070* M-18
● Fairview-Ferndale, Northumberland, 18920 .... I-19
▲ *Fallowfield, Washington, 15022* M-3
Falls Creek, Clearfield/Jefferson, 15840 .... G-9
Farrell, Mercer, 16121 .... F-1
▲ *Fawn, Allegheny, 15065,84* A-35
● Fayetteville, Franklin, 17222 .... O-15
● Feasterville-Trevose, Bucks, 19053 .... J-40
▲ *Fell, Lackawanna, 18421* D-24
Fellsburg, Westmoreland, 15012 F-35
Ferndale, Cambria, 18921 .... L-8
● Fernway, Butler, 16063 .... J-3
▲ *Findley, Mercer, 15026* F-3
Fleetwood, Berks, 19522 .... K-23
Flemington, Clinton, 17745 .... G-15
● Flourtown, Montgomery, 19031 .... J-38
● Flying Hills, Berks, 19607 .... L-8
Folcroft, Delaware, 19032 .... O-26
● Folsom, Delaware, 19033 .... Q-35
Ford City, Armstrong, 16226 .... I-5
Forest City, Susquehanna, 18421 D-24
Forest Hills, Allegheny, 15221 .... C-7
▲ *Forks, Northampton, 18042* J-26
● Fort Washington, Montgomery, 19034 .... J-38
Forty Fort, Luzerne, 18704 .... F-23
▲ Forward, Allegheny, 15020,37,63 .... E-34
▲ Forward, Butler, 16033 .... I-3
▲ *Foster, Mc Kean, 16701* C-10
Fountain Hill, Lehigh, 18015 .... J-25
Fox Chapel, Allegheny, 15238 .... B-34
● Fox Run, Butler, 16042 .... J-3
Frackville, Schuylkill, 17931 .... I-21
▲ *Franklin, Beaver, 16323* I-2
▲ *Franklin, Butler, 16052* H-3
▲ *Franklin, Chester, 16323* O-23
▲ *Franklin, Luzerne, 18640* F-22
Franklin, Venango, 16323 .... F-4
▲ *Franklin, York, 17019* N-18
Franklin Park, Allegheny, 15237 . A-33
▲ *Frankstown, Blair, 16648* K-11
▲ *Frazer, Chester, 19355* B-37
● Fredericksburg, Crawford, 16335 .. D-2
● Fredericksburg, Lebanon, 17026 K-20
● Fredericktown-Millsboro, Washington, 15348 .... N-3
Freedom, Beaver, 15042 .... J-2
▲ *Freedom, Blair, 16637* K-10
Freeland, Luzerne, 18224 .... H-23
Freemansburg, Northampton, 18017 .... J-25
Freeport, Armstrong, 16229 .... J-5
● Friedens, Somerset, 15541 .... N-8
● Fullerton, Lehigh, 18052 .... J-25
▲ *Fulton, Lancaster, 17563* O-22

Explanation of symbols: ●– Census Designated Place (CDP) ● *italics* – Township shown which is also a CDP ▲ *italics* – Townships (shown on the map)

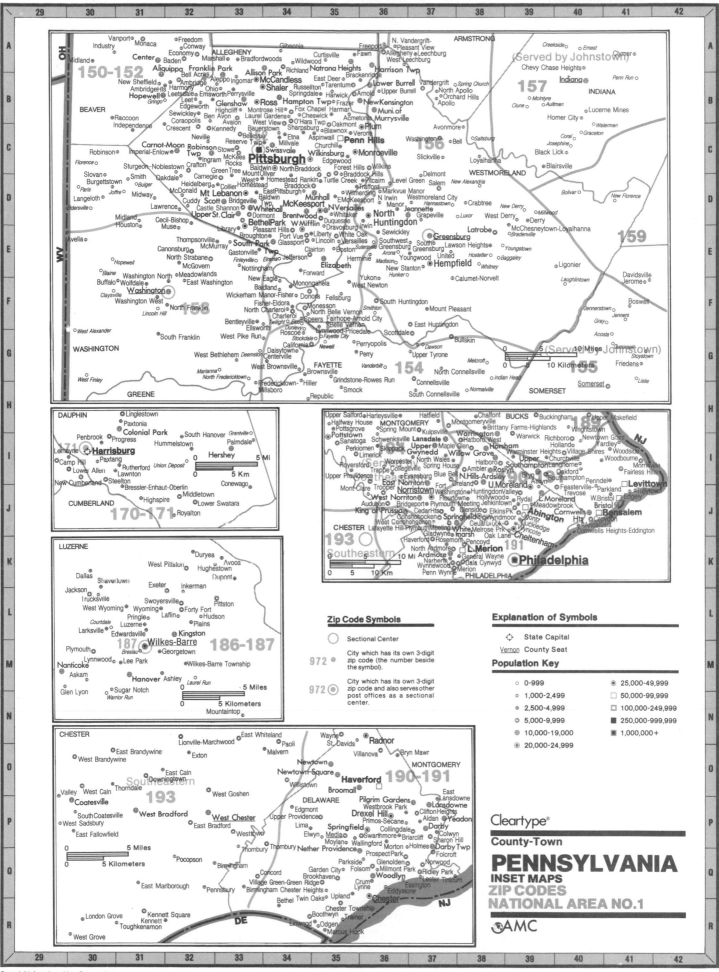

Copyright American Map Corporation

Galeton, Potter, 16922 .... D-14
Gallitzin, Cambria, 16641 .... K-10
• Gap, Lancaster, 17527 .... N-22
Garden City, Delaware, 19086 ... Q-35
• Garden View, Lycoming, 17701 .... G-17
• Gastonville, Washington, 15336 .... E-33
Geistown, Cambria, 15904 .... L-8
▲ *Georges, Fayette, 15478* D-4
Georgetown, Luzerne, 15043 .... M-31
▲ *German, Fayette, 15458* O-4
▲ *Germany, Adams, 17340* P-17
Gettysburg, Adams, 17325 .... O-16
Gibsonia, Allegheny, 15044 .... A-34
• Gilbertsville, Montgomery, 19525 .... L-24
▲ *Gilpin, Armstrong, 15656* J-5
Girard, Erie, 16417 .... B-2
Girardville, Schuylkill, 17935 .... I-21
Gladwyne, Montgomery, 19035 ... J-37
Glassport, Allegheny, 15045 .... E-34
• Glen Lyon, Luzerne, 18617 .... G-22
Glen Rock, York, 17327 .... O-19
• *Glenburn, Lackawanna, 18414* ... E-23
Glenolden, Delaware, 19036 .... Q-36
Glenshaw, Allegheny, 15116 .... K-3
• Glenside, Montgomery, 19038 .... J-38
• Grandview Park, Elk, 15857 .... F-10
• Grantley, York, 17371 .... N-19
▲ *Granville, Mifflin, 17029* K-15
Grapeville, Westmoreland, 15634 .... L-5
Green Tree, Allegheny, 15242 .... G-5
Greencastle, Franklin, 17225 .... O-14
▲ *Greene, Erie, 16509* B-3
Greensburg, Westmoreland, 15601 .... L-5
Greenville, Mercer, 16105 .... E-1
• Greenville East, Mercer, 16105 .... E-2
Greenwood, Blair, 16601 .... K-11
• Grindstone-Rowes Run, Fayette, 15442 .... G-35
Grove City, Mercer, 16127 .... G-3
• Guilford, Franklin, 17201 .... O-15
• Halfway House, Montgomery, 19464 .... L-24
Hallam, York, 17406 .... N-19
Hallstead, Susquehanna, 18822 .... B-23
Hamburg, Berks, 19526 .... K-22
▲ *Hamilton, Adams, 17316* O-16
▲ *Hamilton, Franklin, 17201* N-14
▲ *Hamilton, Monroe, 18354* H-25
▲ *Hampden, Cumberland, 17055* ... M-18
▲ *Hampton, Allegheny, 15101,44* J-3
▲ *Hanover, Lehigh, 17331* J-25
▲ *Hanover, Luzerne, 18702* G-22
▲ *Hanover, Northampton, 18017* ... J-25
Hanover, York, 17331 .... O-18
• Harleysville, Montgomery, 19438 .... L-25
▲ *Harmar, Allegheny, 15024,48* B-35
• *Harmony, Beaver, 15003* J-2
Harmony, Butler, 16037 .... I-3
Harrisburg, Dauphin, 17101-99 ... L-18
• *Harrison, Allegheny, 15065* J-4
Harveys Lake, Luzerne, 18618 ... F-22
Harwick, Allegheny, 15049 .... B-35
• Hasson Heights, Venango, 16301 .... E-5
Hastings, Cambria, 16646 .... J-9
Hatboro, Montgomery, 19040 .... M-27
Hatboro West, Montgomery, 19040 .... I-38
Hatfield, Montgomery, 19440 .... L-26
Haverford, Montgomery, 19041 ... J-37
Hawley, Wayne, 18428 .... E-26
▲ *Haycock, Bucks, 18955* K-26
Hayti, Chester, 19320 .... N-23
Hazleton, Luzerne, 18201 .... H-22
Heidelberg, Allegheny, 15106 .... D-32
▲ *Heidelberg, Berks, 19506* L-22
▲ *Heidelberg, Lebanon, 17088* L-21
▲ *Heidelberg, Lehigh, 18080* J-23
▲ *Heidelberg, York, 17362* O-18
▲ *Hellam, York, 17362* N-20
Hellertown, Northampton, 18055 .... J-25
▲ *Hempfield, Westmoreland, 15601* E-36
▲ *Hepburn, Lycoming, 17101* F-18
▲ *Hereford, Berks, 18056* K-24
Herminie, Westmoreland, 15637 ... L-4
Hermitage, Mercer, 16148 .... F-1
• Hershey, Dauphin, 17033 .... L-19
▲ *Hickory, Lawrence, 15340* H-2
Highcliff, Allegheny, 15229 .... B-33
• Highland Park, Mifflin, 17044 .... J-15
Highspire, Dauphin, 17034 .... J-31
• Hiller, Fayette, 15444 .... N-4
▲ *Hilltown, Bucks, 18927* L-26
• Hokendauqua, Lehigh, 18052 .... J-25
Holland, Bucks, 18966 .... I-40
Hollidaysburg, Blair, 16648 .... L-11
Hollywood, Montgomery, 19117 ... J-39
Holmes, Delaware, 19043 .... P-37
• Homeacre-Lyndora, Butler, 16001 .... I-3
Homer City, Indiana, 15748 .... K-7
Homestead, Allegheny, 15120 ... C-34
• Hometown, Schuylkill, 18252 .... I-22
Honesdale, Wayne, 18431 .... D-25
Honey Brook, Chester, 19344 ... M-23
▲ *Hopewell, Beaver, 16650* J-2
▲ *Hopewell, York, 17363* O-20
• Hopwood, Fayette, 15445 .... O-4
• Horsham, Montgomery, 19044 .... I-38
Houston, Washington, 15342 .... L-2
Houtzdale, Clearfield, 16651 .... I-11
Hudson, Luzerne, 18705 .... L-32
Hughestown, Luzerne, 18640 .... F-23
Hughesville, Lycoming, 17737 ... G-19
• Hummels Wharf, Snyder, 17831 ... I-18
Hummelstown, Dauphin, 17036 ... L-19
▲ *Hunlock, Luzerne, 18621* G-22
Huntingdon, Huntingdon, 16652 .... K-13
Huntingdon Valley, Montgomery, 19006 .... J-39
• Hyde, Clearfield, 16843 .... H-16
Hyndman, Bedford, 15545 .... O-9
• Imperial-Enlow, Allegheny, 15126 .... C-32
▲ *Independence, Beaver, 15026* K-1
▲ *Indiana, Allegheny, 15701* .... B 36
Indiana, Indiana, 15701 .... J-7
Industry, Beaver, 15052 .... J-1
Ingomar, Allegheny, 15127 .... A-33
Ingram, Allegheny, 15205 .... C-32
Inkerman, Luzerne, 18640 .... K-32
Irwin, Westmoreland, 15642 .... L-4
▲ *Jackson, Butler, 18825* I-3
▲ *Jackson, Lebanon, 17042* L-21
▲ *Jackson, Luzerne, 18708* F-22
▲ *Jackson, Monroe, 18352* H-25
▲ *Jackson, York, 17362* O-18
Jacobus, York, 17407 .... O-19
Jeannette, Westmoreland, 15644 ... L-5
Jefferson, Allegheny, 15644 .... E-34
▲ *Jefferson, Butler, 16001* J-3
▲ *Jenkins, Luzerne, 18640* F-24
Jenkintown, Montgomery, 19046 . J-39
Jermyn, Lackawanna, 18433 .... E-24
• Jerome, Somerset, 15937 .... M-8
Jersey Shore, Lycoming, 17723 . G-16
Jessup, Lackawanna, 18434 .... E-24
Jim Thorpe, Carbon, 18229 .... I-23
Johnsonburg, Elk, 15845 .... F-9
Johnstown, Cambria, 15901-09 .... L-8
Kane, Mc Kean, 16735 .... D-9
Kearsarge, Erie, 16509 .... B-3
▲ *Kelly, Union, 17837* H-18
Kenhorst, Berks, 19607 .... L-23
• Kenilworth, Chester, 19464 .... M-24
• Kennedy Township, Allegheny, 15108 .... C-32
▲ *Kennett, Chester, 19348* R-32
Kennett Square, Chester, 19348 O-24
• King of Prussia, Montgomery, 19406 .... J-36
Kingston, Luzerne, 18704 .... F-23
Kittanning, Armstrong, 16201 .... K-5
Kittanning Heights, Armstrong, 16201 .... I-5
▲ *Kline, Schuylkill, 18237* I-22
Knox, Clarion, 16232 .... G-5
Koppel, Beaver, 16136 .... I-2
Kulpmont, Northumberland, 17834 I-20
• Kulpsville, Montgomery, 19443 .... L-25
Kutztown, Berks, 19530 .... K-23
▲ *Lackawannock, Mercer, 16137* G-2
Lafayette Hill-Plymouth Meeting, Montgomery, 19444 .... J-37
Laflin, Luzerne, 18702 .... F-23
▲ *Lake, Wayne, 18436* G-25
Lake City, Erie, 16423 .... B-2
• Lake Wynonah, Schuylkill, 18625 J-21
Lakemont, Blair, 16602 .... K-11
Lancaster, Lancaster, 17601-99 . N-21
Langhorne, Bucks, 19047,53 .... I-40
Lansdale, Montgomery, 19446 .... L-26
Lansdowne, Delaware, 19050 .... N-26
Lansford, Carbon, 18232 .... I-23
Laporte, Sullivan, 18626 .... F-20
Larimer, Westmoreland, 15647 .... L-4
Larksville, Luzerne, 18651 .... F-22
▲ *Latimore, Adams, 17372* N-17
Latrobe, Westmoreland,15650 .... L-6
Laurel Gardens, Allegheny, 15229 .... B-34
Laureldale, Berks, 19605 .... K-23
• Lawnton, Dauphin, 17111 .... H-30
Lawrence, Washington, 15055 .... L-3
• *Lawrence Park, Erie, 18511* A-3
• Lawson Heights, Westmoreland, 15650 .... M-6
▲ *Leacock, Lancaster, 17540* M-21
• Leacock-Leola-Bareville, Lancaster, 17572 .... M-21
Lebanon, Lebanon, 17042 .... L-20
• Lebanon South, Lebanon, 17042 L-20
Lee Park, Luzerne, 18702 .... M-31
Leechburg, Armstrong, 15656 .... J-5
Leesport, Berks, 19533 .... K-22
▲ *Leet, Allegheny, 15009,15143* B-32
Leetsdale, Allegheny, 15056 .... B-32
▲ *Lehigh, Northampton, 18002* I-24
Lehighton, Carbon, 18235 .... I-23
▲ *Lehman, Luzerne, 18627* F-22
• Leith-Hatfield, Fayette, 15401 .... O-4
Lemoyne, Cumberland, 17043 ... M-18
• Lenape Heights, Armstrong, 16226 .... J-5
Lester, Delaware,19029 .... Q-37
Level Green, Westmoreland, 15085 .... K-5
• Levittown, Bucks, 19054-57 .... M-28
Lewisburg, Union, 17837 .... H-18
Lewistown, Mifflin, 17044 .... K-15
Liberty, Allegheny, 15133 .... E-34
Library, Allegheny, 15129 .... D-33
Ligonier, Westmoreland, 15658 .... L-7
Lilly, Cambria, 15938 .... K-10
• Lima, Delaware, 19037 .... P-35
• Lime Ridge, Columbia, 17815 .... H-20
▲ *Limerick, Montgomery, 19468* H-36
Lincoln, Allegheny, 15037 .... E-7
Lincoln Heights, Westmoreland, 15644 .... M-5
Linesville, Crawford, 16424 .... D-1
• Linglestown, Dauphin, 17112 .... L-18
• Linntown, Union, 17837 .... H-18
• Linwood, Delaware, 14061 .... R-35
• Lionville-Marchwood, Chester, 19353 .... N-32
Lititz, Lancaster, 17543 .... M-21
Littlestown, Adams, 17340 .... P-17
Lock Haven, Clinton, 17745 .... G 15
▲ *Logan, Blair, 16602* K-11
▲ *London Britain, Chester, 19350* .. O-23
▲ *London Grove, Chester, 19348* .. R-30
▲ *Londonderry, Chester, 19330* O-23
▲ *Londonderry, Dauphin, 17057* M-19
▲ *Longswamp, Berks, 19539* K-24
• Lorane, Berks, 19606 .... L-9
Loretto, Cambria, 15940 .... K-10
• Lower Allen, Cumberland, 17011 . I-29
▲ *Lower Alsace, Berks, 19606* L-23
Lower Burrell, Westmoreland, 15068 .... K-4
▲ *Lower Heidelberg, Berks, 19604* . L-22
▲ *Lower Milford, Lehigh, 18036* K-25
▲ *Lower Moreland, Montgomery, 19006* M-27
▲ *Lower Mount Bethel, Northampton, 18063* I-26
▲ *Lower Nazareth, Northampton, 18017* J-26
▲ *Lower Oxford, Chester, 19363* O-22
▲ *Lower Saucon, Northampton, 18015* J-26
▲ *Lower Swatara, Dauphin, 17057* . J-32
▲ *Lower Towamensing, Carbon, 18071* I-24
▲ *Lower Windsor, York, 17368* N-20
▲ *Lower Yoder, Cambria, 15906* L-8
▲ *Lowhill, Lehigh, 18080* J-24
▲ *Loyalhanna, Westmoreland, 15661* C-38
▲ *Loyalsock, Lycoming, 17701* F-18
• Lucerne Mines, Indiana, 15754 .... K-7
Luzerne, Luzerne, 18709 .... F-22
▲ *Lycoming, Lycoming, 17728* F-17
Lykens, Dauphin, 17048 .... K-19
Lynnwood, Luzerne, 18702 .... M-30
• Lynnwood-Pricedale, Fayette/ Westmoreland, 19152 .... M-4
Macungie, Lehigh, 18062 .... K-24
Mahanoy City, Schuylkill, 17948 ... I-22
▲ *Mahoning, Carbon, 18235* I-24
▲ *Mahoning, Lawrence, 16132* M-1
▲ *Maidencreek, Berks, 19522* K-23
Malvern, Chester, 19355 .... N-25
Manchester, York, 17345 .... N-19
Manheim, Lancaster, 17545 .... M-20
▲ *Manheim, York, 17545* O-19
▲ *Manor, Lancaster, 17603* N-20
Manor, Westmoreland, 15665 .... L-4
Mansfield, Tioga, 16933 .... C-17
• Maple Glen, Montgomery, 19002 .. I-38
Marcus Hook, Delaware, 19061 . O-25
Marietta, Lancaster, 17547 .... N-20
Markvue Manor, Westmoreland, 15642 .... D-36
▲ *Marlborough, Montgomery, 18084* L-25
Mars, Butler, 16064 .... J-3
▲ *Marshall, Allegheny, 15068* A-33
• Marshallton, Northumberland, 17672 .... I-20
▲ *Martic, Lancaster, 17565* O-21
Martinsburg, Blair, 16662 .... L-11
Marysville, Perry, 17053 .... L-18
Masontown, Fayette, 15461 .... O-3
Matamoras, Pike, 18336 .... F-28
Mather, Greene, 15346 .... N-3
▲ *Maxatawny, Berks, 19538* K-23
Mayfield, Lackawanna, 18433 .... E-24
• Maytown, Lancaster, 17550 .... N-20
McAdoo, Schuylkill, 18237 .... I-22
• *McCandless, Allegheny, 15084* .. J-33
• McChesneytown-Loyalhanna, Westmoreland, 15620 .... L-6
McClure, Snyder, 17841 .... J-16
McConnellsburg, Fulton, 17233 .. N-12
McDonald, Allegheny/ Washington, 15057 .... D-32
• McGovern, Washington, 15342 .. E-32
▲ *McKean, Erie, 16026* B-3
McKees Rocks, Allegheny, 15136 C-33
McKeesport, Allegheny, 15131-35 L-32
• McMurray, Washington, 15317 .... M-3
McSherrystown, Adams, 17344 .. O-17
Meadowbrook, Montgomery, 19046 .... J-39
Meadowlands, Washington, 15347 .... M-2
• Meadowood, Butler, 16045 .... I-4
Meadville, Crawford, 16335 .... D-3
Mechanicsburg, Cumberland, 17055 .... M-18
• Mechanicsville, Montour, 17821 . H-19
Media, Delaware, 19063 .... N-25
Mercer, Mercer, 16137 .... G-2
Mercersburg, Franklin, 17236 .... D-13
• Meridian, Butler, 16001 .... I-3
Merion, Montgomery, 19035 .... K-37
Meyersdale, Somerset, 15552 .... O-8
▲ *Middle Smithfield, Monroe, 18301* G-26
Middleburg, Snyder, 17842 .... I-17
▲ *Middlesex, Butler, 16059* J-3
Middletown, Dauphin, 17057 .... M-19
• Middletown, Northampton, 18017 J-25
Midland, Beaver, 15059 .... J-1
Midland, Washington, 15342 .... L-2
• Midway, Adams, 17331 .... O-18
Midway, Washington, 15060 .... L-2
Mifflinburg, Union, 17844 .... I-17
Mifflintown, Juniata, 17059 .... K-16
• Mifflinville, Columbia, 18631 .... H-21
Milesburg, Centre, 16853 .... H-14
▲ *Milford, Bucks, 18935* K-25
Milford, Pike, 18337 .... F-28
Mill Hall, Clinton, 17751 .... G-15
▲ *Millcreek, Erie, 16505* A-3
Millersburg, Dauphin, 17061 .... K-18
Millersville, Lancaster, 17551 .... N-20
Millvale, Allegheny, 15209 .... C-34
Milmont Park, Delaware,19033 ... Q-35
• Milroy, Mifflin, 17063 .... J-15
Milton, Northumberland,17847 ... H-18
Minersville, Schuylkill, 17954 .... J-21
Mohnton, Berks,19540 .... L-22
Monaca, Beaver, 15061 .... J-2
▲ *Monaghan, York, 17404* M-18
Monessen, Westmoreland, 15062 .... F-34
▲ *Monongahela, Greene, 17404* O-3
Monongahela, Washington, 15063 .... F-34
▲ *Monroe, Cumberland, 17055* M-17
Monroeville, Allegheny, 15146 .... K-4
Mont Alto, Franklin, 17237 .... O-15
Mont Clare, Montgomery,19453 .. J-36
Montgomery, Lycoming, 17752 ... G-18
• Montgomeryville, Montgomery, 18936 .... H-37
▲ *Montour, Columbia, 17815* H-20
Montoursville, Lycoming, 17754 . F-18
Montrose, Susquehanna, 18801 . C-23
Montrose Hill, Allegheny,15238 .. B-34
▲ *Moore, Northampton, 18014* I-25
Moosic, Lackawanna,18507 .... F-23
▲ *Morgan, Greene, 15346* N-3
▲ *Morris, Clearfield, 16821* I-11
Morrisville, Bucks, 19067 .... M-28
• Morrisville, Greene, 15370 .... N-2
Morton, Delaware,19070 .... P-36
Moscow, Lackawanna, 18444 .... F-24
Mount Carmel, Northumberland, 17851 .... I-20
• Mount Cobb, Lackawanna,18436 E-24
Mount Holly Springs, Cumberland, 17065 .... M-17
Mount Jewett, Mc Kean, 16740 .... D-9
▲ *Mount Joy, Adams, 17340* O-16
Mount Joy, Lancaster, 17552 .... M-20
• *Mount Lebanon, Allegheny, 15228* L-3
Mount Oliver, Allegheny, 15210 .. D-33
Mount Penn, Berks,19606 .... L-23
▲ *Mount Pleasant, Adams, 17331* .. O-18
Mount Pleasant, Westmoreland, 15666 .... M-5
Mount Pocono, Monroe, 18344 .. G-25
Mount Union, Huntingdon, 17066 L-13
Mount Wolf, York, 17347 .... N-19
• Mountainhome, Monroe, 18342 .. G-25
Mountaintop, Luzerne,18707 .... N-33
Mountville, Lancaster, 17554 .... N-20
Moylan, Delaware,19065 .... P-35
▲ *Muhlenberg, Berks, 19605* K-23
Muncy, Lycoming, 17756 .... G-18
▲ *Muncy Creek, Lycoming,17756* .. G-19
Munhall, Allegheny, 15120 .... L-3
Municipality of Murrysville, Westmoreland, 15668 .... B-36
Muse, Washington,15350 .... D-32
Myerstown, Lebanon, 17067 .... L-21
Nanticoke, Luzerne, 18634 .... G-22
Nanty-Glo, Cambria, 15943 .... K-9
Narberth, Montgomery, 19072 .... K-37
Natrona Heights, Allegheny,15065 J-4
Nazareth, Northampton,18064 .... I-25
• Nemacolin, Greene, 15351 .... O-3
Nescopeck, Luzerne, 18635 .... H-21
Nesquehoning, Carbon,18240 .... I-23
• *Nether Providence, Delaware, 19013* Q-35
▲ *Neville, Allegheny, 15225* C-32
New Beaver, Lawrence, 16141 .... I-1
New Bethlehem, Clarion, 16242 ... H-6
New Bloomfield, Perry,17068 .... L-17
New Brighton, Beaver, 15066 .... A-31
New Britain, Bucks, 18901 .... L-26
New Castle, Lawrence, 16101-02,05 .... H-2
• New Castle Northwest, Lawrence, 16105 .... H-2
New Cumberland, Cumberland, 17070 .... M-18
New Eagle, Washington, 15067 .... L-3
New Freedom, York, 17349 .... O-19
▲ *New Hanover, Montgomery, 19525* I-35
New Holland, Lancaster, 17557 .. M-22
New Hope, Bucks, 18938 .... L-27
New Kensington, Westmoreland, 15068 .... J-4
▲ *New London, Chester, 19360* O-23
New Oxford, Adams, 17350 .... O-17
New Philadelphia, Schuylkill, 17959 .... J-22
• New Salem-Buffington, Fayette, 15468 .... O-4
▲ *New Sewickley, Beaver, 15074* I-2
New Sheffield, Beaver,15001 .... B-31
New Stanton, Westmoreland, 15672 .... M-6
New Wilmington, Lawrence, 16142 G-2
• Newmanstown, Lebanon, 17073 . L-21
Newport, Perry, 17074 .... K-17
▲ *Newton, Lackawanna, 18411* E-23
Newtown, Bucks, 18940 .... L-27
▲ *Newtown, Delaware, 19073* N-25
• Newtown Grant, Bucks, 18940 .... I-40
Newtown Square, Delaware, 19073 .... O-35
Newville, Cumberland, 17241 .... M-16
• Nixon, Butler, 16001 .... I-4
▲ *Nockamixon, Bucks, 18930* K-27
Norristown, Montgomery, 19401,03 .... M-25
▲ *North Annville, Lebanon, 17038* .. L-20
North Apollo, Armstrong, 15673 .... J-5
North Ardmore, Montgomery, 19525 .... K-37
North Belle Vernon, Westmoreland, 15012 .... F-34
North Braddock, Allegheny, 15104 .... C-34
▲ *North Buffalo, Armstrong, 16201* ... J-5
North Catasauqua, Northampton, 18032 .... J-25
▲ *North Centre, Columbia, 18603* .. H-20
North Charleroi, Washington, 15022 .... F-34
▲ *North Codorus, York, 17362* O-18
North East, Erie, 16428 .... A-4
▲ *North Franklin, Washington, 15301* F-31
North Hills-Ardsley, Montgomery, 19038 .... I-38
▲ *North Hopewell, York, 17322* O-19
▲ *North Huntingdon, Westmoreland, 15642* E-36
▲ *North Londonderry, Lebanon, 17078* L-19
▲ *North Manheim, Schuylkill, 17901* J-22
▲ *North Sewickley, Beaver, 15010* I-2
▲ *North Strabane, Washington, 15317* E-33
• North Vandergrift-Pleasant View, Armstrong, 15690 .... J-5
• *North Versailles, Allegheny, 15137* L-32
North Wales, Montgomery, 19454 .... M-26
▲ *North Woodbury, Blair, 16662* K-11
North York, York, 17404 .... N-19
Northampton, Northampton, 18067 .... J-25
Northumberland, Northumberland, 17857 .... I-18
• Northwest Harborcreek, Erie, 16421 .... A-4
▲ *Norwegian, Schuylkill, 17951* J-22
Norwood, Delaware, 19074 .... Q-37
▲ *Nottingham, Washington, 15332* E-33
• Oak Hills, Butler, 16061 .... I-4
Oak Lane, Montgomery,19012 .... J-39
Oakdale, Allegheny, 15071 .... C-32
Oakford, Bucks,18942 .... I-40
▲ *Oakland, Butler, 16061* I-4
• Oakland, Lawrence, 16101 .... H-1
Oakmont, Allegheny,15139 .... B-35
• Oakwood, Lawrence, 16101 .... H-1
Ogden, Delaware,19061 .... R-35
• *O'Hara Township, Allegheny, 15238* C-35
▲ *Ohio, Allegheny, 15237* B-33
Ohioville, Beaver, 15059 .... J-1
Oil City, Venango, 16301 .... E-5
Old Forge, Lackawanna, 18518 .. F-23
• Old Orchard, Northampton, 18042 I-26
▲ *Oley, Berks, 19547* L-23
• Oliver, Fayette, 15472 .... N-4
▲ *Oliver, Perry, 17074* K-17
Olyphant, Lackawanna, 18447 ... E-24
▲ *Ontelaunee, Berks, 19605* K-23
• Orchard Hills, Armstrong,15713 ... K-6
• Oreland, Montgomery, 19075 .... I-38
Orwigsburg, Schuylkill, 17961 .... J-22
Osceola Mills, Clearfield, 16666 ... I-11
▲ *Overfield, Wyoming, 18414* E-23
▲ *Oxford, Adams, 17350* O-17
Oxford, Chester, 19363 .... O-23
Paint, Somerset, 15963 .... M-8
Palmdale, Dauphin,17033 .... I-33
• Palmer Heights, Northampton, 18042 .... I-26
Palmerton, Carbon, 18071 .... I-24
Palmyra, Lebanon, 17078 .... L-19
Palo Alto, Schuylkill, 17901 .... J-22
• Paoli, Chester, 19301 .... N-25
• Paradise, Lancaster, 17562 .... N-22
▲ *Paradise, Monroe, 18326* G-25
▲ *Paradise, York, 17301* O-18
• Park Forest Village, Centre, 16801 I-13
Parkesburg, Chester, 19365 .... N-23

Explanation of symbols: •– Census Designated Place (CDP) • *italics* – Township shown which is also a CDP ▲ *italics* – Townships (shown on the map)

COUNTIES

(5 Counties)

Name of County	Population	Location on Map
BRISTOL	48,859	G-10
KENT	161,135	G-3
NEWPORT	87,194	I-10
PROVIDENCE	596,270	A-2
WASHINGTON	110,006	I-3
TOTAL	1,003,464	

CITIES AND TOWNS

Note: The first name is that of the city or town, second, that of the county in which it is located, then the zip code area and location on the map.

Anthony, Kent, 02816 .... G-6
• Ashaway, Washington, 02804 .... L-3
Ashton, Providence, 02864 .... B-8
• *Barrington, Bristol, 02806* F-10
Berkeley, Providence, 02864 .... B-8
• Bradford, Washington, 02808 .... M-3
• *Bristol, Bristol, 02809* G-11
Central Falls, Providence, 02863 .... C-9
▲ *Charlestown, Washington, 02813* M-5
Chepachet, Providence, 02814 .... C-4
▲ *Coventry, Kent, 02816* G-4
Cranston, Providence, 02910, 20-21 ...... E-8
• Cumberland Hill, Providence, 02864 ...... A-8
▲ *East Greenwich, Kent, 02818* H-7
East Providence, Providence, 02914 ..... D-9
Esmond, Providence, 02917 .... C-7
Georgiaville, Providence, 02917 .... C-7
▲ *Glocester, Providence, 02814, 28, 57* C-4
• Greenville, Providence, 02828 .... C-6
• Harrisville, Providence, 02830 .... B-4
Harris, Kent, 02816 .... F-6
• Hope Valley, Washington, 02832 .... K-4
Island Park, Newport, 02871 .... H-11
▲ *Jamestown, Newport, 02835* J-9
▲ *Johnston, Providence, 02919* D-7
• Kingston, Washington, 02881 .... K-7
▲ *Lincoln, Providence, 02865* C-8
▲ *Little Compton, Newport, 02837* K-12
Lonsdale, Providence, 02860 .... C-8
Manville, Providence, 02838 .... B-7
• Melville, Newport, 02840 .... I-10
Middletown, Newport, 02840 .... J-10
• Narragansett Pier, Washington, 02882 ... L-8
Newport, Newport, 02840 .... K-10
• Newport East, Newport, 02840 .... K-10
▲ *North Kingstown, Washington, 02852* I-8
• *North Providence, Providence, 02911* D-8
▲ *North Smithfield, Providence, 02896* A-6
North Tiverton, Newport, 02877 .... H-11
• Pascoag, Providence, 02859 .... B-4
Pawtucket, Providence, 02860-61 .... C-9
Portsmouth, Newport, 02871 .... I-11
Providence, Providence, 02903-09 .... D-8
Quidnick, Kent, 02816 .... G-6
▲ *Richmond, Washington, 02812* K-5
Saylesville, Providence, 02865 .... C-8
▲ *Scituate, Providence, 02815, 25, 57* E-6
Slatersville, Providence, 02876 .... A-6
The Anchorage, Newport, 02840 .... J-10
• Tiverton, Newport, 02878 .... H-12
Union Village, Providence, 02895 .... A-7
• Valley Falls, Providence, 02864 .... C-9
• Wakefield-Peacedale, Washington,
  02879, 83 .... L-7
▲ *Warren, Bristol, 02885* F-10
Warwick, Kent, 02886, 88-89 .... G-8
• *West Warwick, Kent, 02893* G-7
• Westerly, Washington, 02891 .... M-2
Woonsocket, Providence, 02895 .... A-7

Explanation of symbols: • – Census Designated Place (CDP)   • *italics* – Township shown which is also a CDP   ▲ *italics* – Townships (shown on the map)

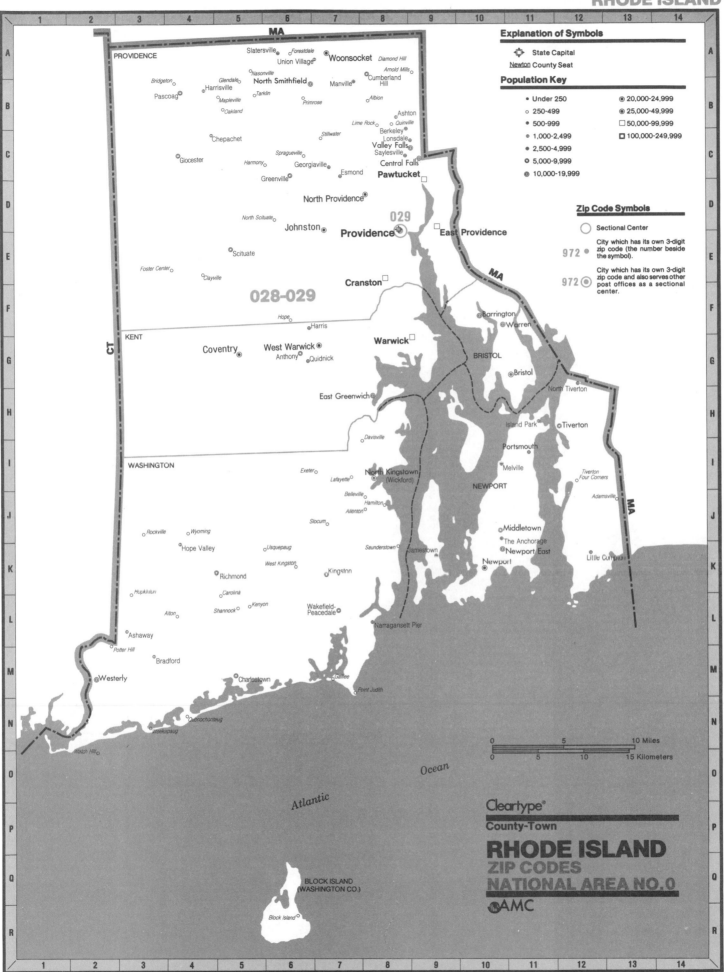

Explanation of Symbols

◇ State Capital

Newton County Seat

Population Key

•	Under 250	◉	20,000-24,999
○	250-499	◉	25,000-49,999
•	500-999	☐	50,000-99,999
◔	1,000-2,499	☐	100,000-249,999
◑	2,500-4,999		
◐	5,000-9,999		
◉	10,000-19,999		

Zip Code Symbols

○ Sectional Center

972 • City which has its own 3-digit zip code (the number beside the symbol).

972 ◉ City which has its own 3-digit zip code and also serves other post offices as a sectional center.

MA

PROVIDENCE

Slatersville
Forestdale
Union Village
Woonsocket
Diamond Hill
Arnold Mills
Bridgeton
Glendale
Nasonville
Harrisville
Mapleville
North Smithfield
Manville
Cumberland Hill
Pascoag
Tarklin
Oakland
Primrose
Albion
Ashton
Lime Rock
Quinville
Chepachet
Stillwater
Berkeley
Lonsdale
Spragueville
Valley Falls
Glocester
Harmony
Georgiaville
Saylesville
Greenville
Esmond
Central Falls
Pawtucket

North Providence

North Scituate
029
Johnston
Providence
East Providence

Scituate

Foster Center
Clayville
028-029
Cranston

CT

KENT

Hope
Harris

Coventry
West Warwick
Warwick
Anthony
Quidnick

Barrington
Warren

BRISTOL

Bristol

East Greenwich

North Tiverton

MA

Davisville

Island Park
Tiverton

Portsmouth

WASHINGTON

Exeter
Lafayette
North Kingstown
(Wickford)
Melville

Tiverton Four Corners

Belleville
Hamilton
NEWPORT
Adamsville
Allenton

Slocum

MA

Rockville
Wyoming
Usquepaug
Middletown
The Anchorage
Hope Valley
Saunderstown
Jamestown
Newport East
West Kingston
Little Compton
Richmond
Kingston
Newport

Hopkinton
Carolina
Alton
Shannock
Kenyon
Wakefield-
Peacedale

Ashaway
Potter Hill
Narragansett Pier
Bradford

Westerly
Charlestown
Galilee
Point Judith

Quonochontaug
Weekapaug

Watch Hill

Ocean

Atlantic

| 0 | | | 5 | | 10 Miles |
| 0 | 5 | | | 10 | 15 Kilometers |

Cleartype®

County-Town

RHODE ISLAND
ZIP CODES
NATIONAL AREA NO.0

◉AMC

BLOCK ISLAND
(WASHINGTON CO.)

Block Island

Copyright American Map Corporation

COUNTIES

(46 Counties)

Name of County	Population	Location on Map
ABBEVILLE	23,862	E-3
AIKEN	120,940	G-6
ALLENDALE	11,722	J-7
ANDERSON	145,196	C-2
BAMBERG	16,902	I-8
BARNWELL	20,293	I-7
BEAUFORT	86,425	M-9
BERKELEY	128,776	H-11
CALHOUN	12,753	H-9
CHARLESTON	295,039	K-11
CHEROKEE	44,506	B-6
CHESTER	32,170	B-7
CHESTERFIELD	38,577	C-10
CLARENDON	28,450	G-11
COLLETON	34,377	J-8
DARLINGTON	61,851	D-11
DILLON	29,114	D-13
DORCHESTER	83,060	I-9
EDGEFIELD	18,375	F-5
FAIRFIELD	22,295	D-7
FLORENCE	114,344	E-12
GEORGETOWN	46,302	G-14
GREENVILLE	320,167	A-3
GREENWOOD	59,567	E-4
HAMPTON	18,191	K-8
HORRY	144,053	E-14
JASPER	15,487	L-8
KERSHAW	43,599	D-9
LANCASTER	54,516	C-9
LAURENS	58,092	C-4
LEE	18,437	E-10
LEXINGTON	167,611	F-7
MARION	33,899	F-13
MARLBORO	29,361	C-12
MCCORMICK	8,868	F-4
NEWBERRY	33,172	D-6
OCONEE	57,494	B-1
ORANGEBURG	84,803	H-8
PICKENS	93,894	B-2
RICHLAND	285,720	E-7
SALUDA	16,357	E-6
SPARTANBURG	226,800	C-5
SUMTER	102,637	E-10
UNION	30,337	B-6
WILLIAMSBURG	36,815	G-12
YORK	131,497	A-7
TOTAL	3,486,703	

CITIES AND TOWNS

Note: The first name is that of the city or town, second, that of the county in which it is located, then the zip code area and location on the map.

Abbeville, Abbeville, 29620 ... E-4
Aiken, Aiken, 29801,03 ... H-6
Allendale, Allendale, 29810 ... J-7
Anderson, Anderson, 29621, 24-25 ... D-3
Andrews, Georgetown/Williamsburg, 29510 ... H-13
•Arial, Pickens, 29640 ... B-3
Baldwin-Aragon Mills, Chester, 29706,30 ... C-7
Bamberg, Bamberg, 29003 ... I-8
Barnwell, Barnwell, 29812 ... I-7
Batesburg, Lexington/Saluda, 29006 ... F-7
Beaufort, Beaufort, 29902 ... L-10
Belton, Anderson, 29627 ... D-3
Belvedere, Aiken, 29841 ... H-5
Bendale, Richland, 29203 ... E-8
Bennettsville, Marlboro, 29512 ... C-13
Bennettsville Southwest, Marlboro, 29512 ... C-12
Berea, Greenville, 29610 ... B-3
Bishopville, Lee, 29010 ... E-11
Blacksburg, Cherokee, 29702 ... A-7
Blackville, Barnwell, 29817 ... I-8
Boiling Springs, Spartanburg, 29316 ... A-5
Bowman, Orangeburg, 29018 ... H-9
Branchville, Orangeburg, 29432 ... I-9
Brandon, Greenville, 29611 ... B-4
Brookdale, Orangeburg, 29115 ... H-9
Bucksport, Horry, 29527 ... G-15
Buffalo, Union, 29321 ... C-6
Burton, Beaufort, 29902 ... L-9
Calhoun Falls, Abbeville, 29628 ... E-3
Camden, Kershaw, 29020 ... E-10
Cayce, Lexington, 29033 ... F-8
Centerville, Anderson, 29565 ... C-3
Central, Pickens, 29630 ... C-2
Charleston, Charleston, 29401-20 ... K-12
Charleston Base, Charleston, 29404 ... K-12
Charleston Yard, Charleston, 29408 ... K-12
Cheraw, Chesterfield, 29520 ... C-12
Cherryvale, Sumter, 29154 ... F-10
Chesnee, Cherokee/Spartanburg, 29323 ... A-5
Chester, Chester, 29706 ... C-8
Chesterfield, Chesterfield, 29709 ... C-11
City View, Greenville, 29611 ... B-3
Clearwater, Aiken, 29822 ... H-5
Clemson, Anderson/Pickens, 29631 ... C-2
Clifton, Spartanburg, 29324 ... A-5
Clinton, Laurens, 29325 ... D-5
Clover, York, 29710 ... A-7
Columbia, Richland, 29201-23, 26-27 ... F-8
Conway, Horry, 29526-27 ... F-15
Cowpens, Spartanburg, 29330 ... A-6
Darlington, Darlington, 29532,40 ... D-12
Denmark, Bamberg, 29042 ... I-8
Dentsville, Richland, 29204 ... E-9
Dillon, Dillon, 29536 ... D-14
Due West, Abbeville, 29639 ... D-4
Duncan, Spartanburg, 29334 ... B-5
Dunean, Greenville, 29601 ... B-4
Dupont, Charleston, 29407 ... K-11
Easley, Pickens, 29640,42 ... B-3
•East Gaffney, Cherokee, 29340 ... A-6
•East Sumter, Sumter, 29150 ... F-11
Eastover, Richland, 29044 ... F-9
•Edgefield, Edgefield, 29824 ... G-5
•Edisto, Orangeburg, 29038 ... H-9
Elgin, Lancaster, 29045 ... C-9
Estill, Hampton, 29918 ... K-8
•Eureka Mill, Chester, 29706 ... C-8
Fairfax, Allendale/Hampton, 29827 ... J-8
Florence, Florence, 29501,05-06 ... E-12
Folly Beach, Charleston, 29439 ... K-12
Forest Acres, Richland, 29206 ... F-8
•Forestbrook, Horry, 29577 ... G-15
Fort Mill, York, 29715 ... B-8
Fountain Inn, Greenville/Laurens, 29644 ... C-4
Gaffney, Cherokee, 29340-41 ... A-6
•Gantt, Greenville, 29605 ... C-4
•Gayle Mill, Chester, 29706 ... C-8
Georgetown, Georgetown, 29440 ... G-14
Glendale, Spartanburg, 29346 ... A-5
•Gloverville, Aiken, 29828 ... H-6
Golden Grove, Greenville, 29673 ... C-4
Goose Creek, Berkeley/Charleston, 29445 ... J-12
Great Falls, Chester, 29055 ... C-9
Greenville, Greenville, 29601-15 ... B-4
Greenwood, Greenwood, 29646,49 ... E-5
Greer, Greenville/Spartanburg, 29650-51 ... B-4
Hampton, Hampton, 29924 ... K-8
Hanahan, Berkeley, 29410 ... J-12
Hardeeville, Jasper, 29927 ... M-8
Hartsville, Darlington, 29550 ... D-11
Hillbrook, Spartanburg, 29307 ... A-5
Hilton Head Island, Beaufort, 29926,28 ... M-9
Holly Hill, Orangeburg, 29059 ... I-10
Hollywood, Charleston, 29449 ... K-11
Homeland Park, Anderson, 29621 ... D-3
Honea Path, Abbeville/Anderson, 29654 ... D-4
India Hook, York, 29730 ... A-8
Inman, Spartanburg, 29349 ... A-5
Inman Mills, Spartanburg, 29349 ... A-5
Irmo, Lexington/Richland, 29063 ... E-8
Isle of Palms, Charleston, 29451 ... K-13
Iva, Anderson, 29655 ... E-3
Jackson, Aiken, 29831 ... I-6
Joanna, Laurens, 29351 ... D-6
Johnsonville, Florence, 29555 ... F-13
Johnston, Edgefield, 29832 ... G-6
Jonesville, Union, 29353 ... B-6
Judson, Greenville, 29611 ... B-4
Kershaw, Lancaster, 29067 ... D-10
Kingstree, Williamsburg, 29556 ... G-12
Ladson, Berkeley/Charleston, 29456 ... J-11
Lake City, Florence, 29560 ... F-12
Lake Wylie, York, 29710 ... A-8
Lamar, Darlington, 29069 ... E-11
Lancaster, Lancaster, 29720 ... C-9
•Lancaster Mill, Lancaster, 29720 ... C-9
Landrum, Spartanburg, 29356 ... A-4
Latta, Dillon, 29565 ... D-13
•Laurel Bay, Beaufort, 29902 ... L-9
Laurens, Laurens, 29360 ... D-5
Leesville, Lexington, 29070 ... F-7
Lexington, Lexington, 29072-73 ... F-8
Liberty, Pickens, 29657 ... B-3
•Little River, Horry, 29566 ... F-16
Loris, Horry, 29569 ... E-15
Lugoff, Kershaw, 29078 ... E-10
Lyman, Spartanburg, 29365 ... A-5
Manning, Clarendon, 29102 ... G-11
Marion, Marion, 29571 ... E-14
Mauldin, Greenville, 29662 ... C-4
•Mayo, Spartanburg, 29368 ... B-5
McColl, Marlboro, 29570 ... C-13
McCormick, McCormick, 28835 ... F-4
Millwood, Sumter, 29150 ... F-10
•Monarch Mill, Union, 29379 ... C-6
Moncks Corner, Berkeley, 29461 ... I-12
Mount Pleasant, Charleston, 29464 ... K-12
•Mulberry, Sumter, 29379 ... F-11
Mullins, Marion, 29574 ... E-14
•Murrells Inlet, Georgetown, 29576 ... G-15
Myrtle Beach, Horry, 29572,75,77 ... G-15
Myrtle Beach Base, Horry, 29579 ... G-15
New Ellenton, Aiken, 29809 ... H-6
Newberry, Newberry, 29108 ... E-6
Ninety Six, Greenwood, 29666 ... E-5
North Augusta, Aiken/Edgefield, 29841 ... H-5
North Charleston, Berkeley/Charleston/Dorchester, 29418 ... J-12
North Hartsville, Darlington, 29550 ... D-11
North Myrtle Beach, Horry, 29582 ... F-16
•Northlake, Anderson, 29624 ... C-3
Oak Grove, Lexington, 29073 ... F-8
•Oakland, Sumter, 29150 ... F-10
Orangeburg, Orangeburg, 29115 ... H-9
Pacolet, Spartanburg, 29372 ... B-6
Pageland, Chesterfield, 29728 ... B-10
Pamplico, Florence, 29583 ... E-13
Paris, Greenville, 29609 ... B-4
Park Place, Greenville, 29608 ... B-4
•Parker, Greenville, 29142 ... B-4
Parris Island, Beaufort, 29905 ... M-10
Pendleton, Anderson, 29670 ... C-3
Pickens, Pickens, 29671 ... B-3
•Piedmont, Anderson/Greenville, 29673 ... C-3
Pineridge, Lexington, 29172 ... F-8
Port Royal, Beaufort, 29935 ... M-9
Prosperity, Newberry, 29127 ... E-7
Ravenel, Charleston, 29470 ... K-11
Red Bank, Lexington, 29073 ... F-7
•Red Hill, Horry, 29526 ... F-15
Ridgeland, Jasper, 29936 ... L-8
Ridgeville, Dorchester, 29472 ... I-11
Rock Hill, York, 29730,32 ... B-8
•Roebuck, Spartanburg, 29376 ... B-5
•Saint Andrews, Richland, 29407 ... F-8
Saint George, Dorchester, 29477 ... I-10
Saint Matthews, Calhoun, 29135 ... G-9
Saint Stephen, Berkeley, 29479 ... H-12
Saluda, Saluda, 29138 ... F-6
•Sans Souci, Greenville, 29609 ... B-4
Saxon, Spartanburg, 29301 ... B-5
Seneca, Oconee, 29678 ... C-2
Seven Oaks, Lexington, 29210 ... E-8
Shannontown, Sumter, 29150 ... F-11
Shell Point, Beaufort, 29902 ... M-9
Simpsonville, Greenville, 29681 ... C-4
Slater-Marietta, Greenville, 29661, 83 ... A-3
•Socastee, Horry, 29575,77 ... G-15
South Congaree, Lexington, 29172 ... F-8
South Sumter, Sumter, 29150 ... F-10
•Southern Shops, Spartanburg, 29303 ... B-5
Spartanburg, Spartanburg, 29301-18 ... B-5
•Springdale, Lancaster, 29720 ... C-9
Springdale, Lexington, 29170 ... F-8
•Startex, Spartanburg, 29377 ... B-5
Sullivan's Island, Charleston, 29482 ... K-12
Summerville, Berkeley/Charleston/Dorchester, 29483,85 ... J-11
Sumter, Sumter, 29150,53-54 ... F-11
Surfside Beach, Horry, 29575 ... G-15
•Taylors, Greenville, 29687 ... B-4
Tega Cay, York, 29715 ... A-8
Timmonsville, Florence, 29161 ... E-12
Travelers Rest, Greenville, 29690 ... B-4
Union, Union, 29379 ... C-6
Utica, Oconee, 29678 ... C-2
•Valencia Heights, Richland, 29205 ... F-8
Valley Falls, Spartanburg, 29303 ... A-5
Varnville, Hampton, 29944 ... K-8
Wade Hampton, Greenville, 29607 ... B-4
Walhalla, Oconee, 29691 ... C-2
Walterboro, Colleton, 29488 ... J-10
Ware Shoals, Abbeville/Greenwood, 29692 ... D-4
Watts Mills, Laurens, 29611 ... D-5
Welcome, Greenville, 29611 ... B-4
Wellford, Spartanburg, 29385 ... A-5
West Columbia, Lexington, 29169-70,72 ... F-8
Westminster, Oconee, 29693 ... C-1
Whitmire, Newberry, 29178 ... D-6
•Wilkinson Heights, Orangeburg, 29115 ... H-9
Williamston, Anderson, 29697 ... C-3
Williston, Barnwell, 29853 ... H-7
Winnsboro Mills, Fairfield, 29180 ... D-8
Woodfield, Richland, 29206 ... F-9
Woodruff, Spartanburg, 29388 ... C-5
York, York, 29745 ... B-7

Explanation of symbols: ● – Census Designated Place (CDP)

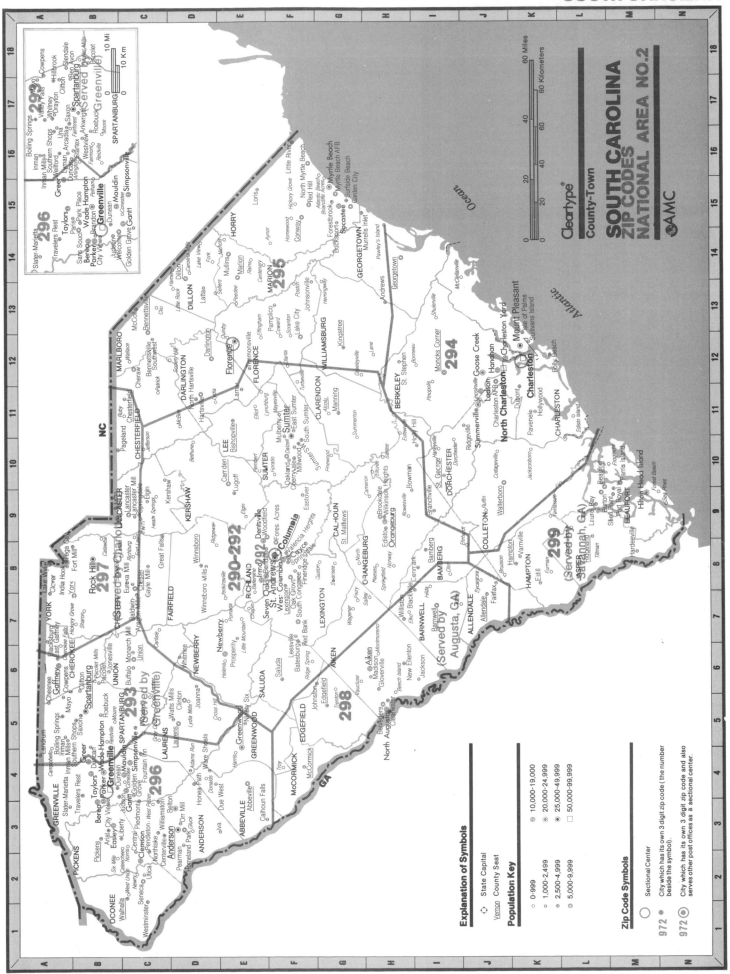

SOUTH CAROLINA
ZIP CODES
NATIONAL AREA NO.2

Cleartype®
County-Town

⊙AMC

Explanation of Symbols

✦ State Capital
Vernon County Seat

Population Key

○ 0-999
⊙ 1,000-2,499
⊕ 2,500-4,999
⊛ 5,000-9,999
⊚ 10,000-19,000
⊛ 20,000-24,999
⊛ 25,000-49,999
☐ 50,000-99,999

Zip Code Symbols

◯ Sectional Center
972 • City which has its own 3 digit zip code (the number beside the symbol).
972 ◉ City which has its own 3 digit zip code and also serves other post offices as a sectional center.

Copyright American Map Corporation

COUNTIES

(66 Counties)

Name of County	Population	Location on Map
AURORA	3,135	H-13
BEADLE	18,253	F-13
BENNETT	3,206	J-5
BON HOMME	7,089	J-14
BROOKINGS	25,207	F-17
BROWN	35,580	A-13
BRULE	5,485	H-12
BUFFALO	1,759	G-11
BUTTE	7,914	C-1
CAMPBELL	1,965	A-9
CHARLES MIX	9,131	I-12
CLARK	4,403	D-15
CLAY	13,186	K-17
CODINGTON	22,698	D-16
CORSON	4,195	A-6
CUSTER	6,179	H-1
DAVISON	17,503	H-14
DAY	6,978	B-15
DEUEL	4,522	D-17
DEWEY	5,523	C-7
DOUGLAS	3,746	I-13
EDMUNDS	4,356	B-11
FALL RIVER	7,353	I-1
FAULK	2,744	C-11
GRANT	8,372	C-16
GREGORY	5,359	J-11
HAAKON	2,624	F-6
HAMLIN	4,974	E-16
HAND	4,272	E-12
HANSON	2,994	H-15
HARDING	1,669	A-1
HUGHES	14,817	F-9
HUTCHINSON	8,262	I-14
HYDE	1,696	E-11
JACKSON	2,811	H-6
JERAULD	2,425	G-13
JONES	1,324	G-8
KINGSBURY	5,925	F-15
LAKE	10,550	G-16
LAWRENCE	20,655	F-1
LINCOLN	15,427	I-17
LYMAN	3,638	G-9
MARSHALL	4,844	A-15
MCCOOK	5,688	H-16
MCPHERSON	3,228	A-11
MEADE	21,878	D-4
MELLETTE	2,137	H-7
MINER	3,272	G-15
MINNEHAHA	123,809	H-17
MOODY	6,507	G-17
PENNINGTON	81,343	G-1
PERKINS	3,932	A-4
POTTER	3,190	C-10
ROBERTS	9,914	A-16
SANBORN	2,833	G-14
SHANNON	9,902	I-4
SPINK	7,981	C-13
STANLEY	2,453	E-8
SULLY	1,589	E-9
TODD	8,352	J-7
TRIPP	6,924	I-10
TURNER	8,576	I-16
UNION	10,189	K-17
WALWORTH	6,087	B-9
YANKTON	19,252	J-16
ZIEBACH	2,220	C-6
TOTAL	**696,004**	

CITIES AND TOWNS

Note: The first name is that of the city or town, second, that of the county in which it is located, then the zip code area and location on the map.

Aberdeen, Brown, 57401	C-14
Alexandria, Hanson, 57311	I-15
Armour, Douglas, 57313	J-14
Belle Fourche, Butte, 57717	E-1
Beresford, Lincoln/Union, 57004	K-17
Bison, Perkins, 57620	B-5
• Blackhawk, Meade, 57718	G-2
Box Elder, Pennington,57719	G-3
Brandon, Minnehaha, 57705	I-18
Britton, Marshall, 57430	B-15
Brookings, Brookings, 57006	F-17
Buffalo, Harding, 57720	B-2
Burke, Gregory, 57523	J-12
Canton, Lincoln, 57013	J-18
Chamberlain, Brule, 57325	H-11
Clark, Clark, 57225	E-15
Clear Lake, Deuel, 57226	E-17
• Colonial Pine Hills, Pennington, 57701	H-2
Custer, Custer,57730	H-2
De Smet, Kingsbury, 57231	F-16
Deadwood, Lawrence, 57732	F-2
Dell Rapids, Minnehaha, 57022	H-18
Dupree, Ziebach, 57623	D-7
Elk Point, Union, 57025	L-18
• Ellsworth AFB, Meade/Pennington, 57706	G-3
Eureka, McPherson, 57437	B-11
Faulkton, Faulk, 57438	D-12
Flandreau, Moody, 57028	G-18
Fort Pierre, Stanley, 57532	F-9
• Fort Thompson, Buffalo, 57339	G-11
Freeman, Hutchinson, 57029	J-16
Gannvalley, Buffalo, 57341	G-12
Gettysburg, Potter, 57442	D-10
Gregory, Gregory, 57533	J-11
Groton, Brown, 57445	C-14
Hartford, Minnehaha, 57033	I-17
Highmore, Hyde, 57345	F-11
Hot Springs, Fall River, 57747	I-2
Howard, Miner, 57349	H-16
Huron, Beadle, 57350	F-14
Ipswich, Edmunds, 57451	C-12
Kadoka, Jackson, 57543	H-7
Kennebec, Lyman, 57544	H-10
Lake Andes, Charles Mix, 57356	J-13
Lake Norden, Hamlin, 57248	E-16
Lead, Lawrence, 57754	F-2
Lemmon, Perkins, 57638	A-5
Lennox, Lincoln, 57039	J-17
Leola, McPherson, 57456	B-13
Madison, Lake, 57042	G-17
Martin, Bennett, 57551	J-6
McIntosh, Corson, 57641	A-7
Milbank, Grant, 57252	C-18
Miller, Hand, 57362	F-12
Mitchell, Davison, 57301	I-15
Mobridge, Walworth, 57601	B-9
Mound City, Campbell, 57646	B-10
Murdo, Jones, 57559	H-9
• North Eagle Butte, Dewey, 57625	D-7
North Sioux City, Union,57049	L-18
• North Spearfish, Lawrence, 57783	F-2
Olivet, Hutchinson, 57052	J-15
Onida, Sully, 57564	E-10
Parker, Turner, 57053	J-17
Parkston, Hutchinson, 57366	J-15
Philip, Haakon, 57567	G-6
Pierre, Hughes, 57501	F-9
Pine Ridge, Shannon, 57770	K-4
Plankinton, Aurora, 57368	I-14
Platte, Charles Mix, 57369	J-13
Rapid City, Pennington, 57701-02	G-3
• Rapid Valley, Pennington, 57701	G-3
Redfield, Spink, 57469	E-13
Rosebud, Todd, 57570	J-8
Salem, McCook, 57058	H-16
Selby, Walworth, 57472	C-10
Sioux Falls, Lincoln/Minnehaha, 57101-99	I-17
Sisseton, Roberts, 57262	B-17
Spearfish, Lawrence, 57783	F-1
Sturgis, Meade, 57785	F-2
Timber Lake, Dewey,57656	C-8
Tyndall, Bon Homme, 57066	K-15
Vermillion, Clay, 57069	L-17
Volga, Brookings, 57071	F-17
Wagner, Charles Mix, 57380	K-14
Watertown, Codington, 57201	D-17
Webster, Day, 57274	C-16
Wessington Springs, Jerauld, 57381	G-13
White River, Mellette, 57579	I-8
Winner, Tripp, 57580	J-10
Woonsocket, Sanborn, 57385	G-14
Yankton, Yankton, 57078	K-16

Explanation of symbols: ● – Census Designated Place (CDP)

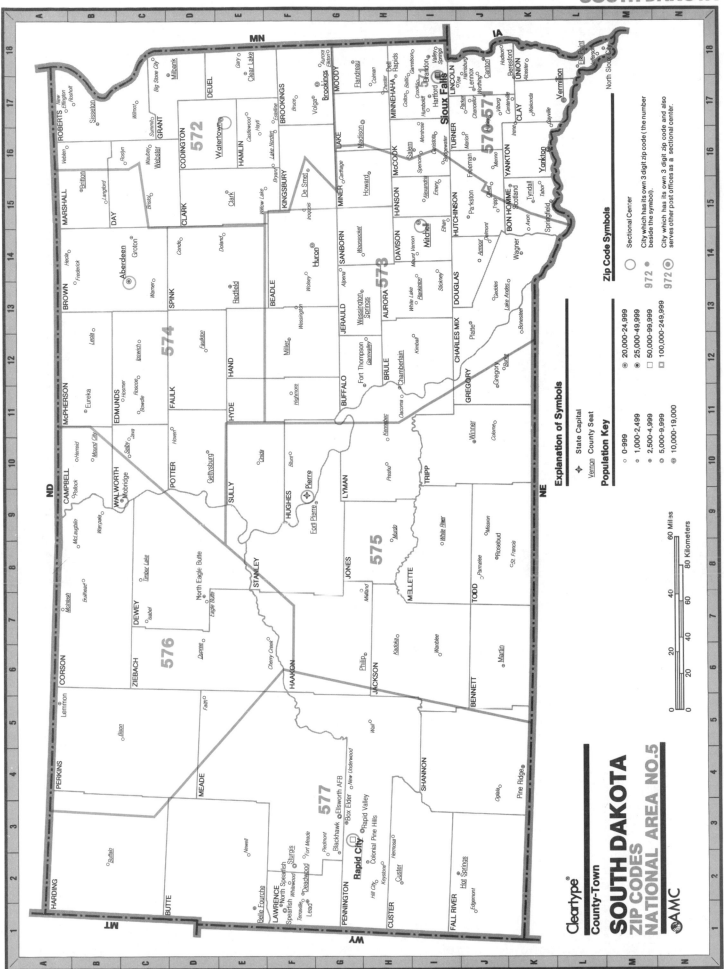

Copyright American Map Corporation

Explanation of symbols: ● – Census Designated Place (CDP)

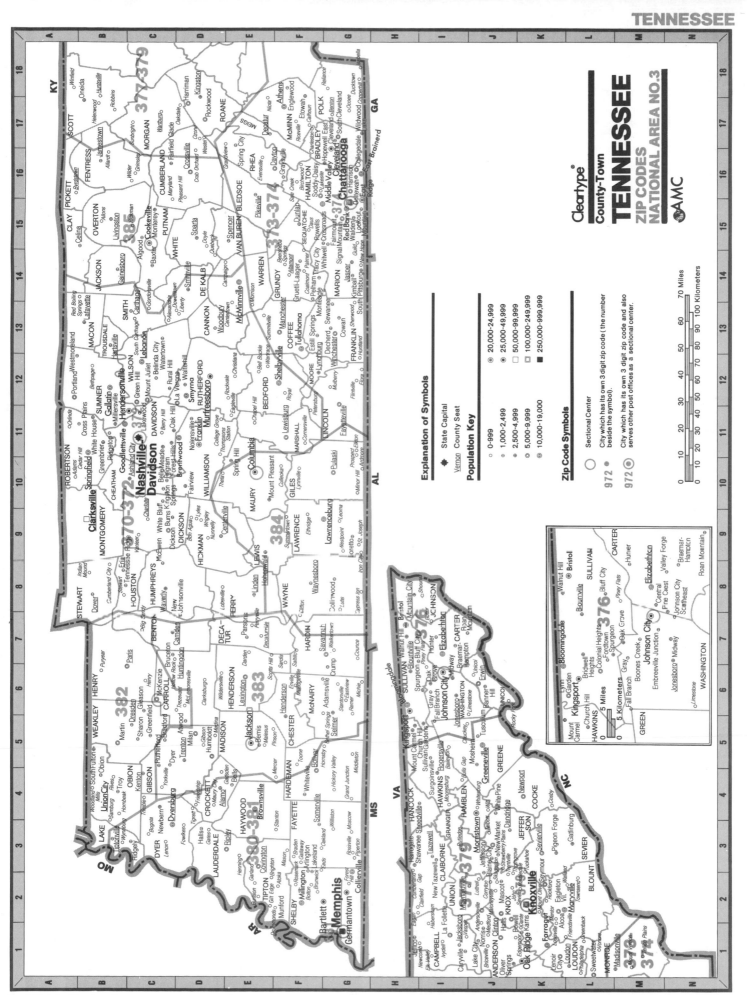

Copyright American Map Corporation

COUNTIES

(254 Counties)

Name of County	Population	Location on Map
ANDERSON	48,024	H-11
ANDREWS	14,338	G-2
ANGELINA	69,884	I-13
ARANSAS	17,892	M-9
ARCHER	7,973	E-7
ARMSTRONG	2,021	C-4
ATASCOSA	30,533	L-7
AUSTIN	19,832	J-10
BAILEY	7,064	D-2
BANDERA	10,562	K-6
BASTROP	38,263	J-9
BAYLOR	4,385	E-6
BEE	25,135	M-8
BELL	191,088	I-9
BEXAR	1,185,394	K-7
BLANCO	5,972	J-8
BORDEN	799	F-3
BOSQUE	15,125	H-8
BOWIE	81,665	F-13
BRAZORIA	191,707	K-12
BRAZOS	121,862	I-11
BREWSTER	8,681	J-1
BRISCOE	1,971	C-4
BROOKS	8,204	O-8
BROWN	34,371	H-7
BURLESON	13,625	J-10
BURNET	22,677	I-8
CALDWELL	26,392	K-9
CALHOUN	19,053	M-10
CALLAHAN	11,859	G-6
CAMERON	260,120	Q-9
CAMP	9,904	F-12
CARSON	6,576	B-4
CASS	29,982	F-13
CASTRO	9,070	C-2
CHAMBERS	20,088	K-13
CHEROKEE	41,049	G-12
CHILDRESS	5,953	C-5
CLAY	10,024	E-8
COCHRAN	4,377	E-2
COKE	3,424	H-5
COLEMAN	9,710	H-6
COLLIN	264,036	F-10
COLLINGSWORTH	3,573	C-5
COLORADO	18,383	K-10
COMAL	51,832	K-8
COMANCHE	13,381	H-7
CONCHO	3,044	I-6
COOKE	30,777	F-9
CORYELL	64,213	I-8
COTTLE	2,247	D-5
CRANE	4,652	H-2
CROCKETT	4,078	I-3
CROSBY	7,304	F-4
CULBERSON	3,407	N-3
DALLAM	5,461	A-2
DALLAS	1,852,810	F-10
DAWSON	14,349	F-3
DEWITT	18,840	L-9
DEAF SMITH	19,153	C-2
DELTA	4,857	E-12
DENTON	273,525	F-9
DICKENS	2,571	E-4
DIMMIT	10,433	M-5
DONLEY	3,696	C-4
DUVAL	12,918	N-7
EASTLAND	18,488	G-7
ECTOR	118,934	H-2
EDWARDS	2,266	J-5
EL PASO	591,610	N-1
ELLIS	85,167	G-10
ERATH	27,991	G-8
FALLS	17,712	I-10
FANNIN	24,804	E-11
FAYETTE	20,095	J-10
FISHER	4,842	G-5
FLOYD	8,497	D-4
FOARD	1,794	E-6
FORT BEND	225,421	K-11
FRANKLIN	7,802	E-12
FREESTONE	15,818	H-11
FRIO	13,472	L-6
GAINES	14,123	F-2
GALVESTON	217,399	K-13
GARZA	5,143	F-4
GILLESPIE	17,204	J-7
GLASSCOCK	1,447	H-3
GOLIAD	5,980	L-9
GONZALES	17,205	K-9
GRAY	23,967	C-4
GRAYSON	95,021	E-10
GREGG	104,948	G-13
GRIMES	18,828	I-11
GUADALUPE	64,873	K-8
HALE	34,671	D-3
HALL	3,905	C-4
HAMILTON	7,733	H-8
HANSFORD	5,848	A-4
HARDEMAN	5,283	D-6
HARDIN	41,320	J-13
HARRIS	2,818,199	K-12
HARRISON	57,483	G-13
HARTLEY	3,634	A-2
HASKELL	6,820	F-6
HAYS	65,614	J-8
HEMPHILL	3,720	A-5
HENDERSON	58,543	G-11
HIDALGO	383,545	O-8
HILL	27,146	H-9
HOCKLEY	24,199	E-2
HOOD	28,981	G-8
HOPKINS	28,833	F-11
HOUSTON	21,375	H-12
HOWARD	32,343	G-3
HUDSPETH	2,915	N-1
HUNT	64,343	F-11
HUTCHINSON	25,689	A-4
IRION	1,629	H-4
JACK	6,981	F-8
JACKSON	13,039	L-10
JASPER	31,102	I-14
JEFF DAVIS	1,946	O-3
JEFFERSON	239,397	K-13
JIM HOGG	5,109	O-7
JIM WELLS	37,679	N-8
JOHNSON	97,165	G-9
JONES	16,490	F-6
KARNES	12,455	L-8
KAUFMAN	52,220	G-11
KENDALL	14,589	K-7
KENEDY	460	O-8
KENT	1,010	F-4
KERR	36,304	J-6
KIMBLE	4,122	J-5
KING	354	E-5
KINNEY	3,119	K-5
KLEBERG	30,274	N-8
KNOX	4,837	E-6
LA SALLE	5,254	M-6
LAMAR	43,949	E-11
LAMB	15,072	D-2
LAMPASAS	13,521	I-8
LAVACA	18,690	L-10
LEE	12,854	J-9
LEON	12,665	I-11
LIBERTY	52,726	J-13
LIMESTONE	20,946	H-10
LIPSCOMB	3,143	A-5
LIVE OAK	9,556	M-8
LLANO	11,631	I-7
LOVING	107	H-1
LUBBOCK	222,636	E-3
LYNN	6,758	F-3
MADISON	10,931	I-11
MARION	9,984	F-13
MARTIN	4,956	G-3
MASON	3,423	I-6
MATAGORDA	36,928	L-11
MAVERICK	36,378	L-5
MCCULLOCH	8,778	I-6
MCLENNAN	189,123	H-9
MCMULLEN	817	M-7
MEDINA	27,312	K-6
MENARD	2,252	I-5
MIDLAND	106,611	H-3
MILAM	22,946	I-10
MILLS	4,531	H-7
MITCHELL	8,016	G-4
MONTAGUE	17,274	E-8
MONTGOMERY	182,201	J-11
MOORE	17,865	B-3
MORRIS	13,200	F-13
MOTLEY	1,532	D-4
NACOGDOCHES	54,753	H-13
NAVARRO	39,926	H-10
NEWTON	13,569	I-14
NOLAN	16,594	G-5
NUECES	291,145	N-8
OCHILTREE	9,128	A-4
OLDHAM	2,278	B-2
ORANGE	80,509	J-14
PALO PINTO	25,055	G-8
PANOLA	22,035	G-13
PARKER	64,785	F-8
PARMER	9,863	C-2
PECOS	14,675	I-2
POLK	30,687	I-13
POTTER	97,874	B-3
PRESIDIO	6,637	P-3
RAINS	6,715	F-11
RANDALL	89,673	C-3
REAGAN	4,514	H-3
REAL	2,412	K-6
RED RIVER	14,317	E-12
REEVES	15,852	H-1
REFUGIO	7,967	M-9
ROBERTS	1,025	A-4
ROBERTSON	15,511	I-10
ROCKWALL	25,604	F-11
RUNNELS	11,294	H-5
RUSK	43,735	H-13
SABINE	9,586	H-14
SAN AUGUSTINE	7,999	H-13
SAN JACINTO	16,372	I-12
SAN PATRICIO	58,749	N-8
SAN SABA	5,401	I-7
SCHLEICHER	2,990	I-4
SCURRY	18,634	F-4
SHACKELFORD	3,316	F-6
SHELBY	22,034	H-13
SHERMAN	2,858	A-3
SMITH	151,309	G-12
SOMERVELL	5,360	G-9
STARR	40,518	O-7
STEPHENS	9,010	G-7
STERLING	1,438	H-4
STONEWALL	2,013	F-5
SUTTON	4,135	J-4
SWISHER	8,133	D-3
TARRANT	1,170,103	F-9
TAYLOR	119,655	G-6
TERRELL	1,410	J-2
TERRY	13,218	F-2
THROCKMORTON	1,880	F-6
TITUS	24,009	F-12
TOM GREEN	98,458	H-5
TRAVIS	576,407	J-8
TRINITY	11,445	I-12
TYLER	16,646	I-13
UPSHUR	31,370	F-12
UPTON	4,447	H-3
UVALDE	23,340	K-5
VAL VERDE	38,721	J-3
VAN ZANDT	37,944	G-11
VICTORIA	74,361	L-10
WALKER	50,917	I-11
WALLER	23,390	J-11
WARD	13,115	H-1
WASHINGTON	26,154	J-10
WEBB	133,239	M-5
WHARTON	39,955	L-10
WHEELER	5,879	B-5
WICHITA	122,378	E-7
WILBARGER	15,121	D-6
WILLACY	17,705	P-9
WILLIAMSON	139,551	I-9
WILSON	22,650	L-8
WINKLER	8,626	H-1
WISE	34,679	F-9
WOOD	29,380	F-12
YOAKUM	8,786	F-2
YOUNG	18,126	F-7
ZAPATA	9,279	O-6
ZAVALA	12,162	L-5
TOTAL	16,986,510	

CITIES AND TOWNS

Note: The first name is that of the city or town, second, that of the county in which it is located, then the zip code area and location on the map.

City, County, Zip	Location
Abernathy, Hale/Lubbock, 79311	E-3
Abilene, Jones/Taylor, 79601-99	G-6
• Abram-Perezville, Hidalgo, 78572	O-16
Addison, Dallas, 75001	C-20
Alamo, Hidalgo, 78516	P-8
Alamo Heights, Bexar, 78516	C-26
Albany, Shackelford, 76430	G-7
• Aldine, Harris, 77039	H-19
Aledo, Parker, 76008	D-16
Alice, Jim Wells, 78332	N-8
Alice Southwest, Jim Wells, 78332	N-8
Alief, Harris, 77411	I-17
Allen, Collin, 75002	B-21
Alpine, Brewster, 79830	J-1
Alta Loma, Galveston, 77510	K-20
Alto, Cherokee, 75925	H-12
Alton, Hidalgo,78572	N-16
Alvarado, Johnson, 76009	G-9
Alvin, Brazoria, 77511	K-19
Amarillo, Potter/Randall, 79101-99	C-3
Anahuac, Chambers, 77514	K-13
Anderson, Grimes, 77830	J-11
• Anderson Mill, Travis/Williamson, 78682	M-25
Andrews, Andrews, 79714	G-2
Angleton, Brazoria, 77515	L-12
Angleton South, Brazoria, 77515	L-12
Anson, Jones, 79501	G-6
Anthony, El Paso, 79821	N-1
Anton, Hockley, 79313	E-3
Aransas Pass, Aransas/Nueces/ San Patricio,78336	N-10
Arcadia, Galveston, 77517	K-20
Archer City, Archer, 76351	E-8
Argyle, Denton, 76226	B-18
Arlington, Tarrant, 76006, 10-18	G-10
Asherton, Dimmit, 78827	M-6
Aspermont, Stonewall,79502	F-5
Athens, Henderson, 75751	G-11
Atlanta, Cass,75551	F-14
Aubrey, Denton, 76227	B-19
Austin, Travis/Williamson, 78701-99	J-9
Azle, Parker/Tarrant,76020	D-17
• Bacliff, Galveston, 77518	J-21
Baird, Callahan,79504	G-6
Balch Springs, Dallas, 75180	D-21
Balcones Heights, Bexar, 78750	C-25
Ballinger, Runnels, 76821	H-6
Bandera, Bandera, 78003	K-7
Bangs, Brown, 76823	H-7
• Barrett, Harris, 77532	H-20
Bartlett, Bell/Williamson, 76511	I-9
Bastrop, Bastrop, 78602	J-9
• Batesville, Zavala, 78829	L-6
Bay City, Matagorda, 77414	L-11
Bayou Vista, Galveston, 77563	K-21
Baytown, Chambers/Harris, 77520-21	I-21
Beaumont, Jefferson, 77701-99	K-14
Beaumont Place, Harris, 77028	H-18
Bedford, Tarrant, 76021-22	D-19
Beeville, Bee, 78102	M-9
Bellaire, Harris, 77401	I-18
Bellmead, McLennan, 76715	N-23
Bellville, Austin, 77418	K-11
Belton, Bell, 76513	I-9
Benavides, Duval, 78341	N-8
Benbrook, Tarrant, 76126	E-17
Benjamin, Knox, 79505	E-6
Beverly Hills, McLennan, 76711	N-22
Bevil Oaks, Jefferson, 77706	G-24
Big Lake, Reagan,76932	I-4
Big Sandy, Upshur, 75755	G-12
Big Spring, Howard, 79720	G-4
Biggs, El Paso, 79908	N-1
Bishop, Nueces, 78343	N-9
Blanco, Blanco, 78606	J-8
• Bloomington, Victoria, 77951	M-10
Blossom, Lamar, 75416	E-12
Blue Mound, Tarrant, 76131	D-18
Boerne, Kendall, 78006	K-7
Bogata, Red River, 75417	E-12
• Boling-Iago, Wharton, 77420	L-16
Bonham, Fannin, 75418	E-11
Booker, Lipscomb/Ochiltree, 79005	A-5
Borger, Hutchinson, 79007	B-4
Bovina, Parmer, 79009	D-2
Bowie, Montague, 76230	E-9
Boyd, Wise, 76023	C-17
Brackettville, Kinney, 78832	L-5
Brady, McCulloch, 76825	I-6
Brazoria, Brazoria, 77422	L-12
Breckenridge, Stephens, 76424	G-7
Bremond, Robertson, 76629	I-10
Brenham, Washington, 77833	J-11
• Briar, Parker/Tarrant/Wise, 76126	C-17
Bridge City, Orange,77611	G-26
Bridgeport, Wise, 76426	B-16
Brookshire, Waller, 77423	I-15
Brookside Village, Brazoria, 77581	J-19
Brownfield, Terry, 79316	F-3
Brownsville, Cameron, 78520	Q-9
Brownwood, Brown, 76801	H-7
Bruceville-Eddy, Falls/McLennan, 76630	O-22
• Brushy Creek, Williamson, 78681	J-9
Bryan, Brazos, 77801-03	J-11
• Buchanan Dam, Llano, 78609	I-8
Buda, Hays,78610	O-11
Buffalo, Leon,75831	H-11
• Buna, Jasper, 77612	J-14
Bunavista, Hutchinson, 79007	B-4
Bunker Hill Village, Harris, 77024	I-17
Burkburnett, Wichita, 76354	E-8
Burleson, Johnson/Tarrant, 76028	E-18
Burnet, Burnet, 78611	I-8
Cactus, Moore, 79013	B-3
Caddo Mills, Hunt, 75135	C-23
Caldwell, Burleson, 77836	J-10
Calvert, Robertson, 77837	I-10
Camden, Polk, 75934	I-13
Cameron, Milam, 76520	I-10
• Cameron Park, Cameron, 76520	O-19
• Camp Swift, Bastrop, 78602	O-27
Canadian, Hemphill, 79014	B-5
Canton, Van Zandt, 75103	G-11
• Canutillo, El Paso, 79835	N-1
Canyon, Randall,79015	C-3
• Canyon Lake, Comal,78133	K-8
Carrizo Springs, Dimmit,78834	M-6
Carrollton, Collin/Dallas/Denton, 75006-08, 10	C-20
Carthage, Panola, 75633	G-13
Castle Hills, Bexar,78213	K-8
Castroville, Medina,78009	L-7
Cedar Hill, Dallas/Ellis, 75104	E-20
Cedar Park, Travis/Williamson, 78613	J-9
Celina, Collin, 75009	A-21
Center, Shelby, 75935	H-14
Centerville, Leon, 75833	I-11
• Central Gardens, Jefferson, 77627	K-14
Chandler, Henderson, 75758	G-12
• Channelview, Harris, 77530	H-20
Channing, Hartley,79018	B-3
Charlotte, Atascosa, 78011	L-7
Chase, Bee, 78103	M-9
Childress, Childress, 79201	D-5
China, Jefferson, 77613	G-24
Cibolo, Bexar/Guadalupe, 78108	B-27
• Circle D-KC Estates, Bastrop, 78602	O-27
Cisco, Eastland, 76437	G-7
Clarendon, Donley,79226	C-5
Clarksville, Red River, 75426	E-12
Claude, Armstrong, 79019	C-4
Clear Lake City, Harris, 77058	J-20
Clear Lake Shores, Galveston, 77565	J-21
Cleburne, Johnson, 76031	G-9
Cleveland, Liberty, 77327	J-12
Clifton, Bosque, 76634	H-9
Clint, El Paso, 79836	N-1
• Cloverleaf, Harris, 77015	I-20
Clute, Brazoria,77531	L-12
Clyde, Callahan, 79510	G-6
Coahoma, Howard, 79511	G-4
Cockrell Hill, Dallas, 75211	D-20
Coldspring, San Jacinto, 77331	J-12
Coleman, Coleman, 76834	H-6
College Station, Brazos, 77840, 43, 45	J-11
Colleyville, Tarrant, 76034	C-19
Collinsville, Grayson, 76233	E-10
Colorado City, Mitchell, 79512	G-4
Columbus, Colorado, 78934	K-10
Comanche, Comanche, 76442	H-8
Combes, Cameron, 78535	N-18
Combine, Dallas/Kaufman, 75159	E-22
• Comfort, Kendall, 78013	K-7
Commerce, Hunt, 75428	F-11
Conroe, Montgomery, 77301-85	J-12
Converse, Bexar, 78109	C-27
Cooper, Delta,75432	F-12
Coppell, Dallas/Denton, 75019	C-20
Copperas Cove, Coryell/ Lampasas,76522	I-8
Corinth, Denton, 76205	B-19
Corpus Christi, Kleberg/Nueces/ San Patricio, 78401-99	N-9
Corrigan, Polk, 75939	I-13
Corsicana, Navarro, 75110	H-10
Cotulla, La Salle, 78014	M-7
Crandall, Kaufman, 75114	E-22
Crane, Crane, 79731	H-3
Crockett, Houston, 75835	I-12
• Crosby, Harris, 77532	H-20
Crosbyton, Crosby, 79322	E-4
• Cross Mountain, Bexar, 78256	B-25
Cross Plains, Callahan, 76443	H-7
Crowell, Foard, 79227	E-6
Crowley, Johnson/Tarrant, 76036	E-18
Crystal City, Zavala, 78839	M-6
Cuero, DeWitt, 77954	L-9
Daingerfield, Morris, 75638	F-13
Dalhart, Dallam/Hartley,79022	A-2
Dallas, Collin/Dallas/Denton/ Kaufman/Rockwall, 75201-99, 75301-99	G-10
Dalworthington Gardens, Tarrant, 76016	E-19
Danbury, Brazoria,77534	I-19
Dayton, Liberty, 77535	G-21
De Kalb, Bowie, 75559	E-13
De Leon, Comanche,76444	H-8
De Soto, Dallas, 75115	E-20
Decatur, Wise, 76234	F-9
Deer Park, Harris, 77536	K-12
Del Rio, Val Verde, 78840	L-4
Denison, Grayson, 75020	E-10
Denton, Denton, 76201, 05	F-9
Denver City, Yoakum, 79323	F-2
Devine, Medina, 78016	L-7
• Deweyville, Newton, 77614	J-14
Diboll, Angelina, 75941	I-13
Dickens, Dickens, 79229	E-5
Dickinson, Galveston, 77539	J-21
Dilley, Frio,78017	M-7
Dimmitt, Castro, 79027	D-3
• Dominion, Bexar,78257	B-26
Donna, Hidalgo, 78537	O-17
Double Oak, Denton, 76221	C-19
Dripping Springs, Hays,78620	N-10
Dublin, Erath, 76446	H-8
Dumas, Moore, 79029	B-3
Duncanville, Dallas, 75116, 37	E-20
Eagle Lake, Colorado, 77434	K-11
• Eagle Mountain, Tarrant, 76135	D-17
Eagle Pass, Maverick, 78852	M-5
Early, Brown, 76801	H-7
Earth, Lamb, 79031	D-3
• East Bernard, Wharton, 77435	K-11
Eastland, Eastland, 76448	G-7
Edcouch, Hidalgo, 78538	N-17
Eden, Concho, 76837	I-6
Edgecliff, Tarrant, 76134	E-18
Edgewood, Van Zandt, 75117	G-11
Edinburg, Hidalgo, 78539	N-16
Edna, Jackson, 77957	L-10
El Campo, Wharton, 77437	L-11
El Campo South, Wharton, 77437	L-11
El Cenizo, Webb, 78043	N-7
El Lago, Harris, 77586	J-21
El Paso, El Paso, 79901-99	N-1
Eldorado, Schleicher, 76936	I-5
Electra, Wichita, 76360	E-7
Elgin, Bastrop, 78621	J-9
Elkhart, Anderson, 75839	H-12
Elsa, Hidalgo, 78543	P-8
Emory, Rains, 75440	F-11
• Encantada-Ranchito El Calaboz, Cameron, 78586	O-18
Ennis, Ellis, 75119	G-10
• Escobares, Starr, 78582	P-7
Euless, Tarrant, 76039	D-19
• Evadale, Jasper, 77615	J-14
Everman, Tarrant, 76140	E-18
• Fabens, El Paso, 79838	N-1
Fair Oaks Ranch, Bexar/Comal/ Kendall, 78006	B-25
Fairfield, Freestone, 75840	H-11
Fairview, Collin, 77266	B-22
Falfurrias, Brooks, 78355	O-8
Farmers Branch, Dallas, 75234	D-20
Farmersville, Collin, 75442	B-23
Farwell, Parmer, 79325	D-2
Ferris, Ellis, 75125	E-22
• First Colony, Fort Bend, 77478	J-17
Flatonia, Fayette, 78941	K-9
Floresville, Wilson, 78114	L-8
Flower Mound, Denton/Tarrant, 75028	C-19
Floydada, Floyd, 79235	E-4
Forest Hill, Tarrant, 76119	E-18
Forney, Kaufman, 75126	D-22
• Fort Bliss, El Paso, 79906	N-1
Fort Davis, Jeff Davis, 79734	P-4
• Fort Hood, Bell/Coryell, 76544	I-9
Fort Sam Houston, Bexar, 78234	C-26
Fort Stockton, Pecos, 79735	I-2
Fort Wolters, Palo Pinto/Parker, 76010	F-8
Fort Worth, Denton/Tarrant, 76101-99	G-9
Franklin, Robertson, 77856	I-11
Frankston, Anderson, 75763	G-12
Fredericksburg, Gillespie, 78624	J-7
Freeport, Brazoria, 77541	L-12
Freer, Duval, 78357	N-7
• Fresno, Fort Bend, 77545	J-18
Friendswood, Galveston/Harris, 77546	J-20
Friona, Parmer, 79035	D-2
Frisco, Collin/Denton, 75034	B-20
Fritch, Hutchinson/Moore, 79036	B-4
Fuller Springs, Angelina, 75901	I-13
Gail, Borden, 79738	G-4
Gainesville, Cooke, 76240	E-9
Galena Park, Harris, 77547	I-19
Galveston, Galveston, 77550-51, 54	L-13
Ganado, Jackson, 77962	L-10
Garden City, Glasscock, 79739	H-4
Garden Ridge, Comal, 78266	B-27
• Gardendale, Ector, 79758	H-3
• Garfield, Bastrop/Travis, 78602	N-26
Garland, Collin/Dallas/Rockwall, 75040-44, 48	C-22
Gatesville, Coryell, 76528	H-9
George West, Live Oak, 78022	M-8
Georgetown, Williamson, 78626, 28	J-9
Giddings, Lee,78942	J-10
Gilmer, Upshur, 75644	G-13
Gladewater, Gregg/Upshur, 75647	G-13
Glen Rose, Somervell, 76043	G-9
Glenn Heights, Dallas/Ellis, 75115	E-20
Goldthwaite, Mills, 76844	H-8
Goliad, Goliad, 77963	M-9
Gonzales, Gonzales, 78629	K-9
Gorman, Eastland, 76454	G-7
Graham, Young, 76450	F-8
Granbury, Hood,76048-49	G-9
Grand Prairie, Dallas/Ellis/ Tarrant, 75050-52	D-19
Grand Saline, Van Zandt, 75140	G-12
Grandview, Johnson, 76050	G-9
Granger, Williamson, 76530	J-9
Granite Shoals, Burnet, 78654	J-8
Grapeland, Houston, 75844	H-12

Explanation of symbols: •– Census Designated Place (CDP)

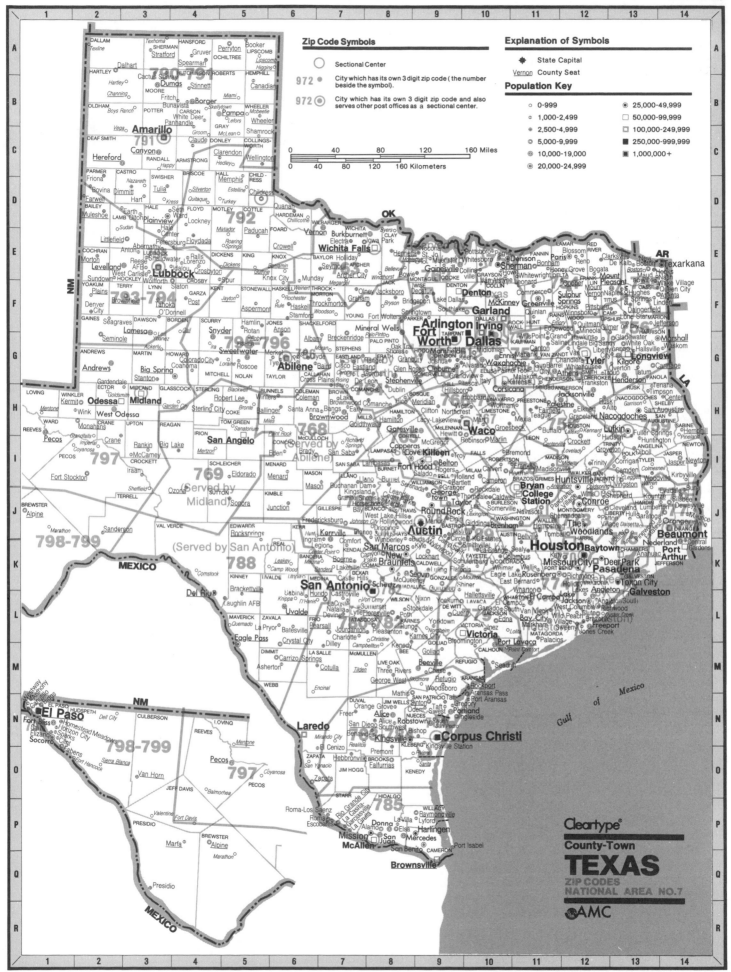

Copyright American Map Corporation

Explanation of symbols: ● – Census Designated Place (CDP)

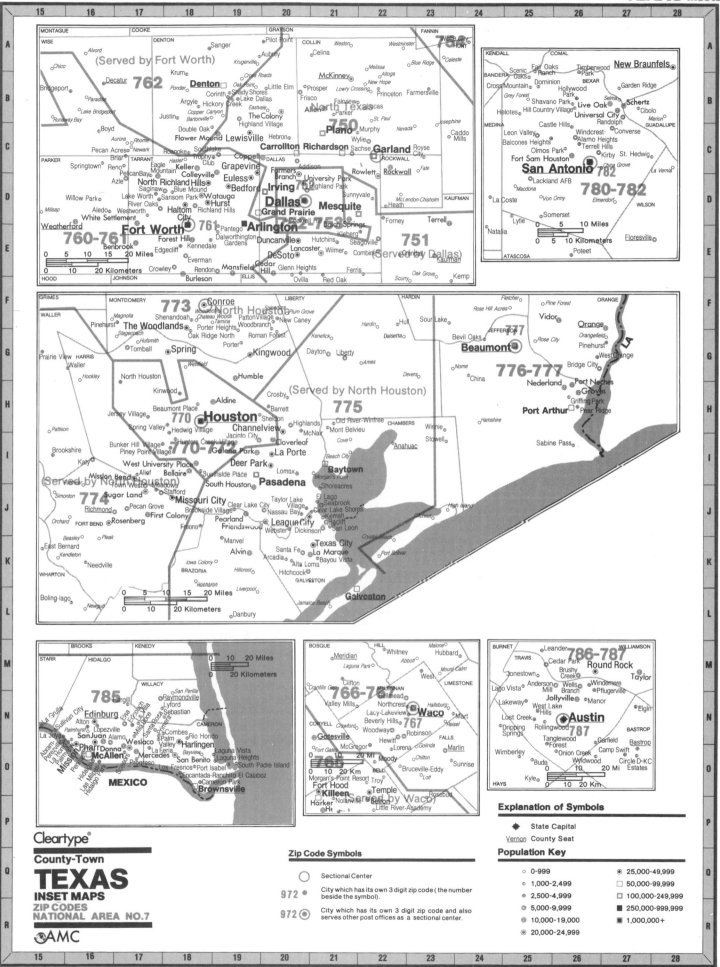

Copyright American Map Corporation

Explanation of symbols: • – Census Designated Place (CDP)

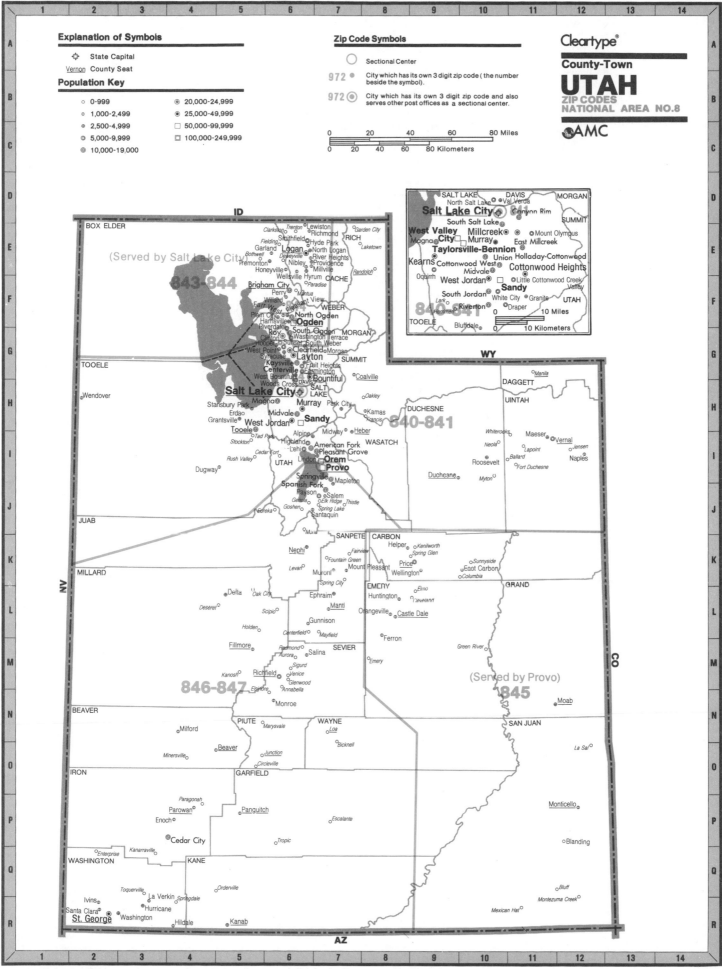

Explanation of Symbols

◈ State Capital

Vernon County Seat

Population Key

- ◦ 0-999
- ⊕ 1,000-2,499
- ⊛ 2,500-4,999
- ⊙ 5,000-9,999
- ⊛ 10,000-19,000
- ⊛ 20,000-24,999
- ⊛ 25,000-49,999
- ☐ 50,000-99,999
- ☐ 100,000-249,999

Zip Code Symbols

○ Sectional Center

972 ● City which has its own 3 digit zip code (the number beside the symbol).

972 ◉ City which has its own 3 digit zip code and also serves other post offices as a sectional center.

Cleartype®
County-Town
UTAH
ZIP CODES
NATIONAL AREA NO.8
⊕AMC

0   20   40   60   80 Miles
0   20   40   60   80 Kilometers

Inset map (Salt Lake City area):

SALT LAKE | DAVIS | MORGAN
North Salt Lake • Val Verda
Salt Lake City◉ ◉ Canyon Rim
SUMMIT
South Salt Lake
West Valley Millcreek ● ● Mount Olympus
City Magna Murray East Millcreek
Taylorsville-Bennion
Union Holladay-Cottonwood
Kearns Cottonwood West Cottonwood Heights
Oquirrh Midvale ● Little Cottonwood Creek
West Jordan● Valley
South Jordan White City ● Granite UTAH
Lark **Sandy**
Hemmatt Riverton ● Draper
TOOELE Bluffdale
844-841
0   10 Miles
0   10 Kilometers

Main map:

ID

BOX ELDER

(Served by Salt Lake City)

843-844

Clarkston • Trenton Lewiston
Richmond Garden City
Fielding Smithfield RICH
Garland Hyde Park North Logan Laketown
Bothwell **Logan**
Tremonton Deweyville River Heights
Honeyville Nibley Providence
Wellsville Millville
Hyrum CACHE
Paradise Randolph
Brigham City
Perry Mantua
Willard Salt View
Farr West WEBER
Plain City North Ogden
Harrisville **Ogden**
Riverdale
Clinton Roy South Ogden MORGAN
Hooper Sunset South Weber
West Point Syracuse Clearfield Morgan
Kaysville **Layton** SUMMIT
Centerville Farmington
West Bountiful **Bountiful** ○ Coalville
Woods Cross DAVIS
SALT Oakley
TOOELE **Salt Lake City**◈ LAKE
Wendover Magna **Murray** Park City
Stansbury Park ○ Kamas
Erdao **Midvale** Kamas
Grantsville **West Jordan** **Sandy**
Tooele Alpine Midway Heber
Stockton Tad Park Highland 840-841
Cedar Fort American Fork WASATCH
Rush Valley Lehi Pleasant Grove
Dugway Lindon
Orem
Utah **Provo**
Springville Mapleton
Spanish Fork Payson Salem
Genola Elk Ridge Thistle
Eureka Goshen Spring Lake
Santaquin
JUAB
Mona
SANPETE CARBON
Nephi Helper Kenilworth
Fairview Spring Glen
MILLARD Fountain Green
Levan Mount Pleasant Price
Moroni Wellington
Delta Spring City EMERY East Carbon
Oak City Ephraim Columbia
Deseret Huntington Elmo GRAND
Scipio Manti Cleveland
Holden Orangeville Castle Dale
Gunnison
Centerfield Mayfield Ferron
Fillmore Redmond SEVIER
Aurora Salina Green River
Sigurd Emery
Kanosh Richfield Venice
(Served by Provo)
846-847 Glenwood
Elsinore Annabella 845
Monroe Moab
BEAVER
Milford PIUTE WAYNE SAN JUAN
Marysvale Loa
Beaver Bicknell
Minersville Junction La Sal
IRON Circleville
GARFIELD
Paragonah
Parowan Monticello
Enoch Panguitch
Escalante
Cedar City Blanding
Enterprise Tropic
Kanarraville
WASHINGTON KANE
Toquerville Orderville Bluff
Ivins La Verkin Springdale Montezuma Creek
Santa Clara Hurricane Mexican Hat
St. George Washington
Hildale Kanab

NV
WY
CO

AZ

COUNTIES

(14 Counties)

Name of County	Population	Location on Map
ADDISON	32,953	G-3
BENNINGTON	35,845	N-3
CALEDONIA	27,846	C-9
CHITTENDEN	131,761	D-3
ESSEX	6,405	A-11
FRANKLIN	39,980	A-3
GRAND ISLE	5,318	A-2
LAMOILLE	19,735	C-6
ORANGE	26,149	H-6
ORLEANS	24,053	A-7
RUTLAND	62,142	J-2
WASHINGTON	54,928	E-6
WINDHAM	41,588	O-6
WINDSOR	54,055	I-5
TOTAL	562,758	

CITIES AND TOWNS

Note: The first name is that of the city or town, second, that of the county in which it is located, then the zip code area and location on the map.

Arlington, Bennington, 05250 .... P-3
Barre, Washington, 05641 .... G-7
Bellows Falls, Windham, 05101 .... O-7
● Bennington, Bennington, 05201 .... Q-3
▲ *Bethel, Windsor, 05032* J-6
▲ *Braintree, Orange, 05060* I-5
● Brandon, Rutland, 05733 .... J-3
● Brattleboro, Windham, 05301 .... Q-6
▲ *Bridport, Addison, 05734* I-2
Bristol, Addison, 05443 .... H-4
▲ *Brookfield, Orange, 05036* H-6
Burlington, Chittenden, 05401 .... E-3
Cabot, Washington, 05647 .... E-8
▲ *Castleton, Rutland, 05735* K-3
Chelsea, Orange, 05038 .... I-7
● Chester-Chester Depot, Windsor, 05143-44 .... N-6
▲ *Colchester, Chittenden, 05446* D-3
▲ *Dummerston, Windham, 05346* Q-6
Enosburg Falls, Franklin, 05450 .... B-5
Essex Junction, Chittenden, 05452 .... E-3
● Fair Haven, Rutland, 05743 .... L-2
▲ *Fairfax, Franklin, 05454* C-4
▲ *Ferrisburg, Addison, 05456* G-3
● Graniteville-East Barre, Washington, 05654, 49 .... G-7
▲ *Guildhall, Essex, 05905* D-12
Hardwick, Caledonia, 05843 .... E-8
▲ *Huntington, Chittenden, 05462* F-4
Hyde Park, Lamoille, 05655 .... D-6
● Island Pond, Essex, 05846 .... B-11
Jericho, Chittenden, 05465 .... E-4
Johnson, Lamoille, 05656 .... D-6
Ludlow, Windsor, 05149 .... M-6
Lyndonville, Caledonia, 05851 .... E-10
● Manchester Center, Bennington, 05255.. .... O-3
Manchester Depot, Bennington, 05254 .... O-4
● Middlebury, Addison, 05753 .... I-3
Milton, Chittenden, 05468 .... D-3
▲ *Monkton, Addison, 05469* G-3
Montpelier, Washington, 05620 .... G-7
Morrisville, Lamoille, 05661 .... D-6
▲ *New Haven, Addison, 05472* H-4
Newfane, Windham, 05345 .... P-6
Newport, Orleans, 05855 .... A-9
North Bennington, Bennington, 05257 ... Q-2
North Hero, Grand Isle, 05474 .... B-2
Northfield, Washington, 05663 .... G-6
Norwich, Windsor, 05055 .... K-8

▲ *Pawlet, Rutland, 05761* N-3
Poultney, Rutland, 05764 .... L-3
▲ *Proctor, Rutland, 05765* K-4
Randolph, Orange, 05060 .... I-6
Richford, Franklin, 05746 .... A-6
▲ *Richmond, Chittenden, 05477* F-4
▲ *Royalton, Windsor, 05068* J-6
Rutland, Rutland, 05701 .... L-4
▲ *Ryegate, Caledonia, 05042* G-9
Saint Albans, Franklin, 05478 .... B-4
● Saint Johnsbury, Caledonia, 05819 ..... E-10
▲ *Salisbury, Addison, 05769* I-4
▲ *Shelburne, Chittenden, 05482* F-3
Shelburne Road Section, Chittenden, 05482 .... E-3
● South Barre, Washington, 05670 .... G-7
South Burlington, Chittenden, 05403 ..... E-3
● Springfield, Windsor, 05156 .... N-7
▲ *Starksboro, Addison, 05487* G-4
Swanton, Franklin, 05488 .... B-3
▲ *Tunbridge, Orange, 05077* I-7
Vergennes, Addison, 05491 .... G-3
● Wallingford, Rutland, 05773 .... M-4
Waterbury, Washington, 05676 .... F-5
● West Brattleboro, Windham, 05301 .... Q-6
● West Rutland, Rutland, 05777 .... L-4
● White River Junction, Windsor, 05001 ... K-8
● Wilder, Windsor, 05088 .... K-8
▲ *Williston, Chittenden, 05495* E-3
▲ *Windsor, Windsor, 05089* L-7
Winooski, Chittenden, 05404 .... E-3
Woodstock, Windsor, 05091 .... K-7

Explanation of symbols: ● – Census Designated Place (CDP)   ● *italics* – Township shown which is also a CDP   ▲ *italics* – Townships (shown on the map)

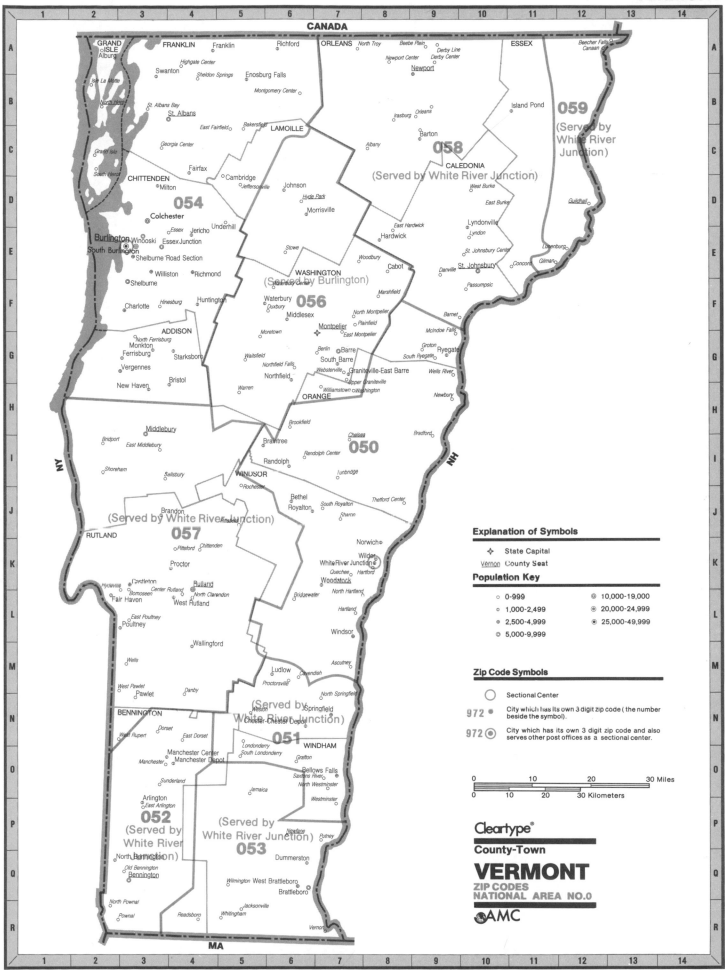

Explanation of Symbols

✛ State Capital
Vernon County Seat

Population Key

○ 0-999
⊙ 1,000-2,499
⊕ 2,500-4,999
◎ 5,000-9,999
◉ 10,000-19,000
◉ 20,000-24,999
◉ 25,000-49,999

Zip Code Symbols

◯ Sectional Center

972 ● City which has its own 3 digit zip code (the number beside the symbol).

972 ◉ City which has its own 3 digit zip code and also serves other post offices as a sectional center.

0 ——— 10 ——— 20 ——— 30 Miles
0 — 10 — 20 — 30 Kilometers

Cleartype®

County-Town

VERMONT

ZIP CODES
NATIONAL AREA NO.0

●AMC

Copyright American Map Corporation

Explanation of symbols: ● – Census Designated Place (CDP)

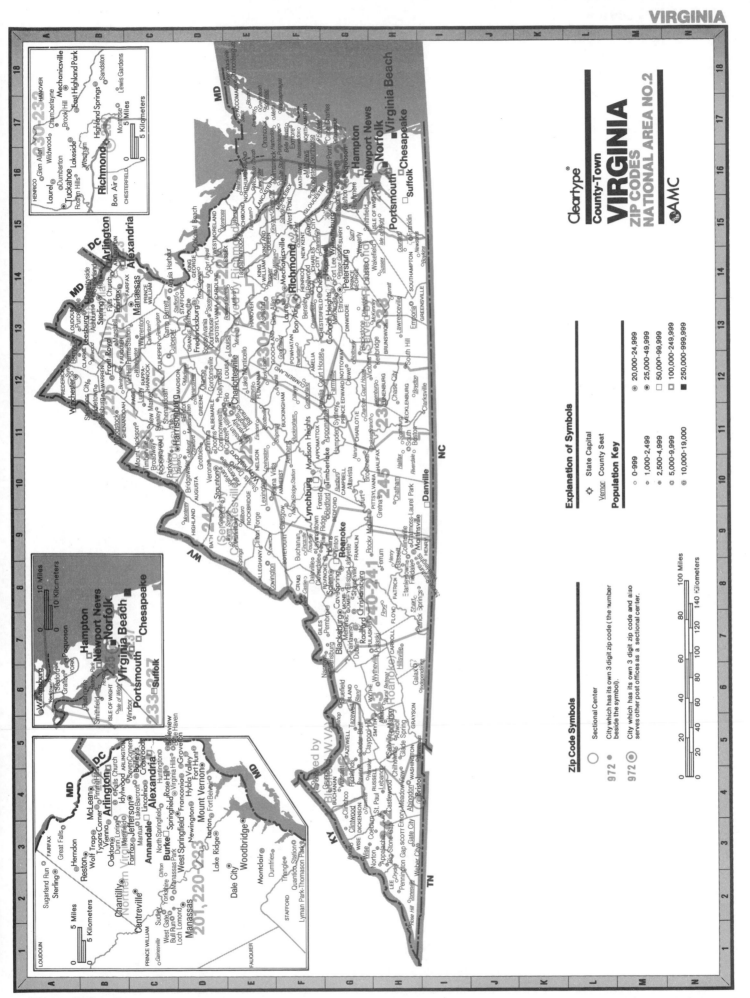

Copyright American Map Corporation

COUNTIES

(39 Counties)

Name of County	Population	Location on Map
ADAMS	13,603	F-15
ASOTIN	17,605	I-16
BENTON	112,560	H-13
CHELAN	52,250	D-11
CLALLAM	56,464	C-4
CLARK	238,053	J-8
COLUMBIA	4,024	H-16
COWLITZ	82,119	H-7
DOUGLAS	26,205	D-13
FERRY	6,295	B-15
FRANKLIN	37,473	G-14
GARFIELD	2,248	H-17
GRANT	54,758	F-13
GRAYS HARBOR	64,175	E-4
ISLAND	60,195	C-7
JEFFERSON	20,146	D-4
KING	1,507,319	D-10
KITSAP	189,731	E-7
KITTITAS	26,725	F-10
KLICKITAT	16,616	J-10
LEWIS	59,358	G-9
LINCOLN	8,864	E-15
MASON	38,341	E-6
OKANOGAN	33,350	A-11
PACIFIC	18,882	H-6
PEND OREILLE	8,915	A-17
PIERCE	586,203	F-9
SAN JUAN	10,035	C-7
SKAGIT	79,555	B-10
SKAMANIA	8,289	H-8
SNOHOMISH	465,642	C-10
SPOKANE	361,364	E-17
STEVENS	30,948	A-16
THURSTON	161,238	G-7
WAHKIAKUM	3,327	H-6
WALLA WALLA	48,439	I-15
WHATCOM	127,780	A-10
WHITMAN	38,775	F-16
YAKIMA	188,823	G-10
TOTAL	4,866,692	

CITIES AND TOWNS

Note: The first name is that of the city or town, second, that of the county in which it is located, then the zip code area and location on the map.

Aberdeen, Grays Harbor, 98520 ... G-5
Airway Heights, Spokane, 99001 ... E-17
• Alderwood Manor-Bothell North, Snohomish, 98036 ... K-4
Algona, King, 98001 ... L-10
• Allyn-Grapeview, Mason, 98524 ... F-7
Anacortes, Skagit, 98221 ... B-8
Appleyard, Chelan, 98816 ... F-12
Arlington, Snohomish, 98223 ... C-8
• Artondale, Pierce, 98335 ... L-7
Asotin, Asotin, 99402 ... H-18
Auburn, King, 98001-02 ... F-8
• Ault Field, Island, 98277 ... C-7
Bainbridge Island, Kitsap, 98110 ... M-3
• Bangor Trident Base, Kitsap, 98315 ... K-1
Battle Ground, Clark, 98604 ... J-8
Bellevue, King, 98004-08 ... E-8
Bellingham, Whatcom, 98225-26 ... B-8
Benton City, Benton, 99320 ... I-13
• Birch Bay, Whatcom, 98230 ... A-7
Black Diamond, King, 98010 ... L-11
Blaine, Whatcom, 98230 ... A-7
Bonney Lake, Pierce, 98390 ... M-10
Bothell, King/Snohomish, 98011-12 ... D-8
Bremerton, Kitsap, 98310,12 ... E-7
Brewster, Okanogan, 98812 ... C-13
Bridgeport, Douglas, 98813 ... D-13
Brier, Snohomish, 98036 ... D-8
• Brush Prairie, Clark, 98606 ... L-13
• Bryn Mawr-Skyway, King, 98178 ... N-4
Buckley, Pierce, 98321 ... F-9
• Burbank, Walla Walla, 99323 ... I-14
• Burien, King, 98166 ... N-3
Burlington, Skagit, 98233 ... B-8
Camas, Clark, 98607 ... K-8
Carnation, King, 98014 ... E-9
• Carson River Valley, Skamania, 94610 ... J-9
• Cascade Park East, Clark, 98055 ... N-13
• Cascade Park West, Clark, 98055 ... N-13
• Cascade Valley, Grant, 98057 ... F-14
• Cascade-Fairwood, King, 98057 ... N-5
Cashmere, Chelan, 98815 ... E-12
Castle Rock, Cowlitz, 98611 ... I-7
Cathlamet, Wahkiakum, 986'2 ... I-6
• Central Park, Grays Harbor, 98520 ... G-6
Centralia, Lewis, 98531 ... G-7
Chehalis, Lewis, 98532 ... H-7
Chelan, Chelan, 98816 ... D-12
Cheney, Spokane, 99004 ... E-17
Chewelah, Stevens, 99109 ... C-17
Clarkston, Asotin, 99403 ... H-18
• Clarkston Heights-Vineland, Asotin, 99403 ... H-18
Cle Elum, Kittitas, 98922 ... F-11
• Clinton, Island, 98236 ... I-3
Clyde Hill, King, 98004 ... M-4
Colfax, Whitman, 99111 ... G-17
College Place, Walla Walla, 99324 ... I-16
Colville, Stevens, 99114 ... B-16
Connell, Franklin, 99326 ... G-15
Cosmopolis, Grays Harbor, 98537 ... G-5
Coulee Dam, Douglas/Grant/Okanogan, 99116 ... D-14
• Country Homes, Spokane, 95218 ... D-17
Coupeville, Island, 98239 ... C-7
• Covington-Sawyer-Wilderness, King, 98042 ... L-10
Darrington, Snohomish, 98241 ... C-9
Davenport, Lincoln, 99122 ... E-16
Dayton, Columbia, 99328 ... H-16
Deer Park, Spokane, 99006 ... D-17
Des Moines, King, 98188 ... E-8
• Dishman, Spokane, 99213 ... E-18
Duvall, King, 98019 ... E-8
• East Hill-Meridian, King, 98042 ... K-9
• East Port Orchard, Kitsap, 98366 ... N-2
• East Renton Highlands, King, 98024 ... N-4
East Wenatchee, Douglas, 98802 ... E-12
• East Wenatchee Bench, Douglas, 98801 ... E-12
• Eastgate, King, 98007 ... M-5
Eatonville, Pierce, 98328 ... G-8
• Edgewood-North Hill, Pierce, 98166 ... L-9
Edmonds, Snohomish, 98020,26 ... D-8
• Elk Plain, Pierce, 98387 ... G-8
Ellensburg, Kittitas, 98926 ... G-11
• Ellsworth North, Clark, 98662 ... N-13
• Ellsworth South, Clark, 98662 ... N-13
Elma, Grays Harbor, 98541 ... G-6
Enumclaw, King, 98022 ... F-9
Ephrata, Grant, 98823 ... F-13
• Erlands Point-Kitsap Lake, Kitsap, 98312 ... M-2
• Esperance, Snohomish, 98043 ... K-4
Everett, Snohomish, 98201-08 ... D-8
• Evergreen, Clark, 98663 ... N-13
Everson, Whatcom, 98247 ... A-8
• Fairchild AFB, Spokane, 99001 ... E-17
• Fairview-Sumach, Yakima, 98903 ... H-12
• Fairwood, Spokane, 99218 ... D-17
• Fall City, King, 98024 ... E-9
• Federal Way, King, 98003,23 ... L-9
• Felida, Clark, 98665 ... M-12
Ferndale, Whatcom, 98248 ... A-8
Fife, Pierce, 98424 ... M-9
• Finley, Benton, 98055 ... I-14
Fircrest, Pierce, 98466 ... M-8
• Five Corners, Clark, 98629 ... M-13
• Fords Prairie, Lewis, 98531 ... G-7
Forks, Clallam, 98331 ... D-4
• Fort Lewis, Pierce, 98433 ... F-8
• Fox Island, Pierce, 98333 ... M-7
• Frederickson, Pierce, 98316 ... F-8
• Freeland, Island, 98249 ... D-8
Friday Harbor, San Juan, 98250 ... B-7
• Fruitvale, Yakima, 98902 ... H-11
• Garrett, Walla Walla, 99326 ... I-16
Geiger Heights, Spokane, 99204 ... E-17
Gig Harbor, Pierce, 98329,32,35 ... F-8
Gold Bar, Snohomish, 98251 ... D-9
Goldendale, Klickitat, 98620 ... J-11
• Grand Mound, Thurston, 98501 ... G-7
Grandview, Yakima, 98930 ... I-13
Granger, Yakima, 98932 ... H-12
Granite Falls, Snohomish, 98252 ... D-9
• Green Acres, Spokane, 99016 ... D-18
• Hadlock-Irondale, Jefferson, 98339 ... D-7
• Harbour Pointe, Snohomish, 98254 ... J-4
• Hazel Dell North, Clark, 98665 ... M-12
• Hazel Dell South, Clark, 98665 ... M-12
• Highland, Benton, 98055 ... I-14
Hoquiam, Grays Harbor, 98550 ... G-5
• Indianola, Kitsap, 98342 ... K-2
• Inglewood-Finn Hill, King, 98011 ... L-4
Issaquah, King, 98027 ... N-5
Kalama, Cowlitz, 98625 ... I-7
Kelso, Cowlitz, 98626 ... I-7
• Kenmore, King, 98028 ... L-4
Kennewick, Benton, 99336-37 ... I-14
Kent, King, 98031-32,42 ... F-8
Kettle Falls, Stevens, 99141 ... B-16
• Kingsgate, King, 98011 ... L-5
• Kingston, Kitsap, 98346 ... K-2
Kirkland, King, 98033-34 ... E-8
Lacey, Thurston, 98503 ... G-7
• Lake Forest North, King, 98155 ... L-4
Lake Forest Park, King, 98155 ... L-4
• Lake Goodwin, Snohomish, 98292 ... C-8
• Lake Serene-North Lynnwood, Snohomish, 98036 ... J-4
• Lake Shore, Clark, 98665 ... M-12
Lake Stevens, Snohomish, 98258 ... D-9
• Lakeland North, King, 98002 ... L-10
• Lakeland South, King, 98002 ... L-10
• Lakewood, Pierce, 98259 ... M-8
• Lea Hill, King, 98015 ... L-9
Leavenworth, Chelan, 98826 ... E-11
• Liberty Lake, Spokane, 99019 ... E-18
Long Beach, Pacific, 98631 ... H-5
Longview, Cowlitz, 98632 ... I-7
• Longview Heights, Cowlitz, 98632 ... I-7
Lynden, Whatcom, 98264 ... A-8
Lynnwood, Snohomish, 98036-37 ... K-4
Mabton, Yakima, 98935 ... I-13
• Manchester, Kitsap, 98353 ... M-2
• Maple Valley, King, 98038 ... E-9
• Marietta-Alderwood, Whatcom, 98225 ... A-8
• Martha Lake, Snohomish, 98012 ... J-4
Marysville, Snohomish, 98270-71 ... D-8
• McChord AFB, Pierce, 98438 ... N-9
McCleary, Grays Harbor, 98557 ... F-6
• Meadow Glade, Clark, 98604 ... L-13
Medical Lake, Spokane, 99022 ... E-17
Medina, King, 98039 ... M-4
Mercer Island, King, 98040 ... M-4
• Midland, Pierce, 98444 ... M-9
Mill Creek, Snohomish, 98012 ... J-4
Millwood, Spokane, 99212 ... D-18
Milton, King/Pierce, 98354 ... M-9
• Minnehaha, Clark, 98661 ... M-12
• Mirrormont, King, 98027 ... N-6
Monroe, Snohomish, 98272 ... D-9
Montesano, Grays Harbor, 98563 ... G-6
Morgan Acres, Spokane, 99207 ... D-17
Morton, Lewis, 98356 ... H-8
Moses Lake, Grant, 98837 ... F-14
• Moses Lake North, Grant, 98837 ... F-14
Mount Vernon, Skagit, 98273 ... C-8
Mountlake Terrace, Snohomish, 98043 ... K-4
Mukilteo, Snohomish, 98275 ... D-8
• Navy Yard City, Kitsap, 98310 ... M-2
Newport, Pend Oreille, 99156 ... C-18
• Newport Hills, King, 98006 ... M-4
Normandy Park, King, 98166 ... K-9
North Bend, King, 98045 ... E-9
• North City-Ridgecrest, King, 98155 ... L-4
• North Creek-Canyon Park, Snohomish, 98035 ... K-5
• North Hill, King, 98166 ... K-9
• North Marysville, Snohomish, 98270 ... D-8
• North Puyallup, Pierce, 98372 ... M-9
• North Yelm, Thurston, 98597 ... G-7
Oak Harbor, Island, 98277 ... C-7
• Ocean Park, Pacific, 98640 ... H-4
Ocean Shores, Grays Harbor, 98569 ... G-5
Okanogan, Okanogan, 98840 ... C-13
Olympia, Thurston, 98501-16 ... F-7
Omak, Okanogan, 98841 ... C-13
• Opportunity, Spokane, 99206 ... E-18
• Orchards North, Clark, 98662 ... M-13
• Orchards South, Clark, 98662 ... M-13
Oroville, Okanogan, 98844 ... A-13
Orting, Pierce, 98360 ... F-8
Othello, Adams, 99344 ... G-14
• Otis Orchards-East Farms, Spokane, 99027 ... D-18
Pacific, King/Pierce, 98047 ... M-10
Packwood, Lewis, 98361 ... H-9
• Paine Field-Lake Stickney, Snohomish, 98251 ... J-4
• Parkland, Pierce, 98444 ... F-8
• Parkwood, Kitsap, 98366 ... N-2
Pasadena Park, Spokane, 99206 ... D-18
Pasco, Franklin, 99301 ... I-14
• Pine Lake, King, 98027 ... M-5
Pomeroy, Garfield, 99347 ... H-17
Port Angeles, Clallam, 98362 ... C-6
• Port Angeles East, Clallam, 98362 ... C-6
Port Orchard, Kitsap, 98366 ... E-7
Port Townsend, Jefferson, 98368 ... C-7
Poulsbo, Kitsap, 98370 ... L-2
• Prairie Ridge, Pierce, 98390 ... M-9
Prosser, Benton, 99350 ... I-13
Pullman, Whitman, 99163 ... G-18
Puyallup, Pierce, 98371-72,74 ... F-8
Quilcene, Jefferson, 98376 ... D-7
Quincy, Grant, 98848 ... F-13
Raymond, Pacific, 98577 ... G-5
Redmond, King, 98052-53 ... E-8
Renton, King, 98055-59 ... E-8
Republic, Ferry, 99166 ... B-15
Richland, Benton, 99352 ... I-14
• Richmond Beach-Innis Arden, King, 98160 ... L-3
• Richmond Highlands, King, 98133 ... K-3
Ridgefield, Clark, 98642 ... J-7
Ritzville, Adams, 99169 ... F-16
• Riverton-Boulevard Park, King, 98188 ... N-4
• Rochester, Thurston, 98579 ... G-7
Royal City, Grant, 99357 ... G-13
• Sahalee, King, 98019 ... L-5
• Salmon Creek, Clark, 98665 ... M-12
• Satus, Yakima, 98911 ... H-12
• Sea-Tac, King, 98188 ... N-4
Seattle, King, 98101-99 ... E-8
Sedro-Woolley, Skagit, 98284 ... B-8
Selah, Yakima, 98942 ... H-11
Sequim, Clallam, 98382 ... D-7
• Shelter Bay, Skagit, 98275 ... B-8
Shelton, Mason, 98584 ... F-7
• Sheridan Beach, King, 98155 ... L-4
• Silver Lake-Fircrest, Snohomish, 98208 ... J-4
• Silverdale, Kitsap, 98315 ... M-2
• Smokey Point, Snohomish, 98223 ... C-8
Snohomish, Snohomish, 98290 ... D-9
Snoqualmie, King, 98065 ... E-9
Soap Lake, Grant, 98851 ... E-13
South Bend, Pacific, 98586 ... H-5
• South Broadway, Yakima, 98902 ... H-11
• South Hill, Pierce, 98373 ... M-9
• South Wenatchee, Chelan, 98801 ... F-12
• Spanaway, Pierce, 98387 ... N-7
Spokane, Spokane, 99201-99 ... E-17
Stanwood, Snohomish, 98292 ... C-8
Steilacoom, Pierce, 98388 ... M-8
Stevenson, Skamania, 98648 ... J-9
• Sudden Valley, Whatcom, 98268 ... B-8
Sultan, Snohomish, 98294 ... D-9
• Summit, Pierce, 98373 ... M-10
Sumner, Pierce, 98390 ... F-8
Sunnyside, Yakima, 98944 ... H-12
• Sunnyslope, Chelan, 98801 ... E-12
• Suquamish, Kitsap, 98392 ... L-2
Tacoma, Pierce, 98401-99 ... F-8
• Tanglewilde-Thompson Place, Thurston, 98506 ... F-7
Tenino, Thurston, 98589 ... G-7
• Terrace Heights, Yakima, 98901 ... H-12
Toppenish, Yakima, 98948 ... H-12
• Town and Country, Spokane, 99210 ... D-17
• Tracyton, Kitsap, 98393 ... M-2
• Trentwood, Spokane, 99215 ... D-18
Tukwila, King, 98188 ... N-4
• Tulalip Bay, Snohomish, 98270 ... D-8
Tumwater, Thurston, 98520 ... G-7
Union Gap, Yakima, 98903 ... H-12
• University Place, Pierce, 98465 ... M-7
Vancouver, Clark, 98660-86 ... J-7
• Vancouver Mall, Clark, 98662 ... M-13
• Veradale, Spokane, 99037 ... E-18
Walla Walla, Walla Walla, 99362 ... I-16
• Walla Walla East, Walla Walla, 99362 ... I-16
• Waller, Pierce, 98301 ... M-8
• Walnut Grove, Clark, 98662 ... M-13
Wapato, Yakima, 98951 ... H-12
Warden, Grant, 98857 ... G-14
Washougal, Clark, 98671 ... K-8
Waterville, Douglas, 98858 ... E-12
Wenatchee, Chelan, 98801-02 ... E-12
• West Clarkston-Highland, Asotin, 99403 ... H-18
• West Lake Sammamish, King, 98232 ... M-5
• West Lake Stevens, Snohomish, 98258 ... D-9
• West Longview, Cowlitz, 98632 ... I-7
• West Pasco, Franklin, 99301 ... I-14
West Richland, Benton, 99352 ... I-14
• West Side Highway, Cowlitz, 93624 ... I-7
• West Valley, Yakima, 98914 ... G-11
• West Wenatchee, Chelan, 98802 ... E-12
Westport, Grays Harbor, 98595 ... G-5
• White Center-Shorewood, King, 98106 ... N-4
White Salmon, Klickitat, 98672 ... J-10
• White Swan, Yakima, 98952 ... H-11
Wiley, Yakima, 98908 ... H-11
Winlock, Lewis, 98596 ... H-7
• Woodinville, King, 98072 ... K-5
Woodland, Clark/Cowlitz, 98674 ... J-7
• Woodmont Beach, King, 98032 ... K-8
Yakima, Yakima, 98901-03,08 ... H-11
Yelm, Thurston, 98597 ... G-8
Zillah, Yakima, 98953 ... H-12

Explanation of symbols: • – Census Designated Place (CDP)

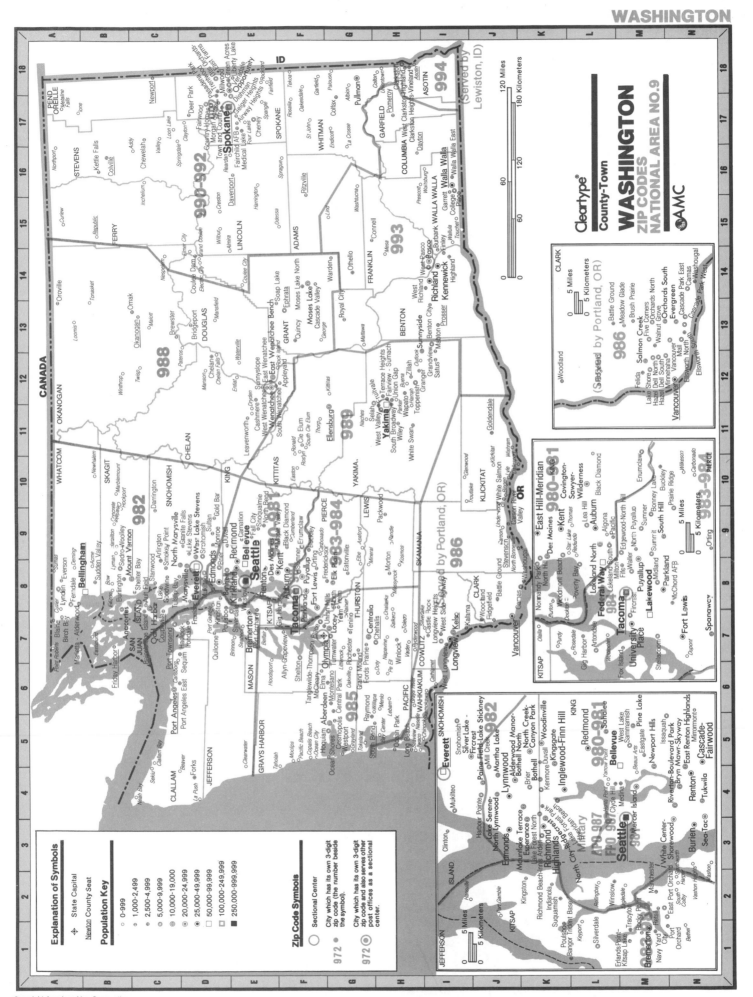

Clertype®
County-Town
WASHINGTON
ZIP CODES
NATIONAL AREA NO.9

AMC

Copyright American Map Corporation

Explanation of Symbols

✦ State Capital

⊙ Newton County Seat

Population Key

○ 0-999
⊙ 1,000-2,499
⊙ 2,500-4,999
⊙ 5,000-9,999
⊙ 10,000-19,000
⊙ 20,000-24,999
⊙ 25,000-49,999
⊙ 50,000-99,999
□ 100,000-249,999
■ 250,000-999,999

Zip Code Symbols

○ Sectional Center

972 • City which has its own 3-digit zip code (the number beside the symbol).

972 ⊙ City which has its own 3-digit zip code and also serves other post offices as a sectional center.

COUNTIES

(55 Counties)

Name of County	Population	Location on Map
BARBOUR	15,699	D-10
BERKELEY	59,253	B-17
BOONE	25,870	I-4
BRAXTON	12,998	F-7
BROOKE	26,992	C-2
CABELL	96,827	H-2
CALHOUN	7,885	E-6
CLAY	9,983	G-6
DODDRIDGE	6,994	C-8
FAYETTE	47,952	J-7
GILMER	7,669	D-7
GRANT	10,428	C-13
GREENBRIER	34,693	I-8
HAMPSHIRE	16,498	B-15
HANCOCK	35,233	A-2
HARDY	10,977	D-14
HARRISON	69,371	B-9
JACKSON	25,938	D-4
JEFFERSON	35,926	C-18
KANAWHA	207,619	G-4
LEWIS	17,223	D-8
LINCOLN	21,382	I-2
LOGAN	43,032	J-2
MARION	57,249	B-9
MARSHALL	37,356	D-2
MASON	25,178	E-3
McDOWELL	35,233	L-3
MERCER	64,980	L-6
MINERAL	26,697	B-14
MINGO	33,739	J-2
MONONGALIA	75,509	A-9
MONROE	12,406	K-8
MORGAN	12,128	B-16
NICHOLAS	26,775	H-7
OHIO	50,871	C-2
PENDLETON	8,054	E-12
PLEASANTS	7,546	C-6
POCAHONTAS	9,008	G-10
PRESTON	29,037	A-11
PUTNAM	42,835	F-4
RALEIGH	76,819	J-5
RANDOLPH	27,803	E-11
RITCHIE	10,233	D-6
ROANE	15,120	E-5
SUMMERS	14,204	K-7
TAYLOR	15,144	C-10
TUCKER	7,728	C-11
TYLER	9,796	D-9
UPSHUR	22,867	D-9
WAYNE	41,636	H-1
WEBSTER	10,729	F-9
WETZEL	19,258	A-7
WIRT	5,192	D-5
WOOD	86,915	D-4
WYOMING	28,990	K-4
TOTAL	1,793,477	

CITIES AND TOWNS

Note: The first name is that of the city or town, second, that of the county in which it is located, then the zip code area and location on the map.

Addison (Webster Springs), Webster, 26288. G-9
Alderson, Greenbrier/Monroe, 24910 K-8
•Alum Creek, Lincoln, 25003 H-4
•Amherstdale-Robinette, Logan,25607 J-3
Ansted, Fayette, 25812 I-6
Barboursville, Cabell, 25504 G-2
Barrackville, Marion, 26559 B-10
Bath (Berkeley Springs), Morgan, 25411 A17
•Beaver, Raleigh, 25813 K-6
Beckley, Raleigh, 25801 J-6
Belington, Barbour, 26250 D-11
Belle, Kanawha, 25015 H-5
Benwood, Marshall, 26031 D-1
•Bethany, Brooke, 26032 C-2
Bethlehem, Ohio, 26003 D-2
•Blennerhassett, Wood, 26101 C-4
Bluefield, Mercer, 24701 M-6
Boaz, Wood, 26187 C-5
Bolivar, Jefferson, 25425 C-18
•Bradley, Raleigh, 25818 J-6
Bridgeport, Harrison, 26330 C-9
Brookhaven, Monongalia, 26505 B-11
Buckhannon, Upshur, 26201 E-9
Cameron, Marshall, 26033 E-2
•Cassville, Monongalia, 26527 A-10
Cedar Grove, Kanawha, 25039 H-5
Ceredo, Wayne, 25507 G-1
Chapmanville, Logan, 25508 I-3
Charles Town, Jefferson,25414 C-18
Charleston, Kanawha, 25301-99 H-4
•Chattaroy, Mingo, 25667 K-2
Cheat Lake, Monongalia, 26505 A-11
Chesapeake, Kanawha, 25315 H-5
Chester, Hancock, 26034 A-2
Clarksburg, Harrison, 26301 C-9
Clay, Clay, 25043 G-6
Clendenin, Kanawha, 25045 G-5
•Coal City, Raleigh, 25823 K-6
Coal Fork, Kanawha, 25147 H-5
Corinne, Wyoming,25826 K-5
Corporation of Ranson, Jefferson, 25438. C-18
•Crab Orchard, Raleigh,25827 K-6
•Craigsville, Nicholas, 26205 H-8
•Cross Lanes, Kanawha, 25313 G-4
•Culloden, Cabell/Putnam, 25510 G-3
•Daniels, Raleigh, 25832 K-6
•Despard, Harrison, 26301 C-9
Dunbar, Kanawha, 25064 G-6
Eleanor, Putnam, 25070 G-5
Elizabeth, Wirt,26143 D-5
Elkins, Randolph, 26241 E-11
•Elkview, Kanawha, 25071 G-5
•Enterprise, Harrison, 26568 B-9
•Fairlea, Greenbrier, 24902 J-9
Fairmont, Marion, 26654 B-10

Fayetteville, Fayette, 25840 I-6
Follansbee, Brooke, 26037 B-2
•Fort Ashby, Mineral, 26719 B-15
Franklin, Pendleton, 26807 F-13
Gary, McDowell, 24836 L-4
•Gilbert Creek, Mingo, 25621 K-4
Glen Dale, Marshall, 26038 D-1
Glen Jean-Hilltop, Fayette,25846 J-6
Glenville, Gilmer, 26351 E-7
Grafton, Taylor, 26354 C-10
Grantsville, Calhoun, 26147 E-6
Hamlin, Lincoln, 25523 H-3
Harrisville, Ritchie, 26362 C-7
•Harts, Lincoln, 25524 I-2
Hinton, Summers,25951 K-7
•Holden, Logan, 25625 J-3
•Hooverson Heights, Brooke, 26037 B-2
Huntington, Cabell/Wayne, 25701-99 G-2
Hurricane, Putnam, 25526 G-3
Institute, Kanawha,25112 G-4
•Inwood, Berkeley, 25428 G-17
Kenova, Wayne, 25530 G-1
Keyser, Mineral, 26726 C-14
Kingwood, Preston, 26537 B-11
Lewisburg, Greenbrier, 24901 J-9
Lilly Grove, Mercer,24740 L-6
Logan, Logan, 25601 J-3
•Lubeck, Wood, 26101 C-4
Lumberport, Harrison, 26386 C-9
Mabscott, Raleigh, 25871 K-6
•MacArthur, Raleigh, 25873 K-6
Madison, Boone, 25130 I-4
•Mallory, Logan, 25634 K-4
Mannington, Marion, 26582 B-9
Marlinton, Pocahontas, 24954 H-10
Marmet, Kanawha, 25365 H-5
Martinsburg, Berkeley, 25401 B-19
Mason, Mason, 25260 D-3
McMechen, Marshall, 26040 D-1
Middlebourne, Tyler,26149 B-7
Milton, Cabell, 25541 G-3
•Mineralwells, Wood, 26150 D-5
Monongah, Marion, 26554 B-10
Montcalm, Mercer, 24737 M-6
Montgomery, Fayette/Kanawha, 25136 I-5
Moorefield, Hardy,26836 D-14
Morgantown, Monongalia, 26505 A-10
Moundsville, Marshall, 26041 D-1
•Mount Gay-Shamrock, Logan, 25637 J-3
Mount Hope, Fayette, 25880 J-6
Mullens, Wyoming,25882 K-5
New Cumberland, Hancock, 26047 A-2
New Haven, Mason, 25265 E-3
New Martinsville, Wetzel, 26155 A-7
•Newell, Hancock, 26050 A-2
Nitro, Kanawha/Putnam, 25143 G-4
Nutter Fort, Harrison, 26301 C-9
Oak Hill, Fayette, 25901 I-6
Oceana, Wyoming, 24870 K-4
Paden City, Tyler/Wetzel, 26159 B-7
Parkersburg, Wood, 26101 C-5
Parsons, Tucker, 26287 D-11
•Pea Ridge, Cabell,25718 G-2

Pennsboro, Ritchie, 26415 C-7
Petersburg, Grant, 26847 E-13
Philippi, Barbour, 26416 D-10
Piedmont, Mineral, 26750 B-14
•Pinch, Kanawha, 25156 G-5
•Pineville, Wyoming, 24874 K-5
•Piney View, Raleigh, 25906 J-6
Poca, Putnam, 26683 G-4
Point Pleasant, Mason, 25550 E-3
•Powellton, Fayette, 25161 I-6
Princeton, Mercer, 24740 L-6
•Prosperity, Raleigh, 25909 J-6
Rainelle, Greenbrier, 25962 I-8
Rand, Kanawha,25306 H-5
Ravenswood, Jackson, 26164 E-4
Richwood, Nicholas, 26261 H-8
Ripley, Jackson, 25271 E-4
Rivesville, Marion, 26588 B-10
Roderfield, McDowell,24881 L-4
Romney, Hampshire, 26757 C-15
Ronceverte, Greenbrier, 24970 K-9
Rupert, Greenbrier, 25984 J-8
Saint Albans, Kanawha, 25177 G-4
Saint Marys, Pleasants, 26170 C-6
Salem, Harrison,26426 C-8
•Shady Spring, Raleigh, 25918 K-6
Shepherdstown, Jefferson, 25443 B-18
Shinnston, Harrison, 26431 C-9
•Sissonville, Kanawha, 25360 G-4
Sistersville, Tyler, 26175 B-7
Smithers, Fayette/Kanawha, 25186 H-6
Sophia, Raleigh, 25921 K-6
South Charleston, Kanawha, 25303 H-4
Spencer, Roane, 25276 E-5
Sprague, Raleigh,25929 J-6
•Stanaford, Raleigh, 25927 J-6
Star City, Monongalia, 26505 A-10
Stonewood, Harrison, 26301 C-9
Summersville, Nicholas,26651 H-7
Sutton, Braxton,26601 F-8
•Switzer, Logan, 25647 J-3
•Teays Valley, Putnam, 25569 G-3
Terra Alta, Preston, 26764 B-12
•Tornado, Kanawha, 25202 H-4
Union, Monroe, 24983 K-8
•Verdunville, Logan, 25649 J-3
Vienna, Wood, 26105 C-5
War, McDowell, 24892 M-4
•Washington, Wood, 26181 C-4
Wayne, Wayne, 25570 H-2
Weirton, Brooke/Hancock, 26062 B-2
Welch, McDowell, 24801 L-4
Wellsburg, Brooke, 26070 C-2
West Liberty, Ohio, 26074 C-2
West Union, Doddridge, 26456 C-8
Weston, Lewis, 26452 D-9
Westover, Monongalia, 26505 A-10
Wheeling, Marshall/Ohio, 26003 D-1
White Sulphur Springs, Greenbrier, 24886 J-9
Williamson, Mingo, 25661 K-2
Williamstown, Wood, 26187 G-5
Winfield, Putnam, 25213 J-3

Explanation of symbols: •– Census Designated Place (CDP)

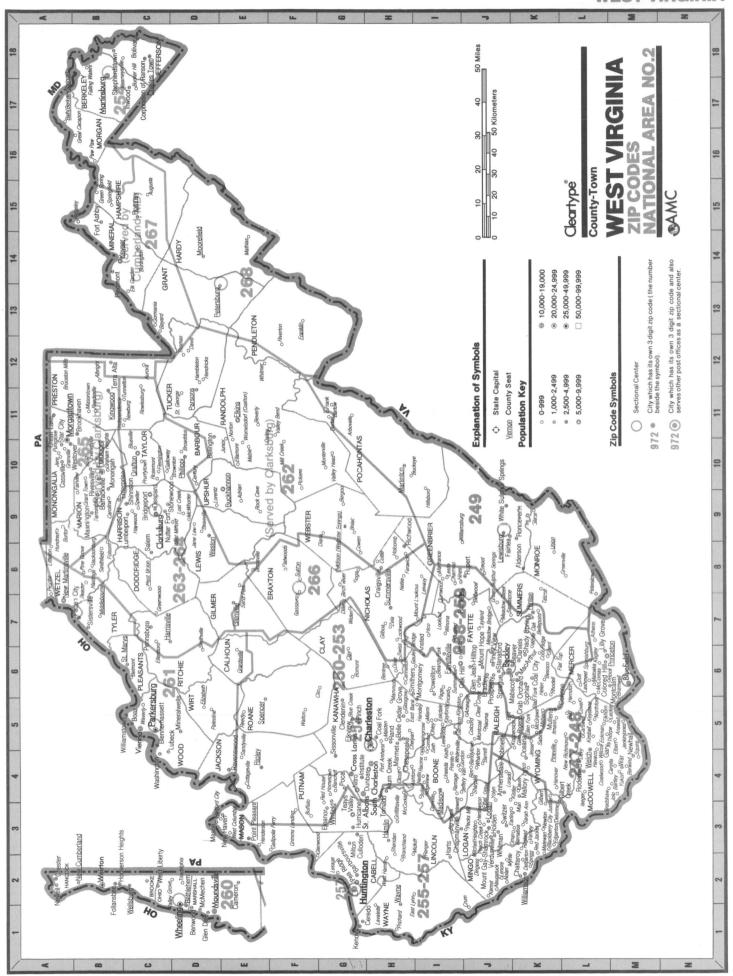

Copyright American Map Corporation

Explanation of symbols: ● – Census Designated Place (CDP)

Explanation of Symbols

State Capital
Vernon County Seat

Population Key

- ○ 0-999
- ⊙ 1,000-2,499
- ⊕ 2,500-4,999
- ◉ 5,000-9,999
- ◎ 10,000-19,000
- ◉ 20,000-24,999
- ◉ 25,000-49,999
- □ 50,000-99,999
- ▢ 100,000-249,999
- ■ 250,000-999,999

Zip Code Symbols

- ○ Sectional Center
- 972 ● City which has its own 3-digit zip code (the number beside the symbol).
- 972 ◉ City which has its own 3-digit zip code and also serves other post offices as a sectional center.

Cleartype®

County-Town

WISCONSIN
ZIP CODES
NATIONAL AREA NO.5

AMC

Copyright American Map Corporation

Explanation of symbols: ●– Census Designated Place (CDP)

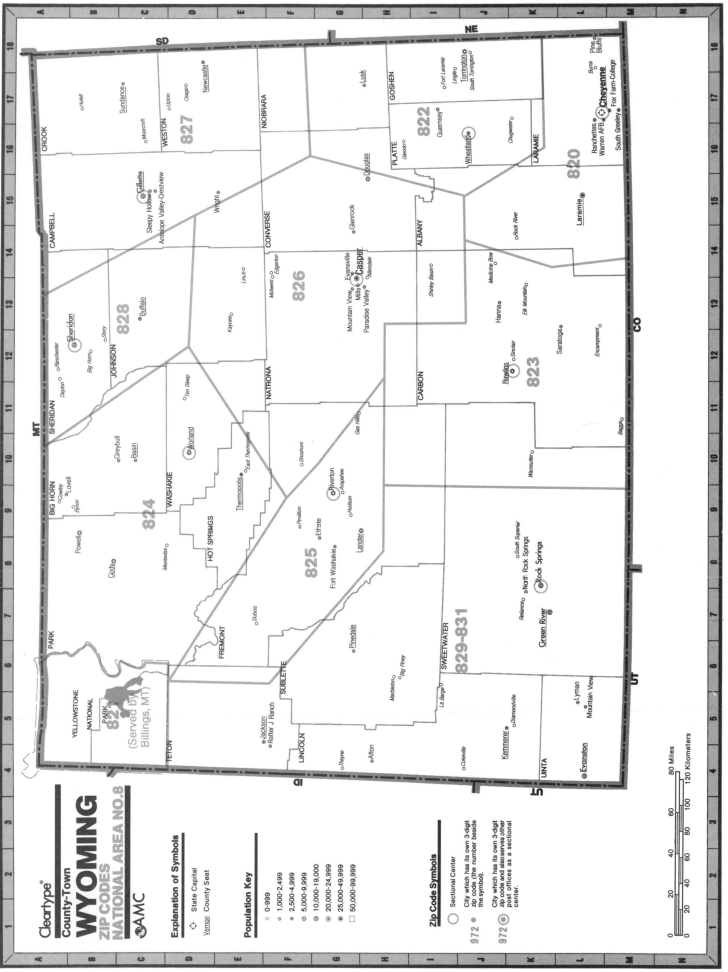

ClearType®
County-Town
WYOMING
ZIP CODES
NATIONAL AREA NO.8

⊙AMC

Explanation of Symbols

✛ State Capital
Vernon County Seat

Population Key

○ 0-999
⊕ 1,000-2,499
⊕ 2,500-4,999
⊚ 5,000-9,999
◉ 10,000-19,000
◉ 20,000-24,999
◉ 25,000-49,999
□ 50,000-99,999

Zip Code Symbols

○ Sectional Center

972 ● City which has its own 3-digit zip code (the number beside the symbol).

972 ◉ City which has its own 3-digit zip code and also serves other post offices as a sectional center.

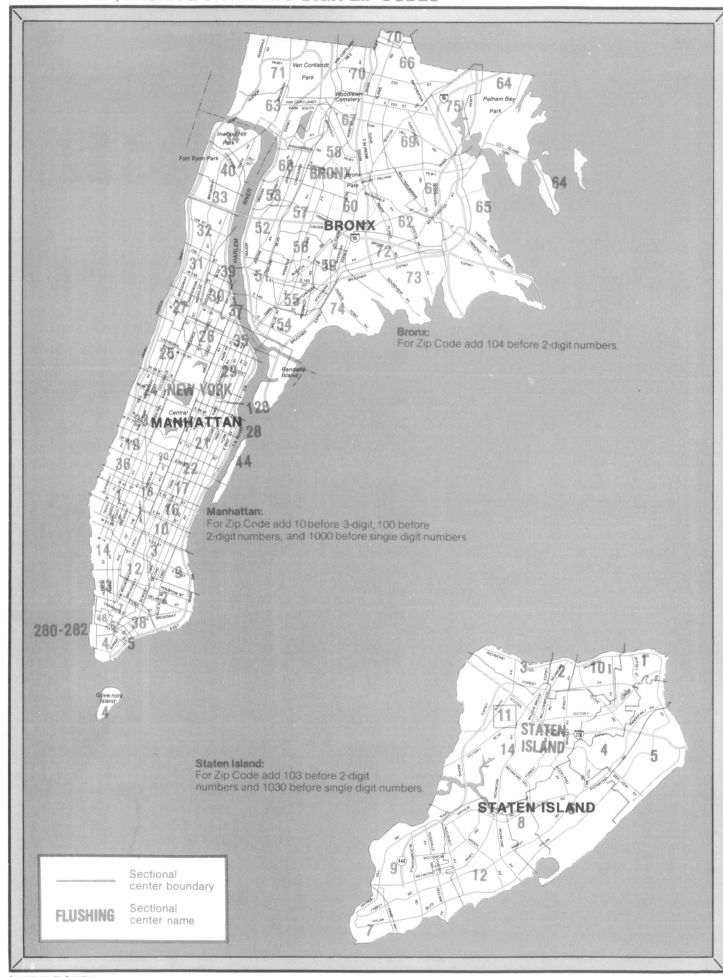

Bronx:
For Zip Code add 104 before 2-digit numbers.

Manhattan:
For Zip Code add 10 before 3-digit, 100 before
2-digit numbers, and 1000 before single digit numbers

Staten Island:
For Zip Code add 103 before 2-digit
numbers and 1030 before single digit numbers.

280-282

	Sectional center boundary
FLUSHING	Sectional center name

Copyright American Map Corporation

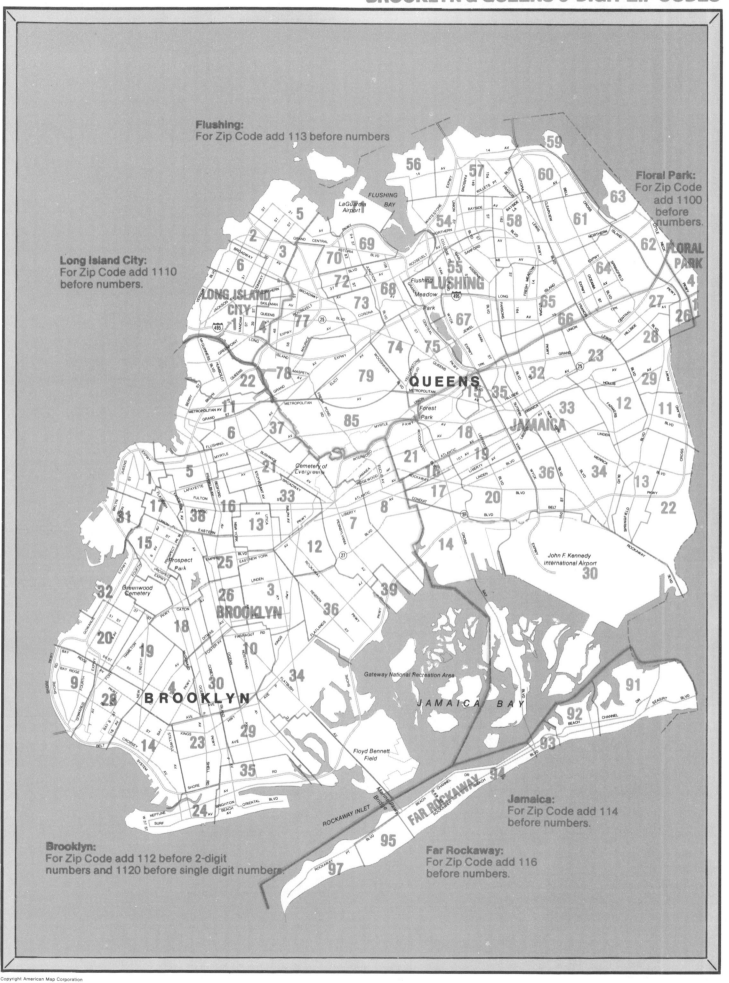

Flushing:
For Zip Code add 113 before numbers

Floral Park:
For Zip Code
add 1100
before
numbers.

Long Island City:
For Zip Code add 1110
before numbers.

Brooklyn:
For Zip Code add 112 before 2-digit
numbers and 1120 before single digit numbers.

Jamaica:
For Zip Code add 114
before numbers.

Far Rockaway:
For Zip Code add 116
before numbers.

Copyright American Map Corporation

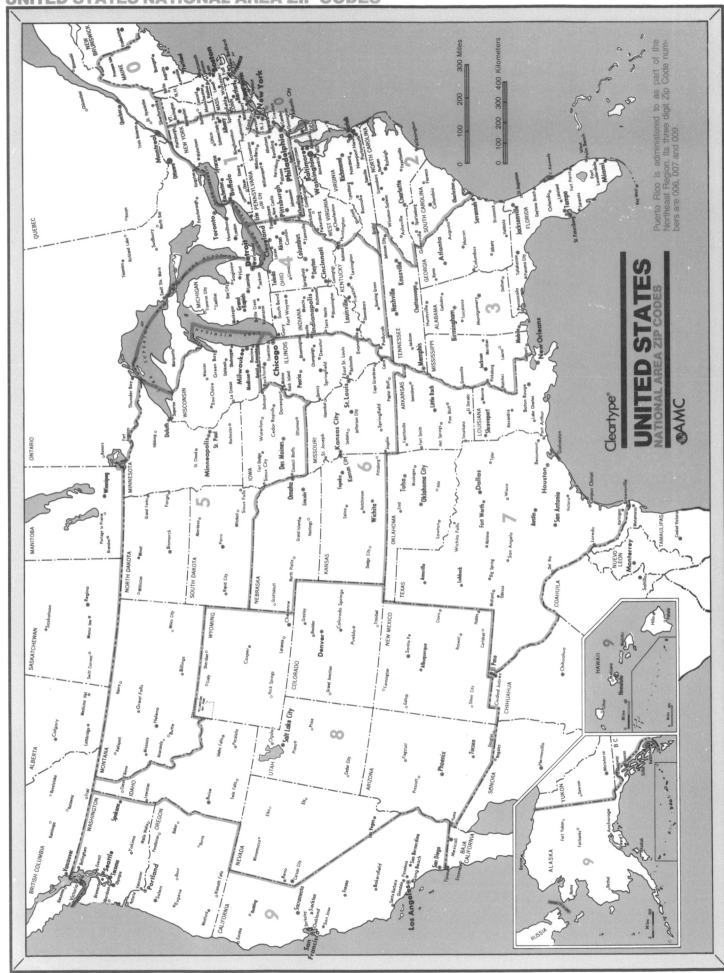

Copyright American Map Corporation

Copyright 1997 American Map Corporation

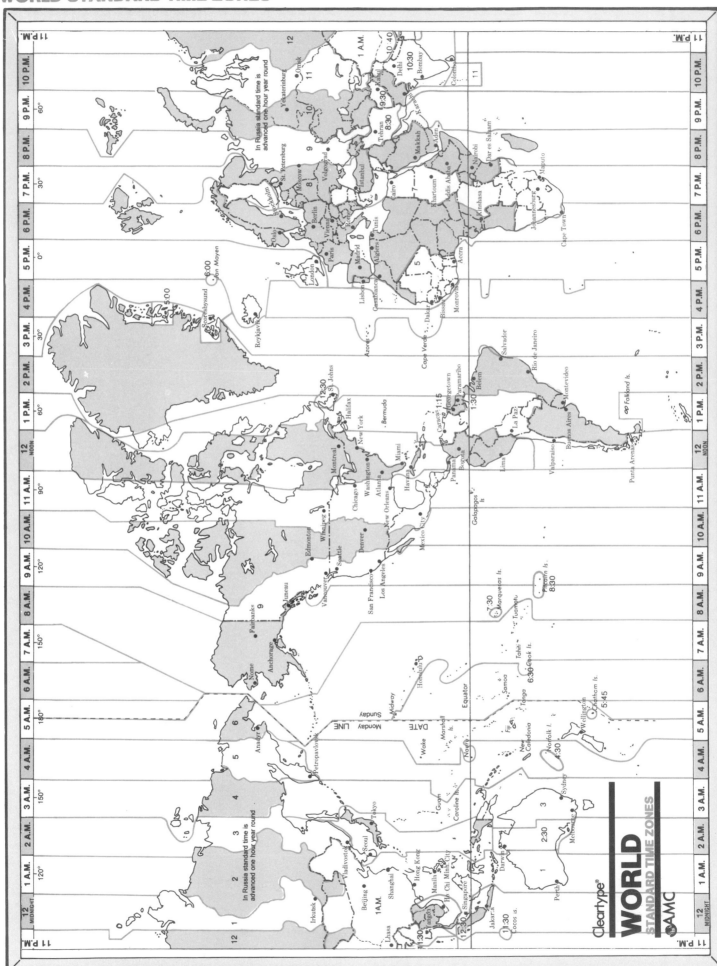

Copyright American Map Corporation

Zip Code	3-Digit Zip Code Areas	Total Households	Median Household Income	Average Household Income	Total Population	Population by Age: 0-5 years	Population by Age: 6-17 years	Population by Age: 18-34 years	Population by Age: 35-49 years	Population by Age: 50-64 years	Gray Markets (65+ years)
010-011	Springfield, MA	236,128	$38,002	$46,620	610,628	53,947	98,104	151,165	143,309	74,876	89,227
012	Pittsfield, MA	54,838	$35,751	$46,524	134,869	10,064	21,352	27,626	31,814	19,348	24,664
013	Springfield, MA	33,313	$35,373	$43,530	81,064	7,419	14,111	15,761	22,016	9,340	12,418
014	Worcester, MA	75,528	$44,596	$57,296	203,673	20,399	33,590	50,804	50,367	23,738	24,776
015-016	Worcester, MA	188,953	$44,136	$56,204	496,776	45,091	78,187	121,957	118,716	61,056	71,770
017	Boston, MA	132,096	$63,666	$88,018	348,006	29,833	48,060	80,212	95,968	53,232	40,701
018	Middlesex-Essex, MA	245,103	$53,428	$68,178	664,276	64,637	105,083	162,314	160,413	90,319	81,510
019	Middlesex-Essex, MA	177,745	$48,854	$66,286	448,897	38,165	63,165	99,191	115,851	64,251	68,274
020, 023-024	Brockton, MA	284,282	$55,953	$71,657	789,964	70,650	124,578	177,396	209,955	112,973	94,413
021-022	Boston, MA	653,072	$46,383	$66,780	1,590,272	117,964	181,737	484,583	364,765	207,493	233,731
025	Buzzards Bay, MA	41,196	$41,035	$54,705	100,366	8,849	15,647	18,861	25,512	14,450	17,048
026	Buzzards Bay, MA	62,797	$36,236	$49,186	141,792	10,658	18,569	24,095	32,676	20,656	35,138
027	Providence, RI	191,643	$37,252	$47,215	498,915	41,387	81,532	113,621	117,559	65,805	79,012
028-029	Providence, RI	389,500	$40,169	$56,148	985,527	80,083	151,506	239,636	230,260	129,614	154,427
030-031	Manchester, NH	181,279	$52,695	$65,427	474,214	47,830	73,858	121,397	126,030	59,126	45,974
032-033	Manchester, NH	81,694	$40,326	$52,650	207,359	18,527	34,171	47,231	54,038	26,856	26,537
034	Manchester, NH	30,009	$39,637	$50,327	77,608	6,760	11,948	18,345	19,282	10,576	10,696
035	White River Junction, VT	18,636	$30,382	$41,079	44,336	3,376	7,282	8,537	10,738	6,933	7,470
036	White River Junction, VT	3,888	$33,614	$41,572	10,770	881	1,695	1,992	2,809	1,739	1,653
037	White River Junction, VT	29,047	$35,708	$46,667	72,485	5,786	11,038	17,416	18,004	9,662	10,491
038	Portsmouth, NH	108,909	$43,633	$57,653	279,982	25,196	39,888	72,771	69,216	38,262	34,650
039	Portsmouth, NH	17,850	$44,992	$58,165	46,204	4,014	8,139	9,783	12,628	6,141	5,498
040-041	Portland, ME	157,457	$40,304	$55,858	398,637	31,906	61,963	97,445	100,849	52,697	53,778
042	Portland, ME	64,559	$30,719	$42,250	164,284	13,450	28,074	38,088	37,644	23,351	23,677
043	Portland, ME	29,164	$35,139	$46,774	75,150	5,448	13,091	15,512	19,802	11,064	10,233
044	Bangor, ME	65,120	$31,435	$43,919	160,464	11,691	28,065	41,415	40,827	25,444	22,022
045	Portland, ME	18,400	$35,138	$49,381	45,003	3,357	7,352	8,474	11,483	6,984	7,354
046	Bangor, ME	29,630	$26,706	$38,314	74,336	5,343	12,528	14,822	18,191	11,664	11,788
047	Bangor, ME	28,694	$24,368	$34,321	74,177	4,929	12,132	16,945	17,240	11,435	11,495
048	Portland, ME	15,225	$29,458	$42,195	37,408	2,901	5,978	6,726	9,827	5,487	6,488
049	Portland, ME	60,895	$28,360	$39,506	156,650	11,358	28,044	34,847	37,984	23,233	21,183
050	White River Junction, VT	24,127	$35,617	$47,793	59,510	4,582	10,428	11,817	15,820	8,787	8,075
051	White River Junction, VT	11,793	$30,957	$41,023	27,989	2,093	4,787	5,040	7,046	4,122	4,900
052	White River Junction, VT	13,282	$34,039	$46,761	32,303	2,549	5,534	7,080	7,779	5,202	5,159
053	White River Junction, VT	14,852	$32,797	$43,349	36,416	2,812	6,098	7,517	10,233	4,994	4,763
054	Burlington, VT	83,866	$42,383	$55,009	212,419	17,461	33,553	60,191	52,873	28,271	20,070
056	Burlington, VT	32,514	$34,572	$45,958	81,077	6,095	13,838	17,897	21,250	12,119	9,877
057	White River Junction, VT	32,231	$34,253	$44,602	81,013	5,981	12,685	19,016	20,516	11,636	11,178
058	White River Junction, VT	21,232	$27,596	$36,553	54,893	3,897	11,044	10,481	13,866	7,970	7,635
059	White River Junction, VT	1,361	$25,797	$29,292	3,441	241	665	594	859	607	476
060-061	Hartford, CT	359,914	$50,872	$67,832	903,338	70,226	145,503	205,498	215,902	129,979	136,231
062	Hartford, CT	50,982	$45,893	$56,424	139,964	10,833	24,233	36,661	34,270	18,051	15,916
063	New Haven, CT	95,644	$44,305	$56,832	248,096	20,302	41,388	62,501	56,748	33,918	33,239
064-066	New Haven, CT	458,111	$52,390	$70,435	1,185,659	94,689	190,737	268,987	288,979	164,657	177,609
067	Waterbury, CT	123,775	$48,324	$63,423	310,899	25,794	51,865	69,361	75,803	41,704	46,373
068-069	Stamford, CT	182,742	$73,013	$115,865	473,723	35,247	70,673	103,793	120,849	80,231	62,929
070-073	Newark, NJ	832,648	$46,034	$66,637	2,280,173	194,751	339,173	566,527	525,310	329,439	324,969
074-075	Paterson, NJ	210,795	$59,627	$84,687	621,837	58,156	100,623	138,847	154,990	93,867	75,354
076	Hackensack, NJ	171,207	$64,177	$89,966	469,117	37,976	64,805	97,489	115,803	78,991	74,052
077	Monmouth, NJ	217,261	$59,176	$82,265	574,087	54,019	91,819	122,601	150,590	83,101	71,956
078	West Jersey, NJ	117,266	$63,213	$83,282	333,781	32,241	54,946	70,586	96,390	46,965	32,653
079	West Jersey, NJ	87,221	$83,590	$124,567	231,829	18,283	29,440	48,928	60,462	42,540	32,175
080-084	South Jersey, NJ	633,150	$44,070	$58,024	1,702,691	162,851	290,949	381,352	399,802	235,395	232,341
085-086	Trenton, NJ	189,208	$54,297	$74,275	510,476	46,930	76,945	127,275	126,384	67,136	65,806
087	Trenton, NJ	157,859	$40,986	$53,753	389,200	31,186	58,854	69,194	81,248	51,498	97,220
088-089	New Brunswick, NJ	317,039	$59,904	$75,895	862,848	79,934	119,417	226,692	212,532	120,777	103,496

Zip Code	3-Digit Zip Code Areas	Total Households	Median Household Income	Average Household Income	Total Population	Population by Age: 0-5 years	Population by Age: 6-17 years	Population by Age: 18-34 years	Population by Age: 35-49 years	Population by Age: 50-64 years	Gray Markets (65+ years)
100-102	New York, NY	752,031	$46,178	$88,606	1,517,203	99,566	176,066	397,747	410,405	236,430	196,990
103	Staten Island, NY	146,426	$60,224	$76,298	400,987	36,234	66,375	93,900	100,627	57,192	46,659
104	Bronx, NY	422,446	$28,449	$40,651	1,177,877	127,357	229,554	296,542	241,326	149,739	133,359
105-108	Westchester, NY	371,237	$69,936	$106,107	982,784	84,668	143,415	220,205	237,467	155,414	141,615
109	Rockland, NY	157,109	$64,060	$85,147	470,325	43,865	86,216	104,441	112,013	74,480	49,310
110	Queens, NY	83,928	$70,982	$106,788	236,213	17,122	33,747	47,283	54,731	38,086	45,244
111	Long Island City, NY	80,165	$37,068	$48,342	187,098	12,332	24,128	54,577	42,574	26,853	26,634
112	Brooklyn, NY	811,260	$33,476	$49,727	2,226,576	200,630	429,673	531,108	491,655	286,183	287,327
113	Flushing, NY	399,184	$45,539	$60,809	1,009,933	71,230	138,720	250,536	237,888	149,377	162,182
114	Jamaica, NY	218,009	$48,533	$60,326	650,940	54,432	109,078	163,303	147,487	95,313	81,326
115	Western Nassau, NY	233,213	$71,155	$102,935	692,397	55,828	105,182	153,040	162,583	109,553	106,212
116	Far Rockaway, NY	34,424	$38,432	$55,390	99,758	9,764	19,194	22,145	19,922	12,115	16,618
117-118	Mid-Island, NY	503,231	$68,252	$90,294	1,540,663	124,268	243,571	365,906	372,410	259,123	175,385
119	Mid-Island, NY	73,077	$53,317	$73,739	202,065	17,015	32,240	42,140	46,516	28,097	36,057
120-123	Albany, NY	354,585	$40,599	$53,647	886,717	76,118	143,629	207,739	214,546	115,855	128,830
124	Mid-Hudson, NY	58,221	$38,525	$51,373	147,893	13,146	23,576	29,982	36,371	22,180	22,638
125-126	Mid-Hudson, NY	172,904	$50,994	$63,422	482,442	45,337	80,078	116,046	116,365	66,721	57,895
127	Mid-Hudson, NY	32,524	$35,991	$47,267	91,194	8,851	16,502	19,392	21,586	12,020	12,844
128	Glens Falls, NY	79,310	$37,604	$49,895	209,543	17,699	36,195	48,590	49,964	28,674	28,420
129	Plattsburgh, NY	57,819	$29,786	$38,379	159,768	14,369	27,119	42,200	35,272	21,649	19,159
130-132	Syracuse, NY	307,496	$37,948	$49,292	806,724	75,608	143,352	194,177	183,377	103,799	106,410
133-135	Utica, NY	156,319	$30,916	$40,979	407,966	35,535	72,688	92,685	88,010	53,477	65,571
136	Watertown, NY	82,653	$29,592	$37,930	237,241	22,206	45,002	66,948	48,005	28,314	26,767
137-139	Binghamton, NY	146,198	$33,864	$44,523	366,745	32,201	62,691	84,364	80,133	51,886	55,469
140-143	Buffalo, NY	521,747	$33,618	$45,292	1,317,210	115,665	218,383	294,882	292,176	186,920	209,185
144-146	Rochester, NY	410,358	$42,798	$56,089	1,072,448	104,348	183,475	249,354	259,005	138,774	137,492
147	Jamestown, NY	73,212	$28,355	$36,995	193,748	17,403	39,050	38,647	42,193	27,619	28,835
148-149	Elmira, NY	127,914	$31,524	$43,546	335,821	27,098	59,769	84,038	74,195	44,573	46,147
150-152	Pittsburgh, PA	651,039	$33,628	$51,734	1,590,427	113,313	228,558	340,874	370,381	238,246	299,056
153	Pittsburgh, PA	70,739	$31,096	$46,509	184,064	11,746	32,320	35,413	46,295	27,659	30,631
154	Pittsburgh, PA	61,219	$21,775	$31,823	157,736	9,377	27,771	31,132	36,624	23,293	29,539
155	Johnstown, PA	34,277	$25,221	$36,242	89,899	5,739	16,575	17,659	20,262	14,254	15,410
156	Greensburgh, PA	124,060	$31,883	$44,826	318,289	20,307	50,693	60,893	80,246	50,578	55,572
157	Johnstown, PA	41,938	$25,932	$35,699	113,832	6,707	20,110	28,205	25,767	14,963	18,080
158	DuBois, PA	37,820	$27,282	$35,919	95,427	6,831	17,557	19,103	20,570	15,013	16,352
159	Johnstown, PA	63,045	$24,379	$34,332	160,920	8,823	27,827	28,964	37,842	24,886	32,578
160	New Castle, PA	67,015	$36,010	$46,964	181,191	13,031	31,544	40,200	45,338	25,663	25,416
161	New Castle, PA	91,407	$26,924	$37,353	232,943	15,042	40,210	45,383	51,956	36,392	43,959
162	New Castle, PA	35,908	$25,434	$34,008	92,784	5,660	16,411	21,231	20,062	13,902	15,518
163	Oil City, PA	62,997	$27,622	$38,526	160,581	10,939	29,519	30,928	38,375	24,673	26,141
164-165	Erie, PA	116,473	$31,656	$44,094	311,797	24,364	57,992	70,813	72,872	40,591	45,164
166	Altoona, PA	79,176	$27,221	$36,380	209,788	13,544	37,558	43,403	49,938	31,454	33,890
167	Bradford, PA	20,243	$27,650	$35,534	52,853	3,737	9,385	10,799	12,169	8,129	8,634
168	Altoona, PA	63,835	$29,948	$44,435	171,254	10,798	22,444	61,357	35,167	21,857	19,630
169	Williamsport, PA	23,729	$26,962	$36,826	63,297	4,447	11,752	12,946	14,030	10,270	9,853
170-171	Harrisburg, PA	282,096	$38,744	$51,580	715,896	52,810	116,391	158,425	177,879	104,210	106,181
172	Harrisburg, PA	65,662	$33,696	$45,553	171,140	12,226	28,562	39,849	39,637	25,620	25,246
173-174	Lancaster, PA	164,442	$39,966	$51,564	429,288	33,868	70,325	96,900	107,910	61,970	59,314
175-176	Lancaster, PA	160,171	$41,971	$56,333	429,246	37,914	79,871	97,137	97,190	57,980	59,155
177	Williamsport, PA	66,254	$29,632	$39,358	172,323	12,243	30,649	36,958	39,811	25,432	27,230
178	Harrisburg, PA	88,846	$29,351	$40,522	232,060	16,667	37,696	53,985	51,823	34,083	37,806
179	Reading, PA	53,118	$28,250	$36,428	130,552	8,137	21,190	25,990	29,352	19,539	26,345
180-181	Lehigh Valley, PA	235,622	$42,576	$56,968	606,360	47,322	96,617	136,001	147,810	82,580	96,030
182	Wilkes-Barre, PA	50,951	$29,206	$39,033	127,903	8,240	19,781	25,357	28,139	19,689	26,697
183	Lehigh Valley, PA	46,345	$42,092	$53,526	130,710	11,614	22,834	30,234	31,692	17,577	16,759
184-185	Scranton, PA	116,014	$31,251	$44,395	298,109	20,835	48,487	61,052	67,149	43,042	57,544

Zip Code	3-Digit Zip Code Areas	Total Households	Median Household Income	Average Household Income	Total Population	Population by Age: 0-5 years	Population by Age: 6-17 years	Population by Age: 18-34 years	Population by Age: 35-49 years	Population by Age: 50-64 years	Gray Markets (65+ years)
186-187	Wilkes-Barre, PA	127,046	$29,581	$40,580	314,626	20,737	48,813	64,720	71,798	45,986	62,573
188	Scranton, PA	28,902	$30,530	$41,037	75,716	5,646	14,481	14,585	17,979	11,728	11,298
189	Southeastern, PA	114,021	$62,108	$84,304	311,991	24,862	52,342	66,443	83,494	46,244	38,605
190-191	Philadelphia, PA	1,009,926	$41,346	$60,326	2,603,458	216,731	413,547	637,953	582,138	349,074	404,016
193	Southeastern, PA	127,138	$66,168	$91,215	351,290	30,257	58,735	80,396	93,800	48,519	39,583
194	Southeastern, PA	167,773	$57,718	$79,745	425,553	35,026	63,252	101,397	105,479	59,795	60,603
195-196	Reading, PA	140,282	$41,860	$55,627	361,048	28,309	58,736	80,979	84,150	52,032	56,841
197-198	Wilmington, DE	179,371	$52,019	$69,713	471,518	40,450	73,046	124,410	115,252	61,125	57,235
199	Wilmington, DE	97,415	$35,429	$48,697	258,584	22,388	42,465	57,536	58,324	40,176	37,695
200, 202-205	Washington, DC	230,464	$42,407	$69,093	536,290	46,925	64,485	143,500	127,491	76,606	77,282
201, 220-223	Northern Virginia, VA	649,125	$69,038	$88,811	1,697,481	143,217	248,712	459,643	475,556	236,394	133,959
206-207	Southern, MD	405,663	$53,727	$63,725	1,111,519	109,486	170,916	309,757	281,869	153,335	86,155
208-209	Suburban, MD	324,452	$68,593	$97,141	854,279	83,731	116,124	203,408	221,382	112,585	97,048
210-212, 214	Baltimore, MD	884,867	$43,869	$58,618	2,282,157	222,437	338,883	551,122	565,843	315,529	288,343
215	Cumberland, MD	41,365	$25,311	$33,847	101,400	7,548	16,321	21,318	21,404	16,584	18,226
216	Easton, MD	58,474	$36,312	$50,450	145,754	12,995	22,070	29,374	33,607	23,513	24,195
217	Frederick, MD	141,871	$44,404	$55,526	385,162	36,897	62,451	89,890	98,762	53,822	43,340
218	Salisbury, MD	56,120	$31,497	$41,479	144,035	11,833	22,065	34,718	32,754	21,207	21,458
219	Baltimore, MD	28,849	$42,845	$50,730	78,570	7,925	13,628	18,004	19,830	10,926	8,257
224-225	Richmond, VA	102,587	$43,456	$53,942	287,115	25,799	51,468	69,613	68,321	40,657	31,257
226	Winchester, VA	54,984	$36,501	$45,436	140,778	11,848	21,810	33,036	32,751	22,721	18,612
227	Culpepper, VA	21,239	$40,925	$51,192	59,484	5,500	10,255	13,835	13,878	8,855	7,162
228	Charlottesville, VA	49,355	$31,582	$41,146	129,492	8,891	18,700	35,602	27,540	19,647	18,111
229	Charlottesville, VA	79,402	$36,561	$50,057	202,272	16,226	29,373	53,945	46,506	30,191	26,031
230-232	Richmond, VA	369,711	$41,572	$55,346	915,256	76,264	143,335	221,015	231,286	130,920	113,435
233-237	Norfolk, VA	555,952	$36,248	$46,418	1,472,933	145,302	253,520	431,616	318,576	177,902	146,016
238	Richmond, VA	106,646	$34,649	$43,251	283,664	23,898	47,530	65,785	67,503	44,310	34,639
239	Farmville, VA	34,552	$25,115	$31,463	94,050	6,177	14,683	21,716	19,928	15,701	15,845
240-241	Roanoke, VA	211,190	$30,994	$40,402	517,707	34,980	70,523	130,868	121,433	84,852	75,052
242	Bristol, VA	76,848	$21,670	$29,867	191,391	11,118	33,082	37,916	45,858	34,217	29,200
243	Roanoke, VA	60,973	$24,819	$29,657	151,027	9,098	22,861	30,470	34,663	28,612	25,323
244	Charlottesville, VA	51,760	$29,924	$36,937	133,361	8,718	19,876	29,622	31,106	23,477	20,562
245	Lynchburg, VA	139,949	$29,752	$38,749	356,590	25,869	55,785	77,158	81,415	60,480	55,883
246	Bluefield, WV	30,277	$21,387	$30,432	77,247	4,026	14,960	15,390	19,410	13,438	10,023
247-248	Bluefield, WV	45,246	$22,294	$35,125	116,268	7,150	20,979	24,274	27,461	17,719	18,684
249	Lewisburg, WV	19,747	$24,896	$35,563	51,044	3,376	7,725	10,647	12,112	8,840	8,344
250-253	Charleston, WV	135,639	$30,381	$45,502	335,880	22,184	55,338	70,843	79,827	54,922	52,767
254	Martinsburg, WV	47,912	$38,050	$49,377	125,039	11,053	19,243	32,286	28,586	18,321	15,550
255-257	Huntington, WV	107,620	$27,779	$41,516	277,629	18,016	47,713	64,791	62,707	44,523	39,881
258-259	Beckley, WV	54,972	$23,996	$36,982	137,487	8,158	25,106	25,967	33,231	22,033	22,992
260	Wheeling, WV	56,492	$32,896	$45,247	144,779	9,316	21,397	29,964	33,517	24,355	26,231
261	Parkersburg, WV	53,863	$32,549	$41,843	136,018	9,877	21,282	28,827	31,213	23,672	21,147
262	Clarksburg, WV	32,037	$22,984	$33,367	86,135	6,032	14,161	19,007	20,217	13,258	13,460
263-264	Clarksburg, WV	56,646	$25,238	$36,306	146,944	10,252	24,227	32,210	32,865	23,089	24,301
265	Clarksburg, WV	61,734	$29,088	$42,478	156,663	9,861	22,115	46,244	34,700	20,779	22,965
266	Gassaway, WV	13,123	$23,214	$32,185	32,396	2,513	5,783	6,694	7,556	5,149	4,702
267	Cumberland, MD	19,212	$27,563	$36,625	50,623	3,887	8,130	11,432	11,617	8,066	7,490
268	Petersburg, WV	12,642	$27,972	$35,914	32,016	2,530	4,693	7,124	7,178	5,271	5,221
270-274	Greensboro, NC	591,250	$35,249	$52,819	1,462,698	118,971	222,727	348,278	353,245	219,791	199,685
275-277	Raleigh, NC	485,670	$41,037	$59,335	1,242,695	108,805	192,926	352,289	309,076	153,434	126,165
278	Rocky Mount, NC	185,235	$26,644	$39,941	486,471	40,082	90,718	111,597	112,262	66,889	64,923
279	Rocky Mount, NC	62,099	$26,959	$39,278	164,110	14,287	30,077	33,923	36,412	23,825	25,586
280-282	Charlotte, NC	574,270	$39,098	$57,028	1,459,903	131,450	236,989	362,740	353,336	200,343	175,045
283	Fayetteville, NC	257,687	$27,747	$39,707	703,198	65,037	135,419	178,839	150,256	93,058	80,588
284	Fayetteville, NC	129,469	$28,938	$43,386	331,190	25,044	55,038	72,643	77,816	53,022	47,627
285	Kinston, NC	143,361	$27,958	$39,878	419,167	38,898	70,179	126,327	83,108	52,132	48,522

Zip Code	3-Digit Zip Code Areas	Total Households	Median Household Income	Average Household Income	Total Population	Population by Age: 0-5 years	Population by Age: 6-17 years	Population by Age: 18-34 years	Population by Age: 35-49 years	Population by Age: 50-64 years	Gray Markets (65+ years)
286	Hickory, NC	216,803	$30,334	$42,550	548,861	38,626	86,173	127,956	130,204	88,934	76,968
287-289	Asheville, NC	227,766	$28,902	$41,777	560,601	38,152	84,194	108,878	130,094	93,780	105,502
290-292	Columbia, SC	336,705	$34,200	$47,810	921,974	79,166	158,231	236,835	222,176	120,135	105,431
293	Greenville, SC	132,958	$32,738	$44,049	345,502	27,591	54,703	81,420	82,370	52,738	46,680
294	Charleston, SC	228,155	$35,473	$48,424	585,317	60,785	100,308	162,600	131,269	68,621	61,735
295	Florence, SC	190,960	$28,821	$42,591	499,504	38,179	91,161	111,454	116,636	75,026	67,048
296	Greenville, SC	306,359	$35,361	$48,586	776,981	61,759	120,513	191,586	182,501	118,285	102,338
297	Charlotte, NC	94,276	$37,358	$48,909	248,610	21,903	41,185	60,813	58,712	37,001	28,996
298	Augusta, GA	72,590	$37,766	$48,035	192,206	16,889	34,916	45,966	44,959	26,050	23,426
299	Savannah, GA	51,650	$36,661	$56,941	138,112	13,811	23,147	35,813	27,434	18,467	19,440
300-302	North Metro, GA	1,133,977	$46,395	$63,429	3,013,850	281,260	534,497	788,055	775,706	394,147	240,187
303	Atlanta, GA	335,761	$39,256	$71,430	793,482	64,394	112,159	234,574	196,403	103,188	82,764
304	Swainsboro, GA	70,548	$22,734	$31,710	189,856	15,591	35,659	49,176	39,026	25,630	24,775
306	Athens, GA	110,060	$27,660	$40,476	286,174	22,804	48,898	80,866	61,136	39,022	33,447
307	Chattanooga, TN	113,150	$29,478	$39,789	294,697	21,905	52,640	68,398	67,567	49,037	35,151
308-309	Augusta, GA	129,834	$32,398	$46,189	351,653	33,149	69,428	85,000	82,324	46,374	35,378
310,312	Macon, GA	226,341	$29,427	$41,474	613,635	52,084	115,205	143,527	135,056	91,061	76,702
313-314	Savannah, GA	133,445	$30,614	$43,831	364,262	35,389	68,578	98,707	77,738	44,400	39,449
315	Waycross, GA	103,931	$27,640	$38,525	281,489	24,777	54,853	66,874	61,961	39,500	33,523
316	- Valdosta, GA	55,943	$24,791	$35,642	154,879	14,237	29,830	40,115	32,519	21,408	16,771
317	Albany, GA	168,045	$24,218	$35,186	459,837	39,236	96,841	99,901	99,340	64,244	60,275
318-319	Columbus, GA	96,053	$27,675	$41,389	262,730	24,220	48,266	69,699	55,146	34,960	30,439
320-322	Jacksonville, FL	611,985	$32,688	$47,528	1,554,844	125,494	270,484	357,195	349,955	224,998	226,719
323	Tallahassee, FL	129,118	$29,794	$45,891	344,087	24,969	62,402	97,004	81,190	43,027	35,496
324	Panama City, FL	110,198	$25,729	$37,131	286,576	20,794	52,962	62,585	62,253	47,961	40,021
325	Pensacola, FL	204,631	$31,724	$44,353	551,295	46,548	99,771	131,838	119,050	87,784	66,304
326,344	Gainsville, FL	243,720	$25,425	$38,482	594,793	41,080	92,076	131,090	117,972	91,588	120,986
327	Mid-Florida, FL	304,626	$38,413	$55,275	757,779	59,240	130,452	168,168	171,849	108,309	119,761
328	Orlando, FL	234,671	$37,060	$51,694	599,806	51,801	99,118	182,416	132,980	73,168	60,323
329	Orlando, FL	206,705	$37,727	$52,562	490,760	36,633	71,710	103,236	95,715	80,380	103,086
330	South Florida, FL	477,136	$37,189	$54,921	1,263,720	107,569	210,625	279,113	285,718	177,738	202,957
331-332	Miami, FL	575,234	$33,417	$57,560	1,597,660	134,488	275,033	361,494	346,764	238,001	241,879
333	Fort Lauderdale, FL	279,595	$39,568	$59,649	676,192	52,582	97,728	151,466	164,510	85,803	124,102
334	West Palm Beach, FL	489,372	$43,153	$69,156	1,090,705	77,969	147,195	211,985	225,262	150,571	277,723
335-336	Tampa, FL	414,695	$34,037	$50,627	1,011,200	83,611	170,004	242,392	234,555	140,889	139,748
337	Saint Petersburg, FL	250,207	$31,273	$47,391	536,999	34,839	67,598	105,062	119,943	77,946	131,611
338	Lakeland, FL	212,197	$28,032	$41,124	532,684	40,527	89,155	96,515	101,788	86,591	118,108
339	Fort Meyers, FL	215,515	$33,018	$50,049	481,179	31,477	66,262	83,432	89,128	80,797	130,082
342	Manasota, FL	262,040	$33,971	$52,805	572,385	34,985	70,888	93,473	109,020	91,562	172,458
346	Tampa, FL	309,387	$29,571	$43,516	679,128	41,705	89,140	118,068	135,264	104,536	190,415
347	Orlando, FL	111,710	$30,617	$42,968	289,711	22,658	51,294	59,209	59,367	44,568	52,416
349	West Palm Beach, FL	122,970	$34,639	$53,319	304,103	21,584	47,028	54,746	57,936	49,293	73,516
350-352	Birmingham, AL	440,131	$33,250	$52,150	1,139,452	89,810	202,675	262,675	273,841	157,708	152,939
354	Tuscaloosa, AL	76,078	$27,614	$42,140	199,342	14,252	35,125	56,317	42,019	26,286	25,345
355	Birmingham, AL	61,228	$23,836	$34,886	157,755	10,457	27,984	33,273	35,864	25,862	24,316
356	Huntsville, AL	134,011	$31,323	$43,440	345,431	26,148	57,723	80,514	79,537	54,459	47,051
357-358	Huntsville, AL	132,170	$42,122	$57,754	333,486	27,961	51,943	90,693	73,587	53,676	35,627
359	Birmingham, AL	99,366	$26,314	$37,489	251,308	16,758	45,256	53,357	57,946	39,900	38,091
360-361	Montgomery, AL	171,242	$30,047	$44,710	467,026	40,126	90,030	114,728	103,918	59,994	58,231
362	Anniston, AL	66,905	$27,994	$37,956	175,385	12,192	31,556	41,340	39,746	25,789	24,762
363	Dothan, AL	80,626	$29,466	$41,142	211,744	17,307	39,632	49,069	47,544	30,141	28,051
364	Evergreen, AL	41,787	$23,301	$33,062	111,765	8,417	22,319	23,534	23,716	16,680	17,099
365-366	Mobile, AL	212,594	$29,541	$45,527	577,049	48,317	113,705	127,955	132,184	80,240	74,648
367	Montgomery, AL	43,698	$20,400	$33,314	124,902	10,792	29,014	26,434	24,484	16,715	17,464
368	Montgomery, AL	77,369	$26,727	$40,152	201,889	15,345	33,087	60,708	42,308	26,809	23,632
369	Meridian, MS	8,603	$19,536	$32,639	23,255	1,805	5,160	4,970	4,799	3,218	3,303

Zip Code	3-Digit Zip Code Areas	Total Households	Median Household Income	Average Household Income	Total Population	Population by Age: 0-5 years	Population by Age: 6-17 years	Population by Age: 18-34 years	Population by Age: 35-49 years	Population by Age: 50-64 years	Gray Markets (65+ years)
370-372	Nashville, TN	576,181	$37,054	$53,261	1,479,050	132,175	245,353	385,508	353,455	201,625	160,935
373-374	Chattanooga, TN	261,829	$30,694	$44,862	664,735	49,433	108,467	149,920	158,375	106,257	92,284
376	Johnson City, TN	151,110	$29,014	$41,258	371,743	24,658	53,144	85,055	89,534	62,610	56,743
377-379	Knoxville, TN	423,652	$29,473	$43,836	1,067,318	78,625	162,322	252,050	257,042	171,012	146,267
380-381	Memphis, TN	409,142	$34,608	$53,549	1,078,090	106,097	192,092	271,137	256,999	132,468	119,298
382	McKenzie, TN	44,850	$26,058	$36,122	111,936	7,439	18,086	25,304	24,542	18,039	18,526
383	Jackson, TN	104,436	$26,079	$36,263	264,834	20,006	44,911	58,288	59,941	40,615	41,074
384	Columbia, TN	64,944	$28,399	$37,973	167,641	14,200	29,062	38,152	37,814	25,704	22,709
385	Cookeville, TN	75,760	$24,076	$33,971	190,889	13,243	29,588	44,429	42,194	31,994	29,443
386	Memphis, TN	111,759	$27,272	$39,141	312,122	24,705	63,240	79,731	65,713	42,730	36,003
387	Greenville, MS	46,506	$20,537	$35,153	143,933	12,268	35,948	34,307	29,465	15,644	16,300
388	Tupelo, MS	92,152	$26,057	$37,792	299,558	17,837	45,244	54,205	53,175	35,854	33,243
389	Grenada, MS	43,144	$21,261	$53,316	117,950	9,409	26,414	25,603	24,259	15,272	16,994
390-392	Jackson, MS	271,876	$28,975	$46,661	757,418	58,741	155,074	174,540	162,969	97,262	88,832
393	Meridian, MS	76,867	$23,319	$56,069	206,327	15,904	44,846	45,165	43,259	28,174	28,978
394	Hattiesburg, MS	121,187	$23,116	$36,638	329,635	25,019	69,387	79,026	69,758	44,842	41,603
395	Gulfport, MS	129,221	$29,696	$42,880	360,593	28,934	70,267	85,309	79,631	54,350	42,102
396	McComb, MS	47,547	$19,356	$51,514	128,720	9,224	29,554	26,853	26,690	18,017	18,381
397	Columbus, MS	60,597	$26,314	$39,650	163,411	13,180	33,063	44,936	33,084	20,549	18,600
400-402	Louisville, KY	387,390	$34,533	$53,830	986,687	77,515	170,610	234,678	238,242	140,032	125,609
403-406	Lexington, KY	285,071	$31,099	$48,265	730,322	53,704	119,851	195,674	174,109	101,910	85,073
407-409	London, KY	78,920	$17,275	$30,609	211,651	15,436	41,713	49,089	49,488	30,045	25,880
410	Cincinnati, OH	152,807	$36,886	$50,730	412,362	36,760	77,053	100,492	94,850	54,825	48,383
411-412	Ashland, KY	71,984	$23,241	$37,339	188,964	11,836	35,416	40,106	45,253	31,323	25,031
413-414	Campton, KY	23,861	$14,258	$23,230	63,861	4,432	13,223	14,812	14,461	9,779	7,153
415-416	Pikeville, KY	44,664	$18,823	$32,098	119,970	7,782	24,633	26,771	29,634	17,082	14,069
417-418	Hazard, KY	29,717	$16,808	$26,781	80,937	5,268	16,944	19,035	19,569	11,373	8,747
420	Paducah, KY	87,342	$25,342	$39,867	215,760	14,438	35,180	46,730	49,348	33,845	36,219
421-422	Bowling Green, KY	119,633	$24,661	$36,384	321,698	24,520	55,583	85,819	68,802	45,790	41,185
423	Owensboro, KY	63,158	$25,923	$38,771	162,592	12,462	30,419	34,640	37,646	24,723	22,702
424	Evansville, IN	52,653	$27,715	$40,352	135,531	9,859	25,532	29,018	31,839	19,790	19,494
425-426	Somerset, KY	51,022	$18,618	$28,847	129,449	9,012	23,176	28,252	29,189	21,458	18,361
427	Elizabethtown, KY	61,187	$23,511	$34,913	154,653	11,137	27,729	33,760	34,159	25,319	22,549
430-432	Columbus, OH	647,683	$38,233	$54,032	1,633,876	132,955	272,220	449,249	381,553	229,009	173,890
433	Columbus, OH	68,813	$32,114	$41,653	173,246	13,661	34,372	37,881	39,970	27,728	24,634
434-436	Toledo, OH	321,446	$36,791	$51,445	812,249	64,656	148,177	196,404	183,091	112,076	107,845
437-438	Zanesville, OH	98,892	$26,450	$35,015	243,893	18,739	47,842	51,429	53,567	39,315	36,001
439	Steubenville, OH	78,269	$23,320	$32,686	192,333	11,450	33,388	35,397	43,253	33,084	35,761
440-441	Cleveland, OH	855,095	$37,925	$55,406	2,131,768	169,426	351,110	481,456	485,110	316,934	327,732
442-443	Akron, OH	307,530	$38,272	$54,407	801,037	60,838	135,144	191,712	188,665	118,007	106,671
444-445	Youngstown, OH	217,755	$30,605	$42,976	547,437	37,945	94,689	107,639	126,137	86,815	94,212
446-447	Canton, OH	243,491	$32,606	$45,816	632,686	48,561	115,605	132,235	146,726	96,566	92,992
448-449	Mansfield, OH	172,841	$33,479	$44,263	442,931	32,911	84,844	92,955	99,149	70,736	62,337
450-452	Cincinnati, OH	632,257	$39,667	$57,675	1,607,741	137,101	286,977	396,992	356,229	232,428	198,014
453-455	Dayton, OH	441,253	$37,779	$51,122	1,096,696	85,215	188,088	256,483	248,030	170,915	147,966
456	Chillicothe, OH	135,835	$23,367	$33,613	349,321	23,706	67,928	77,078	76,338	56,841	47,429
457	Athens, OH	60,504	$25,127	$35,774	157,123	9,575	26,687	44,837	33,099	23,426	19,499
458	Lima, OH	140,204	$35,280	$44,987	369,668	29,781	73,738	82,162	80,194	52,420	51,373
460-462	Indianapolis, IN	635,289	$40,020	$57,311	1,605,781	142,994	273,448	398,012	382,941	221,775	186,611
463-464	Gary, IN	278,926	$37,688	$50,332	761,350	56,679	148,310	163,766	184,646	110,835	97,114
465-466	South Bend, IN	217,760	$35,564	$49,835	572,962	53,107	104,952	133,393	131,552	74,706	75,252
467-468	Fort Wayne, IN	219,644	$37,465	$50,420	571,885	51,690	110,685	129,379	135,524	74,157	70,450
469	Kokomo, IN	123,970	$32,222	$42,698	310,717	23,448	56,027	64,702	71,359	49,934	45,246
470	Cincinnati, OH	40,298	$34,159	$44,424	109,315	8,951	21,799	23,127	25,598	16,072	13,768
471	Louisville, KY	102,799	$31,504	$41,520	262,455	19,298	48,572	56,390	65,589	39,199	33,407
472	Columbus, IN	76,575	$33,276	$45,350	195,736	15,031	35,260	42,922	46,893	31,312	24,319

Zip Code	3-Digit Zip Code Areas	Total Households	Median Household Income	Average Household Income	Total Population	Population by Age: 0-5 years	Population by Age: 6-17 years	Population by Age: 18-34 years	Population by Age: 35-49 years	Population by Age: 50-64 years	Gray Markets (65+ years)
473	Muncie, IN	135,205	$28,783	$39,691	334,580	22,899	54,849	78,950	74,710	52,644	50,528
474	Bloomington, IN	97,087	$29,331	$41,236	248,870	17,077	37,394	75,585	54,531	34,572	29,710
475	Washington, IN	61,978	$29,784	$39,591	162,271	13,112	29,768	37,572	35,177	23,323	23,319
476-477	Evansville, IN	117,893	$33,520	$47,504	289,485	23,004	50,279	63,883	68,468	41,459	42,393
478	Terre Haute, IN	70,561	$27,768	$39,635	180,503	13,028	30,707	42,759	41,541	24,924	27,543
479	Lafayette, IN	101,809	$32,537	$44,818	270,576	20,720	43,589	80,373	57,183	35,623	33,089
480, 483	Royal Oak, MI	774,068	$55,190	$75,654	1,962,129	159,856	306,939	468,296	497,901	280,754	248,383
481-482	Detroit, MI	997,079	$40,270	$54,499	2,620,042	240,741	461,258	640,598	630,286	326,611	320,550
484-485	Flint, MI	250,910	$39,346	$49,770	655,519	54,632	126,138	146,045	158,890	96,728	73,086
486-487	Saginaw, MI	250,385	$30,886	$42,876	629,872	49,896	115,802	128,252	144,009	97,900	94,013
488-489	Lansing, MI	268,501	$39,332	$51,057	714,355	57,971	127,732	194,933	171,909	88,089	73,721
490-491	Kalamazoo, MI	327,198	$35,521	$48,380	836,648	69,918	155,134	187,797	198,694	117,017	108,087
492	Jackson, MI	124,932	$36,479	$46,294	344,047	28,292	65,166	76,266	83,087	47,399	43,837
493-495	Grand Rapids, MI	421,508	$38,447	$51,287	1,129,739	112,088	218,440	275,150	255,890	136,913	131,258
496	Traverse City, MI	95,362	$29,867	$40,362	236,015	19,727	45,219	45,635	55,086	36,223	34,124
497	Gaylord, MI	84,931	$27,429	$37,263	214,401	16,490	38,648	44,136	47,340	34,221	33,566
498-499	Iron Mountain, MI	109,541	$26,321	$34,455	264,866	18,386	49,145	54,525	59,957	37,258	45,595
500-503, 509	Des Moines, IA	301,618	$38,162	$55,937	770,537	58,320	129,328	192,847	175,298	108,162	106,581
504	Mason City, IA	45,354	$29,546	$40,921	110,846	7,967	20,317	21,476	23,056	16,817	21,213
505	Fort Dodge, IA	53,602	$28,125	$39,357	133,443	9,666	24,880	25,193	26,268	21,035	26,401
506-507	Waterloo, IA	95,490	$30,961	$44,737	244,187	16,004	45,380	50,855	54,315	36,735	40,899
508	Creston, IA	14,890	$24,171	$31,232	35,903	2,211	7,046	6,106	7,197	5,596	7,746
510-511	Sioux City, IA	65,678	$31,217	$48,697	175,521	13,436	36,508	36,379	37,122	24,376	27,701
512	Sheldon, IA	15,861	$29,189	$40,626	44,524	3,366	9,872	8,973	8,199	6,469	7,645
513	Spencer, IA	19,629	$29,022	$43,535	48,080	2,959	9,419	8,409	10,341	7,658	9,293
514	Carroll, IA	19,589	$26,953	$40,363	49,971	3,855	10,245	9,186	9,899	7,379	9,407
515	Omaha, NE	54,373	$31,270	$42,617	140,775	10,496	26,503	29,202	30,591	22,265	21,716
516	Omaha, NE	10,260	$27,490	$38,274	25,767	1,537	5,172	4,303	5,621	3,859	5,275
520	Dubuque, IA	50,640	$32,966	$49,619	137,852	9,929	26,128	29,563	29,827	21,245	21,160
521	Decorah, IA	22,736	$27,464	$39,166	59,258	4,301	10,678	13,411	11,326	8,952	10,589
522-524	Cedar Rapids, IA	153,452	$38,917	$57,787	396,901	29,075	63,395	111,381	89,540	53,988	49,522
525	Ottumwa, IA	46,466	$26,188	$38,123	115,073	8,010	20,648	22,005	26,586	17,030	20,794
526	Burlington, IA	43,881	$32,108	$42,937	112,344	7,744	20,684	22,404	26,744	16,544	18,223
527-528	Rock Island, IL	102,079	$38,476	$52,873	265,230	20,377	50,327	57,661	63,575	38,817	34,472
530-532, 534	Milwaukee, WI	807,998	$41,671	$56,827	2,096,265	185,120	367,653	493,416	487,273	289,241	273,563
535, 537	Madison, WI	284,263	$40,141	$55,062	708,384	59,648	113,435	187,093	175,417	91,344	81,447
538	Madison, WI	22,003	$28,806	$39,475	58,880	4,374	11,597	13,998	11,750	8,548	8,614
539	Portage, WI	68,449	$31,058	$40,829	177,721	13,820	32,385	36,408	39,538	27,034	28,536
540	Saint Paul, MN	41,422	$43,428	$55,477	111,875	9,854	22,697	26,294	27,271	13,859	11,900
541-543	Green Bay, WI	196,351	$34,864	$46,972	508,276	43,035	93,268	114,699	117,614	69,795	69,866
544	Wausau, WI	144,106	$33,864	$46,183	375,437	30,098	72,247	83,500	83,651	52,646	53,295
545	Rhinelander, WI	38,878	$25,906	$35,860	92,480	6,778	15,344	15,389	19,812	16,967	18,190
546	LaCrosse, WI	85,589	$30,056	$40,136	221,017	18,742	40,446	50,133	49,641	29,856	32,198
547	Eau Claire, WI	89,535	$30,383	$41,337	235,015	19,020	42,792	57,502	53,046	29,533	33,121
548	Spooner, WI	70,338	$25,565	$34,112	173,037	13,279	33,144	32,388	39,767	25,410	29,049
549	Oshkosh, WI	167,943	$36,551	$49,152	431,657	35,463	75,661	102,335	99,489	59,458	59,251
550-551	Saint Paul, MN	462,382	$45,065	$61,613	1,202,564	110,033	215,803	300,220	304,472	148,540	123,496
553-555	Minneapolis, MN	682,564	$45,877	$66,852	1,700,681	150,146	276,742	442,757	440,530	212,230	178,277
556-558	Duluth, MN	115,796	$27,607	$36,865	286,151	17,031	52,340	53,708	71,879	42,534	48,658
559	Rochester, MN	112,318	$34,997	$50,158	287,803	24,119	53,461	65,844	64,803	39,197	40,377
560	Mankato, MN	93,696	$30,141	$39,949	241,190	16,889	45,511	56,402	51,725	32,427	38,236
561	Windom, MN	38,321	$26,456	$34,556	96,065	6,505	19,218	15,556	19,918	14,803	20,066
562	Willmar, MN	59,391	$26,926	$35,625	150,224	10,744	30,240	29,444	31,375	20,921	27,500
563	Saint Cloud, MN	98,214	$28,942	$35,521	263,154	19,818	51,938	68,220	54,246	33,072	35,859
564	Brainerd, MN	49,743	$24,212	$31,841	124,930	8,813	24,478	20,860	27,381	20,847	22,552
565	Detroit Lakes, MN	62,954	$26,399	$34,559	163,071	11,507	31,376	34,062	34,239	24,318	27,569

HOUSEHOLDS/HOUSEHOLD INCOME/POPULATION STATISTICAL DATA FOR 3-DIGIT ZIP CODE AREAS

Zip Code	3-Digit Zip Code Areas	Total Households	Median Household Income	Average Household Income	Total Population	Population by Age: 0-5 years	Population by Age: 6-17 years	Population by Age: 18-34 years	Population by Age: 35-49 years	Population by Age: 50-64 years	Gray Markets (65+ years)
566	Bemidji, MN	30,878	$24,500	$32,107	82,901	6,635	17,275	17,256	18,283	11,835	11,617
567	Thief River Falls, MN	27,903	$27,434	$33,416	71,420	5,513	14,813	14,097	15,703	9,817	11,477
570-571	Sioux Falls, SD	102,336	$32,347	$48,173	269,955	20,209	50,408	69,940	61,227	32,646	35,525
572	Dakota Central, SD	28,448	$24,792	$34,774	71,971	5,113	15,359	12,784	15,005	10,257	13,453
573	Dakota Central, SD	33,082	$23,728	$33,434	84,531	6,206	18,075	14,890	16,650	12,314	16,396
574	Aberdeen, SD	25,440	$27,016	$40,646	62,358	4,237	11,372	12,707	13,198	9,583	11,261
575	Pierre, SD	20,222	$25,076	$38,626	55,616	4,885	13,601	10,222	12,041	7,717	7,151
576	Mobridge, SD	8,482	$20,841	$34,437	23,044	2,148	5,483	4,276	4,187	3,476	3,474
577	Rapid City, SD	64,100	$30,244	$44,430	172,910	15,517	35,939	39,754	39,074	22,610	20,015
580-581	Fargo, ND	60,832	$34,210	$52,527	157,059	12,631	26,013	43,228	37,159	18,872	19,155
582	Grand Forks, ND	40,490	$30,934	$44,693	108,014	9,391	17,787	32,117	22,766	12,432	13,523
583	Devils Lake, ND	21,250	$23,216	$34,113	55,131	4,985	11,071	10,422	11,043	7,851	9,761
584	Jamestown, ND	20,642	$25,642	$39,261	51,904	3,450	9,143	8,909	10,756	8,603	11,043
585	Bismarck, ND	46,788	$35,187	$47,900	121,579	9,769	23,791	24,271	29,886	17,253	16,610
586	Dickinson, ND	15,980	$25,811	$35,924	41,185	3,242	8,089	7,574	9,015	6,113	7,152
587	Minot, ND	33,755	$27,691	$39,362	86,861	7,223	15,782	20,736	18,607	11,680	12,834
588	Williston, ND	9,840	$29,852	$42,135	25,418	2,038	5,296	4,393	6,127	3,450	4,114
590-591	Billings, MT	76,075	$30,880	$43,507	192,918	14,370	37,931	39,832	46,735	28,359	25,690
592	Wolf Point, MT	15,069	$24,023	$30,857	39,649	3,061	8,854	7,019	8,336	5,953	6,427
593	Miles City, MT	15,244	$27,869	$37,150	38,875	2,416	8,606	6,702	8,946	5,964	6,242
594	Great Falls, MT	50,336	$28,795	$42,831	132,378	11,047	26,215	28,476	27,714	20,242	18,685
595	Havre, MT	12,342	$28,177	$39,138	33,666	2,786	7,556	6,758	7,343	4,483	4,739
596	Helena, MT	25,407	$34,438	$43,949	65,279	4,802	12,799	12,417	17,943	9,715	7,602
597	Butte, MT	52,818	$28,888	$43,624	133,138	9,065	22,688	34,929	31,602	18,224	16,631
598	Missoula, MT	64,460	$27,396	$40,333	163,422	11,812	31,132	35,771	40,224	24,292	20,190
599	Kalispell, MT	37,931	$29,824	$42,472	95,700	6,522	19,619	16,002	25,301	15,606	12,650
600, 602	Palatine, IL	627,666	$60,702	$93,433	1,561,191	136,219	261,274	368,188	394,927	227,764	172,819
601, 603	Carol Stream, IL	484,051	$55,535	$74,535	1,297,400	118,690	230,392	336,620	324,884	162,849	123,965
604	South Suburban, IL	473,091	$47,801	$62,077	1,254,739	103,212	233,396	281,646	296,582	171,719	148,185
605	Fox Valley, IL	281,452	$60,510	$84,970	765,435	71,017	141,299	174,755	201,441	98,373	78,549
606-607	Chicago, IL	937,407	$34,880	$54,081	2,873,976	250,927	506,602	779,793	612,247	369,391	355,016
609	Kankakee, IL	58,753	$32,397	$41,932	161,037	12,555	33,011	31,446	35,802	23,410	24,813
610-611	Rockford, IL	191,784	$36,851	$49,653	505,092	41,053	92,993	106,457	118,626	74,305	71,658
612	Rock Island, IL	85,320	$32,125	$44,042	217,105	15,168	41,992	41,743	51,009	33,710	33,483
613	La Salle, IL	59,836	$31,309	$40,492	157,041	11,391	30,206	29,608	33,867	23,698	28,271
614	Galesburg, IL	60,947	$26,850	$36,359	157,571	9,553	28,294	35,577	33,524	23,740	26,883
615-616	Peoria, IL	142,935	$34,820	$47,239	369,717	25,665	71,802	72,906	87,242	56,739	55,363
617	Bloomington, IL	74,377	$38,331	$50,677	206,376	15,123	36,935	58,921	45,162	25,768	24,467
618-619	Champaign, IL	143,866	$31,046	$43,641	369,780	26,544	63,697	104,205	78,361	48,576	48,395
620, 622	Saint Louis, MO	282,175	$33,811	$43,634	752,372	60,631	145,492	167,860	163,319	107,201	107,868
623	Quincy, IL	44,747	$27,258	$37,794	115,918	8,459	22,248	22,351	25,002	17,399	20,460
624	Effingham, IL	57,185	$28,061	$37,311	149,927	11,679	30,320	29,297	30,951	22,808	24,872
625-627	Springfield, IL	193,977	$33,935	$45,965	490,565	35,693	92,684	98,987	115,402	72,909	74,889
628	Centralia, IL	86,212	$25,790	$35,459	220,222	15,494	43,033	42,463	47,717	32,762	38,753
629	Carbondale, IL	91,587	$23,270	$33,409	231,017	15,254	39,554	57,948	49,287	33,412	35,562
630-631	Saint Louis, MO	660,622	$42,347	$64,058	1,647,207	141,869	273,935	383,317	386,954	232,026	229,105
633	Saint Louis, MO	127,954	$46,198	$55,346	343,707	34,680	68,984	83,753	84,627	45,346	32,317
634	Quincy, IL	26,395	$24,115	$32,725	67,376	5,017	13,352	13,345	14,673	9,531	11,458
635	Quincy, IL	24,618	$20,119	$30,404	61,890	4,092	9,998	15,953	12,181	8,706	10,960
636	Cape Girardeau, MO	45,350	$23,605	$32,228	123,718	9,227	23,646	27,055	26,049	19,171	18,569
637	Cape Girardeau, MO	43,729	$27,445	$39,751	110,746	8,423	19,741	26,027	24,706	15,190	16,660
638	Cape Girardeau, MO	52,604	$20,503	$31,823	133,774	10,379	26,843	26,705	29,077	19,777	20,994
639	Cape Girardeau, MO	32,602	$18,389	$28,235	79,902	5,790	14,880	15,304	16,240	14,076	13,611
641	Kansas City, MO	221,447	$35,880	$52,224	523,328	44,788	82,868	130,255	122,280	72,376	70,761
644-645	Saint Joseph, MO	68,404	$26,535	$37,779	179,005	13,428	32,088	41,483	37,413	24,754	29,840
646	Chillicothe, MO	29,420	$22,243	$32,063	74,178	5,351	14,311	12,688	15,230	11,566	15,031

Zip Code	3-Digit Zip Code Areas	Total Households	Median Household Income	Average Household Income	Total Population	Population by Age: 0-5 years	Population by Age: 6-17 years	Population by Age: 18-34 years	Population by Age: 35-49 years	Population by Age: 50-64 years	Gray Markets (65+ years)
647	Harrisonville, MO	43,067	$24,500	$34,450	109,598	8,524	20,944	20,791	23,085	17,534	18,720
648	Springfield, MO	65,000	$24,526	$36,677	162,085	13,003	29,913	35,793	35,835	23,932	23,608
650-651	Mid-Missouri, MO	74,303	$30,024	$43,368	193,299	15,161	34,477	40,824	44,362	29,463	29,011
652	Mid-Missouri, MO	83,828	$28,722	$42,472	224,309	18,047	36,749	65,797	49,315	26,950	27,453
653	Mid-Missouri, MO	37,602	$24,142	$34,245	94,851	7,703	17,487	20,387	19,352	14,852	15,070
654-655	Springfield, MO	68,157	$22,855	$32,219	179,588	14,870	33,894	41,942	37,183	26,807	24,892
656-658	Springfield, MO	231,671	$24,719	$38,335	588,278	42,931	102,080	134,384	127,656	92,156	89,072
661-662,664	Kansas City, MO	211,230	$46,122	$72,493	531,084	47,600	92,067	122,688	131,960	72,539	64,229
665-666	Topeka, KS	107,331	$33,639	$47,926	283,207	23,092	48,133	78,734	62,271	36,380	34,596
667	Fort Scott, KS	48,465	$24,428	$33,221	121,341	8,748	22,562	24,925	25,721	17,317	22,068
668	Topeka, KS	24,889	$28,478	$39,104	64,428	5,025	12,562	14,322	13,980	8,488	10,051
669	Salina, KS	12,347	$24,091	$30,091	29,806	1,916	5,173	4,556	5,583	5,051	7,527
670-672	Witchita, KS	248,186	$36,613	$52,561	632,154	58,065	120,482	139,740	143,094	85,720	85,053
673	Independence, KS	27,160	$25,534	$34,853	67,144	5,140	11,994	12,708	14,292	9,968	13,042
674	Salina, KS	54,216	$29,325	$41,266	135,960	10,335	25,357	26,137	29,639	20,483	24,010
675	Hutchinson, KS	50,066	$28,110	$38,446	126,586	9,382	23,260	23,703	27,071	19,686	23,484
676	Hays, KS	24,680	$25,879	$36,945	60,580	4,110	11,232	11,971	12,712	9,216	11,339
677	Colby, KS	14,191	$25,253	$33,765	35,085	2,663	6,698	5,930	7,069	5,848	6,878
678	Dodge City, KS	40,144	$31,174	$43,833	113,785	11,522	25,130	26,341	23,309	13,986	13,499
679	Liberal, KS	9,653	$30,489	$44,736	27,001	2,546	5,973	6,431	5,364	3,507	3,178
680-681	Omaha, NE	248,871	$41,148	$60,269	652,779	60,730	116,665	161,709	153,588	87,319	72,768
683-685	Lincoln, NE	145,586	$34,300	$48,845	371,729	29,780	61,969	95,427	84,405	47,479	52,669
686	Norfolk, NE	27,807	$28,875	$40,822	74,147	6,532	15,513	13,567	15,041	10,881	12,613
687	Norfolk, NE	51,312	$26,121	$37,423	137,583	12,021	28,066	27,630	27,951	19,107	22,807
688	Grand Island, NE	57,965	$28,361	$41,649	151,767	11,937	29,728	32,915	33,232	20,651	23,305
689	Grand Island, NE	30,108	$28,085	$41,030	76,513	5,792	13,827	14,483	16,435	11,408	14,568
690	McCook, NE	11,268	$24,092	$35,793	28,005	1,957	5,770	4,632	5,665	4,463	5,519
691	North Platte, NE	31,828	$28,028	$38,874	79,803	6,006	16,234	13,390	17,647	12,851	13,675
692	Valentine, NE	3,947	$20,948	$37,050	9,918	839	1,933	1,570	2,026	1,680	1,870
693	Alliance, NE	29,111	$25,921	$39,628	75,027	5,422	15,824	13,749	16,757	10,882	12,394
700-701	New Orleans, LA	431,181	$30,720	$47,530	1,137,696	98,748	206,763	277,975	267,343	149,797	137,070
703	Thibodaux, LA	93,894	$23,417	$35,027	263,901	24,473	54,723	65,762	56,188	36,664	26,092
704	Hammond, LA	124,751	$30,164	$47,786	344,871	30,061	71,971	75,474	83,649	47,515	36,201
705	Lafayette, LA	210,024	$32,868	$37,758	576,436	56,190	119,101	140,335	118,153	78,834	63,824
706	Lake Charles, LA	92,587	$28,076	$41,602	257,402	23,259	50,401	66,394	53,742	36,002	27,604
707-708	Baton Rouge, LA	239,320	$34,167	$49,096	654,574	57,178	124,047	172,593	155,760	82,027	62,970
710-711	Shreveport, LA	175,535	$27,609	$41,234	457,282	41,110	87,246	102,609	97,829	66,760	61,728
712	Monroe, LA	124,394	$23,538	$37,150	338,852	28,302	68,690	87,194	66,278	45,599	42,788
713-714	Alexandria, LA	145,549	$22,118	$33,864	388,389	33,830	77,650	92,856	78,549	54,638	50,865
716	Pine Bluff, AR	65,935	$22,444	$38,050	183,019	15,039	36,159	41,320	38,871	25,958	25,675
717	Camden, AR	46,016	$23,306	$37,448	119,946	10,086	22,946	25,400	24,964	16,566	19,984
718	Texarkana, TX	46,482	$21,838	$34,426	123,495	10,149	23,993	26,757	26,116	17,658	18,821
719	Hot Springs National Park, AR	59,997	$22,468	$36,329	147,824	10,111	22,554	29,061	29,476	25,302	31,320
720-722	Little Rock, AR	308,002	$29,814	$48,276	788,485	65,697	140,410	189,608	180,567	111,245	100,958
723	Memphis, TN	67,609	$19,342	$32,427	189,932	18,591	42,016	42,030	38,264	24,925	24,106
724	Jonesboro, AR	76,684	$22,094	$36,463	193,147	15,073	32,143	45,636	40,992	30,357	28,946
725	Batesville, AR	41,136	$20,632	$33,835	101,145	6,757	16,990	18,342	20,719	18,242	20,096
726	Harrison, AR	49,778	$21,530	$34,751	123,207	8,585	20,387	22,037	26,220	21,274	24,704
727	Fayetteville, AR	101,697	$29,678	$47,217	275,464	23,864	46,900	68,954	59,069	39,431	37,246
728	Russellville, AR	40,187	$23,488	$36,694	106,245	8,939	18,714	25,936	21,887	15,825	14,943
729	Fort Smith, AR	75,377	$26,013	$42,022	196,099	16,839	36,053	43,972	44,318	28,118	26,798
730-731	Oklahoma City, OK	428,317	$32,374	$46,609	1,115,781	92,402	207,751	277,194	251,110	155,519	131,806
734	Ardmore, OK	30,139	$23,835	$34,883	78,542	5,693	15,260	15,403	16,770	12,262	13,155
735	Lawton, OK	77,710	$27,004	$36,386	215,995	18,799	41,460	56,762	42,142	29,524	27,308
736	Clinton, OK	22,138	$22,513	$33,947	57,214	4,420	12,324	10,794	11,378	8,146	10,152
737	Enid, OK	41,674	$25,991	$37,227	104,798	7,590	20,311	21,497	21,014	16,130	18,255

Zip Code	3-Digit Zip Code Areas	Total Households	Median Household Income	Average Household Income	Total Population	Population by Age: 0-5 years	Population by Age: 6-17 years	Population by Age: 18-34 years	Population by Age: 35-49 years	Population by Age: 50-64 years	Gray Markets (65+ years)
738	Woodward, OK	12,268	$24,970	$35,347	31,350	1,965	6,720	5,620	6,514	5,081	5,450
739	Liberal, KS	10,006	$28,356	$36,539	25,762	1,814	5,561	5,091	5,506	4,073	3,717
740-741	Tulsa, OK	348,128	$33,066	$49,433	868,497	72,728	157,258	205,619	202,750	123,097	107,046
743	Tulsa, OK	46,423	$22,980	$34,557	117,147	8,156	20,565	22,700	23,935	20,665	21,126
744	Muskogee, OK	77,440	$23,441	$33,529	201,578	15,392	39,090	41,976	42,095	31,834	31,190
745	McAlester, OK	34,898	$19,898	$28,949	89,396	6,190	16,883	17,795	18,373	14,781	15,374
746	Ponca City, OK	23,558	$29,114	$40,953	59,051	4,705	11,662	11,138	12,862	8,564	10,120
747	Durant, OK	32,092	$19,250	$28,736	81,884	6,558	16,092	17,624	16,499	12,502	12,609
748	Shawnee, OK	70,274	$23,882	$33,976	187,737	13,966	37,175	40,460	38,533	29,302	28,302
749	Poteau, OK	38,526	$21,976	$30,024	104,472	8,452	20,842	23,104	22,023	16,259	13,794
750	North Texas, TX	490,581	$52,304	$69,723	1,286,160	128,174	241,234	345,442	346,013	147,877	77,420
751	North Texas, TX	201,334	$39,501	$52,374	550,169	53,502	112,191	125,992	130,305	73,688	54,490
752-753	Dallas, TX	449,510	$39,303	$67,308	1,111,943	100,298	175,474	330,279	254,805	133,801	117,286
754	Greenville, TX	104,171	$29,511	$41,388	270,427	21,351	51,110	54,809	58,343	42,117	42,695
755	Texarkana, TX	46,702	$29,106	$40,844	119,503	8,566	23,822	23,206	28,368	17,016	18,525
756	Longview, TX	119,199	$28,928	$39,849	309,484	23,445	64,031	61,191	68,971	46,758	45,088
757	Tyler, TX	107,072	$29,631	$42,929	277,464	21,534	52,069	58,315	60,530	42,125	42,891
758	Palestine, TX	39,178	$25,733	$35,213	114,017	7,756	20,630	29,009	23,661	15,469	17,492
759	Lufkin, TX	89,157	$24,253	$35,548	232,983	16,964	44,870	52,923	47,124	35,899	35,203
760-761	Fort Worth, TX	593,226	$42,217	$56,582	1,546,994	149,091	283,729	411,464	368,609	189,881	144,221
762	Fort Worth, TX	84,823	$36,865	$52,555	222,163	18,438	39,576	61,143	50,344	28,148	24,515
763	Wichita Falls, TX	63,946	$28,141	$39,253	169,872	14,154	31,908	39,158	34,366	25,563	24,724
764	Fort Worth, TX	50,456	$24,737	$36,023	128,689	9,676	24,165	26,836	26,112	19,981	21,920
765	Waco, TX	128,964	$29,372	$40,051	383,311	37,167	75,631	111,214	77,949	44,625	36,725
766-767	Waco, TX	109,563	$27,778	$38,921	289,087	23,822	54,466	69,681	59,794	38,461	42,863
768	Abilene, TX	34,032	$22,336	$32,202	85,941	6,408	16,944	14,903	18,088	12,870	16,728
769	Midland, TX	48,046	$29,515	$41,707	126,852	11,182	25,691	29,589	27,093	16,703	16,594
770-772	Houston, TX	872,076	$38,789	$61,199	2,342,898	222,648	440,452	618,116	588,449	282,222	191,012
773	North Houston, TX	234,801	$43,987	$62,586	675,969	59,625	140,927	144,855	183,464	91,548	55,550
774	North Houston, TX	193,408	$49,820	$66,815	576,254	56,719	130,326	120,525	158,340	65,274	45,069
775	North Houston, TX	324,491	$41,610	$54,592	905,386	82,078	187,475	209,191	225,363	119,292	81,987
776-777	Beaumont, TX	144,185	$31,366	$43,504	394,682	30,096	78,889	79,897	88,651	61,785	55,365
778	Bryan, TX	85,684	$26,254	$40,614	226,107	17,603	37,058	81,647	41,875	24,280	23,644
779	Victoria, TX	59,586	$29,160	$41,952	157,377	12,562	33,415	29,786	35,231	23,272	23,110
780-782	San Antonio, TX	658,861	$31,932	$46,136	1,906,524	178,219	394,831	458,721	422,537	242,257	209,960
783-784	Corpus Christi, TX	176,125	$28,479	$41,615	519,284	44,468	114,826	112,413	116,828	71,135	59,613
785	McAllen, TX	240,704	$20,594	$32,156	904,429	85,458	252,169	206,587	170,197	99,933	90,085
786-787	Austin, TX	441,213	$36,034	$52,679	1,114,333	98,113	195,467	328,315	274,981	122,761	94,696
788	San Antonio, TX	52,481	$19,222	$29,573	166,172	15,298	40,721	35,387	32,707	23,039	19,019
789	Austin, TX	23,161	$26,015	$36,534	58,570	4,316	11,767	10,069	12,428	8,493	11,497
790-791	Amarillo, TX	153,109	$29,344	$42,358	408,100	35,690	89,689	84,935	85,069	59,305	53,411
792	Childress, TX	14,661	$21,756	$32,083	36,764	2,714	7,692	6,067	6,914	6,095	7,281
793-794	Lubbock, TX	130,201	$28,656	$43,100	356,001	29,948	72,354	91,559	71,238	48,525	42,378
795-796	Abilene, TX	82,924	$27,874	$39,132	220,056	18,582	44,044	49,324	44,881	31,208	32,018
797	Midland, TX	130,262	$30,525	$46,036	360,983	35,254	84,062	74,879	76,009	49,431	41,348
798-799	El Paso, TX	221,860	$27,908	$41,053	726,936	69,333	170,277	181,130	147,456	91,615	67,125
800-803	Denver, CO	827,314	$43,140	$58,525	2,005,124	172,769	328,836	497,717	537,942	275,143	192,718
804	Denver, CO	68,367	$47,664	$54,864	171,491	13,005	28,301	35,719	56,362	25,667	12,438
805	Longmont, CO	129,442	$39,957	$51,909	328,679	27,452	58,732	81,579	85,549	43,547	31,819
806	Brighton, CO	56,446	$32,236	$42,290	158,499	13,176	30,376	40,254	36,633	21,910	16,150
807	Brighton, CO	23,676	$26,088	$36,259	60,332	4,416	12,330	11,295	12,283	9,980	10,028
808-809	Colorado Springs, CO	197,083	$36,118	$48,043	517,989	48,384	93,306	141,921	120,452	69,100	44,827
810	Pueblo, CO	78,771	$23,771	$32,552	203,967	14,385	38,532	39,882	44,702	32,768	33,698
811	Alamosa, CO	22,133	$23,611	$34,127	60,824	5,284	13,381	12,092	13,732	9,177	7,158
812	Salida, CO	27,587	$24,920	$34,307	74,071	4,190	11,901	16,173	18,115	12,947	10,746
813	Durango, CO	21,047	$29,971	$40,444	55,729	4,110	10,847	12,896	13,717	7,986	6,173

Zip Code	3-Digit Zip Code Areas	Total Households	Median Household Income	Average Household Income	Total Population	Population by Age: 0-5 years	Population by Age: 6-17 years	Population by Age: 18-34 years	Population by Age: 35-49 years	Population by Age: 50-64 years	Gray Markets (65+ years)
814	Grand Junction, CO	26,183	$27,051	$36,990	66,421	4,031	12,490	9,888	16,287	12,653	11,073
815	Grand Junction, CO	42,705	$27,650	$38,647	108,093	7,610	20,938	19,882	25,537	17,355	16,771
816	Glenwood Springs, CO	41,468	$40,758	$59,619	105,024	9,203	19,021	24,252	31,538	13,141	7,870
820	Cheyenne, WY	43,913	$35,055	$46,307	111,250	8,287	18,820	34,577	24,888	14,149	10,530
821	Billings, MT	134	$36,829	$44,092	268	19	45	52	102	41	8
822	Wheatland, WY	9,497	$28,688	$40,694	24,283	1,555	5,080	4,577	5,290	3,799	3,982
823	Rawlins, WY	6,733	$34,366	$41,404	17,680	1,075	3,935	3,511	4,692	2,585	1,881
824	Worland, WY	19,748	$32,152	$43,825	51,641	3,434	10,869	9,970	11,859	7,920	7,589
825	Riverton, WY	12,587	$28,059	$38,973	35,690	2,657	8,025	6,734	8,148	5,859	4,267
826	Casper, WY	31,159	$34,272	$47,880	78,522	5,635	16,392	16,247	18,835	12,118	9,295
827	Gillette, WY	15,782	$43,941	$51,062	45,215	3,636	11,733	9,663	11,520	5,599	3,064
828	Sheridan, WY	12,979	$32,440	$44,074	32,013	1,722	6,307	5,483	8,601	4,833	5,067
829-831	Rock Springs, WY	33,757	$42,895	$52,693	95,934	7,491	25,313	19,754	25,302	10,967	7,108
832	Pocatello, ID	55,037	$31,321	$43,674	162,637	13,839	44,303	33,698	33,533	19,872	17,393
833	Twin Falls, ID	57,450	$29,383	$49,244	158,860	13,169	37,402	32,095	34,666	21,009	20,520
834	Pocatello, ID	48,267	$33,822	$47,813	151,030	13,168	39,071	38,379	28,589	17,610	14,214
835	Lewiston, ID	27,390	$28,527	$41,899	67,689	4,550	11,920	13,680	15,475	11,339	10,725
836-837	Boise, ID	177,416	$33,706	$51,750	483,305	41,674	98,604	114,968	114,379	61,369	52,311
838	Spokane, WA	78,257	$29,259	$44,630	201,814	15,092	37,632	45,350	49,330	30,235	24,174
840-842	Salt Lake City, UT	438,986	$39,956	$59,250	1,357,446	141,197	341,113	339,114	284,666	144,529	106,828
843-844	Salt Lake City, UT	89,647	$36,424	$49,179	272,697	27,636	65,563	70,924	50,200	30,722	27,652
845	Provo, UT	18,115	$26,956	$36,758	53,799	4,834	14,770	10,082	11,241	6,933	5,939
846-847	Provo, UT	103,371	$28,525	$42,916	348,065	31,775	84,161	109,632	51,372	33,450	37,676
850, 852-853	Phoenix, AZ	1,109,825	$38,488	$55,623	2,850,559	297,546	483,509	702,999	625,488	361,699	379,316
855	Globe, AZ	30,503	$24,939	$34,448	84,721	7,666	17,869	13,542	17,082	14,550	14,012
856-857	Tuscon, AZ	365,616	$30,994	$46,064	946,094	92,761	158,642	224,232	209,328	128,095	133,036
859	Show Low, AZ	16,456	$27,678	$35,319	52,548	6,814	13,188	9,092	10,321	7,861	5,274
860	Flagstaff, AZ	47,833	$29,666	$41,134	162,684	19,969	38,040	43,763	34,142	17,764	9,005
863	Prescott, AZ	60,087	$27,843	$40,777	141,939	9,581	21,356	21,139	30,057	25,893	33,913
864	Kingman, AZ	49,608	$28,860	$39,865	125,610	9,550	17,678	20,796	25,391	24,998	27,197
865	Gallup, NM	15,634	$12,785	$21,417	61,081	9,407	16,805	13,821	9,801	7,244	4,004
870-872	Albuquerque, NM	266,595	$37,251	$50,955	728,426	63,861	138,222	171,939	180,439	93,889	80,075
873	Gallup, NM	19,108	$22,238	$32,345	67,764	8,220	18,123	15,896	13,183	7,868	4,474
874	Farmington, NM	33,825	$28,878	$40,055	104,659	10,154	28,897	21,014	22,360	12,936	9,298
875	Albuuquerque, NM	82,686	$39,513	$56,260	205,011	16,316	38,484	40,581	57,439	30,603	21,588
877	Las Vegas, NM	16,611	$23,874	$32,856	44,169	3,542	9,585	9,129	9,725	6,320	5,868
878	Socorro, NM	7,112	$26,537	$35,631	17,996	1,356	3,952	4,018	3,985	2,524	2,160
879	Truth or Consequences, NM	6,343	$19,667	$29,558	15,092	1,138	2,686	2,372	2,377	2,739	3,781
880	Las Cruces, NM	79,104	$27,494	$37,782	223,030	19,476	49,351	55,375	43,450	29,503	25,876
881	Clovis, NM	26,125	$26,041	$36,308	70,786	6,483	15,207	19,102	13,048	8,962	7,984
882	Roswell, NM	63,550	$29,544	$40,673	175,521	14,745	43,215	35,448	35,456	22,965	23,693
883	Carrizozo, NM	28,228	$28,157	$37,872	74,432	7,151	14,866	17,389	15,174	10,994	8,857
884	Tucumcari, NM	7,435	$21,128	$29,931	17,918	1,375	3,659	2,995	3,912	2,937	3,040
890-891	Las Vegas, NV	437,460	$39,425	$56,079	1,112,147	96,508	179,915	281,737	253,448	170,705	129,833
893	Ely, NV	4,454	$33,572	$42,346	12,318	1,058	2,460	2,688	2,908	1,762	1,443
894-895, 897	Reno, NV	199,052	$40,650	$56,724	476,689	42,227	78,466	111,421	121,734	66,343	56,499
898	Elko, NV	17,157	$43,568	$53,100	49,232	5,428	11,845	12,986	11,534	4,960	2,479
900-901	Los Angeles, CA	795,903	$33,689	$60,204	2,326,583	248,035	408,574	698,800	478,559	250,826	241,789
902-905	Inglewood, CA	544,920	$48,336	$77,642	1,553,130	162,337	272,530	423,736	352,767	192,353	149,408
906	Long Beach, CA	211,298	$49,908	$66,190	663,889	71,773	121,456	172,543	135,305	90,970	71,842
907-908	Long Beach, CA	371,613	$44,990	$63,907	1,053,470	113,579	184,314	287,511	229,234	122,532	116,301
910-912	Pasadena, CA	241,341	$50,239	$79,326	643,856	57,929	99,525	155,906	155,262	87,799	87,435
913-916	Van Nuys, CA	633,489	$53,604	$80,055	1,734,827	168,663	280,986	470,977	416,015	221,502	176,684
917-918	Alhambra, CA	639,326	$48,976	$64,575	2,020,109	231,413	408,004	531,757	453,320	233,284	162,331
919-921	San Diego, CA	997,253	$44,084	$63,034	2,666,052	268,341	438,523	746,336	596,460	311,879	304,513
922	Palm Springs, CA	192,235	$32,675	$52,649	531,228	55,019	105,356	118,671	96,134	73,546	82,502

Zip Code	3-Digit Zip Code Areas	Total Households	Median Household Income	Average Household Income	Total Population	Population by Age: 0-5 years	Population by Age: 6-17 years	Population by Age: 18-34 years	Population by Age: 35-49 years	Population by Age: 50-64 years	Gray Markets (65+ years)
923-925	San Bernadino, CA	682,310	$40,080	$53,371	1,337,766	238,202	417,108	469,631	391,368	217,301	204,156
926-928	Santa Ana, CA	816,413	$62,240	$86,725	2,355,615	232,435	368,814	665,489	547,409	316,396	225,073
930	Oxnard, CA	199,038	$57,359	$74,549	504,136	60,681	110,836	147,300	141,922	80,173	63,224
931, 934	Santa Barbara, CA	222,128	$42,258	$62,295	595,999	54,160	93,039	159,319	131,992	75,661	81,828
932-933	Bakersfield, CA	311,953	$30,832	$44,457	367,875	115,736	226,528	224,411	194,710	112,447	94,043
935	Mojave, CA	148,780	$44,036	$57,191	416,419	52,669	86,544	105,885	92,519	46,967	31,835
937-938	Fresno, CA	165,694	$30,805	$47,673	487,641	59,229	109,667	112,590	98,720	54,757	52,678
939	Salinas, CA	113,734	$41,008	$59,841	326,813	35,275	60,154	87,753	70,126	36,032	37,474
940-941, 943-944	San Fransisco, CA	691,607	$54,386	$80,191	1,723,563	130,146	209,528	437,632	452,777	250,052	243,427
942, 956-958	Sacramento, CA	678,469	$41,408	$55,839	1,733,507	172,736	318,337	404,246	414,368	229,391	194,429
945-948	Oakland, CA	1,017,178	$53,019	$71,366	2,519,176	257,025	427,272	613,718	683,760	343,190	294,210
949, 954	North Bay, CA	329,924	$47,276	$71,384	794,661	68,677	124,910	146,292	230,737	112,705	111,340
950-951	San Jose, CA	543,845	$61,208	$80,126	1,594,049	157,988	258,306	417,547	397,099	214,178	148,931
952-953	Stockton, CA	426,068	$34,859	$48,146	1,231,092	138,763	268,666	273,012	262,734	150,848	137,069
955	Eureka, CA	60,861	$27,154	$38,934	151,954	13,308	29,883	31,067	38,784	19,791	19,121
959	Marysville, CA	180,178	$28,971	$42,121	459,818	44,245	88,379	91,963	100,892	64,086	70,253
960	Redding, CA	110,274	$28,588	$40,097	275,993	24,671	55,587	44,960	64,538	44,179	42,059
961	Reno, NV	37,432	$33,691	$46,739	98,048	8,822	17,986	21,254	27,010	12,842	10,133
967-968	Honolulu, HI	402,761	$49,494	$68,194	1,196,228	110,008	196,709	283,345	285,319	162,238	158,608
970-972	Portland, OR	629,526	$40,672	$58,809	1,575,944	130,968	268,941	375,903	398,189	212,754	189,188
973	Salem, OR	202,631	$33,325	$46,448	519,674	40,400	91,446	124,454	118,611	75,013	69,750
974	Eugene, OR	208,351	$29,930	$43,746	504,730	36,253	84,544	108,333	117,998	79,886	77,716
975	Medford, OR	102,662	$30,334	$43,325	246,606	18,064	41,663	45,037	57,541	41,647	42,654
976	Klamath Falls, OR	27,463	$28,517	$40,750	67,325	5,163	12,131	14,018	14,673	11,365	9,974
977	Bend, OR	58,023	$32,938	$48,291	-43,132	11,698	26,099	27,877	34,191	24,321	18,947
978	Pendleton, OR	54,058	$27,392	$38,359	-34,435	10,235	26,797	28,169	28,739	21,372	19,123
979	Boise, ID	11,163	$25,254	$40,610	29,689	2,676	6,463	5,683	5,546	4,935	4,386
980-981	Seattle, WA	786,908	$50,567	$71,314	1,843,326	144,584	269,276	486,417	501,588	243,512	197,949
982	Everett, WA	251,347	$41,492	$57,017	657,073	55,584	119,377	156,776	161,706	87,234	76,396
983-984	Tacoma, WA	369,087	$38,659	$51,338	967,812	82,775	178,209	243,993	226,932	127,950	107,954
985	Olympia, WA	155,379	$34,792	$45,708	395,868	28,706	76,645	80,217	99,253	58,839	52,209
986	Portland, OR	165,654	$38,641	$50,660	436,858	32,814	85,744	91,041	113,274	64,378	49,607
988	Wenatchee, WA	69,968	$29,094	$42,366	181,742	15,281	37,738	36,093	41,593	26,978	24,058
989	Yakima, WA	86,519	$29,052	$42,549	245,226	21,764	50,500	59,294	52,751	31,970	28,947
990-992	Spokane, WA	203,682	$31,934	$45,045	520,551	38,202	96,902	126,104	124,970	71,795	62,578
993	Pasco, WA	92,266	$35,801	$47,187	263,931	22,345	58,079	57,217	60,943	37,022	28,325
994	Lewiston, ID	8,565	$28,113	$41,193	20,941	1,626	4,176	4,073	4,568	3,338	3,160
995-996	Anchorage, AK	145,215	$54,109	$69,637	407,522	42,379	82,170	101,245	107,926	52,377	21,425
997	Fairbanks, AK	39,253	$45,989	$57,072	113,742	13,301	23,899	32,124	26,820	12,402	5,195
998	Juneau, AK	17,828	$56,748	$66,759	47,567	4,476	9,361	10,199	13,875	6,538	3,117
999	Ketchikan, AK	8,815	$54,223	$64,841	23,334	2,135	4,747	5,111	6,484	3,230	1,627
	TOTAL	100,742,770	$39,112	$55,462	264,652,292	22,802,237	46,179,135	63,509,524	61,573,464	36,503,274	34,084,681

135

Zip Code	3-Digit Zip Code Areas	Black Markets	Hispanic Markets	Total Retail Sales ($Millions)	Retail Sales: Apparel & Accessories ($Millions)	Retail Sales: Automotive ($Millions)	Retail Sales: Drugs, First Aid & Health Care Products ($Millions)	Retail Sales: Food ($Millions)	Retail Sales: Furniture & Major Appliances ($Millions)	Retail Sales: General Merchandise ($Millions)	Retail Sales: Hardware, Lumber & Garden Supplies ($Millions)
010-011	Springfield, MA	42,180	64,367	5,515	260	57	235	1,057	251	651	330
012	Pittsfield, MA	3,044	1,804	1,430	85	11	63	295	57	133	78
013	Springfield, MA	670	1,542	580	15	10	22	126	25	49	39
014	Worcester, MA	7,452	12,485	1,891	100	18	83	334	97	216	83
015-016	Worcester, MA	13,488	30,865	4,694	217	45	203	836	234	554	212
017	Boston, MA	9,053	14,383	3,451	238	31	153	596	194	358	143
018	Middlesex-Essex, MA	15,430	64,259	6,171	415	51	284	1,077	324	637	281
019	Middlesex-Essex, MA	14,591	24,495	4,263	249	29	207	759	191	453	232
020, 023-024	Brockton, MA	34,648	18,520	8,432	463	67	329	1,404	447	763	468
021-022	Boston, MA	207,317	128,470	16,509	1,256	118	786	2,790	902	1,511	577
025	Buzzards Bay, MA	2,163	2,287	1,482	104	10	49	290	68	77	140
026	Buzzards Bay, MA	2,655	2,160	2,064	157	13	77	429	130	124	136
027	Providence, RI	10,158	16,575	4,999	345	79	221	942	215	747	286
028-029	Providence, RI	34,893	57,200	8,505	411	109	460	1,603	381	907	394
030-031	Manchester, NH	5,774	8,852	6,170	327	47	188	1,091	392	1,054	407
032-033	Manchester, NH	797	1,423	2,484	101	23	85	500	96	236	153
034	Manchester, NH	311	417	974	33	10	26	195	32	74	79
035	White River Junction, VT	68	258	524	14	5	17	111	17	47	31
036	White River Junction, VT	18	43	106	3	1	3	22	4	9	8
037	White River Junction, VT	439	542	869	30	11	25	197	27	87	58
038	Portsmouth, NH	3,004	2,450	3,605	216	29	103	754	195	488	223
039	Portsmouth, NH	367	359	379	33	3	12	79	19	17	21
040-041	Portland, ME	2,691	2,800	4,867	409	41	130	841	186	456	271
042	Portland, ME	806	1,223	1,567	40	23	50	309	49	186	97
043	Portland, ME	262	362	785	23	12	25	169	27	84	49
044	Bangor, ME	801	1,000	1,796	66	32	57	346	62	276	138
045	Portland, ME	324	334	406	10	5	13	102	12	21	34
046	Bangor, ME	231	393	769	22	9	24	216	18	53	80
047	Bangor, ME	981	580	671	21	12	31	165	18	70	42
048	Portland, ME	81	147	363	20	5	12	95	9	29	42
049	Portland, ME	372	722	1,341	35	22	48	297	47	132	117
050	White River Junction, VT	133	324	467	6	6	12	93	9	18	54
051	White River Junction, VT	24	186	268	7	3	6	55	6	13	22
052	White River Junction, VT	89	290	467	51	3	15	82	16	33	33
053	White River Junction, VT	151	347	419	17	3	15	90	13	20	31
054	Burlington, VT	870	1,989	2,518	137	20	75	516	125	196	183
056	Burlington, VT	187	843	865	26	8	30	200	26	52	77
057	White River Junction, VT	227	512	809	22	10	33	175	27	58	60
058	White River Junction, VT	118	252	489	13	5	20	120	8	43	48
059	White River Junction, VT	3	25	17	1	0	0	2	1	0	2
060-061	Hartford, CT	109,166	88,586	9,700	552	114	404	1,584	558	1,139	556
062	Hartford, CT	2,598	6,536	1,005	28	25	48	237	26	64	45
063	New Haven, CT	14,956	11,330	2,349	125	45	80	436	112	243	136
064-066	New Haven, CT	139,770	98,297	12,649	719	124	498	2,291	661	1,338	686
067	Waterbury, CT	20,902	21,304	2,916	130	33	125	596	131	261	188
068-069	Stamford, CT	49,541	38,785	6,367	430	54	196	1,046	352	669	337
070-073	Newark, NJ	541,774	455,240	19,860	1,523	192	907	3,713	1,519	1,668	735
074-075	Paterson, NJ	61,514	87,501	6,672	463	59	235	1,088	509	771	316
076	Hackensack, NJ	40,307	37,738	5,914	518	47	222	1,030	362	589	236
077	Monmouth, NJ	50,266	27,821	6,445	459	88	227	1,255	423	729	267
078	West Jersey, NJ	7,189	17,512	3,527	143	33	110	690	175	280	209
079	West Jersey, NJ	9,536	12,148	2,913	137	27	91	516	177	243	152
080-084	South Jersey, NJ	244,758	103,761	16,944	869	194	689	3,168	979	2,078	757
085-086	Trenton, NJ	80,111	31,447	5,258	287	52	217	976	387	584	230
087	Trenton, NJ	11,587	14,479	3,819	163	42	155	836	204	355	275
088-089	New Brunswick, NJ	72,922	73,383	9,240	659	93	288	1,690	745	1,160	510

Zip Code	3-Digit Zip Code Areas	Black Markets	Hispanic Markets	Total Retail Sales ($Millions)	Retail Sales: Apparel & Accessories ($Millions)	Retail Sales: Automotive ($Millions)	Retail Sales: Drugs, First Aid & Health Care Products ($Millions)	Retail Sales: Food ($Millions)	Retail Sales: Furniture & Major Appliances ($Millions)	Retail Sales: General Merchandise ($Millions)	Retail Sales: Hardware, Lumber & Garden Supplies ($Millions)
100-102	New York, NY	388,150	372,751	22,410	3,220	19	920	2,216	2,140	2,265	293
103	Staten Island, NY	40,741	32,172	2,431	158	28	151	674	125	299	123
104	Bronx, NY	537,720	521,457	3,847	308	45	280	945	289	298	133
105-108	Westchester, NY	157,065	98,188	10,175	658	103	427	1,858	728	1,087	493
109	Rockland, NY	52,704	31,664	4,280	244	53	188	903	184	396	257
110	Queens, NY	20,317	16,839	3,012	204	21	131	453	225	254	140
111	Long Island City, NY	23,957	43,999	995	61	11	67	217	67	77	32
112	Brooklyn, NY	1,028,859	434,484	8,353	749	96	574	1,919	697	693	351
113	Flushing, NY	105,787	218,434	5,017	309	52	337	1,093	338	389	159
114	Jamaica, NY	348,179	109,073	2,743	169	28	184	598	185	213	87
115	Western Nassau, NY	124,628	54,395	9,057	614	61	383	1,337	682	768	427
116	Far Rockaway, NY	55,327	15,262	428	26	4	29	93	29	33	14
117-118	Mid-Island, NY	97,776	97,501	16,675	1,017	171	662	2,892	1,067	1,742	1,108
119	Mid-Island, NY	16,806	9,990	2,220	126	27	87	413	128	250	167
120-123	Albany, NY	54,361	17,636	8,571	413	80	387	1,627	422	979	511
124	Mid-Hudson, NY	8,170	5,381	1,239	35	21	56	312	31	134	87
125-126	Mid-Hudson, NY	51,528	25,850	4,416	234	60	174	967	168	491	289
127	Mid-Hudson, NY	8,407	6,137	716	28	7	33	179	19	57	65
128	Glens Falls, NY	6,008	3,504	2,084	107	15	82	437	84	156	135
129	Plattsburgh, NY	11,554	5,134	1,456	76	15	63	302	25	167	127
130-132	Syracuse, NY	56,947	11,888	7,451	373	106	325	1,468	388	780	478
133-135	Utica, NY	21,523	8,818	3,286	120	37	195	637	154	314	214
136	Watertown, NY	17,757	7,365	2,078	103	22	110	396	38	196	163
137-139	Binghamton, NY	8,578	4,526	3,248	98	42	164	648	130	291	220
140-143	Buffalo, NY	157,326	32,165	12,130	590	132	564	2,411	736	1,411	595
144-146	Rochester, NY	122,399	35,131	9,913	407	98	348	1,970	515	1,206	552
147	Jamestown, NY	3,090	2,835	1,403	42	17	70	281	54	144	101
148-149	Elmira, NY	13,261	5,033	2,695	90	34	142	545	94	308	182
150-152	Pittsburgh, PA	184,204	11,080	15,296	773	181	728	2,636	865	2,005	651
153	Pittsburgh, PA	5,735	867	380	39	18	62	293	57	120	88
154	Pittsburgh, PA	5,695	497	1,396	57	22	66	301	53	178	75
155	Johnstown, PA	301	308	640	18	8	25	112	25	46	32
156	Greensburgh, PA	4,326	1,140	2,564	68	44	116	509	96	310	182
157	Johnstown, PA	1,616	480	861	24	12	36	182	26	104	47
158	DuBois, PA	124	228	728	19	8	36	167	23	66	45
159	Johnstown, PA	3,976	973	1,245	37	16	60	270	48	163	66
160	New Castle, PA	1,085	652	1,527	37	30	61	247	99	209	120
161	New Castle, PA	10,521	1,075	1,841	62	34	89	357	78	237	122
162	New Castle, PA	500	228	653	19	11	32	151	19	64	46
163	Oil City, PA	2,016	592	1,835	33	18	55	245	35	158	77
164-165	Erie, PA	17,805	4,651	2,906	110	29	128	538	139	402	136
166	Altoona, PA	4,380	830	1,848	58	18	91	345	92	231	112
167	Bradford, PA	1,017	925	366	7	5	21	99	11	29	17
168	Altoona, PA	4,378	1,776	1,575	72	13	54	274	70	204	103
169	Williamsport, PA	324	239	435	9	6	24	93	14	38	49
170-171	Harrisburg, PA	49,210	13,702	7,234	241	77	261	1,170	317	890	374
172	Harrisburg, PA	4,162	1,682	1,401	41	16	60	237	65	166	101
173-174	Lancaster, PA	14,966	8,391	4,185	111	39	127	658	145	506	224
175-176	Lancaster, PA	13,098	18,831	4,097	222	37	144	750	283	383	300
177	Williamsport, PA	4,267	999	1,551	69	18	63	292	53	150	88
178	Harrisburg, PA	2,284	2,370	1,917	48	23	82	344	57	215	127
179	Reading, PA	1,389	756	912	27	9	78	206	35	112	44
180-181	Lehigh Valley, PA	16,485	34,724	5,782	240	62	242	1,071	284	704	308
182	Wilkes-Barre, PA	1,033	1,165	967	26	15	54	195	46	107	74
183	Lehigh Valley, PA	2,494	3,288	1,210	53	13	45	250	59	151	91
184-185	Scranton, PA	3,318	2,870	2,682	124	37	147	535	84	315	184

Zip Code	3-Digit Zip Code Areas	Black Markets	Hispanic Markets	Total Retail Sales ($Millions)	Retail Sales: Apparel & Accessories ($Millions)	Retail Sales: Automotive ($Millions)	Retail Sales: Drugs, First Aid & Health Care Products ($Millions)	Retail Sales: Food ($Millions)	Retail Sales: Furniture & Major Appliances ($Millions)	Retail Sales: General Merchandise ($Millions)	Retail Sales: Hardware, Lumber & Garden Supplies ($Millions)
186-187	Wilkes-Barre, PA	5,265	2,369	2,800	102	45	141	505	122	418	168
188	Scranton, PA	248	345	555	11	7	28	110	19	46	37
189	Southeastern, PA	4,121	4,893	3,801	126	34	121	596	195	374	184
190-191	Philadelphia, PA	756,756	114,286	23,387	1,421	226	1,203	4,177	1,326	2,377	853
193	Southeastern, PA	27,303	9,791	4,198	113	32	118	593	138	178	189
194	Southeastern, PA	29,599	7,029	5,758	338	49	213	880	370	725	243
195-196	Reading, PA	12,939	22,367	3,655	295	38	129	581	196	492	167
197-198	Wilmington, DE	88,255	16,501	5,553	218	64	215	915	408	846	261
199	Wilmington, DE	48,759	6,474	3,064	138	39	108	486	152	432	285
200, 202-205	Washington, DC	347,196	30,459	4,140	369	25	231	669	318	236	61
201, 220-223	Northern Virginia, VA	153,611	144,167	19,465	1,394	219	573	3,205	1,570	2,192	848
206-207	Southern, MD	526,093	42,054	10,610	503	168	330	1,993	620	1,461	522
208-209	Suburban, MD	133,606	76,187	9,826	674	78	297	1,710	944	903	382
210-212, 214	Baltimore, MD	651,569	32,284	21,381	1,134	255	766	3,962	1,237	2,520	1,078
215	Cumberland, MD	2,095	445	983	34	12	49	211	40	119	71
216	Easton, MD	26,969	1,535	1,245	64	19	46	271	52	83	83
217	Frederick, MD	23,347	4,142	3,693	97	57	121	669	184	498	247
218	Salisbury, MD	38,741	1,382	1,843	103	19	66	319	53	211	120
219	Baltimore, MD	3,652	796	682	35	6	16	109	12	35	45
224-225	Richmond, VA	41,372	4,661	2,657	73	36	98	525	117	277	186
226	Winchester, VA	5,609	1,410	1,488	45	16	55	282	90	169	103
227	Culpepper, VA	6,712	525	442	6	8	18	101	24	34	23
228	Charlottesville, VA	3,379	1,788	1,305	32	12	41	225	50	162	87
229	Charlottesville, VA	23,340	2,298	2,126	88	28	78	394	115	191	141
230-232	Richmond, VA	224,585	9,675	9,115	492	128	349	1,736	538	998	415
233-237	Norfolk, VA	403,722	42,192	13,172	598	189	441	2,179	723	1,679	638
238	Richmond, VA	100,295	3,746	2,569	99	34	101	446	121	350	160
239	Farmville, VA	32,219	397	746	15	8	29	139	33	82	41
240-241	Roanoke, VA	54,048	3,479	5,355	152	71	185	916	302	641	322
242	Bristol, VA	2,660	572	1,691	42	24	65	406	79	137	117
243	Roanoke, VA	3,963	705	1,316	35	16	48	255	60	67	97
244	Charlotesville, VA	7,664	696	1,205	26	13	38	194	51	131	75
245	Lynchburg, VA	82,313	1,959	3,512	95	59	87	579	189	449	187
246	Bluefield, WV	1,154	353	720	9	7	45	176	29	91	66
247-248	Bluefield, WV	8,335	502	922	26	15	51	182	27	135	51
249	Lewisburg, WV	1,760	328	310	4	5	22	73	12	24	21
250-253	Charleston, WV	16,306	1,359	3,251	101	42	156	595	119	467	225
254	Martinsburg, WV	5,508	1,331	946	70	16	28	185	47	108	44
255-257	Huntington, WV	6,153	1,252	2,220	69	37	126	391	99	201	167
258-259	Beckley, WV	8,486	718	1,179	22	13	60	243	32	193	76
260	Wheeling, WV	2,867	757	1,078	26	19	54	217	62	134	62
261	Parkersburg, WV	901	376	1,288	47	18	57	220	46	209	78
262	Clarksburg, WV	423	402	581	8	8	27	132	19	70	54
263-264	Clarksburg, WV	1,413	1,360	1,166	34	17	63	225	33	174	75
265	Clarksburg, WV	4,116	1,309	1,355	55	18	63	252	37	230	107
266	Gassaway, WV	50	79	285	2	3	14	60	8	30	28
267	Cumberland, MD	873	280	280	3	6	14	50	15	32	17
268	Petersburg, WV	516	148	177	1	3	9	39	7	9	16
270-274	Greensboro, NC	320,425	15,503	14,580	645	259	568	2,369	983	1,597	923
275-277	Raleigh, NC	349,669	19,299	12,114	603	179	447	2,004	704	1,391	864
278	Rocky Mount, NC	214,906	3,833	4,311	175	73	153	798	186	480	391
279	Rocky Mount, NC	57,944	1,169	1,475	55	25	47	316	58	140	142
280-282	Charlotte, NC	318,910	14,965	14,679	663	253	519	2,407	793	1,713	1,022
283	Fayetteville, NC	234,465	21,675	5,845	220	127	187	1,043	239	735	453
284	Fayetteville, NC	85,273	3,057	3,240	125	46	131	579	127	429	236
285	Kinston, NC	110,904	15,661	3,504	132	75	124	613	198	435	276

Zip Code	3-Digit Zip Code Areas	Black Markets	Hispanic Markets	Total Retail Sales ($Millions)	Retail Sales: Apparel & Accessories ($Millions)	Retail Sales: Automotive ($Millions)	Retail Sales: Drugs, First Aid & Health Care Products ($Millions)	Retail Sales: Food ($Millions)	Retail Sales: Furniture & Major Appliances ($Millions)	Retail Sales: General Merchandise ($Millions)	Retail Sales: Hardware, Lumber & Garden Supplies ($Millions)
286	Hickory, NC	44,611	4,403	5,030	180	108	198	939	338	564	430
287-289	Asheville, NC	27,634	4,395	5,263	196	103	215	1,015	230	581	424
290-292	Columbia, SC	379,571	10,255	7,837	330	158	253	1,350	413	933	633
293	Greenville, SC	88,246	2,358	2,781	120	50	117	525	137	326	185
294	Charleston, SC	203,683	9,658	5,622	257	82	188	946	314	645	361
295	Florence, SC	186,662	2,829	5,212	360	81	172	977	235	585	334
296	Greenville, SC	147,029	6,494	7,343	280	135	257	1,354	372	920	547
297	Charlotte, NC	64,395	1,359	1,893	61	41	79	428	87	191	114
298	Augusta, GA	66,729	1,716	1,398	60	30	57	313	44	192	93
299	Savannah, GA	51,273	2,828	1,588	136	21	36	262	71	139	86
300-302	North Metro, GA	431,523	65,537	30,555	1,324	524	972	4,877	1,785	4,264	1,682
303	Atlanta, GA	365,536	28,506	9,756	627	121	307	1,342	543	1,110	442
304	Swainsboro, GA	50,040	4,301	1,466	51	29	58	309	75	180	95
306	Athens, GA	54,242	3,765	2,422	53	53	82	389	119	279	157
307	Chattanooga, TN	6,888	4,865	2,637	85	53	83	543	169	311	122
308-309	Augusta, GA	102,587	5,743	3,414	141	64	95	531	189	511	280
310, 312	Macon, GA	188,354	5,828	5,629	206	103	197	887	219	576	336
313-314	Savannah, GA	100,690	9,050	3,305	169	57	111	486	122	370	203
315	Waycross, GA	47,146	3,926	2,410	88	43	95	467	115	271	168
316	Valdosta, GA	37,518	3,157	1,404	84	25	44	296	94	170	86
317	Albany, GA	151,831	9,986	3,739	92	69	137	693	182	402	206
318-319	Columbus, GA	83,991	9,356	2,347	125	40	68	286	88	359	137
320-322	Jacksonville, FL	272,560	60,926	15,336	533	233	543	2,692	728	2,022	833
323	Tallahassee, FL	100,921	10,797	3,165	121	51	101	619	134	455	185
324	Panama City, FL	39,070	6,222	2,712	105	41	82	532	98	397	158
325	Pensacola, FL	78,925	16,077	5,311	171	85	178	785	257	680	263
326, 344	Gainsville, FL	75,828	24,419	5,585	146	87	203	998	249	871	367
327	Mid-Florida, FL	68,764	65,904	8,389	362	118	272	1,361	496	1,095	455
328	Orlando, FL	102,876	94,504	7,888	441	126	228	1,105	387	924	358
329	Orlando, FL	37,738	22,562	5,719	162	63	207	855	259	661	242
330	South Florida, FL	223,091	434,914	15,234	907	187	651	2,143	952	1,457	648
331-332	Miami, FL	366,341	959,610	17,875	1,401	259	895	2,584	1,519	1,930	757
333	Fort Lauderdale, FL	150,553	83,336	9,168	456	107	350	1,217	497	841	361
334	West Palm Beach, FL	144,528	118,103	14,039	839	150	547	2,086	868	1,715	596
335-336	Tampa, FL	132,058	164,944	11,036	420	173	392	1,721	644	1,141	473
337	Saint Petersburg, FL	55,688	19,704	6,556	244	58	261	1,007	348	664	260
338	Lakeland, FL	66,391	37,440	5,078	151	78	187	887	362	643	308
339	Fort Meyers, FL	32,154	32,538	5,604	241	55	215	952	372	721	391
342	Manasota, FL	34,552	30,339	6,321	323	72	278	1,093	426	697	343
346	Tampa, FL	22,772	26,662	6,886	222	74	289	1,191	334	848	310
347	Orlando, FL	24,547	37,930	3,080	118	40	102	548	115	310	149
349	West Palm Beach, FL	35,057	23,687	3,123	118	42	146	602	155	367	201
350-352	Birmingham, AL	346,782	5,548	10,793	546	211	394	1,793	598	1,521	582
354	Tuscaloosa, AL	75,034	1,210	1,687	84	40	71	298	88	216	115
355	Birmingham, AL	11,693	522	1,142	31	29	53	257	45	141	80
356	Huntsville, AL	50,989	1,682	3,054	104	60	102	539	139	477	205
357-358	Huntsville, AL	70,656	4,582	3,242	178	64	76	506	139	410	218
359	Birmingham, AL	23,552	1,041	2,173	124	51	73	396	98	278	139
360-361	Montgomery, AL	215,414	3,208	4,068	172	83	145	653	164	476	198
362	Anniston, AL	39,704	1,647	1,347	40	26	46	230	63	198	77
363	Dothan, AL	55,231	2,878	1,971	72	37	54	321	75	211	143
364	Evergreen, AL	34,973	520	823	32	19	37	149	30	92	58
365-366	Mobile, AL	187,698	5,447	5,208	233	105	215	950	234	699	325
367	Montgomery, AL	80,174	327	808	26	20	35	190	32	95	35
368	Montgomery, AL	72,574	1,243	1,534	45	29	42	313	70	205	90
369	Meridian, MS	13,827	88	137	2	4	6	33	6	9	5

Zip Code	3-Digit Zip Code Areas	Black Markets	Hispanic Markets	Total Retail Sales ($Millions)	Retail Sales: Apparel & Accessories ($Millions)	Retail Sales: Automotive ($Millions)	Retail Sales: Drugs, First Aid & Health Care Products ($Millions)	Retail Sales: Food ($Millions)	Retail Sales: Furniture & Major Appliances ($Millions)	Retail Sales: General Merchandise ($Millions)	Retail Sales: Hardware, Lumber & Garden Supplies ($Millions)
370-372	Nashville, TN	193,304	12,663	15,559	609	239	487	2,411	905	2,064	859
373-374	Chattanooga, TN	67,738	3,925	6,459	245	106	219	1,137	283	890	409
376	Johnson City, TN	6,616	1,273	3,629	103	56	117	547	173	597	214
377-379	Knoxville, TN	46,771	4,050	11,085	458	200	368	1,823	511	1,331	733
380-381	Memphis, TN	438,130	8,504	10,588	521	163	427	1,537	485	1,457	427
382	McKenzie, TN	10,079	365	857	32	19	34	155	34	92	76
383	Jackson, TN	44,351	957	2,183	75	49	85	366	114	284	147
384	Columbia, TN	13,841	692	1,325	45	30	50	274	52	156	99
385	Cookeville, TN	1,789	588	1,584	70	33	50	337	66	160	134
386	Memphis, TN	93,096	1,894	2,058	56	52	87	482	81	270	93
387	Greenville, MS	84,731	1,060	941	46	22	30	227	45	146	38
388	Tupelo, MS	37,573	1,281	1,959	91	51	64	370	87	344	147
389	Grenada, MS	53,853	524	797	31	21	28	166	31	79	41
390-392	Jackson, MS	312,263	3,986	6,305	227	130	224	1,135	242	984	343
393	Meridian, MS	71,356	1,077	1,494	40	37	57	308	56	236	106
394	Hattiesburg, MS	78,416	1,912	2,266	88	59	90	462	89	364	152
395	Gulfport, MS	63,104	5,867	2,700	60	58	85	513	91	487	144
396	McComb, MS	50,309	508	835	36	23	39	158	34	108	51
397	Columbus, MS	61,227	1,426	1,134	60	29	38	231	56	167	66
400-402	Louisville, KY	123,784	8,415	9,301	321	138	369	1,526	465	1,277	494
403-406	Lexington, KY	46,549	5,309	7,064	296	93	248	1,231	355	982	378
407-409	London, KY	2,554	466	1,690	44	30	64	328	56	246	134
410	Cincinnati, OH	7,242	1,788	3,989	108	39	172	640	117	520	241
411-412	Ashland, KY	1,178	804	1,628	49	21	70	322	55	251	115
413-414	Campton, KY	255	76	375	3	9	25	66	17	32	16
415-416	Pikeville, KY	675	245	987	32	19	45	213	32	146	65
417-418	Hazard, KY	612	125	586	19	11	23	119	21	88	36
420	Paducah, KY	10,598	973	2,072	90	36	81	328	92	285	204
421-422	Bowling Green, KY	29,767	4,429	2,666	89	46	95	481	104	285	203
423	Owensboro, KY	4,707	444	1,352	32	24	61	279	61	219	78
424	Evansville, IN	8,619	558	1,108	32	17	46	199	40	142	56
425-426	Somerset, KY	1,063	320	989	29	26	38	217	46	128	89
427	Elizabethtown, KY	5,282	920	1,268	45	26	45	219	49	125	102
430-432	Columbus, OH	198,985	13,696	17,529	610	224	488	2,482	908	2,429	806
433	Columbus, OH	4,758	1,092	1,379	33	25	52	227	59	231	77
434-436	Toledo, OH	79,726	36,238	7,808	224	105	313	1,376	383	1,133	391
437-438	Zanesville, OH	5,956	572	1,958	69	35	79	369	110	200	132
439	Steubenville, OH	7,785	724	1,591	52	29	90	343	65	231	72
440-441	Cleveland, OH	420,505	60,988	19,551	904	238	1,169	3,286	1,172	2,343	978
442-443	Akron, OH	74,577	4,603	7,420	241	105	316	1,328	299	725	533
444-445	Youngstown, OH	60,667	8,500	4,894	191	70	244	833	294	682	235
446-447	Canton, OH	31,775	3,249	5,651	157	99	231	1,059	238	550	373
448-449	Mansfield, OH	22,165	6,312	3,775	112	58	178	642	162	510	228
450-452	Cincinnati, OH	224,221	8,338	15,231	622	183	573	2,770	586	1,918	919
453-455	Dayton, OH	140,515	8,492	9,870	313	150	335	1,404	556	1,777	469
456	Chillicothe, OH	12,131	1,124	2,660	49	43	114	529	117	426	180
457	Athens, OH	3,085	708	1,149	25	22	48	258	54	99	65
458	Lima, OH	15,671	7,217	3,407	76	54	124	535	160	549	226
460-462	Indianapolis, IN	223,527	14,753	17,329	574	219	717	2,357	990	2,329	939
463-464	Gary, IN	149,905	47,553	6,750	314	95	353	1,121	324	820	394
465-466	South Bend, IN	41,774	12,629	5,490	162	77	244	855	252	786	406
467-468	Fort Wayne, IN	39,953	9,718	5,555	178	83	226	855	303	811	352
469	Kokomo, IN	13,779	4,465	2,634	62	37	118	442	111	365	178
470	Cincinnati, OH	466	258	758	15	12	38	141	34	101	48
471	Louisville, KY	10,242	1,278	2,481	48	40	95	389	99	411	171
472	Columbus, IN	2,344	893	1,789	83	30	67	298	60	267	119

RETAIL SALES REPORTS/BLACK AND HISPANIC MARKETS STATISTICAL DATA FOR 3-DIGIT ZIP CODE AREAS

Zip Code	3-Digit Zip Code Areas	Black Markets	Hispanic Markets	Total Retail Sales ($Millions)	Retail Sales: Apparel & Accessories ($Millions)	Retail Sales: Automotive ($Millions)	Retail Sales: Drugs, First Aid & Health Care Products ($Millions)	Retail Sales: Food ($Millions)	Retail Sales: Furniture & Major Appliances ($Millions)	Retail Sales: General Merchandise ($Millions)	Retail Sales: Hardware, Lumber & Garden Supplies ($Millions)
473	Muncie, IN	14,303	2,026	2,828	56	51	127	488	118	412	153
474	Bloomington, IN	3,997	2,097	1,992	65	26	80	362	99	296	113
475	Washington, IN	1,355	863	1,448	49	19	54	223	42	203	118
476-477	Evansville, IN	17,131	1,470	2,966	126	43	107	432	114	383	178
478	Terre Haute, IN	7,488	1,476	2,620	30	20	64	251	66	224	100
479	Lafayette, IN	4,165	3,553	2,430	61	29	95	371	87	292	142
480, 483	Royal Oak, MI	96,699	30,915	25,422	1,361	295	1,092	3,041	1,755	3,962	1,240
481-482	Detroit, MI	923,981	61,747	22,219	1,012	325	1,045	3,078	1,158	3,265	1,085
484-485	Flint, MI	91,670	13,085	6,502	242	98	273	891	315	1,082	438
486-487	Saginaw, MI	42,211	20,342	6,093	273	93	229	960	283	924	408
488-489	Lansing, MI	42,189	24,027	6,682	194	79	173	894	345	1,285	459
490-491	Kalamazoo, MI	71,952	15,729	7,433	232	112	242	1,060	331	1,328	486
492	Jackson, MI	18,896	9,893	2,803	59	52	122	374	102	609	178
493-495	Grand Rapids, MI	73,498	38,500	10,866	430	147	277	1,400	638	2,027	761
496	Traverse City, MI	1,076	1,960	2,846	118	44	92	455	130	368	232
497	Gaylord, MI	4,212	1,266	2,456	99	32	69	477	57	180	239
498-499	Iron Mountain, MI	2,008	1,500	2,432	82	41	61	479	74	252	177
500-503, 509	Des Moines, IA	18,141	9,625	7,636	272	92	237	1,369	325	1,057	531
504	Mason City, IA	412	1,613	943	24	19	28	156	35	149	62
505	Fort Dodge, IA	1,127	968	1,085	31	15	37	225	41	151	72
506-507	Waterloo, IA	9,063	1,415	2,171	52	36	67	364	96	285	176
508	Creston, IA	13	179	280	5	4	8	66	11	24	12
510-511	Sioux City, IA	2,586	4,109	1,560	42	19	50	278	67	150	96
512	Sheldon, IA	17	79	274	7	5	12	48	12	24	20
513	Spencer, IA	68	177	451	20	6	15	83	15	42	33
514	Carroll, IA	118	184	416	17	6	14	80	15	56	27
515	Omaha, NE	536	1,833	1,327	40	18	58	208	56	105	51
516	Omaha, NE	128	281	200	6	3	9	35	8	31	13
520	Dubuque, IA	504	606	1,219	33	20	49	214	64	177	95
521	Decorah, IA	79	188	405	12	7	11	82	18	31	30
522-524	Cedar Rapids, IA	7,129	4,056	3,854	134	42	133	648	208	547	298
525	Ottumwa, IA	522	646	946	32	13	27	197	36	113	57
526	Burlington, IA	3,089	1,531	998	27	13	37	192	35	166	51
527-528	Rock Island, IL	10,683	8,751	2,713	93	39	99	427	162	438	126
530-532, 534	Milwaukee, WI	281,855	85,718	20,065	766	235	778	3,413	1,257	2,489	1,296
535, 537	Madison, WI	26,510	11,895	8,873	252	118	208	1,168	508	940	606
538	Madison, WI	167	224	459	9	5	11	84	13	58	33
539	Portage, WI	2,809	2,131	1,518	31	16	41	246	40	163	111
540	Saint Paul, MN	189	580	869	8	15	21	141	45	90	59
541-543	Green Bay, WI	2,133	3,957	4,859	150	44	91	728	251	814	405
544	Wausau, WI	816	2,281	3,628	98	28	56	589	154	573	258
545	Rhinelander, WI	311	370	971	23	10	20	180	30	84	79
546	LaCrosse, WI	1,150	1,815	2,205	53	26	41	351	75	214	155
547	Eau Claire, WI	642	1,342	2,269	74	26	69	314	88	319	179
548	Spooner, WI	579	1,062	1,596	28	19	38	282	52	174	147
549	Oshkosh, WI	2,003	4,773	4,344	151	52	103	684	226	573	335
550-551	Saint Paul, MN	35,040	25,791	11,981	465	129	337	1,898	652	1,709	856
553-555	Minneapolis, MN	82,669	23,071	19,327	884	190	493	2,712	1,258	2,480	1,213
556-558	Duluth, MN	1,410	1,423	2,732	86	27	90	472	110	405	179
559	Rochester, MN	1,519	2,672	2,749	106	28	65	411	154	392	258
560	Mankato, MN	532	3,405	2,001	82	28	62	338	79	269	174
561	Windom, MN	120	812	695	27	10	27	121	25	79	65
562	Willmar, MN	395	3,173	1,199	31	16	43	206	40	159	112
563	Saint Cloud, MN	1,087	1,132	3,306	48	24	63	398	92	220	282
564	Brainerd, MN	243	397	1,192	21	13	34	206	38	156	126
565	Detroit Lakes, MN	272	2,272	1,259	33	17	39	212	51	156	88

Zip Code	3-Digit Zip Code Areas	Black Markets	Hispanic Markets	Total Retail Sales ($Millions)	Retail Sales: Apparel & Accessories ($Millions)	Retail Sales: Automotive ($Millions)	Retail Sales: Drugs, First Aid & Health Care Products ($Millions)	Retail Sales: Food ($Millions)	Retail Sales: Furniture & Major Appliances ($Millions)	Retail Sales: General Merchandise ($Millions)	Retail Sales: Hardware, Lumber & Garden Supplies ($Millions)
566	Bemidji, MN	254	575	721	26	8	18	137	21	87	52
567	Thief River Falls, MN	96	1,802	516	13	7	22	99	22	39	35
570-571	Sioux Falls, SD	1,623	1,412	2,942	79	38	103	392	119	291	148
572	Dakota Central, SD	45	233	630	30	12	16	97	26	99	52
573	Dakota Central, SD	125	329	755	27	14	29	125	29	64	51
574	Aberdeen, SD	66	164	620	26	11	12	88	23	97	40
575	Pierre, SD	71	457	477	16	8	11	72	18	59	25
576	Mobridge, SD	44	206	163	5	4	4	27	8	20	9
577	Rapid City, SD	2,246	3,653	1,824	57	28	48	265	93	268	104
580-581	Fargo, ND	403	1,119	1,746	58	18	40	238	66	307	153
582	Grand Forks, ND	1,536	2,157	1,152	41	14	24	150	42	215	76
583	Devils Lake, ND	81	250	442	11	8	14	63	17	41	27
584	Jamestown, ND	76	203	422	12	8	15	71	17	51	24
585	Bismarck, ND	108	791	1,210	31	13	41	178	50	123	67
586	Dickinson, ND	22	234	382	9	6	11	55	13	55	15
587	Minot, ND	1,546	1,230	862	29	15	27	113	28	156	43
588	Williston, ND	28	194	217	8	4	7	32	8	20	12
590-591	Billings, MT	733	4,607	2,106	65	36	46	320	105	291	146
592	Wolf Point, MT	40	529	274	10	5	8	59	11	12	23
593	Miles City, MT	55	408	291	10	5	11	63	12	10	24
594	Great Falls, MT	969	1,792	1,234	43	20	27	215	36	163	82
595	Havre, MT	34	349	250	10	4	7	61	10	22	15
596	Helena, MT	71	828	590	13	11	15	120	33	68	35
597	Butte, MT	173	2,187	1,307	48	16	46	219	80	99	111
598	Missoula, MT	248	2,288	1,625	44	31	31	300	91	213	123
599	Kalispell, MT	74	1,005	991	26	17	23	197	59	112	105
600, 602	Palatine, IL	79,342	123,671	17,833	1,021	164	875	2,675	1,219	1,787	904
601, 603	Carol Stream, IL	103,023	116,157	14,275	879	122	675	2,084	1,034	1,658	752
604	South Suburban, IL	219,835	85,702	11,203	585	108	600	1,739	710	1,250	517
605	Fox Valley, IL	34,457	59,341	8,730	532	71	392	1,211	641	1,049	485
606-607	Chicago, IL	1,127,860	592,791	22,552	1,418	217	1,258	3,598	1,546	2,471	923
609	Kankakee, IL	17,154	3,797	1,335	40	40	53	207	75	182	80
610-611	Rockford, IL	34,695	19,659	4,290	120	78	187	712	178	508	296
612	Rock Island, IL	12,914	9,857	1,939	70	26	85	337	93	247	99
613	La Salle, IL	1,033	5,151	1,300	40	33	48	215	54	185	73
614	Galesburg, IL	6,651	2,725	1,243	31	16	45	211	62	207	54
615-616	Peoria, IL	32,438	4,179	3,593	109	50	147	533	186	388	178
617	Bloomington, IL	9,059	3,049	1,990	96	35	72	277	114	231	102
618-619	Champaign, IL	29,129	6,274	3,166	118	40	123	482	154	481	169
620, 622	Saint Louis, MO	102,649	9,088	6,066	160	88	201	1,002	303	936	350
623	Quincy, IL	3,199	568	901	33	14	30	152	48	161	52
624	Effingham, IL	689	606	1,247	27	18	37	182	36	168	95
625-627	Springfield, IL	39,019	3,142	4,608	135	63	185	663	221	579	216
628	Centralia, IL	6,089	1,035	1,652	40	27	62	278	55	251	95
629	Carbondale, IL	19,662	2,739	1,900	53	33	65	292	57	399	140
630-631	Saint Louis, MO	346,489	19,349	17,327	818	227	610	2,700	1,042	2,479	722
633	Saint Louis, MO	10,500	4,451	3,064	94	43	85	512	157	417	280
634	Quincy, IL	2,207	242	529	7	7	13	79	19	97	32
635	Quincy, IL	650	363	468	13	6	14	85	18	68	26
636	Cape Girardeau, MO	2,741	661	849	17	12	28	158	33	125	40
637	Cape Girardeau, MO	4,375	651	1,170	38	15	29	171	32	243	85
638	Cape Girardeau, MO	19,082	656	1,026	20	14	40	169	38	142	52
639	Cape Girardeau, MO	2,282	451	673	16	9	17	101	23	88	43
641	Kansas City, MO	140,106	22,224	5,655	196	79	164	869	281	823	270
644-645	Saint Joseph, MO	5,267	3,294	1,495	28	23	28	261	56	222	63
646	Chillicothe, MO	814	446	520	9	8	11	100	21	91	33

RETAIL SALES REPORTS/BLACK AND HISPANIC MARKETS STATISTICAL DATA FOR 3-DIGIT ZIP CODE AREAS

Zip Code	3-Digit Zip Code Areas	Black Markets	Hispanic Markets	Total Retail Sales ($Millions)	Retail Sales: Apparel & Accessories ($Millions)	Retail Sales: Automotive ($Millions)	Retail Sales: Drugs, First Aid & Health Care Products ($Millions)	Retail Sales: Food ($Millions)	Retail Sales: Furniture & Major Appliances ($Millions)	Retail Sales: General Merchandise ($Millions)	Retail Sales: Hardware, Lumber & Garden Supplies ($Millions)
647	Harrisonville, MO	662	883	818	12	12	19	137	32	136	47
648	Springfield, MO	1,630	1,647	1,620	52	24	29	269	48	192	99
650-651	Mid-Missouri, MO	6,390	1,282	1,817	73	18	29	284	83	324	134
652	Mid-Missouri, MO	18,259	2,085	2,104	65	19	44	304	99	355	160
653	Mid-Missouri, MO	3,863	1,206	774	23	10	23	131	29	119	57
654-655	Springfield, MO	6,532	3,378	1,403	42	18	20	199	50	202	109
656-658	Springfield, MO	5,529	4,907	6,008	172	67	112	920	173	730	404
661-662,664	Kansas City, MO	67,429	21,069	5,586	208	73	160	833	416	890	236
665-666	Topeka, KS	25,527	12,608	2,550	97	40	80	373	137	448	136
667	Fort Scott, KS	1,914	1,470	830	17	17	26	152	31	120	53
668	Topeka, KS	993	2,487	462	14	9	15	83	17	56	22
669	Salina, KS	82	141	198	4	4	7	36	8	26	12
670-672	Witchita, KS	48,853	27,515	5,193	215	94	129	1,056	286	736	368
673	Independence, KS	3,857	1,513	500	12	9	16	106	18	82	24
674	Salina, KS	2,869	2,369	1,190	34	19	25	200	51	181	78
675	Hutchinson, KS	3,246	4,680	1,044	33	18	30	190	37	172	56
676	Hays, KS	664	512	568	20	9	14	106	16	93	29
677	Colby, KS	106	784	318	14	5	9	51	9	37	18
678	Dodge City, KS	1,450	19,912	950	40	14	19	146	27	156	57
679	Liberal, KS	1,633	5,211	283	15	3	6	49	7	25	10
680-681	Omaha, NE	59,997	18,213	6,452	272	76	201	1,056	566	799	250
683-685	Lincoln, NE	6,257	5,375	3,284	137	38	120	520	167	358	195
686	Norfolk, NE	146	1,026	544	14	9	12	97	16	74	47
687	Norfolk, NE	707	2,799	1,005	18	17	31	193	31	153	61
688	Grand Island, NE	493	4,815	1,518	61	18	39	219	52	273	105
689	Grand Island, NE	269	822	567	13	10	21	109	17	82	36
690	McCook, NE	14	445	242	7	4	7	43	6	38	12
691	North Platte, NE	161	3,436	967	18	11	23	122	18	103	45
692	Valentine, NE	6	54	82	3	1	2	16	2	11	6
693	Alliance, NE	196	8,117	635	21	10	16	111	17	108	34
700-701	New Orleans, LA	456,208	52,961	10,700	526	157	470	1,952	616	1,423	424
703	Thibodaux, LA	52,847	3,705	2,099	55	38	86	475	73	326	140
704	Hammond, LA	67,118	5,184	2,992	97	57	120	596	97	426	144
705	Lafayette, LA	162,685	5,847	4,803	178	81	203	913	214	674	282
706	Lake Charles, LA	56,572	4,721	2,140	75	35	65	410	76	326	137
707-708	Baton Rouge, LA	214,274	8,439	6,059	205	102	196	1,122	207	882	313
710-711	Shreveport, LA	168,409	5,293	3,874	146	62	139	659	191	635	186
712	Monroe, LA	121,667	2,556	2,821	98	49	108	494	111	461	131
713-714	Alexandria, LA	105,724	7,201	2,793	76	49	105	574	95	473	141
716	Pine Bluff, AR	62,530	1,897	1,290	48	27	36	255	42	175	72
717	Camden, AR	34,462	594	895	37	17	36	190	25	117	50
718	Texarkana, TX	24,256	2,721	889	13	17	25	184	28	132	37
719	Hot Springs National Park, AR	8,738	1,976	1,321	32	18	38	230	33	208	102
720-722	Little Rock, AR	117,887	6,914	7,739	295	118	188	1,129	363	1,339	425
723	Memphis, TN	69,181	2,044	1,423	35	25	47	248	40	192	52
724	Jonesboro, AR	4,567	1,157	1,602	63	28	42	243	65	325	127
725	Batesville, AR	629	548	726	15	15	21	140	22	102	61
726	Harrison, AR	36	932	972	19	18	23	186	27	119	85
727	Fayetteville, AR	1,819	4,898	2,629	71	28	40	363	115	401	194
728	Russellville, AR	1,966	1,511	844	23	15	22	158	22	127	55
729	Fort Smith, AR	5,648	3,158	1,874	48	32	50	293	55	410	134
730-731	Oklahoma City, OK	123,832	42,206	10,476	423	165	296	1,604	561	1,512	421
734	Ardmore, OK	4,430	1,848	594	26	9	19	121	11	89	28
735	Lawton, OK	28,775	14,004	1,547	52	26	45	264	54	289	71
736	Clinton, OK	1,620	3,103	445	16	7	13	89	8	64	19
737	Enid, OK	3,317	2,301	383	24	18	28	159	28	160	35

Zip Code	3-Digit Zip Code Areas	Black Markets	Hispanic Markets	Total Retail Sales ($Millions)	Retail Sales: Apparel & Accessories ($Millions)	Retail Sales: Automotive ($Millions)	Retail Sales: Drugs, First Aid & Health Care Products ($Millions)	Retail Sales: Food ($Millions)	Retail Sales: Furniture & Major Appliances ($Millions)	Retail Sales: General Merchandise ($Millions)	Retail Sales: Hardware, Lumber & Garden Supplies ($Millions)
738	Woodward, OK	215	1,020	244	9	4	7	51	4	32	15
739	Liberal, KS	95	2,423	167	5	3	5	32	4	26	10
740-741	Tulsa, OK	67,018	17,392	8,959	361	108	232	1,354	436	1,128	392
743	Tulsa, OK	882	965	786	14	14	28	169	16	118	38
744	Muskogee, OK	17,772	2,432	1,411	40	31	38	304	50	234	62
745	McAlester, OK	2,869	941	552	17	11	14	116	12	72	25
746	Ponca City, OK	997	977	487	16	7	17	81	9	86	20
747	Durant, OK	5,990	1,037	513	13	10	15	114	11	81	27
748	Shawnee, OK	6,870	2,781	1,331	39	23	42	217	33	198	54
749	Poteau, OK	1,943	1,019	671	10	12	15	157	17	109	23
750	North Texas, TX	91,426	177,540	13,538	627	207	359	2,083	837	1,985	565
751	Dallas, TX	70,977	68,525	5,347	221	89	157	836	296	709	216
752-753	Dallas, TX	311,090	286,159	13,581	703	210	326	1,896	940	1,776	519
754	Greenville, TX	25,153	16,329	2,264	90	46	79	426	71	289	116
755	Texarkana, TX	25,705	2,277	1,122	59	18	27	188	37	138	55
756	Longview, TX	64,270	13,487	2,807	90	69	96	479	92	340	136
757	Tyler, TX	46,276	22,346	2,510	92	58	78	423	85	458	163
758	Palestine, TX	25,185	10,391	730	17	17	35	167	20	77	36
759	Lufkin, TX	43,316	15,918	1,812	85	45	68	403	47	211	101
760-761	Fort Worth, TX	161,571	220,786	15,857	564	320	429	2,540	908	2,087	748
762	Fort Worth, TX	10,008	18,714	1,825	57	31	49	360	60	261	78
763	Wichita Falls, TX	13,567	19,578	1,511	46	24	37	224	68	276	79
764	Fort Worth, TX	1,501	14,546	1,013	26	22	37	198	27	89	39
765	Waco, TX	69,733	55,531	2,665	69	48	50	472	110	422	119
766-767	Waco, TX	43,770	40,832	2,395	102	53	61	495	98	359	126
768	Abilene, TX	2,186	17,073	626	19	15	23	137	18	51	38
769	Midland, TX	4,665	41,777	1,128	41	23	23	219	57	171	42
770-772	Houston, TX	550,383	708,119	24,944	1,268	465	791	4,405	1,704	3,419	977
773	North Houston, TX	52,744	75,080	5,581	251	111	159	1,048	257	689	255
774	North Houston, TX	91,616	109,929	4,774	148	82	124	869	217	642	230
775	North Houston, TX	95,339	207,350	8,160	374	152	254	1,623	404	1,132	325
776-777	Beaumont, TX	91,961	19,035	3,681	137	66	114	626	126	490	180
778	Bryan, TX	34,001	33,268	1,897	69	38	41	381	66	309	88
779	Victoria, TX	10,883	49,953	1,375	48	34	40	301	43	157	75
780-782	San Antonio, TX	103,923	995,207	17,269	1,003	350	390	3,232	956	2,567	638
783-784	Corpus Christi, TX	16,540	292,902	4,378	165	80	99	984	142	586	186
785	McAllen, TX	2,186	736,654	6,785	508	165	113	1,353	332	1,411	350
786-787	Austin, TX	95,060	252,925	11,746	500	159	267	2,024	709	1,447	600
788	San Antonio, TX	1,562	121,479	1,174	81	23	23	298	27	159	58
789	Austin, TX	6,262	7,969	433	9	10	12	107	13	46	21
790-791	Amarillo, TX	16,232	101,708	3,647	149	65	86	632	171	411	166
792	Childress, TX	1,672	9,594	222	4	6	8	56	8	25	8
793-794	Lubbock, TX	22,878	113,150	3,213	134	59	78	605	152	488	133
795-796	Abilene, TX	11,671	44,785	1,853	65	38	64	349	61	306	81
797	Midland, TX	17,484	138,760	3,145	116	63	106	653	104	477	123
798-799	El Paso, TX	25,566	539,122	6,229	354	134	131	1,120	390	1,154	286
800-803	Denver, CO	96,780	264,655	22,103	829	305	399	3,893	1,524	2,669	1,168
804	Denver, CO	667	7,939	2,070	136	32	33	400	97	221	116
805	Longmont, CO	1,519	27,979	3,369	114	44	63	543	204	520	260
806	Brighton, CO	752	36,940	1,114	21	16	14	210	57	146	61
807	Brighton, CO	86	8,052	501	12	12	11	100	25	54	24
808-809	Colorado Springs, CO	30,476	44,742	5,159	143	80	99	749	312	708	292
810	Pueblo, CO	2,669	70,483	1,636	32	33	39	333	87	255	74
811	Alamosa, CO	129	24,440	520	11	11	13	115	25	45	39
812	Salida, CO	1,590	4,598	577	12	14	13	106	29	67	41
813	Durango, CO	75	4,962	590	23	9	13	122	28	41	58

RETAIL SALES REPORTS/BLACK AND HISPANIC MARKETS STATISTICAL DATA FOR 3-DIGIT ZIP CODE AREAS

Zip Code	3-Digit Zip Code Areas	Black Markets	Hispanic Markets	Total Retail Sales ($Millions)	Retail Sales: Apparel & Accessories ($Millions)	Retail Sales: Automotive ($Millions)	Retail Sales: Drugs, First Aid & Health Care Products ($Millions)	Retail Sales: Food ($Millions)	Retail Sales: Furniture & Major Appliances ($Millions)	Retail Sales: General Merchandise ($Millions)	Retail Sales: Hardware, Lumber & Garden Supplies ($Millions)
814	Grand Junction, CO	185	5,506	626	13	13	13	125	27	78	77
815	Grand Junction, CO	427	9,632	1,057	26	24	15	207	55	198	62
816	Glenwood Springs, CO	241	9,364	1,710	135	21	37	264	74	122	121
820	Cheyenne, WY	2,905	10,476	1,180	32	19	16	155	42	160	40
821	Billings, MT	0	4	5	0	0	0	1	0	1	0
822	Wheatland, WY	75	1,638	187	2	4	4	32	7	21	9
823	Rawlins, WY	118	2,539	185	2	3	4	31	5	11	9
824	Worland, WY	69	2,488	454	11	9	11	83	15	64	23
825	Riverton, WY	79	1,480	285	8	6	6	48	9	43	16
826	Casper, WY	560	2,743	763	24	16	11	131	32	96	31
827	Gillette, WY	66	1,191	380	9	7	7	69	12	45	17
828	Sheridan, WY	50	482	318	10	6	6	49	10	48	15
829-831	Rock Springs, WY	411	5,275	1,109	55	16	13	201	26	121	68
832	Pocatello, ID	429	9,637	1,195	25	33	37	245	59	117	81
833	Twin Falls, ID	165	14,036	1,553	67	40	29	300	66	119	119
834	Pocatello, ID	370	7,944	1,340	42	29	36	231	74	196	115
835	Lewiston, ID	61	830	692	18	19	19	126	21	91	40
836-837	Boise, ID	1,946	27,283	4,687	141	96	105	787	283	581	354
838	Spokane, WA	390	2,994	2,000	77	55	46	420	82	176	179
840-842	Salt Lake City, UT	8,481	72,232	12,358	565	205	201	2,391	837	1,549	716
843-844	Salt Lake City, UT	2,222	15,119	2,201	78	54	38	444	109	359	133
845	Provo, UT	74	3,158	395	3	9	9	97	16	36	15
846-847	Provo, UT	510	10,411	2,716	85	48	50	508	132	351	201
850, 852-853	Phoenix, AZ	100,813	569,802	28,927	1,042	534	1,028	5,296	1,643	3,652	1,342
855	Globe, AZ	526	17,475	617	12	15	18	157	21	77	34
856-857	Tuscon, AZ	32,319	279,894	8,775	431	164	332	1,583	424	1,330	453
859	Show Low, AZ	112	4,206	348	7	10	6	87	11	48	16
860	Flagstaff, AZ	2,256	16,349	1,520	46	32	31	311	35	197	102
863	Prescott, AZ	427	8,292	1,336	39	23	37	319	42	134	118
864	Kingman, AZ	493	6,604	1,447	31	33	47	271	69	155	91
865	Gallup, NM	52	1,266	242	2	8	6	68	10	18	7
870-872	Albuquerque, NM	22,674	299,931	7,109	225	88	267	1,071	379	1,020	342
873	Gallup, NM	345	11,491	674	26	18	8	121	16	89	29
874	Farmington, NM	625	19,126	949	28	27	21	190	44	134	75
875	Albuuquerque, NM	1,468	118,309	2,427	117	35	61	388	107	182	158
877	Las Vegas, NM	311	31,117	415	7	11	13	66	14	31	28
878	Socorro, NM	202	8,517	137	2	5	3	25	6	6	2
879	Truth or Consequences, NM	82	6,194	121	2	4	3	24	6	8	9
880	Las Cruces, NM	3,377	130,605	1,696	53	38	38	303	98	201	94
881	Clovis, NM	4,384	20,462	602	25	17	16	95	23	85	45
890-891	Las Vegas, NV	85,748	162,308	12,138	523	172	355	2,120	664	1,315	577
893	Ely, NV	322	1,558	112	3	2	2	23	4	16	3
894-895, 897	Reno, NV	7,849	64,714	5,900	191	90	167	1,089	303	906	449
898	Elko, NV	336	9,777	504	25	8	13	99	17	65	32
900-901	Los Angeles, CA	444,693	1,229,503	19,903	1,110	331	775	3,527	1,502	2,443	879
902-905	Inglewood, CA	193,196	721,686	13,945	795	224	532	2,428	1,072	1,707	602
906	Long Beach, CA	12,499	346,375	5,674	323	90	212	964	438	715	256
907-908	Long Beach, CA	109,768	381,604	6,495	534	154	364	1,659	724	1,170	418
910-912	Pasadena, CA	52,905	192,092	6,165	351	98	237	1,076	473	754	267
913-916	Van Nuys, CA	65,084	663,161	16,413	905	264	626	2,845	1,238	2,013	724
917-918	Alhambra, CA	102,997	864,189	15,933	818	286	591	2,851	1,068	2,089	754
919-921	San Diego, CA	178,944	667,216	24,922	1,383	432	910	4,255	1,819	3,260	1,276
922	Palm Springs, CA	18,597	234,857	4,690	214	124	180	1,002	186	697	243

145

Zip Code	3-Digit Zip Code Areas	Black Markets	Hispanic Markets	Total Retail Sales ($Millions)	Retail Sales: Apparel & Accessories ($Millions)	Retail Sales: Automotive ($Millions)	Retail Sales: Drugs, First Aid & Health Care Products ($Millions)	Retail Sales: Food ($Millions)	Retail Sales: Furniture & Major Appliances ($Millions)	Retail Sales: General Merchandise ($Millions)	Retail Sales: Hardware, Lumber & Garden Supplies ($Millions)
923-925	San Bernadino, CA	167,598	592,075	16,071	681	344	593	3,091	756	2,294	892
926-928	Santa Ana, CA	47,319	683,783	24,757	1,467	382	864	3,934	1,988	3,290	1,171
930	Oxnard, CA	16,050	207,124	5,560	186	96	227	968	312	696	315
931, 934	Santa Barbara, CA	18,323	159,443	5,462	263	74	300	1,074	308	520	310
932-933	Bakersfield, CA	45,248	381,123	6,969	213	164	345	1,487	325	993	392
935	Mojave, CA	26,055	108,286	3,741	183	66	149	684	246	461	174
937-938	Fresno, CA	34,729	170,524	4,139	149	91	201	826	213	535	229
939	Salinas, CA	22,239	128,006	2,985	175	42	137	546	154	416	140
940-941, 943-944	San Fransisco, CA	117,761	298,008	19,658	1,540	188	851	3,076	1,776	2,296	789
942, 956-958	Sacramento, CA	129,271	245,651	17,327	675	341	628	3,272	1,067	1,906	1,102
945-948	Oakland, CA	365,667	402,066	24,992	1,202	413	1,102	4,679	1,817	3,415	1,395
949, 954	North Bay, CA	18,738	99,604	8,835	364	115	436	1,797	583	1,064	677
950-951	San Jose, CA	54,569	426,258	15,866	829	247	687	2,672	1,445	1,866	784
952-953	Stockton, CA	49,644	330,416	9,907	286	219	522	2,023	498	1,332	621
955	Eureka, CA	2,950	9,952	1,356	46	24	93	347	46	114	119
959	Marysville, CA	7,493	61,170	3,888	110	70	191	824	211	551	281
960	Redding, CA	2,569	18,607	2,530	60	54	98	557	119	347	199
961	Reno, NV	2,706	13,089	873	25	17	35	193	31	97	69
967-968	Honolulu, HI	26,511	95,222	14,789	1,122	168	788	2,470	710	2,415	460
970-972	Portland, OR	41,638	74,145	17,676	836	280	329	2,477	1,110	3,082	1,027
973	Salem, OR	4,228	26,715	4,770	169	95	146	823	207	689	326
974	Eugene, OR	2,820	13,384	5,046	162	107	140	896	215	752	331
975	Medford, OR	660	9,817	2,794	64	49	71	427	121	469	183
976	Klamath Falls, OR	409	4,160	667	17	20	18	116	28	128	40
977	Bend, OR	173	4,753	1,706	57	47	61	337	89	224	170
978	Pendleton, OR	720	9,006	1,154	35	39	54	259	44	103	68
979	Boise, ID	62	5,709	305	14	7	12	68	7	41	20
980-981	Seattle, WA	73,303	68,378	21,778	1,253	330	766	3,561	1,592	2,728	1,088
982	Everett, WA	5,485	25,725	7,157	290	130	240	1,254	381	899	529
983-984	Tacoma, WA	48,512	39,355	8,893	302	186	274	1,476	513	1,243	711
985	Olympia, WA	4,630	12,698	3,612	106	72	131	729	187	518	281
986	Portland, OR	3,952	13,479	3,442	93	72	140	730	129	468	260
988	Wenatchee, WA	732	30,456	1,687	50	45	71	407	72	103	158
989	Yakima, WA	1,950	75,475	2,163	78	51	54	458	78	320	170
990-992	Spokane, WA	5,572	12,533	5,078	211	94	137	927	290	666	339
993	Pasco, WA	2,926	49,714	2,388	66	44	89	425	122	409	161
994	Lewiston, ID	48	399	173	1	5	10	44	8	13	19
995-996	Anchorage, AK	22,367	13,759	4,620	226	56	132	926	190	665	287
997	Fairbanks, AK	8,156	3,784	1,129	26	16	30	211	35	160	58
998	Juneau, AK	503	1,256	553	21	7	16	123	17	53	29
999	Ketchikan, AK	85	464	262	14	4	7	77	8	15	22
	TOTAL	33,237,676	27,845,140	2,534,043	117,170	36,606	92,880	434,236	141,288	319,943	138,424

The statistical data for 3-digit Zip Code areas on pages 125 through 146 are based on 1997 demographic and zip code data. The data are copyrighted by National Decision Systems, a national demographic company located in San Diego, California (Toll Free 1-800-866-6511) and are reproduced here by permission. Direct all other questions to the American Map Corporation at 718-784-0055.

Zip code areas provided by American Map Corporation are based on 1997 National Postal Service information.